Managing Collective Investment Funds

Managing Collective Investment Funds

Second Edition

Mark St Giles
Ekaterina Alexeeva
and
Sally Buxton

WILEY

First edition published by Cadogan Financial © 2000

Copyright © 2003   John Wiley & Sons, Ltd, The Atrium, Southern Gate,
Chichester, West Sussex PO19 8SQ, England
Telephone (+44) 1243 779777

Email (for orders and customer service enquiries): cs-books@wiley.co.uk
Visit our Home Page www.wileyeurope.com or www.wiley.com

Reprinted January 2006

Other Wiley Editorial Offices

John Wiley & Sons Inc., 111 River Street, Hoboken, NJ 07030, USA

Jossey-Bass, 989 Market Street, San Francisco, CA 94103-1741, USA

Wiley-VCH Verlag GmbH, Boschstr. 12, D-69469 Weinheim, Germany

John Wiley & Sons Australia Ltd, 33 Park Road, Milton, Queensland 4064, Australia

John Wiley & Sons (Asia) Pte Ltd, 2 Clementi Loop #02-01, Jin Xing Distripark, Singapore 129809

John Wiley & Sons (Canada) Ltd, 22 Worcester Road, Etobicoke, Ontario M9W 1L1

Wiley also publishes its books in a variety of electronic formats. Some content that appears in print may not be available in electronic books.

Library of Congress Cataloging-in-Publication Data

St. Giles, Mark.
    Managing collective investment funds / Mark St. Giles, Ekaterina Alexeeva, and Sally Buxton.—2nd ed.
      p. cm.
    Includes bibliographical references and index.
    ISBN 0-470-85695-5 (cloth : alk. paper)
    1. Mutual funds. 2. Investments. I. Alexeeva, Ekaterina. II. Buxton, Sally. III. Title.

    HG4530.S75   2003
    332.63′27—dc21   2003009132

British Library Cataloguing in Publication Data

A catalogue record for this book is available from the British Library

ISBN-10: 0-470-85695-5 (hbk)
ISBN-13: 978-0-470-85695-6 (hbk)

Typeset in 11/13pt RotisSerif by TechBooks, New Delhi, India
Printed and bound in Great Britain by Biddles Ltd, King's Lynn, Norfolk
This book is printed on acid-free paper responsibly manufactured from sustainable forestry, in which at least two trees are planted for each one used for paper production.

Contents

Contents

Contents

Preface

Over the last decade the authors of this book have worked in over 30 emerging and developed financial markets worldwide, training thousands of people entering the collective investment fund business to understand how it works.

Throughout that time people have asked us what reference books exist on the subject and what further reading they could do. While we have been able to suggest books that covered isolated aspects of the business – portfolio management or financial marketing, for instance – we have not been able to find one that is both specific to collective investment funds and that covers how the whole business works.

So we decided to write that book ourselves, and here it is. Aimed at those who wish to learn about the collective investment funds sector for academic or business reasons, or those who work in one part of the sector but want to know more about the other parts, it is designed as a generic explanation of the concepts and principles of collective investment funds and of how the collective investment fund business works.

We would never have been able to write this book were it not for the experience we have gained through working with government officials, regulators, practitioners, service providers and trade associations both at home and abroad, which has largely been funded by bilateral and multilateral government assistance programmes. Our thanks therefore go to these organisations (primarily the UK Department for International Development and the World Bank), and to the taxpayers worldwide who fund them, as well as to the clients from whom we have learned so much – and of course to John Wiley & Sons Ltd for publishing the fruits of this experience. We are also indebted to the many fund-related trade associations who have helped us with information and contacts over the years, particularly the European Federation of Investment Funds and Companies (FEFSI), the Investment Company Institute of the USA and the Investment Management Association of the UK.

We hope you find the book useful and would welcome any feedback via our website at www.cadoganeducation.co.uk, which also serves as a portal to information on collective investment funds worldwide.

Ekaterina Alexeeva, Sally Buxton and Mark St Giles

About the authors

Mark St Giles is Chairman of Cadogan Education. An authority on the investment management market worldwide, he has extensive experience of investment management, both as an investment manager and as managing director of investment management companies managing substantial sums for institutional and private clients. Following an early career in securities markets, working with the stockbroking firm Laurence Keen and Gardner, he moved into asset management in the 1970s, becoming managing director successively of Jessel Britannia Group (1969–74), Allied Hambro Group (1975–83) and GT Management plc (1983–88).

Other posts held include: Chairman of the British Unit Trust Association, President of the European Federation of Investment Funds and Companies, Member of the UK Takeover Panel, Chairman of the Financial Intermediaries, Managers and Brokers Regulatory Association, Board Member of the Life Assurance and Unit Trust Regulatory Organisation. From 1990–96 he was Chairman and then a non-executive director of Framlington Group plc; until 1997 a member of the Board of National Savings.

Recently Mark has been carrying out advisory work on the development of financial institutions in China.

Ekaterina Alexeeva is Director of Cadogan Education. With a degree in Sociology from Moscow State Management Academy, she was involved in creating the legal basis for voucher privatisation work on correspondence and monitoring social aspects of the privatisation process, as well as devising workshop programmes on privatisation in Russia, which has included working with the GKI, RFCSM, Presidentail Audit Commission, Ministry of Finance and ROSKMOSTAT.

She recently worked in the UK, firstly project-managing import-export operations involving adminstration work, translating and interpreting; and secondly working under the Chancellor's Scheme for Cadogan Financial. During her time with Cadogan in London she worked o Russian investment funds regulation and practice and assisted in reviews of Russian and Ukrainian funds law and decrees. She worked with Cadogan in Moscow for several years, advising the RFCSM on a variety of projects including development of fund laws, decrees and regulations, unit investment fund management and depositary training courses. She is now responsible for researching Cadogan's website and for continuing liaison with

Slavic countries and has undertaken training courses for Cadogan in London and Tashkent.

Sally Buxton is a Director of Cadogan Education and specialises in advisory work in asset management and securities markets internationally, with a particular focus on the development of investment funds within emerging and established markets. She has worked in asset management and securities markets since 1982, when she became responsible for all aspects of the UK Unit Trust Association's (now AUTIF) public information and lobbying programme including data collection and publication, PR, government relations, publications and so on. She was public relations and strategic adviser to the UK Association of Investment Trust Companies from 1988 to 1993. Sally worked in Russia from 1992–2000, first on the development of voucher investment funds and latterly on the development of unit investment funds, advising the Russian State Duma on a new law on investment funds. She has recently completed projects on advising and reviewing the development of asset management in Pakistan, providing training for the Egyptian Capital Markets Authority, and advising on privatisation in Yugoslavia.

Introduction

'COLLECTIVE INVESTMENT FUNDS'

Broadly, a 'fund' is a pool of money contributed by a range of investors who may be individuals or companies or other organisations, which is managed and invested as a whole, on behalf of those investors. Generically such funds are sometimes known as 'collective investments' since they collect people's money together. Traditionally, most collective investments fell into one of three main categories: pension funds – that is, funds into which people save during their working life, which can only normally be accessed upon their retirement, in order to receive a pension (in some countries provident funds fulfil a similar role); insurance funds – that is, funds into which people save whereby the fund agrees to pay them a specific sum upon the occurrence of certain events (such as the inappropriately named life insurance which actually pays out on death, to the deceased's nominated beneficiaries); and investment funds into which people save, but where money can be put into and taken out of the fund at any time and where payouts are not specifically related to any one event occurring. This book is about this last category – known as collective investment funds.

However, much of this book will also apply to some forms of pension and insurance funds. Until the 1970s a key difference between investment funds and most life and pension funds was that in the case of life and pension funds the sponsor of the fund (usually the employer or an insurance company) guaranteed the payment to be made by the fund upon certain events: either in terms of a cash sum (e.g. $50 000 upon death) in the case of insurance or in terms of a proportion of salary in the case of pension schemes (e.g. two-thirds of the final salary earned by the worker – hence the term 'defined benefit' pension). Investment funds made no such guarantees: people simply saved into them, their money was invested, and when they wanted to take their money out, they got back the current value of the investments that had been made.

However, in the last 30 or so years forms of pension (known as 'money purchase' or 'defined contribution') and life insurance (unit-linked funds) have developed where there are no guarantees of the amount of money to be paid out – either upon retirement or upon specific events occurring – and which operate in broadly the same way as the collective investment funds: the saver's subscriptions buys units in the fund and the money the investor can take out of the fund upon retirement or upon the end of a period of saving is simply the current value of the units owned. These defined contribution pensions or unit-linked funds, therefore, are simply collective investment funds – though they are hedged around with some different legal and fiscal requirements, such as those that prevent exit from the fund before retirement, for instance. An early example of this form of defined contribution pension fund is the famous Chilean system, introduced in 1981 whereby Chileans are required to save 10% of their salary into a private sector operated pension plan, which has been much emulated elsewhere (primarily Latin America and Central and Eastern Europe).

The term 'collective investment funds' has been adopted for this book because it covers all forms of such funds, whereas the only other term generically used – 'collective investment schemes', which is used by the International Organisation of Securities Commissions, the organisation which establishes common international standards of securities regulation – refers only to one form of fund, which is open ended (that is, funds that buy back their shares or units from holders). All these terms, and their significance, will be explained further in Chapters 2 and 3. Unfortunately there is something of an embarrassment of riches in terms of different names used for different forms of collective investment funds in different countries, which aren't rehearsed here since confusion would abound as a result – suffice it simply to say that probably the most commonly used term is 'mutual funds'.

MANAGING COLLECTIVE INVESTMENT FUNDS

Anyone thinking of creating a business to market and operate collective investment funds will first have to consider the potential for such a business (existing legal and fiscal framework, economic environment, etc.) as any other business would do. Then they will have to create funds and offer them to potential investors (marketing), invest the money they raise (investment management) and operate both the funds and investors' holdings in these funds (administration). They will need to monitor both the market and how taxation or other changes may affect competitiveness of products. And they will need to manage and direct the business, ensuring that the three core activities of marketing, investment management and administration interact effectively and that a profit is produced for shareholders, who may not continue to support the business otherwise.

The chapters of this book broadly follow this pattern. The first four chapters of the book are descriptive, setting out:

- Why the business is worth entering – Chapter 1.
- What the key functions, roles and responsibilities are – Chapter 2.

- What the main fund structures are, and their implications – Chapter 3.
- Why regulation is needed and what it covers – Chapter 4.

The next two chapters relate to investment management, explaining:

- What investment management entails, with a comparison of different styles and their implications and a review of the implications of restrictions imposed by investment and borrowing powers – Chapter 5.
- How investment performance measurement is done and why it matters – Chapter 6.

In the next four chapters the four key elements of fund administration are reviewed. Starting with valuation, which creates the basis for creating a price for shares or units, the chapters then cover charging, since charges are then added or deducted from the resulting valuation to create prices for dealing, which is covered in the following chapter. Finally, how dealing in shares or units is done and how investors are serviced are reviewed. Summarising, the administration-related chapters explain:

- How valuation is done and how common problems can be dealt with – Chapter 7.
- What charges may be levied on a fund and how – Chapter 8.
- How fund prices are created – Chapter 9.
- What issue and redemption is, and how it is done – Chapter 10.

Four chapters on key areas of marketing follow, outlining:

- The activities involved in marketing funds – Chapter 11.
- How funds are sold (often known as distribution) – Chapter 12.
- How communication with investors is handled – Chapter 13.
- What product development entails – Chapter 14.

The next three chapters review three factors that may greatly influence the success or failure of collective investment funds, which are:

- Why fund accounting methods matter – Chapter 15.
- Why taxation matters – Chapter 16.
- How funds are governed and how conflicts of interest between funds and their service providers are commonly dealt with – Chapter 17.

And in the last chapter, we bring this all together, outlining:

- How the business is managed – Chapter 18.

Since the main function of investment funds is to service ordinary investors (also known as the 'retail' market) as opposed to institutional (also known as 'wholesale') investors, this book has a greater focus on the former than the latter.

It is worth bearing in mind, however, that every institutional investor actually represents the savings of individuals, or of companies that are owned by individuals, so it all comes down to retail business in the end. Someone has coined the term 'instividual' for collective investments, which – if ungrammatical – accurately reflects the real nature of funds.

It is perhaps a commonplace to state that without the individual customer there is no business: but this is a fact that some in the financial sector seem to forget from time to time. Even institutional money derives from individuals in the end. These individuals entrust financial institutions with management of their money and if such institutions fail to live up to this trust, or abuse that trust, the penalties can (and should) be very high. It is well known that those who work in the fund management sector are well paid for their task (which may well be why you are reading this book); what is less clear, in some cases, is that this level of remuneration – in terms of investment management and service delivered to the customer – is justified. There are around 2000 collective investment funds and over 130 operators of such funds in the UK alone; and yet the number of operators that provide consistently good standards of performance and service is probably much less than one-third of these.

This sort of trend could not persist in a retail business (e.g. shops or restaurants or garages), but then consumption of retail goods and services is immediate, and results are known; whereas consumption of financial services is deferred as results of saving for retirement, etc. may only become known decades in the future. Perhaps it is simply much more discriminating customers that are needed, who can winnow out the seeds from the chaff. Or perhaps fund management companies – that always advise the public to invest for the long term – should do some long-term thinking for themselves too.

The first chapter of this book looks at why so many companies enter this business and why the business expanded strongly in the 1990s, though the early 2000s have brought a contraction in many countries.

For those who wish to assess their grasp of the subject matter covered by the book, a series of self-test questions for each chapter (with separate answers) are given at the back of the book.

1

Why Enter the Business

INTRODUCTION

In this chapter the role of collective investment funds (henceforth just 'funds' – where reference is to another form of fund this will be specified) is elaborated, as are the reasons why the collective investment funds business has expanded internationally, though falls in many stock markets worldwide have seen the total value of the industry contract in recent years.

Many countries have been experiencing depressed equity markets in the early 2000s, which has caused the amount of money invested in funds globally to fall from its peak of US$12.25 trillion ($12 250 000 000 000) at the end of March 2000 to US$11.217 trillion at the end of December 2002[1] – the most recent global figures available at the time of writing.[2] Even the latter figure represents substantial revenues to managers of these funds, whose fees are usually based on a percentage of the amount they manage. At a 1% annual fee, which is not uncommon, this would represent fund management revenues of US$112.17 billion – which is one reason for entering this business. Actual total funds under management in collective investment funds worldwide will be higher than this, since not all countries report their data and since closed-ended funds are not included within this figure.

This recent contraction follows a period when the industry expanded strongly – partly attributable to increased sale of funds, but also partly attributable to strong performance, with the rising equity markets of the 1990s: always keep in mind when looking at values of funds under management that increases can be due to either of these factors or both. The most recent comparative figures from the Organisation for Economic Co-operation and Development (OECD)[3] show that collective investment funds in OECD countries had an average annual growth rate of 20% in the years 1991–1998, by comparison with 13% for pension funds and 11% for insurance companies.

While the total value of collective investment funds worldwide has been contracting, the number of funds has continued to rise: even since the peak value of funds in 2000 there has been a rise of around 3%, so that the US$11.217 trillion value quoted above reflects statistics for just over 53 000 funds – and there are many other funds in countries whose figures are not yet included in this calculation, though their value is not large in relative terms.

WHY FUNDS HAVE BEEN EXPANDING

It was in the United Kingdom in 1868 that the first collective investment fund was created – the Foreign & Colonial Government Trust – whose purpose, quoted in its prospectus,[4] remains as true of collective investment funds today as it was then:

> 'To provide the investor of moderate means the same advantage as the large capitalist in diminishing risk... by spreading the investment over a number of stocks'.

This fund is still in existence today, with a current value of around $4 billion. Clearly the founders' belief – that there were enough people with enough money and enough confidence in the future to invest in the fund – proved to be correct. Such sufficiency of demand is a prerequisite for the success of a collective investment funds market.

It is worth considering why such demand might not exist – which at its simplest is where funds are irrelevant because a country's population is polarised between a small number of very rich people, who do not need funds to make investments on their behalf, and a large number of very poor people who cannot afford to save. This is a common feature of pre-emerging and emerging markets.[5]

However, in other countries there may be people with savings – but there may still be very little demand for funds. Russia is just one example of such a scenario, where there are reputedly over a hundred billion cash dollars stashed under the mattress ('in the sock' being the equivalent Russian term) or in safety deposit boxes. Why, it might be asked, are these dollars not invested – particularly when the Russian economy and Russian stock markets have been improving? The answer is that despite the fact that well-regulated collective investment funds have existed in Russia now for some five years, people lack trust in the government and the general financial system and have little confidence in the future. From their point of view, what is the point of saving or investing if government may arbitrarily snatch money from them (as it has done in the past, most recently during the Russian financial crisis of 1998) and when the future is so uncertain that saving would be to meet unknowable needs?

So collective investment funds only develop successfully where legal systems provide for clear and fair mechanisms of asset ownership and transfer and for redress if things go wrong – basically, where rights can be predictably sustained. In such an environment, people can be reasonably sure that if they hand over their money to someone else for management, that it will be properly looked after and that they will be able to get their money back subject to the terms stated in the contract. Such a legal system generally derives from the development of a stable and fair system of democratic government, which also gives people the confidence to plan and save for the medium to longer term. In these circumstances a growing middle class emerges – the key target market for collective investment funds since this group has money it can invest and has future needs to save for, but little understanding of investment and little time to learn about it. The development of regulation of funds, which often starts as a response to scandals (e.g. the US Investment Company Act of 1940 which followed problems associated with the Wall Street Crash), plays a major role in creating and sustaining such confidence.

As countries develop, regulation improves and people's confidence in the future improves, collective investment funds develop more strongly. It is interesting to note that – for example – the Spanish collective investment funds' sector was almost non-existent at the time of Spain's accession to the EU in 1985; legislation governing funds was only introduced in 1984 as part of the EU accession process. Today, however, the Spanish funds industry is the seventh largest in Europe[6] – though this is in part due to fiscal incentives to save offered by the government.

WHY GOVERNMENTS ENCOURAGE DEVELOPMENT OF FUNDS

Both governments and companies need to be able to borrow money in order to finance their current and future operations: this is why both companies and governments issue bonds (whereby generally they agree to repay the amount borrowed upon a certain date, and pay a stated level of interest over the period of the life of the bond), which represent fixed-term borrowing; and why companies issue shares (also known as equities since they broadly represent equal proportions of ownership or rights of ownership of a company), which represent indefinite or permanent borrowing, since the shares will remain in existence for ever unless the company is shut down. Companies try to incentivise people to buy and hold their shares by growing the company and its profits, resulting in the payment of rising dividends to holders, which in turn should increase demand for their shares, and thus achieve a rising share price: holders can then make capital gains from selling these shares at a higher price than they bought them for.

If smaller savers keep their money under the mattress, this money is clearly not available to finance government or commerce and thus the development of an economy; and if they keep it on term deposit it will generally only be available to fund bank lending over a stated term, which often will be relatively short. Therefore money available to fund borrowing for the longer term could be restricted. However, if smaller savers invest through funds, their money will become available to finance longer term borrowing through purchase of bonds and shares

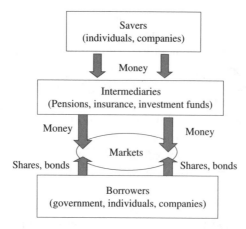

Figure 1.1 *Investment funds intermediate*

and thus help to develop countries' economies – and this is a key reason why governments encourage collective investment (and indeed insurance and pension) funds: they 'mobilise capital'. Insurance, pension and collective investment funds are often characterised as 'non-bank financial institutions'[7] since they provide non-banking finance.

This role of collective investment funds – that of standing between the investor with spare cash and the entity (the government or company) that wants to borrow it – is known as 'intermediation' and is illustrated in Figure 1.1.

The other reason that governments wish to stimulate the development of collective investment funds is to encourage people to save, thus reducing the likelihood of future dependency on the state and consequent drain on state budgets: particularly in relation to retirement. This is explored further later in this chapter.

WHY PEOPLE SAVE THROUGH FUNDS

So the question arises: why do people in developed economies prefer to invest indirectly in securities via funds rather than directly purchase those securities? The answer is that investors find funds attractive because of five factors:

- Reduction of risk through diversification.
- Reduction of cost through economies of scale.
- Professional management.
- Investor protection.
- Flexibility.

Each of these factors is explored in more detail below.

Reduction of risk

An ordinary investor might only be able to afford to invest between US$1000 and US$10000. If the investor were buying securities directly, it would be difficult to buy a holding in several companies for such a sum, even though this money might be the only amount available for investment. Thus investors putting a small sum directly into securities are unlikely to be able to diversify their risk: and if the one company they choose to invest in goes bankrupt, they can lose all their money (all the eggs are in one basket so if the basket is dropped they are all broken).

Investing through funds reduces risk:

- Firstly, because funds usually invest in 20 or more different investments (the eggs are in many different baskets, so if one is dropped some eggs are broken but others are not). Broadly, mathematical studies have shown[8] that holding shares of about 20 randomly selected companies will completely eliminate 'unsystematic' or 'specific' risk (which is the risk attaching to any one company – where there may be value-destroying management, uncompetitive products or natural disasters for instance). Systematic risk[9] is that risk that derives from general and market economic conditions, which cannot be diversified away (see more in Chapter 5).
- Secondly, because increasing the risks of investing by concentrating on just a few securities does not necessarily generate higher returns.

On the first point, once investors understand clearly that diversification pays – in that it lowers risk in relation to return – then they will value this diversification and seek it out. This is almost certainly the major factor in the recent success of funds in developed markets. It is even more relevant to emerging markets, where the risks involved in individual securities are usually higher, so that the advantages of diversification are greater.

On the second point, investors in securities also will become aware that securities whose perceived returns are high often carry correspondingly high risks (many investors in the 'dot-com' or technology/media/telecommunications ('TMT') sector recently learnt this at some cost). This contradicts the naive expectation of the novice investor that he can secure very high returns by finding the right high-risk securities. Essentially, the reality is that any investor with a small portfolio of risky securities is taking on far more risk in relation to return than he needs to. From the perspective of the individual investor, diversification is valuable. It is worth paying for, because it reduces risk.

This diversified risk can be taken through funds with a comparatively small amount of money – around US$1000 would be a normal minimum investment – whereas to achieve a personal portfolio spread of 20 or more securities in a way that minimised transaction costs, most investors would need to invest US$100000 or more.

Reduction of cost

The second major factor in attracting investors to funds is cost. The details of the comparison will vary from one market to another, but the average small investor will usually incur higher total costs in buying and selling a portfolio of individual securities for himself than a fund would.

The reason is that transaction costs in most markets have historically been related to the size of the transaction. The individual investor's transaction costs on small purchases or sales are typically much higher as a percentage of the value of each transaction than those for institutional investors dealing in large quantities, such as funds. The extent of the cost advantage this gives the fund, as opposed to direct purchases of securities, will depend on the time for which the investment is held, the extent to which a portfolio is subject to changes, and the total charges levied by the fund.

The cost factor is, as far as the individual is concerned, aggravated by risk. In order to reduce risk, diversification is necessary. Yet the greater the diversification, the greater the transaction costs: and the greater the relative advantage of the fund with its economies of scale.

This is not to say, however, that costs of investing through funds may not be quite high – a topic covered in Chapter 8.

Professional management

The evolution of developed markets has included a phase (ongoing in some cases) in which inadequate supply of public information gave possessors of 'inside information' a definite advantage. As regulation has reduced such imbalances, the possession and analysis of publicly available information has become the key to the selection and management of investments.

The volume and complexity of the information available mean that the scope for the amateur investor has become more limited. As developed markets show, there is a minority of people – often retired – who devote a good deal of time and energy to managing their own investments. But the majority of people lack the time, inclination or professional skills to do this. They therefore prefer to delegate the task of selecting and managing investments to professional investment fund managers.

Collective investment funds provide such full-time professional management in direct and simple form. This is valuable even in developed markets where information is widely available and financial markets are well regulated. It is even more valuable in countries where this is not the case.

This is to leave to one side, of course, the ongoing debate as to whether such professional managers produce returns commensurate with the fees that they are paid: an issue which is discussed in Chapters 5 and 18 and which commonly rears its head whenever markets are depressed.

Investor protection

The success of funds in many developed markets depends fundamentally on a framework of law and regulation, applied fairly, evenly and consistently. People must have confidence that their money is protected from fraud, theft and other abuses and, if these do occur, that there are reliable means of redress for those affected. In the absence of this confidence, individuals simply will not invest in funds in any volume.

Governments therefore require that in return for the privilege of being permitted to attract money from the public, collective investment funds must be transparent: that is, the terms on which the investment in a fund is made must be absolutely clear, investors should be able to find out at all times what their investment is worth, and be able to enter and exit the investment without undisclosed charges or penalties being levied. This contrasts with many life insurance and pension funds, which historically can be characterised as opaque. In addition, those that offer such collective investment funds, and provide services to them, are required to be of good repute and to meet requirements regarding their conduct of business, covered in Chapter 4.

In addition, for funds to have a chance of success, tax law must put fund investors in a position that is no worse tax-wise than that of direct investors in securities. Failure to address this problem, which is often an accident of legal and fiscal history, has frequently adversely affected developing fund sectors.

Putting such legal and fiscal regimes in place is a demanding agenda and one that has taken developed countries many decades to achieve. Specific regulation of funds did not really begin to take shape in the US or in Europe until the 1930s or even later, when funds had been in operation for 70 years or more; and it was only developed after some major scandals following the Wall Street Crash of 1929. Even today, amendments continue to be made to aspects of tax law and fund supervision and regulation in most jurisdictions, often associated with preventing re-occurrence of a scandal, or the development of new financial instruments or technological developments.

It is vital to appreciate that without a reliable regulatory system, the public will lack the confidence in funds that is crucial to the long-term development of a profitable collective investment fund sector. Practitioners may see regulation as an unnecessary evil, but – provided it is of high standard, is not unduly onerous and is consistently and fairly applied – it has considerable benefits for them.

Flexibility

Collective investment funds also offer flexibility: generally they can be bought and sold on any business day so it is easy to invest and disinvest. This is in contrast to many life insurance and pension fund products where it may take time to exit a fund and where undisclosed penalties or levies may be payable upon early withdrawal.

Further, there are collective investment funds to meet a wide variety of different needs: for capital preservation; for capital growth, income, or a mixture of both; for a stable or a rising income; for exposure only to domestic markets or world-wide; for those with ethical, religious or environmental concerns etc: the list is almost endless. In addition, collective investment funds are commonly available which:

- Enable people to provide for retirement: for instance, it is estimated that around a quarter of net new cash inflows to mutual funds in the USA derives from retirement-related savings[10] and that 80% of money invested in Australian funds is also retirement-related.[11]
- Enable people to save for the medium to long term: many governments in-centivise such savings (additionally to retirement savings) in order to decrease citizens' reliance on the State and to increase flows of capital available to finance governments and companies. Often this is done through creation of tax-privileged 'wrappers' (whereby individuals entitled to do so may hold in-vestments in funds or other assets within tax-privileged 'envelopes' – such as UK Individual Savings Accounts or ISAs and French Employee Savings Plans – 'Fonds Communs de Placement d'Entreprise' or 'FCPE').
- Provide a substitute for bank accounts: this is done by funds known as 'money market funds' whose basic principle, like bank accounts, is that they should be able to pay back not less than the amount originally invested at any time (hence the American term that these funds should not 'break the dollar' that has been invested). These funds are particularly successful where, by pooling together investors' money and investing in bulk, they can access the higher wholesale money market interest rates that are not usually available to ordinary investors: this was true in the USA in the 1970s and later in France, where the government capped interest rates on retail savings accounts: in these countries and many others such funds are a substantial part of the funds market, as illustrated in Figure 1.3.

The collective investment fund proposition – lower risk, lower cost, professional management, investor protection and flexibility – is the foundation of funds'

End 2002–Total value US$ 11 217 billion

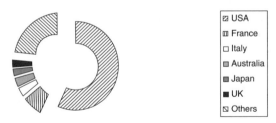

Figure 1.2 *The six largest domestic collective investment funds markets*
Source: *Worldwide Mutual Fund Assets and Flows, Fourth Quarter 2002.* Reproduced by permission of FEFSI (the European Federation of Investment Funds and Companies) and the Investment Company Institute (www.ici.org)

success in every market. However, local factors, such as culture, taxation, regulation and the relative stage of development of financial infrastructure, such as securities exchanges and markets, will shape the pace of their evolution and result in the varying scale of different domestic funds markets as illustrated in Figure 1.2.

The majority of funds invest exclusively in money market instruments, bonds or equities. The extent to which the five factors of risk, cost, professional management, investor protection and flexibility apply to these different types of investment varies according to the regulation, taxation, quality of assets and level of competition within any one market.

For instance, in the case of money market funds versus deposits, whether funds offer a reduction in risk to individual investors or companies depends on the nature of the banking system and the extent to which bank depositors are protected by law in the event of bank failures. On the upside, money market funds, due to their diversification, may even achieve a higher credit rating than the banks or companies whose debt they hold; but on the downside, investors in them are not entitled to the compensation available to depositors in banks through deposit guarantee schemes.

The reduction in risk provided by funds is more significant in the case of bonds, particularly for those that are not of the highest grade, but it is most valuable in respect of equity investments. The cost advantage of funds is also potentially greatest with equities, where individual transaction costs are normally higher than in bonds. Also the selection of equities through good professional management can over time provide greater incremental returns than is possible in managing a portfolio of bonds.

In the long run, one might therefore expect equity funds to be the largest category of funds. However, individual investors start with portfolio preferences of their own in respect of the proportion of their assets they wish to hold in

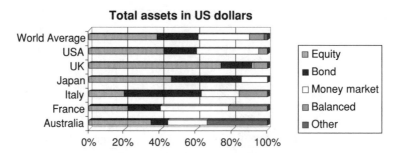

Figure 1.3 *Asset preferences of the six largest domestic collective investment fund markets as at end December 2002*
Source: *Worldwide Mutual Fund Assets and Flows, Fourth Quarter 2002.* Reproduced by permission of FEFSI (the European Federation of Investment Funds and Companies) and the Investment Company Institute (www.ici.org)

deposits, bonds and equities. Where investors can choose funds for each type of investment, then the total assets invested in each type of fund will reflect these portfolio preferences as well as the relative advantages of funds as compared with direct investment. Such portfolio preferences also account for the higher volumes of assets invested in bond-invested funds than equity-invested funds in most of the EU, and for the higher volumes of assets in equity-invested funds than bond-invested funds in the UK, though it should be noted that tax incentives attached to investing in different assets can also have a strong influence on investment preferences. Figure 1.3 shows the variations in asset preferences in the six largest domestic fund markets, compared with a world average.

The advantages of funds versus direct investment are even more pronounced when investing outside a domestic market, as people increasingly do in the interests of diversification of risk. Few individual investors could research foreign markets effectively for themselves, and dealing with the currency and other complexities of investing abroad – as well as the cost of this – is something few people would wish to take upon themselves. This is particularly true of investing in emerging markets, where there may be little information available on companies and no alternative to personal meetings with companies to 'look them in the eye'. This largely accounts for the recent rapid growth rate in funds investing outside their domestic market.

WHO INVESTS IN FUNDS

Most collective investment funds are designed to attract ordinary people to invest and are commonly known as 'publicly offered' or more rarely 'non-specialised' or 'diversified' funds. However, these funds may also attract institutional investors, such as pension funds or insurance or other collective investment funds that may wish to use funds for many of the same reasons as individuals do: to achieve diversification; or to lower the costs of portfolio management; or to utilise professional management – they may lack the expertise to invest in specialist areas so choose to attain this exposure through a fund instead.

In the UK, at any one time in the five years to end 2002, the proportion of collective investment funds owned by institutional investors was between 45% and 57% of total funds under management;[12] while in the USA institutional investment was estimated to account for a little under 50% of total funds under management at the end of 2001.[13] Institutional investors therefore can be an important sales channel for funds. Other legal entities which may invest in funds include companies and charitable organisations.

The pervasiveness of individuals' investment in collective investment funds varies enormously between countries and can be artificially high when funds have been used for privatisation (at one point, for instance, in theory at any rate, all adult citizens of Kazakhstan held funds – technically the highest penetration in the world; but not 'real' since no money was invested, since 'vouchers' which had to be invested in privatisation funds were distributed free). In general terms, levels of ownership of funds by households in any one country will be anything upwards of zero to around 50%; in the USA, with the largest fund market in the world, 52% of all households held collective investment funds in 2001, the highest figure ever recorded – a remarkable achievement when compared with the same figure for 1980: 5.7%.[14] In the three biggest domestic fund markets in Europe, it is estimated that French households hold 20% of their financial assets in funds; German households around 12% and Italian households around 21%.[15]

Research indicates that the typical owner of funds is usually 45 or older, is often (though increasingly less so) male and has a higher than average income. The reason for this older age profile is that this is more normally an age at which people begin to have more disposable income, since their children are beginning to leave home: also, as retirement approaches, people become more anxious to save for it. However, these trends are changing, with younger savers of both sexes affecting trends: the increasing tendency to divorce and have second or even third families could also affect developments.

It should be noted that the figures given in this chapter do not include the substantial number of funds that are designed only for institutional and professional investors and for rich people (sometimes referred to as 'high net worth individuals' or 'HNWI'). These funds, which may only be offered to this limited audience, are known as 'privately offered funds' or sometimes 'specialised funds' or 'non-diversified funds' since they are not permitted to be authorised for public offer. This means that they can take greater investment and borrowing risks than are permitted to publicly offered funds and can have more sophisticated charging structures: 'hedge funds', which are discussed further in Chapter 14, fall within this category.

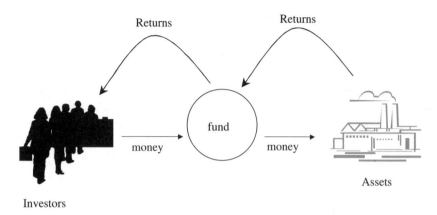

Returns

Returns

fund

money

money

Investors

Assets

Figure 1.4 *The function of a collective investment fund*

However, whoever or whatever the investor may be, a collective investment fund performs the same function: gathering sums of money from a variety of investors, pooling it together, and using a professional management company to invest the money in a spread of investments which will, in turn, hopefully achieve capital growth or bring in an income, in the form of dividends from companies or interest from bonds or deposits (or more rarely rental on real estate) (Figure 1.4). These returns (capital gain, income) belong to fund investors.

BUILDING A SUCCESSFUL FUND MANAGEMENT BUSINESS

The key to building a successful funds business is consistently to give fund investors a good return; ideally this return should be competitive in relation to other savings products and relevant indices, and should outpace inflation. Since those who operate funds – fund management companies – make their money by charging fees, which are related in percentage terms to the value of the funds they manage, they have a strong incentive to increase the value of fund assets by pursuing successful investment strategies and thus to both enhance returns to investors and fees paid to themselves. Also, the happier investors are about their investment returns, the greater their readiness to invest more money with the same management company.

However, consistently making money from fund management involves rather more than simply attracting customers, choosing investments and administering investors' money. If a fund business loses clients as fast as it gains them, or chooses bad investments and only gives poor returns, or is inefficient and unreliable, it will fail. On the other hand, if it is successful, the business can reach a very large scale: the largest independent collective investment fund management business in the world is Fidelity® Investments of the USA, founded in 1946 by Edward C. Johnson II and still controlled by the Johnson family – its total funds under management were over $737.7 billion at the end of November 2002.[16]

The remainder of this book seeks to explain how such a business operates, and within what constraints, with the next chapter exploring the key roles and functions that have to be undertaken in order for funds to operate.

Those who would like to test their grasp of the contents of this chapter should turn to the self-test questions at the back of the book.

NOTES

1. *Worldwide Mutual Funds Assets and Flows, Fourth Quarter 2002*, Investment Company Institute, Washington.
2. To check if more recent figures are available, visit our website www.cadoganeducation.co.uk.
3. *Institutional Investors Statistical Yearbook 2001*, OECD, Paris, 2002.
4. As quoted in *Put Not Your Trust in Money*, John Newlands, Chappin Kavanagh, London, 1997 (a history of the investment trust company movement in the UK).
5. Broadly, countries which are deemed not to be 'developed markets'.
6. European Federation of Investment Funds and Companies (FEFSI), Brussels.
7. *The Development and Regulation of Non Bank Financial Institutions*, Jeffrey Carmichael and Michael Pomerleano, World Bank, Washington 2002.
8. The effect of diversification of risk, Wayne H. Wagner and Sheila Lau, *Financial Analysts Journal*, November/December 1981; Portfolio selection, Harry M. Markowitz, *Journal of Finance*, March 1952.
9. The portion of an asset's variability that can be attributed to a common factor: refer to A simplified model for portfolio analysis, William F. Sharpe, *Management Science*, January 1963.
10. *Fundamentals*, Vol II No 2, Investment Company Institute, Washington as at 2001.
11. *Country Report for Australia*, IIFC Conference, Investment and Financial Services Association, Sydney October 2002.
12. Investment Management Association, London.
13. Assets of Fiduciary, Business and Other Institutional Investors, Mutual Funds Yearbook, p. 96, Investment Company Institute, Washington, 2002.
14. *Fundamentals*, 11(5), October, Investment Company Institute, Washington 2002.
15. European Federation of European Investment Funds & Companies (FEFSI), Brussels.
16. Fidelity® Investments.

2

Key Functions, Roles and Responsibilities

INTRODUCTION

This chapter sets out the key functions that must be performed in order for funds to operate, identifying which result from operational or regulatory requirements. It then explores the implications of fund structures for the roles and responsibilities of key organisations including management companies; trustees, depositaries and custodians; auditors; and regulators.

KEY OPERATIONAL FUNCTIONS

The fundamental purpose of funds is to make money for their investors. Stated at its simplest, this is done through:

- Creating and promoting the fund so it attracts money, making sales, keeping investors informed (known as marketing).
- Receiving subscriptions and paying out proceeds, recording transactions, valuing and pricing the fund and reporting to investors (known as administration or customer servicing).
- Investing subscribers' money in assets that align with the investment objective of the fund and which it is anticipated will give a good return, and adjusting that portfolio as necessary (known as investment management).

These functions must be carried out in order for funds to operate. However, regulation also requires three other key functions to be undertaken.

ADDITIONAL FUNCTIONS REQUIRED BY REGULATION

To allow any person or company to have unlimited access to the scale of the money that can flow through funds is asking for trouble – there is potentially too great a temptation to use fund assets to the benefit of those other than fund investors. Regulation therefore requires certain precautions to be taken in this respect.

The first precaution is to prevent fund management companies or directors stealing fund assets. This is done by a requirement that a fund's assets, including its cash, should be held for safekeeping by an entity other than the management company or directors of a fund. This entity is known as a 'custodian' and under law and regulation it has the responsibility of keeping safe the assets of a fund. A custodian is required by law and regulation to be at least operationally independent of the management company or wholly independent from it. Many countries, particularly those with a Civil Code legal system, permit the management company and the custodian to be a part of the same organisation owned by a single ultimate parent, but require that the organisations may not share personnel or systems, nor may they own any shares in each other. Some argue that this offers weaker investor protection than a requirement for absolute independence – the counter argument being that in most instances both management company and custodian are owned by large banks or financial holding companies that will be keen to ensure that their reputation is maintained, so their custody operation has every incentive to be vigilant.

The net outcome of this requirement for a custodian is that while the management company (or an appointed investment adviser) takes the investment decisions, it cannot carry out those decisions without the co-operation of the custodian, which has to release money or securities to complete a purchase or sale transaction respectively. Equally, the custodian cannot initiate a transaction, only being able to undertake a transaction with fund assets upon the instructions of the management company. In effect, it is as if the management company and custodian each have a 'key' to the box that holds fund assets but neither can open the box without the other's key also being used.

The second precaution is the regulatory requirement for a fund to be audited by a professional qualified auditor who is independent of the management company of the fund (though generally it may also act as auditor to the management company). The auditor's task is to check that the financial statements made about any one fund accurately reflect its real financial position, and to undertake random tests to validate this. They may also be required to report any irregularities they find to the regulator.

These two requirements – for custody and for independent audit of funds – are sometimes known as 'third-party regulation' – since a third party, other than the regulator, is fulfilling a regulatory-type role.

The third precaution is not always the norm, but is increasingly so: that a management company (and a custodian) are required by law and regulation to have a compliance function in place. The responsibility of this function is to ensure that the company concerned is operating in compliance with law and regulation and that its systems and procedures are designed in such a way that it remains in compliance on a continuing basis.

So to summarise – while collective investment funds operate in different ways in different countries, they all need the following functions to be undertaken in order for them to work effectively:

- marketing
- administration
- investment management
- custody
- audit
- compliance.

KEY ROLES AND RESPONSIBILITIES

The structures in which collective investment funds have developed around the world are largely a function of the particular environment within which they operate. While the functions outlined above are key to funds everywhere, how these functions are carried out, by whom, and what rights and responsibilities pertain to those who fulfil the functions, will vary from country to country. The legal and fiscal frameworks of the countries concerned are usually key factors influencing the form that collective investment funds take and in defining who is responsible for what.

As discussed in more detail in Chapter 3, collective investment funds can take the legal form of:

- Companies, whose directors are responsible to shareholders – i.e. fund investors; or
- Trusts, which have a trustee that is the legal owner of the fund's assets: the trustee also has a duty to look after the interests of the beneficiaries of the trust – i.e. the fund's investors; or
- Contractual pools, where duties on the management company and depositary (see below) to look after fund investors' interests are specified in law or regulation; or
- Limited partnerships, where the managing partner (the fund management company) is responsible to the limited partners (the investors) for the conduct of the business of the fund. This form is commonly used for funds whose investors are institutional or professional investors but is not used for funds offered to the general public so its governance structure is not discussed here (refer to Chapter 3).

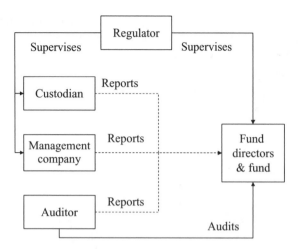

Figure 2.1 *Roles – classical corporate investment funds*

In essence, the corporate and trust forms of funds are similar in that both place a clear fiduciary duty to look after the interests of fund investors either upon the company's directors or the trust's trustee, respectively. Contractual funds can only seek to impose this fiduciary duty through law and regulation and the terms of the management company contract.

The legal structure of each type of fund outlined above has an impact on the roles and responsibilities of the organisations involved in operating funds, which are also influenced by the requirements set by the domestic regulator.

In order to explore these roles and responsibilities, a common allocation of functions for each different legal structure of fund is shown in Figures 2.1 and 2.2.

Figure 2.1 shows the typical roles relating to a classical corporate investment fund that has a board of directors, responsible to the fund's shareholders. Essentially, all contracted parties report to the directors of the fund who are responsible to fund shareholders.

However, there is an alternative and rather unusual structure found in the UK (please contact the authors if you know of other examples) whereby the management company can and does act as the 'authorised corporate director' or 'ACD' – which may be the only director of the corporate fund. Please note an ACD is only possible for an investment company with variable capital, or 'ICVC', which is an open-ended fund, and not for an investment company of fixed capital, which is a closed-ended fund – refer to Chapter 3 for further information on this. Clearly in this unusual structure the management company, as a director of the fund, cannot supervise its own conduct as a director of the fund; so this task is given by law and regulation to the depositary of the fund instead. In this structure the depositary not only fulfils the functions of the custodian, i.e. safekeeps the assets,

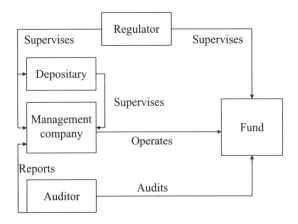

Figure 2.2 *Roles – classical contractual or trust*[1] *fund (and UK ICVC)*
[1]In which case, replace 'depositary' with 'trustee'.

but has additional duties to supervise that the management company is correctly undertaking its obligations under fund laws and regulations (more below).

The outcome of the single ACD supervised by a depositary is roles and responsibilities that more closely resemble those undertaken for contractual or trust funds, which are illustrated in Figure 2.2.

Figure 2.2 shows the typical roles relating to a classical contractual or trust form fund, where the outcome of law and regulation is that the trustee (trust fund) or depositary (contractual fund) has the responsibility of supervising the activities of the management company on behalf of fund investors.

However, there are numerous variations on these themes that may occur within different types of fund within each country, as well as between countries: these are explored further in Chapter 3.

ROLE OF THE FUND MANAGEMENT COMPANY

Essentially the term 'fund management company' is used in this book for the entity that usually causes a fund to be created (to add to revenues) and operates the fund. Technically this entity does not always have to be formed as a company – partnerships are also possible in some regulatory environments. Other names commonly applied to this entity are 'fund sponsor' or fund 'investment adviser'. The functions that are carried out by the fund management company will vary from quite narrow (such as fund initiation and marketing only) to very wide (all tasks except audit and custody) and will depend upon the structure of the fund being formed as well as the commercial choices made about its operation. For the purposes of clarity, the functions listed under the sub-headings below are those that, at a maximum, are carried out by the fund management company.

There is an unusual variant on the management company/trustee theme in Australia, whereby the management company and trustee roles have been required by law to be combined into a 'single responsible entity' or SRE, which is the management company; custody usually is still undertaken by another organisation, however.

Fund management companies have been started by a wide range of people and organisations, ranging from individual specialists such as fund managers, lawyers, stockbrokers or accountants through to international financial houses and consumer brands. Provided regulatory requirements for fitness and properness and competence are met, in theory anyone can start a fund management firm – though some regulatory regimes may be more restrictive.

Investment management

Investment management (home to the 'prime donne' of the fund management world – on a passing note, why is there no male equivalent for this term?) will generally cover the following activities:

- defining investment objectives and styles
- research
- investment analysis
- portfolio selection and management.

Some or all of these activities may be subcontracted.

Administration

Administration includes two different areas of activity: the first being outward facing, which is servicing the fund's investors; the second, being inward facing, which is administration and accounting for the fund's investments. At a maximum, these cover:

- Outward facing:
  - administering the flow of money into and out of a fund
  - creating and maintaining individual accounts for fund investors
  - confirming contractual details
  - creating and maintaining fund registers
  - recording all payments to and from investors
  - paying dividends to investors.

- Inward facing:
  - fund valuation and pricing
  - advising fund managers of money available (or not available) for investment
  - recording fund portfolio transactions
  - operating the accounts of the fund including income received and gains or losses realised
  - liaison with the custodian and auditor.

A management company may, however, subcontract these activities to another party.

Marketing

This is a broad title, which at its most extensive, covers the following activities:

- Market research.
- Branding.
- Product development – design of funds and related services.
- Promotion of funds to potential and existing investors, including general information provision.
- Sales of funds to investors.
- Communications with investors.

Again, some or all of these functions may be subcontracted to other entities. In addition, of course, the business itself must be managed, which is discussed in Chapter 18.

ROLE OF THE CUSTODIAN

The role and responsibilities of the entity that fulfils the role of custodian to a fund will vary according to the legal structure of the fund; i.e., whether the fund is constituted as a company, a trust or a contractual pool. It will also vary according to the duties placed upon the function in governing law and regulation. This gives rise to the fact that a number of different terms are used for this entity, each of which has been allocated a particular meaning in the context of this book:

- 'Trustee': in this book this term is used only to refer to the capacity of a single trustee whose responsibilities under a trust deed of a fund are to protect the interests of beneficiaries under that deed – i.e. the fund investors – and to keep safe the assets of the fund (it does not refer to multiple trustees of funds structured as business trusts in the USA or elsewhere, where the trustees are equivalent to directors of the fund and there is a separate custodian). It has both safekeeping and supervisory functions (see below).

- 'Custodian': in this book this refers to an entity that only safekeeps fund assets, also known as a 'bare custodian'. A custodian has no supervisory duties.
- 'Depositary': in this book – and generally in many legislative frameworks – this term is used to refer to an entity which not only safekeeps fund assets (i.e. acts as a custodian) but also has certain supervisory duties to ensure that the management company is operating the fund in compliance with regulation and founding documents of funds. Basically a fund depositary is similar to a fund trustee, but its powers derive only from fund law and regulation; whereas a trustee's duty to the beneficiaries of the trust derives from legal precedent as well as from fund law and regulation.

Essentially the entity carrying out the role of custodian, trustee or depositary may undertake between one and three of the functions outlined below, only two of which are linked to regulatory requirements.

Safekeeping of assets

Regulation makes a custodian, trustee or depositary responsible for the safekeeping of all the assets of a fund, whether cash or near cash, securities, title to real estate or other assets. In a dematerialised system (where securities ownership is recorded in electronic rather than paper form) these assets are registered in the nominal ownership of the relevant organisation and in a materialised system (where securities ownership is recorded by a certificate and/or registers, both of which are paper-based) the certificates are physically held by the custodian, depositary or trustee, so the management company is unable to buy or sell assets without its assent and co-operation. To repeat: this is designed to prevent theft of fund assets by the management company or by the directors of the fund.

Supervision of the conduct of business of the fund

Supervision of the compliance of the management company's conduct of business of a fund with its founding documents and with regulation is a duty that is imposed upon a depositary or a trustee of contractual or trust (or ICVC) form funds, in addition to safekeeping of assets. This supervisory role is not imposed on custodians, however, since the funds for which they act (classical corporate funds) have directors who are responsible for such supervision. Except in cases of classical corporate funds, the supervisory role can cause conflicts of interest, since it means that an entity chosen and contracted by a fund management company (which usually creates the fund and chooses the contractors to it) is being called upon to monitor the conduct of the business of the organisation which chose it

Table 2.1 *Summary of safekeeping and supervisory roles — by fund legal structure*

Fund type	Safekeeping role	Supervisory role
Corporate fund	Undertaken by a custodian	Undertaken by fund directors (except for UK ICVCs where the depositary is responsible)
Trust fund	Undertaken by a trustee, trustee can subcontract role to a custodian	Undertaken by a trustee
Contractual fund	Undertaken by a depositary	Undertaken by a depositary

and which can replace it; this is why a duty placed on both the fund management company and depositary to act only in the interests of fund investors can be a useful clarifying measure in a regulatory framework.

Provision of additional commercial services
This third element is the provision of additional commercial services which may be required by the fund or fund management company to support the operations of the fund, and which can conveniently be provided by the custodian, depositary or trustee if so desired. These would normally include money management services, such as currency management, and fund administration services such as registration.

A summary of the usual nature of regulatory requirements for custodians, depositaries or trustees is given in Table 2.1.

Some fund regulatory regimes require the appointment of a supervisory committee to a fund, whose task is to monitor the performance of the fund management company and also sometimes the depository, thus providing another form of 'third-party supervision'. In some Latin American countries this is termed the 'Comite de Vigilancia'; and in a slightly different legal construction the individual trustees required under Indian law fulfil a similar function. The effectiveness of such committees, whose access to information is dependent upon the management company and depositary, which are unlikely to voluntarily expose themselves to criticism, is perhaps questionable.

Trustee, depositary and custodian operations have been founded by a variety of individuals and organisations. Today the increasingly global nature of the business, the information technology investment needed and its transaction orientation has resulted in the majority of custody, trustee and depositary work being undertaken by banks or banking subsidiaries. In addition, custody fits naturally alongside the other financial services that such institutions also offer.

ROLE OF THE AUDITOR

The requirement that independent and qualified auditors undertake at least annual fund audits is standard to most regulatory environments. Such auditors may, or may not (regulatory regimes vary on this) be permitted to be the same auditor as that which provides audit services to the fund management company. Regulation or accounting professional ethics generally require that auditors must be independent of the funds and the management companies they audit.

The standards to which audits must be undertaken will be set by domestic accounting standards. Special accounting standards are usually set for funds, since their operation is not comparable with that of ordinary companies or other trusts (see Chapter 15): regrettably at the time of writing no international standard for fund accounting exists.

Regulation also may place on a fund auditor the responsibility of reporting any discrepancies found during the audit to the regulator, as an additional element of supervision; it may also require the auditor to undertake a fixed number of random spot checks on funds during the audit year and report on any problems discovered.

ROLE OF THE REGULATOR

In this book, the role of the regulator is taken broadly to mean that of whichever regulatory body has the responsibility for supervising funds. In general this is the body:

- Whose authorisation or registration or approval is needed prior to a fund being publicly offered for sale.
- Whose authorisation or registration is required prior to a fund management company being permitted to seek approval for any funds it wishes to offer.
- That monitors and supervises the operation of funds, their management companies and some other service providers.
- That has powers to discipline those responsible for malpractice within funds or fund management companies, and to order compensation to be paid for any damage to fund investors.

The regulator may also regulate the conduct of custody business (which is sometimes covered by bank-related law or regulation instead) and usually regulates the conduct of fund depositaries and trustees. This regulator is often the regulator of securities markets in general, since fund units, shares or participations are usually defined as securities.

ABILITY TO DELEGATE TASKS BUT NOT RESPONSIBILITIES

It is noted above that fund management companies, trustees and depositaries may subcontract some tasks to other parties – as indeed may custodians who could appoint sub-custodians to hold non-domestic assets on behalf of funds. A key requirement of fund regulation internationally (refer to Chapter 4) is that a fund management company, custodian, depositary or trustee remains responsible for the fulfilment of all its tasks under law and regulation irrespective of whether it appoints a subcontractor to undertake that task on its behalf. In other words, liability to fund investors rests with the delegator of the task and not with the delegatee, though the delegator may seek redress from the delegatee for any breach of contract.

In the next chapter the structures in which funds may be created and the implications these have for those that operate and service such funds are explained and explored in detail.

Those who would like to test their grasp of the contents of this chapter should turn to the self-test questions at the back of the book.

3

Main Fund Structures

INTRODUCTION

The different legal structures of funds – corporate, trust, contractual and limited partnership – have already been mentioned in Chapter 2. In this chapter the implications of the different structures of funds that have developed in different legal environments, are examined more closely.

When the first fund was formed in the UK in 1868 there was, unsurprisingly, no fund-specific legislation. However, then, as today, the creators of the fund examined the legal structures available to them, and the relative merits of each structure in operational and fiscal terms, and chose what they considered to be the most attractive to potential investors. They had the choice of being a company, or a trust; they chose the latter, since the reputation of companies was at that time poor (limited liability companies could not be formed in the UK before 1855, so shareholders had suffered dire personal consequences if companies became insolvent): it was also felt that choosing 'great and good' trustees would enhance confidence in the vehicle. Also, interestingly, the creators of the fund decided to lodge the stocks held by the fund with bankers: this early use of a custodian[1] was also designed to build investor confidence: a key aim of funds to this day.

However, a fund's legal structure is only one of a series of structural choices that have to be made when deciding in what form to create a fund. The complete list of structural choices when considering the creation of a new fund is:

- Which legal structure – company, trust, contractual pool or partnership.
- Which operating structure – open, interval or closed-ended.
- Which management structure – internal or external.

The list given above identifies the widest range of possibilities that will not necessarily be available in every country (for instance as noted elsewhere, commonly domestic trust and contractual form funds do not co-exist within single countries): the range of structures actually available to be used for a fund will depend on the law and regulation of the country in which the fund is to be legally created and will be affected by the acceptability of different structures in any other country into which it is hoped the fund will be marketed. In addition, the tax treatment of different structures can be a key influence: managers are unlikely to offer a choice of a contractual fund that suffers no tax and a corporate fund that suffers tax when they can predict that investors would opt for the former.

Some countries' legal frameworks offer a wider range of structural choices than others, the widest often being found in the 'low tax' or 'offshore' domiciles. These may be countries, or designated areas within countries, or sometimes islands (respective examples being Luxembourg, Ireland's 'International Financial Services Centre' based in Dublin and Bermuda), which have made a strategic decision to create a legal and fiscal environment that is attractive to funds. Such funds will be based in their territory legally but will be marketed in other countries so all the investors in such funds will be foreign rather than domestic. The merit of this from the offshore domiciles' point of view is that servicing funds will create employment and bring in revenues to domestic service providers to funds.

FUND LEGAL STRUCTURES AND THEIR IMPLICATIONS

The three main legal structures in which funds are created are corporate, trust or contractual. Corporate form funds can be operated under most legal systems so this form of fund is found throughout the world: though taxation treatment and inability to operate variable capital companies (see below) can restrict their development. Trust form funds are only found in countries that have a common law system, or which have been influenced by such countries (the main example being the English common law system which has influenced the legal systems of former British colonies including America). Contractual form funds are found in countries which have a Civil Code based legal system and are common in Continental European countries and their former colonies. While corporate and trust funds may co-exist in a single country, as may corporate and contractual funds, trust and contractual form funds hardly ever co-exist in a single country since they derive from different legal traditions.

By value, corporate funds dominate the fund sector worldwide, largely due to the scale of the US market where open-ended (see below) corporate funds known as 'mutual funds' predominate: however, contractual and trust funds are common in many countries, and may be greater in number than corporate funds.

Corporate funds

Funds formed as companies generally operate on the basis of company law in the country in which they are created, though they are usually subject to specific additional regulatory and fiscal provisions or exemptions relating to funds (refer to Chapters 4 and 16, respectively) that distinguish them from ordinary companies. This is because corporate funds are not ordinary companies, which usually seek to make profits from producing goods or providing services: instead corporate funds aim to give their shareholders good returns from making investments.

The practicalities of funds' operation, which entail attracting large numbers of investors, dictate that such companies must be:

- Formed in the 'open', and not 'closed',[2] company type, since 'closed' companies require any shareholder who wishes to sell shares to seek the approval of other shareholders prior to so doing. Seeking such permission clearly would not be feasible for funds which may have thousands, or even hundreds of thousands of investors (the Unit Trust of India's Scheme US-64 is probably the largest fund, by number of investors, in the world with over 20 million investors).
- Formed as limited companies: that is, the liability of their shareholders is limited to the amount paid to buy shares in that company; clearly unlimited liability would not be attractive to potential investors.

As a company, a corporate fund has a board of directors that is responsible to shareholders for the performance of the company in which they have invested. Such directors have a fiduciary duty to their shareholders, which essentially places a responsibility on them to treat shareholders' money as carefully as they would their own. The board is legally responsible for contracting the services of a fund management company, a custodian and any other provider of services to the fund, such as the auditor, and monitoring their performance of their obligations. It can also terminate the contracts of such organisations, including the management company, and appoint replacements.

It should be noted, however, that since it is normally the fund management company that stimulates the creation of new funds (the motivation being to bring in more management fees and potentially enhance profitability), it is normally the management company that selects the directors of the fund, also. An example of regulation of fund directors to correct any biases thus created is to be found in the USA, where a minimum of 40% of fund directors are required to be independent of the fund management company (though best practice, which is common, is that two-thirds of directors should be independent) and where certain decisions (such as selecting and nominating new independent director where funds levy a 12b-1 plan) must be made by independent directors only. In fact, in the USA, best practice is for independent directors only to sit on audit committees and to select and nominate other independent directors.

The shares issued by corporate funds are securities, as are those issued by other companies. The rights of investors in corporate funds are the same as investors in other companies – they buy shares in the fund and are referred to as shareholders – though fund law may give them additional rights and require them to vote on additional issues to those required under company law. Such issues would

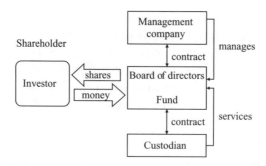

Figure 3.1 *Corporate fund relationships*

usually include a change in investment objectives of a fund and an increase in fees charged to the fund.

Unusually, as far as companies generally are concerned, corporate funds may be created with a finite life – generally of between 5 and 35 years – at the end of which they will be liquidated and assets paid out to shareholders (although shareholders may vote to extend the life of the fund, also). Such funds are usually closed-ended and are able to create more complex share structures (see below). These can be very useful in enabling 'guaranteed' type funds to be operated (refer to Chapter 14).

In principle the purchaser of shares in a corporate fund acquires rights over the returns made by the fund in proportion to their contribution to the total value of the fund (as also applies to trust and contractual funds), though where the fund has the ability to issue several different types of share (see below) this becomes more complicated. An illustration of the relationships between the investor, fund, fund management firm and custodian of a corporate fund is shown in Figure 3.1.

This fund structure is the most common in the world, the largest group by value being American open-ended investment companies, commonly known as 'mutual funds'. It is worth remembering that funds formed as companies are corporations in law and are taxable as such unless they are given special dispensations.

While some corporate funds have a very simple structure, with a single class of ordinary shares in issue, all with the same rights, it is possible to create more complex funds, both in closed-ended fund and open-ended fund forms (the features of open-ended and closed-ended funds are explored later in this chapter). Essentially this means that these more complex funds can issue different securities or different classes of shares.

Complex corporate structures: closed-ended funds

Closed-ended funds formed as companies (unless fund law precludes this) can issue all the securities that any other company can issue, which commonly includes:

- Ordinary shares representing an equal proportion of ownership of a company and having standardised voting rights.
- Debenture stocks (a form of loan capital with a fixed annual rate of interest and a fixed repayment value, usually secured on company assets and taking precedence over ordinary and preferred shareholders if a firm is wound up), loan stocks (similar to debenture stocks, repayable on or by a certain date but unsecured) and convertible loan stocks (fixed interest loans that may be converted into ordinary shares at a future date upon terms fixed at the date of the issue of the loan) which enable these funds to borrow long term, as other companies do: all these are generally described as 'bonds'.
- Preference shares (a class of share capital that receives a fixed rate of return and comes ahead of ordinary shares in order of priority in a winding up), redeemable preference shares (which are repaid at a certain date in the future), cumulative preference shares (where if payments due are missed these securities have priority when the next payment is made and arrears must be made good before dividends can be paid to ordinary shareholders) or stepped preference shares (where dividend or capital entitlements increase annually by a predetermined amount).
- Warrants (which give the right, but not the obligation, to buy shares at a specified price in the future).

A further complexity is that a corporate closed-ended fund *with a fixed life* can take the form of a simple or complex split capital fund – that is, the fund's capital is 'split' into different types. A simple 'split' (as these funds are known in the UK – they are called 'dual purpose' funds in the USA) issues two forms of share: income and capital. For the sake of example: a split might issue 5 million income shares and 5 million capital shares, totalling 10 million shares in issue, all at $1 each ($10 million capital in total). Essentially the concept is that the 5 million income shares have the right to most or all of the income earned by fund assets and the 5 million capital shares have the right to most or all of the capital growth earned by fund assets. Thus the income shareholders have paid 5 million dollars, but will receive all the income from all of the 10 million dollars invested; and the capital shareholders have paid 5 million dollars, but will get capital gains on all of the 10 million dollars invested. This increases the potential return to each share class (which is termed 'gearing' or 'leveraging') which can be attractive to those needing a high income or high capital return (relative tax treatment can be significant here).

Complex splits may issue other forms of share such as zero dividend preference shares, similar in concept to zero coupon fixed income securities, that have no rights to dividends but are entitled to a fixed sum on repayment, usually based on an annual percentage rate of interest, accruing annually. Each type of share appeals to investors with particular needs but the complexities of such structures can lead to situations where one class of securities benefits to the detriment of another class, which can prove unpopular with investors – who may have grasped the upside, but not the downside, to their investment.

On a cautionary note, the fact that these closed-ended corporate funds can borrow extensively can also be their undoing: if a fund raises $60 million and borrows a further $40 million and buys $100 million of assets with the cash thus raised, then if the value of those assets halves to $50 million the fund can only just repay its borrowings and has only $10 million of assets left for investors who originally invested $60 million. This is not common, but is not unknown either.

Complex corporate structures: open-ended funds
The complexity of open-ended corporate funds' capital structure is more restricted, since they are not permitted to borrow long term so cannot issue loan stock or bonds (unlike closed-ended corporate funds) and can only borrow up to 10% of the fund for a limited period (refer to Chapter 5).

In addition, the general principle is applied that open-ended funds are not permitted to issue any share that has advantages that would prejudice the holders of other shares in the fund. As a result, only the following different categories of share have generally been issued in open-ended corporate funds:

- Income shares, which distribute dividends to their holders.
- Accumulation shares, where dividends are not paid out, but retained and accumulated within the value of the share.
- Currency shares, essentially where the price of a share, and related payments, are expressed in, and transacted in, the currency of that class of share (e.g. dollar share, yen share, pound sterling share, euro share).
- Variable charging structure shares – these are shares with the same rights and of the same type (e.g. accumulation, income, currency), but which are subject to different charging structures: so an 'A' share may have an initial charge of 5% and an annual charge of 1.5%; and a 'B' share may have no initial charge and an annual management fee of 1.5%; etc. (for more explanation about charges, refer to Chapter 8). These different shares are usually marketed to different types of client – the first to retail clients and the second to institutional clients, for instance (Chapter 11 has more on this subject).

Trust funds

Trust funds are formed under trust law or precedent: trusts are essentially an arrangement recognised by law under which one person (the trustee) holds property for the benefit of another (the beneficiary). As such, a trust is a legal person and may be therefore be taxable.

Funds formed as trusts are often known as 'unit trusts' and holdings in them, which are generally defined as securities by fund or securities legislation, are known as 'units' (or sometimes, if these are issued, 'certificates'). They are created by a trust deed, to which the signatories are the management company and the trustee. The investor becomes a beneficiary of the trust upon subscription of money to the fund, in return for which he receives a holding of units. The beneficiary has rights to the returns earned by the fund in proportion to his contribution to the total value of the fund.

The trustee of a unit trust is entitled, in the final analysis, to sack the management company if it fails adequately to perform its duties as required by the trust deed and by fund regulation. Thus the task of the trustee is as onerous in this form of fund as is the directorship of a corporate form fund, with approximately the same liability to fund investors.

Voting rights of unitholders in unit trusts are more limited than those of shareholders in corporate funds. In contrast to corporate funds, unit trusts do not have annual general meetings; though they are required to call extraordinary general meetings to vote on specified issues, such as an increase in fees or a change in investment objective (this is because such changes have the effect of altering the basis on which the original contract was entered into and were unknown to the investor at that time).

Most unit trusts are open-ended funds, though theoretically there is no reason why interval or closed-ended unit trusts should not be formed. If law and regulation permits, they may be able to issue a variety of classes of unit along the lines of those outlined for complex open-ended corporate funds above though in the authors' experience this is relatively uncommon.

An illustration of the relationships between the investor, fund, fund management company and trustee of a trust type fund is shown in Figure 3.2.

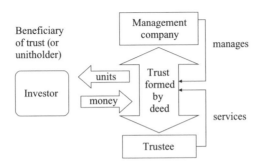

Figure 3.2 *Unit trust fund relationships*

Contractual funds

This form of fund is created by a standardised contract between the investor and the fund management company, whereby the management company contracts to provide management of the pool of assets collected according to the contract and the founding documents of the fund (sometimes called fund rules or constitution). The management company is required to have a contract with a depositary to provide custody and supervisory services in order for the fund to be approved by the regulator.

Investors buy 'units' or 'participations' or 'certificates' in the fund (henceforward described as 'units') and are known as 'participants' or 'unitholders' or 'certificate holders' (henceforward described as 'unitholders'). Holdings in contractual funds are usually (but not always) defined as securities by securities or fund regulation. The unitholder's right to returns made by the fund is proportionate to his contribution to the total value of the fund.

The rights of investors in such funds are defined by the contract with the management company: investment fund laws and regulation establish these rights and often specify requirements for the mandatory content of such contracts. The voting rights of investors in contractual funds are often weaker than those of shareholders in corporate-type funds or beneficiaries of trust-type funds; unlike them, contractual fund investors will have no vote on changes to the fund which substantially affect their interests (e.g. an increase in charges) – unless fund law and regulation specifically mandates such rights, which is the case in some countries. Without the right to vote unitholders can only express their disagreement with any proposed change by 'voting with their feet' and asking for their units to be redeemed; most regulatory regimes require that sufficient notice is given to such unitholders to exercise this right before the changes come into effect, and that no redemption fees are imposed on such redemptions (again, because the terms of the contract on the basis of which the investor entered the fund have been changed).

However, the downside of the fact that the contractual pool has no legal persona – unlike a corporate or trust fund – has an upside: since the fund has no legal existence, it cannot be taxed: hence the popularity of such funds in many countries. German 'investmentfonds' are of this type; as are French 'fonds communs de placement' or 'FCPs'.

An illustration of the relationships between the investor, fund, fund management firm and depositary of a contractual-type fund is shown in Figure 3.3.

Partnership funds

Another form of fund uses the partnership structure, which is not usually permitted (or practical, since maximum numbers of partners are often limited by law) to

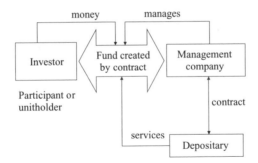

Figure 3.3 *Contractual fund relationships*

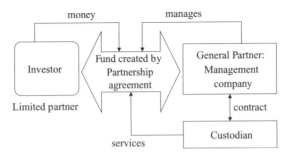

Figure 3.4 *Partnership fund relationships*

be used for funds offered to the public, but is quite often used for funds designed to attract only institutional or professional investors. Partnership structure funds can occur both in common law and Civil Code countries: their operation is governed by the legislation governing other similar partnerships, but fund law and regulation often does not apply since the funds are not publicly offered.

In this form, the management company is the general partner, offering partnerships to a relatively small number of investors who become limited partners. The liability of limited partners is limited to the sum of their investment and the life of the partnership is usually also limited (5–25 years or so), in order to ensure the ability to exit from the fund at some point (never forget that the first thing institutional investors will want to know about a fund is how they can exit from it – if they cannot get out they cannot take their profits nor can they cut their losses). Limited partners who wish to redeem before the end of the fund's life have to rely on the general partner's ability, but not obligation, to find a replacement investor.

Partnership-type funds are commonly formed in offshore or low tax domiciles and are often used by so-called 'hedge' funds (refer to Chapter 14).

An illustration of the relationships between the investor (the limited partner), the fund management company (the general partner) and the custodian in a partnership-type fund is shown in Figure 3.4.

Table 3.1 *Summary of the implications of the main legal structures*

	Corporate fund	Trust fund	Contractual fund
Legal form	Joint stock company (corporation)	Trust	Not a legal entity: contractual pool
Governing law	Company law or commercial code, fund law	Trust law or precedent, fund law	Law of contract or commercial code, fund law
Investors buy	Shares	Units	Units or certificates or participations
Investor status	Shareholder	Beneficiary of trust (unitholder)	Unitholder or participant
Voting rights of holders	As per ordinary shareholder plus those set by fund law and regulation	As per trust deed plus those set by fund law and regulation	None or those set by fund law and regulation
Meetings of holders	Annual and extraordinary	Extraordinary only	None or extraordinary only
Fiduciary duty to investors	Fund directors	Trustee	None unless specified in fund law or contract with investors
Holder of fund assets	Custodian	Trustee or custodian on trustee's behalf	Depositary
Assets registered in the name of	Fund or custodian on behalf of fund	Trustee or custodian on trustee's behalf	Management company or depositary on behalf of fund
Founding documents	Memorandum and Articles of Association or equivalent e.g. Charter	Trust deed	Contract and rules of fund

The advantage of this structure taxwise is that the partnership itself is not taxable as an entity, so each partner pays only that tax that is appropriate to them depending on their tax obligations in their country of residence.

Since this structure is not commonly used for funds to be sold to the general public, it is not included in Table 3.1 nor is it extensively covered in this book. However, broadly all the principles of operation of funds covered in Chapters 5 to 17 will apply to partnership, as well as other, funds.

FUND OPERATIONAL STRUCTURES AND THEIR IMPLICATIONS

Funds, whether of company, trust or contractual type, generally operate either in 'open-ended' or in 'closed-ended' form; some regulatory frameworks also permit an 'interval' or 'limited' or 'clopen' form – a sort of halfway house between open-ended and closed-ended.

Open-ended funds

An 'open-ended' fund is a fund which has the absolute obligation under fund law and regulations to redeem (buy back) its shares or units on a regular, stated basis. Subject to local law permitting it, these funds can be formed in corporate, trust or contractual form. As a general rule, most open-ended funds both issue and redeem daily: the minimum requirement is always set by regulation and may be less frequent – for instance, a common provision is that an open-ended fund must redeem at least once every two weeks on a clearly disclosed day and time.

This constant issue and redemption means that the capital (number of shares or units in issue) of the fund changes from day to day as new investors arrive and other investors leave the fund. Thus any fund with the term 'variable capital' in its name is likely to be open-ended (though it could also be interval) – for example, 'an investment company with variable capital'.

Open-ended funds have to be able to create and cancel shares or units in the fund every day to meet demand to sell units or buy them back; so corporate open-ended funds can be difficult to operate in countries where company laws do not recognise the concept of a company with variable capital – this is quite common, since company laws normally only provide for ordinary companies that, like closed-ended funds, have a fixed capital. Special laws may therefore be needed in order for open-ended corporate funds to be able to operate.

Another key factor is that since an open-ended fund has to take in new money every day and pay out existing investors every day in cash, it must be able to buy and sell assets for the fund quickly and reliably. This is why open-ended funds are required by regulation to hold mostly liquid assets (that is, assets which can be bought and sold reasonably quickly and easily in substantial quantities without such transactions moving market prices).

Reference is sometimes made to 'UCITS' or 'UCITS funds'. These initials stand for 'Undertakings for Collective Investment in Transferable Securities', which are open-ended funds that meet the requirements of the 'UCITS Directive' issued by the European Union in 1985[3] (since updated, most recently in 2002). This Directive establishes requirements for open-ended funds that must be met if such funds are to be registered to be sold across borders with the European Economic Area (EEA – the EU countries plus Norway, Iceland and Liechtenstein). However, provided that

UKP Billion

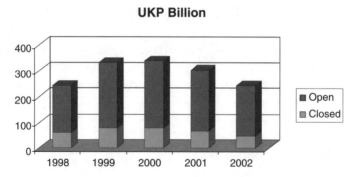

Figure 3.5 *Value of funds under management in the UK: closed-ended v. open-ended funds*
Reproduced by permission of the Association of Investment Trust Companies and Investment Management Association

open-ended funds do not wish to be sold across borders within the EEA, they do not have to meet these requirements. Closed-ended funds do not meet UCITS requirements.

Open-ended funds constitute the largest proportion of funds internationally: they are more popular than closed-ended funds largely because investors can buy or sell shares or units quickly and easily at their full net asset value or NAV (see section on dealing prices below and Chapter 7 for a fuller explanation). However, they cannot operate efficiently or effectively in illiquid markets since they cannot easily buy or sell assets to meet purchase and redemption orders; nor can they easily find prices to create accurate valuations (refer to Chapter 7 for more on this).

In general, closed-ended fund sectors, even if they do exist, amount to at best, less than half the size of open-ended fund sectors in OECD[4] countries; around a third of OECD countries do not have closed-ended funds at all. The UK has one of the larger closed-ended fund sectors, whose ratio to open-ended funds has been fairly consistent over the last few years as illustrated in Figure 3.5. Regrettably statistics on closed-ended funds are also rather harder to come by in many countries than statistics on open-ended funds.

Closed-ended funds

A 'closed-ended' fund is one that, like a company, has a fixed amount of capital (number of shares or units) in issue. Closed-ended funds can operate in corporate, trust or contractual form though the corporate form is most common. These funds have an initial offer period to raise capital and then at the end of that offer they close to further subscription: usually no further issues may be made unless existing holders agree to an increase in capital (similarly to ordinary companies).

There is no duty on closed-ended funds to redeem – i.e., to buy back shares or units from investors – so there are no demands on them to sell assets for cash; this also makes these funds more able to borrow or 'gear' or 'leverage', since their asset base is more stable. This structure is therefore suited to investing in illiquid as well as liquid assets, being commonly used to invest in emerging markets and in unlisted and untraded companies. Many countries' early funds were formed as closed-ended corporate funds, since these fitted more easily within laws governing companies than open-ended corporate funds did, and since assets available at that time were relatively illiquid. Closed-ended funds continue to be formed in (and to invest in) liquid financial markets, too, since their form has additional uses: in creating fixed-life funds, which invest in bonds which can provide a specified return to investors or guaranteed funds, for instance (see Chapter 14 for more on these).

'Interval' funds

There is, in addition, a further variant; the so-called 'interval' fund which is also referred to as a 'limited' or 'clopen' fund. This is a fund that opens for sale or redemption on an occasional, though regular, basis; but is otherwise closed. That is, its capital does not change, except that when it periodically opens for issue and/or redemption when the capital changes; then the fund closes again and has fixed capital for a further period. The usual minimum requirement is that such funds must 'open' at least once a year. Some funds may open at more frequent intervals.

These have the advantages that:

- They can enable occasional redemptions at net asset value (see section on dealing prices below), which is more attractive than closed-ended funds whose shares or units can rarely be realised at net asset value except upon winding up of a fund. Sometimes the amount of net redemptions at any one dealing date may also be limited in order to prevent runs on a fund whose assets may be relatively illiquid.
- They do not have to meet regular redemptions, so can invest in less liquid assets than open-ended funds, which is helpful in emerging economies.
- They can enable funds that offer investors a guaranteed minimum return over a defined period (usually through investment of a proportion of the fund in bonds which mature at a specified time, which matches an opening period, with the balance invested in other types of security).

This last category of 'guaranteed' funds has been becoming more popular in recent years in a number of countries, particularly given the bearish conditions prevailing in equity markets in the early years of the new millennium.

Table 3.2 *Summary of key characteristics of operating structures*

Characteristic	open-ended	Interval	closed-ended
Capital	Variable	Fixed, temporarily varying when open	Fixed
Duration	Usually indefinite	Indefinite or finite life	Indefinite or finite life
Investments	90% liquid	Illiquid or liquid	Illiquid or liquid
Borrowing	Limited (10% of fund)	May be limited	Often unlimited
Share (or unit) classes	Must not disadvantage other shareholders	Must not disadvantage other shareholders	May have varying rights to income and capital
Listing on stock exchange	Not required	Not required	Usually required
Pricing	At net asset value	At net asset value	At market price
Dealing frequency	Daily	Intervals	As per listing
Transactions	Through fund management company or sometimes on stock market	Through fund management company or sometimes on stock market	On stock market
Managed	Externally	Externally	Internally or externally

Key differences between open-ended and closed-ended funds

The most important distinction between the operation of open-ended and closed-ended funds is that open-ended funds are required to redeem their shares or units from fund investors, while closed-ended funds are not. All the key differences in the operation of open- and closed-ended funds, as outlined below and summarised in Table 3.2, arise from this distinction.

Requirement to redeem
An open-ended fund usually issues and redeems shares or units every day. At any one time, it therefore has to balance the interests of new investors buying, existing investors selling and ongoing investors continuing to hold, while contending with the fact that the value of assets which it owns changes from day to day. This

change in value has to be taken into account, so that new investors – who buy shares or units representing ownership of an equal slice of all the assets in the fund – do not pay too much, damaging themselves, or too little, damaging on-going fund investors; or leaving investors – who sell shares or units representing an equal slice of all the assets in the fund – do not receive too little, damaging them, or too much, disadvantaging ongoing holders.

Dealing prices for fund shares or units

The principle which is required by law and regulation to be applied to buying and selling shares or units in open-ended funds is that of equality: a fund must receive in payment for a sale, or pay out for a redemption, the net asset value of the share or unit adjusted for charges (see Chapter 8) only as permitted by regulation. 'Net asset value per share (or unit)' is calculated by taking the total value of the assets of the fund and deducting its liabilities, which results in the 'fund net asset value'. This figure is then divided by the total number of units or shares in issue at the time of the calculation of the value, resulting in the 'net asset value per share (or unit)'. In principle, there is no limit to the number of shares or units that may be issued and redeemed by an open-ended fund.

By contrast, closed-ended funds have only a limited number of shares or units in issue, which are issued only within a specified period prior to a closing date. Thereafter the owner of a share or unit in closed-ended fund can only sell it if he can find a buyer for it. This is usually done through a secondary market such as a stock exchange or trading system – otherwise the chances of sellers being able to find a buyer would be low and the funds would, therefore, not be attractive to many investors. It is often a regulatory or fiscal requirement that closed-ended funds' shares or units be listed or quoted. The price that the buyer of a share or unit in such a market will pay will depend upon the level of supply and demand for that share or unit. If few fund shares are available, but demand is high, prices will be higher; where many fund shares are available and demand is low, prices will be lower. Thus the price paid per share or unit is not the net asset value of the share or unit; it could be more but commonly it will be less than the net asset value since there is usually an oversupply of such shares or units.

Ability to borrow

The fixed capital base of a closed-ended fund makes it less risky for it to borrow money that it can use to buy more assets and 'gear' or 'leverage' its performance, than it is for open-ended funds. Open-ended funds, whose capital is variable, are only permitted to borrow within narrow limits, due to the risk of the proportion of borrowing relative to value of the fund rising, which can occur both as a result of redemptions as well as market falls.

Pros and cons of different operating structures for fund management companies

Each operating structure has implications for the way that a fund has to conduct its business. For a fund management company, open-ended, interval and closed-ended funds each have advantages and disadvantages. Open-ended and interval funds can be promoted consistently over time, and assets under management within a single fund can expand substantially thus causing management fees to rise; however, investors can easily leave in droves if fashions change or markets fall and fees may plummet as a result.

Closed-ended funds are usually only promoted once on the first issue and their capital does not change so only an increase in the value of assets managed will bring in higher fees; however, if fashions change or markets fall investors can only leave if they find a buyer, which does not affect the fund's issued capital. Management fees on closed-ended funds therefore generally have a more limited upside; but also have a more limited downside.

Pros and cons of different operating structures for investors

While open-ended, interval and closed-ended funds are designed to offer the same service to investors – essentially, diversified portfolio management – the operational differences between them have some pros and cons for investors.

Generally, investing in an open-ended fund is the most straightforward: usually the management company sells and buys back units and shares every day, at a price which is required by regulation to be based on net asset value per share or unit. An interval fund operates on the same principle although the investor cannot enter and exit so frequently.

By contrast, unless investors subscribe to an initial offer of a closed-ended fund, if they wish to buy a holding in an existing closed-ended fund, they have to find an existing investor willing to sell. Prices of fund shares or units in the stock market are set by supply and demand, and do not necessarily relate to the value of the share or unit of the fund in which a holding is being bought. This can have advantages for incoming investors, since most closed-ended funds' shares or units can be bought at a price which is lower than NAV (this being known as being 'at a discount to NAV', the discount being the difference between the price and the NAV, expressed as a percentage of NAV per share or unit – the reverse, where share or unit prices are higher than NAV, is referred to as being 'at a premium to NAV', and again is the difference between the price and the NAV, also expressed as a percentage of NAV). So an investor may pay 100 for a share that has a NAV of 120 and which will pay dividends on assets of 120, and not 100. Of course, investors may face the discount problem when they come to sell their holding, which is that they may have to sell it for less than its value – and the discount may have increased (or 'widened') or decreased (or 'narrowed') in the meantime.

Dealing in the stock market also may mean that the investor has to use a stockbroker, which some find off-putting.

MANAGEMENT STRUCTURES AND THEIR IMPLICATIONS

There are essentially two ways of managing a fund: known as 'internal' (or sometimes self-management) or 'external' management.

Internal management

Essentially, internal management is where, like other companies, the fund owns or rents its own offices, employs its own staff, buys its own equipment, etc. This is a very rare form of management structure internationally; an example is the Alliance Trust and its sister the Second Alliance Trust, both of Dundee, whose origins go back to the 1880s.

While there are no figures available in this area, the authors estimate that well over 99% of collective investment funds by value are managed externally, even if they are legally permitted to be internally managed – which is why this book focuses throughout on the more normal structure – external management.

External management

External management is where a separate company from the fund, a fund management company, is contracted to operate the fund. The fund itself therefore has no employees or offices or equipment. All these are provided by the management company, which is paid a specific fee, usually based on a percentage of the value of the fund, to operate the fund.

A variant – external management with a twist – is where the investment funds operated by a management company own that management company of which a well-known example is The Vanguard Group® of the USA. However, such an arrangement may only be made if it is in compliance with investment powers permitted to funds.

The reasons why external management predominates are as follows:

- Future value: fund management companies hold contracts for the management of funds, from which they derive a stream of revenue of between 0.20% and 3% of the value of the funds they manage. As such, a management company has a commercial value and can be sold. A management structure that is internal to a fund cannot be sold unless it is separately incorporated first; and anyway will only have a contract for a single fund, which is a much less attractive proposition – revenues from a single fund are vulnerable to its performance and continuing existence.

- Economies of scale: multiple funds contracting a single management company for services spreads the cost of the management company across a series of funds, rather than focusing all the costs of its operation within a single fund; and funds with lower costs will reduce investment returns less, so are more likely to be attractive to investors.
- Diversification of revenue flows: a variety of funds to meet different needs can be provided by an external management company, ensuring that when one product is out of favour, another is in favour and so will maintain revenues; a single self-managed fund cannot cater for a series of different investment needs or changes in the popularity of different forms of fund or fund investment objectives.

In general, regulators are not particularly keen on internally managed structures, either. Reasons for this include:

- Operational considerations: the impossibility of operating an internal management company within an open-ended fund structure is a major consideration. A fund which has varying capital could find that sustaining costs of internal management of $250000 – a relatively acceptable cost of 2.5% of the value of a fund of $10 million, could become 25% of the value if the fund shrinks to $1 million, due to market movements or redemptions reducing the value of the fund on which management costs are levied. This would clearly adversely affect the interests of fund investors.
- Licensing considerations: withdrawing the licence of a management company for regulatory failures can be done relatively easily where that management is external – the management company can simply be replaced by another licensed firm and the funds continue to operate under the new management; but removing the management of a fund which is internally managed could mean having to take away the fund's license, so that the fund would have to cease to operate which could adversely affect the interests of its investors.
- Cost control considerations: assets of a self-managed fund can easily be eroded through excessive costs of operation which may be difficult to identify from outside; also off-balance sheet contingent liabilities can build up which can become problematic (employee contracts, leases, pensions). Contracts for external management specify what fees are payable and their payment from the fund to the management company is easily traced; identifying flows of money and levels of cost of operation within an internally managed fund is much more difficult.
- Clarity of responsibilities and liabilities: contracts between management companies and funds clearly identify responsibilities and liability; if the

management company makes an error or omits to act, it may have to compensate for any loss. If an internal management team of a fund makes an error or omits to act the only sanction is against the individuals involved, who are unlikely to be able to finance large sums; or against the fund itself, which would further damage the interests of investors.

- Valuation considerations: valuation of funds can become problematic if fixed assets are owned by the self-managed fund which are not investments – e.g. office buildings.
- Lack of incentive to perform: there is less of an incentive for internal managers to perform well, since their salaries are less likely to rise or fall in line with fund net asset value; whereas external managers' fees will rise if the value of assets rises or will fall if they fall, since their fee is a percentage of net asset value. Also, there is little downside in poor performance, whereas an external management company could be replaced or fees renegotiated.
- Resistance to change: internally managed funds are more likely to be resistant to takeovers or liquidation due to loss of jobs, so failing funds may continue in existence rather than being taken over or liquidated.

Thus while there are some successful internally managed funds, of good reputation, the self-managed structure is not the one most commonly adopted internationally.

The impact of regulation on these funds and their service providers is examined in the next chapter.

Those who would like to test their grasp of the contents of this chapter should turn to the self-test questions at the back of the book.

NOTES

1. *Put Not Your Trust in Money*, John Newlands, Chappin Kavanagh, London, 1997.
2. The use of 'open' and 'closed' in this context refers to the transferability of securities issued by the fund.
3. COUNCIL DIRECTIVE of 20 December 1985 on the coordination of laws, regulations and administrative provisions relating to undertakings for collective investment in transferable securities (UCITS) (85/611/EEC), as amended.
4. *Institutional Investors Yearbook*, OECD, Paris, 2001.

4

Regulation

If people do not have confidence in collective investment funds then they simply will not invest in them and the market will fail to thrive. For a start, why would anyone in their right mind hand over their money to someone if they were not certain that they could get it back?

At its most basic, regulation seeks to create and maintain confidence: in the case of collective investment funds by ensuring that those who are permitted to attract money from the public and profit from servicing this business – funds, fund management companies and other service providers – are reputable; that they conduct their business in such a way that confidence is maintained or enhanced; and that redress is available to those who suffer damage from any failure in this respect. This chapter outlines typical regulatory requirements applying to funds and their service providers and explores the implications of these.

INTRODUCTION

The term 'regulation' is used here to encompass the body of laws, regulations and other regulatory requirements governing funds and their service providers, which are applied by a regulator (and sometimes a self-regulatory organisation or 'SRO') that is also empowered by law. As a general rule, funds are governed either by laws that are specific to funds (such as the US Investment Company Act of 1940) or by more general laws governing financial or securities markets (such as the UK Financial Services and Markets Act 2000). Usually laws empower a regulator both to apply them and to issue regulations, which set more detailed requirements under those laws (this is more flexible than putting everything in a law which is cumbersome and is more difficult to update than regulations issued by the regulator). Such regulators generally have the objectives of maintaining market confidence, protecting consumers and reducing financial crime – a relatively recent formal addition to such objectives in some cases is to promote public awareness.

Typically a regulator will be required and empowered to:

- Set requirements for the approval (also known as 'authorisation' or 'registration' or 'licensing') of funds to be publicly offered, and for the approval of service providers to funds such as management companies, custodians, depositaries and trustees (and sometimes other service providers also) prior to their being able to undertake fund-related business.
- Set requirements for the ongoing operation of funds and the conduct of business of fund management companies, custodians, depositaries and trustees.
- Approve funds before they can be publicly offered.
- Approve fund management companies, custodians, depositaries and trustees before they can offer funds or services to funds.
- Monitor and supervise ongoing compliance of funds and their service providers including the operation of funds and the conduct of business of fund management companies, custodians, depositaries and trustees – usually done through requiring submission of regular reports and by inspection visits, but also by tracking market news and events, advertising, etc.
- Investigate possible malpractice.
- Take disciplinary action against those who fail to comply with regulation (here the powers of the regulator can vary from the weak – minor fines, say – to the draconian – banning an individual from the business for life, for instance).
- Require compensation to be paid to those whose interests have been damaged by failure to comply with regulation.

Some regulatory regimes set out to protect investors by being highly prescriptive, setting out in great detail how everything must be done. Others take the view that investors are best protected by transparency – that is, requiring clear and full disclosure of all relevant information and terms and conditions – leaving investors to make their own choices advisedly. The authors favour the latter approach, since prescriptiveness can never cope with every contingency and can stifle innovation; it also has a tendency to mollycoddle consumers who may come to place undue emphasis on regulatory approval (which after all only signifies that certain tests have been passed) and insufficient emphasis on understanding their own needs and making educated choices about meeting them.

The absolute keys to good regulation are:

- Unambiguous and consistent rules are set that are appropriate to the stage of development of the market and are clearly disclosed.
- Fair, even, consistent, timely and transparent application of the rules.
- Cost of regulation does not outweigh its benefits.

It is also very important that the regulator itself is of good repute: it is very difficult to build confidence in markets, which is what a fund business needs, if the regulator of that market is arbitrary, biased or inconsistent (the same is true of public governance as a whole, of course).

WHAT ENTITIES ARE REGULATED

Funds

In regulatory terms, the key distinction is between publicly offered and privately offered funds. The most onerous regulation applies to those funds that wish to offer their shares or units to the general public, in order to provide investor protection. These are generally known as 'publicly offered funds'. In most countries open-ended funds are the commonest form of publicly offered fund, since most ordinary investors value the facility of redemption on demand. Such funds invest almost entirely in listed securities, good quality bonds and short-term paper or deposits.

A 'privately offered fund' is one which is not required to meet the regulation applying to publicly offered funds because it is only offered to certain qualifying investors such as wealthy individuals and investment institutions, who are adjudged sophisticated enough to look after themselves. Various specialist, venture capital or private equity funds and that amorphous group of funds known as 'hedge funds' usually fall under this category. Such funds are usually formed as joint stock companies or limited partnerships and are forbidden to market directly to the public, with an additional proviso that all marketing materials and fund documentation must specify that these funds are not for public distribution and that fund distributors or advisers must reassure themselves that the persons to whom they are considering offering such funds are qualifying persons. Most regulators exempt such funds entirely from the provisions of the regulatory regime that is applied to publicly offered funds provided that they do not act in such a way as to require them to achieve 'publicly offered fund' status.

An additional layer of regulation of funds may derive from another source: if funds are to be given a privileged tax status in order to encourage investment into them, there is room for the abuse of fund status by entities, which are not really funds, but call themselves funds in order to enjoy more favourable tax treatment. This is a concern of the tax authorities. That is why in some countries the tax authority may set up additional definitions of the characteristics of qualifying funds to those established by regulation. The definitions may concern 'qualifying holdings' (requirements for types or sizes of permitted investments), characteristics of assets in which such funds are allowed to invest, listing of such funds on a stock exchange, diversification and distribution of income. If an entity does not operate within these limitations, it may be deprived of the tax privileges given to funds.

Fund management companies and service providers

Fund management companies and service providers (including custodians, depositaries, trustees, third-party service providers such as administrators and registrars who undertake the tasks outlined in Chapters 7 to 10, fund supermarkets[1] and sometimes information providers[2]) are almost always subject to regulation. There may also be some regulatory requirements for the qualifications and suitability of individuals who work within these organisations. Different countries have different requirements, notably about the qualifications and suitability of directors and senior personnel.

THE REGULATORY SYSTEM

The components of the regulatory system are:

- Primary legislation.
- The government department, executive agency or agencies responsible for regulation.
- The set of rules lawfully promulgated by the regulator.
- The criminal and civil courts and any independent arbiters of consumer complaints such as ombudsmen or financial services arbitration tribunals.

The regulatory systems in force around the world differ in many respects. In some, the primary legislation contains considerable detail while in others all the detail is left to the rules that the regulator is specifically empowered or required to make. In some systems, the adjudication and enforcement mechanisms of the regulator are highly formalised, while in others they are more informal. The civil and criminal courts may play a larger or smaller role depending on the penalties the regulator is able to impose under its own authority, on the adequacy of means available within the rules for investors to obtain redress without going to court, and on the ability of, and means by which, regulated entities may appeal against the decisions of the regulator.

The following sections outline the essential features of a regulatory system for funds, leaving open the issue of precisely how they are achieved.

The legal framework

The matters normally covered in primary legislation specific to funds are outlined in Table 4.1.

Table 4.1   *Elements of legislation for funds*

1. Definitions	The characteristics of regulated funds are defined as are exclusions
2. Classification	At a minimum by public or private offer, by legal structure and by operational structure (refer to Chapter 3)
3. Management structure	The legal and contractual relationships between management companies, investment advisers and custodians, depositaries and trustees are defined
4. Fees and charges, valuation and pricing	Principles are established governing charging, valuation and pricing
5. Authorisation and licensing	Requirements and procedures are laid down for authorising fund management companies and funds and service providers and for ongoing compliance with these requirements
6. Authority of the regulator	The regulator's authority is defined, as is the procedure for the regulator to delegate responsibility for specific functions
7. Affiliated persons	Provisions to bar or limit affiliates from occupying positions or carrying out transactions in which conflicts of interest arise
8. Investment definitions and restrictions	Restrictions on permitted investments and borrowing and on percentages of particular assets which may be included in a fund portfolio
9. Capital structure	Rights of different classes of shares or units are defined
10. Reporting	The content and frequency of reports to investors is defined
11. Records, accounts	Content and frequency of records and procedures for accounting are laid down
12. Depositary	The duties of the custodian, depositary or trustee are defined
13. Share/unitholders' rights	The rights of holders of shares or units to redeem or vote are defined
14. Duties and legal obligations of directors or depositaries or trustees	If a fund has directors, their legal obligations are laid down in general terms, although usually reliance can be placed on company law in addition or instead
15. Prospectus, publicity	Requirements for disclosure of information are established

(continues overleaf)

Table 4.1 (*Continued*)

16. Mergers and acquisitions	There are specific rules for fund mergers and acquisitions
17. Change of managers and liquidation	Conditions and procedures for changing the management company and liquidating a fund
18. Cross border funds	Sets criteria and requirements for funds created in other countries, which wish to distribute to investors in the country concerned, as well as requirements for domestic funds, which intend to distribute in other countries

The existence of a law governing funds and their operation is vital, because:

- It is the law, on the basis of which judges in the courts base their judgement: courts are the institutions of the last resort, where legal and physical persons apply for protection of their rights.
- It is the law that defines what a fund is and what it is not – this makes it possible to require all institutions which behave as funds to be officially licensed and regulated; enabling action against those unlicensed entities resembling funds which defraud or mislead investors (which damage market confidence) and the exclusion of entities that seek to misuse fund status to enjoy taxation or other benefits.

The regulator

The law usually states which entity will regulate particular activities though much of the detail is normally found in the rules of the regulator authorised by the primary legislation. To regulate effectively a regulator should:

- Be politically independent – since market stability should not be dependent on the political orientation of the ruling party. In order to ensure political independence a regulator must have special safeguards in its structure.
- Have sufficient resources – the regulator must have resources to do the job properly. Funding exclusively by the State may not provide enough resources to the regulator and makes it dependent on politicians – funding (fully or partially) out of levies imposed on the regulated entities may be a solution.
- Have appropriate skills – having well-trained, properly paid and competent personnel.

- Be impartial – should not grant privileges to any regulated entities.
- Be accountable – should have clearly defined lines of responsibility to a government body or to a national parliament, which gives the regulator its mandate and assesses its performance.

In most countries these days funds are regulated by Securities Commissions or consolidated mega-regulators, which usually have a special status in that they may be State bodies or independent agencies of government. However, some other forms of regulation are also possible. Below we briefly examine the pros and cons of different models.

Statutory regulation or self-regulation
Self-regulation can be described as a system of regulation and supervision undertaken by an organisation whose members are the practitioners of the business being regulated and who finance that organisation. While in theory an attractive idea in that it provides many of the benefits of state regulation without being a burden on the taxpayer (the cost basically lands on the buyers of the products or services offered by the self-regulated) and that it utilises industry specific expertise – 'it takes a thief to catch a thief' – in practice self-regulation is not easy to apply. The UK experiment, known as 'self-regulation within a statutory framework', which began with the Financial Services Act of 1986 was abandoned and replaced by a single statutory mega-regulator under the Financial Services and Markets Act 2000: the main problem being that self-regulation tended to result in protection of self-interest rather than investors. Funding of self-regulation can also be problematic – if there are several SROs, people will tend to opt for the cheapest which may be the least effective; and some industries are simply not large enough to sustain the cost of even a single self-regulator.

Ensuring an SRO's impartiality and objectivity is the greatest obstacle to the successful use of this form of regulation and is the main reason why – in the view of the authors – only exchanges and their members are suitable candidates for self-regulation. Their members have a strong self-interest in ensuring the good behaviour of other members since they are counter-parties to transactions. Self-regulation is not generally effective in relation to fund management business, because fund management companies, although interested in the good reputation of the industry, are not dependent on each other.

Regulation by function or by institution
Regulation by function is where all financial services of a particular type – fund management, for example – are regulated by a single body, regardless of the ownership of the company or the type of corporate group of which it is a part. An example of regulation by function is where a Securities Commission regulates a

fund offered by the subsidiary of a bank as part of its task to regulate securities markets, of which funds form a part, despite the fact that banks may be under the supervision of a Central Bank.

Regulation by institution is where a single body regulates all the financial services offered by a certain type of institution, irrespective of their nature. An example of this would be that funds offered by a bank would be regulated by the banking regulator, since the service is offered by the bank.

Who is responsible for fund-related regulation within the regulator's structure?

Different regulatory bodies have different structures. It is not uncommon, however, to have a special department within the regulator, which provides licensing and authorisation of funds and their management companies and service providers, which also undertakes routine monitoring and inspections. This department usually reports to a senior person within the regulator who has a board status (member of the board or a commissioner). Investigations and enforcement, which are undertaken where malpractice is suspected or identified, are usually duties of a separate department, which provides investigation and enforcement in relation to the whole range of regulated entities.

KEY REGULATORY PRINCIPLES

Most of the detailed aspects of regulation of specific aspects of fund operations will be dealt with in the relevant chapters of this book. This section focuses on the principles underlying regulation and summarises the essential content of any regulatory system.

Most governments give support to the development of collective investments, since they help to mobilise private savings in a constructive way. Funds and their investors are often given specific incentives, for example in the form of tax concessions: in exchange the State by law requires that funds are used only for the purposes for which they have been originally designed, that investors are not defrauded and that privileged fund status is not misused by quasi funds.

To achieve all of this different countries use a variety of mechanisms to govern funds. Whatever the form of the regulatory systems and the nature of the bodies involved, certain common principles underlie the rules and procedures. Thanks to the efforts of the International Organisation of Securities Commissions (IOSCO), there is a set of generally agreed principles for the regulation of funds.[3] These principles constitute a useful and universal checklist either for those charged with drafting new legislation or analysing existing laws. They were designed to apply to open-ended funds. Many, but not all, apply equally to closed-ended funds.

These are 10 in number and are itemised below.

Fund structures

Funds must conform to certain defined legal forms and structures and it must be impossible to set up or promote a fund that does not conform to these. Investors must be certain of their rights. Funds must be clearly segregated and independent and where this is not the case – for example where a certain set of funds may share some liabilities, in the case of umbrella funds for instance – this must be made clear to investors. For more detail on fund structures see Chapters 3 and 14.

Custodians, depositaries and trustees

The system should separate the assets of funds from the assets of management companies or other entities, and the assets of an individual fund from all other funds. A custodian, depositary or trustee should hold all these assets and must be at least operationally independent of the fund management company; it should be liable without limit to investors for any loss incurred by investors resulting from its failure to perform its obligations. The qualifying requirements for custodians, trustees and depositaries should ensure they have financial and management resources adequate to meet their obligations.

Eligibility of operators[4]

The system should impose standards of conduct and minimum eligibility for fund management companies. These should include capital adequacy and financial resources, the integrity of directors (at a minimum through the proven lack of any criminal convictions), competence and the ability to meet minimum standards of systems and procedures.

Delegation

Law or regulation must state that any entity responsible under law or regulation for fulfilment of a responsibility or duty remains responsible for this, even if they delegate performance of the task or duty to another entity. This ensures provision of a consistent level of investor protection while allowing flexibility that may reduce costs to investors.

Supervision

A single regulatory authority should have paramount responsibility for funds within its jurisdiction. Funds should be registered with or authorised by the regulator before the operator begins marketing activity. The regulator must have the power to promulgate and apply regulations, and inspect and investigate fund management companies; it also should have adequate powers to protect the interests of investors, including revocation of licences, suspension of dealing, freezing of fund or fund management companies' assets, levying fines, withdrawing fund authorisations, commencing civil proceedings and recommending criminal prosecutions.

Conflicts of interest

The system must recognise the existence of potential conflicts of interest between a fund management company and its affiliates and investors. This may be dealt with by the definition of an operator's general 'fiduciary responsibility' to investors or by the adoption of specific conduct of business rules.

Asset valuation and pricing

The prime requirement here is that the system of valuation and pricing must be fair to ongoing investors, incoming investors and outgoing investors in funds. The price of an open-ended or interval fund share or unit must be closely related to the net asset value of the fund share or unit calculated on a regular basis in accordance with specific rules or accepted accounting practice.

Limits on investment and borrowing

The system should place limits on the investment and borrowing capabilities of a fund. Rules should require portfolio diversification, provision of liquidity to meet redemptions, and containment of risk within defined parameters and lay down requirements for dealing with any breaches of such limits.

Investor rights

The regulatory framework should confer specific rights on investors, including the right to withdraw their money from a fund within a reasonable period of time or to be able to sell shares in a secondary market. Investors should have the right to participate in significant decisions affecting a fund, or to have their interests protected by a regulator or other independent third party. Investors should be able to refer complaints to the regulator or an independent complaints arbitrator.

Marketing and disclosure

The key requirement is that operators provide existing and prospective investors with all the information they need to make informed investment decisions (usually in a prospectus) and that this information should be neither misleading nor inaccurate. Detailed requirements should also be set for the required content of prospectuses, disclosure of prices, and content and frequency of reports (including financial data) to investors. Advertising should be required to be consistent with the prospectus. In addition, information on matters such as charges and returns should be provided in such a way that they can be quickly understood and that comparisons can easily be made.

Principles on the 'Eligibility of operators', and 'Supervision', were expanded by IOSCO later in *Principles for the Supervision of Operators of Collective Investment Schemes*.[5] This paper contains 10 principles dedicated specifically to supervision of fund operators. Each of these principles states what supervision should seek to achieve in the following areas of operators' activities:

- conduct of business
- connected party transactions
- valuation of fund assets
- safekeeping and segregation of investments
- fees and expenses
- internal control and compliance arrangements
- disclosure
- accounts and record keeping
- continuous eligibility.

The *Principles for the Supervision of Operators of Collective Investment Schemes* does not specify which entity should be responsible for any particular supervisory activity and does not specify regulatory techniques to be applied.

REGULATORY ACTIVITIES

In order to achieve its objectives the regulator uses a whole range of regulatory tools, as discussed below.

Establishing detailed rules and regulations

Depending on the regulatory system, the regulator issues more or less detailed guidelines on how to apply the law, in the form of regulations – it may or may not consult practitioners (often through trade associations) as part of the development process. Once regulations are issued and gazetted dates are set by which all those subject to regulation must achieve compliance: time often has to be allowed to change all necessary documentation and systems (known as 'transitional periods'). Sometimes to avoid unnecessarily long and detailed regulations, regulators keep them short, but issue explanatory letters and legal opinions in relation to regulatory issues whose interpretation is uncertain. Some regulators consult with practitioners or their trade associations more formally through standing committees.

Licensing and authorising

In most jurisdictions, the fund management company of a fund must be licensed independently of the licensing (or authorisation) of the fund itself. Because depositaries or trustees usually carry responsibility for the protection of investors too, they also are required to be licensed, though some regimes do not require fund depositaries or trustees to be specifically licensed as such, relying on the fact that they are usually banks, which are subject to Central Bank supervision. The licence is the regulatory permission issued to the company to run a specific business: the management of investment funds or trustee or depositary work. The purpose of licensing is to ensure that those who obtain licenses are honest, competent and solvent. To obtain a licence an applicant has to demonstrate that it satisfies all the licensing requirements and also to pay a licensing fee that may be nominal or substantial.

Authorisation of a fund constitutes regulatory approval for the fund to be offered to the public, indicating that it conforms in all respects with the structure laid down by law and regulation.

Setting licensing requirements
Regulatory systems will always set rules for the capital of a fund management company and sometimes for the custodian, depository or trustee (though if they are banks, the capital of the parent bank may be relied upon); they will also set qualification rules for their directors and senior managers and sometimes also for those advising people on choosing funds.

As a general rule, regulators tend to require that management of funds is carried out by separate and specifically constituted companies, not simply the departments of other financial institutions, and that operating funds is the sole and exclusive activity of such companies. In some jurisdictions a licence issued to a fund management company also covers management of pension funds and investment management for life and non-life insurance companies and private portfolio management; in other words a full asset management licence. In other jurisdictions special licenses are required for the management and operation of investment funds, separately from other asset management activities. There is some debate about the convenience of granting licences to cover all asset management and investment advisory functions.

Requirements for directors and personnel of licensed entities generally focus on:

- Honesty: the individuals who are going to manage the activity should not have had previous convictions for fraud or financial crimes, or failed to comply with regulations of the securities or other regulator at home or abroad. In some jurisdictions, regulators rely on an individual's declaration that he or she has no criminal convictions, on the basis that discovery of a false statement will result in immediate disqualification and other penalties. In other jurisdictions, the regulator will make its own investigations through police or court records.

- Competence: directors should preferably have some relevant experience, if not in the management of funds then in other relevant fields such as securities markets, banking or commercial law. To ensure that individuals are competent to carry out the proposed activities, some systems require the test of competence by means of examination.

In some jurisdictions a management company or depositary or trustee cannot be granted licences unless members of their personnel hold specific individual qualifications. Where the character and qualifications of individuals are a factor in granting a licence, the regulator will normally keep a file of all such individuals, noting any regulatory transgressions. Fraud is almost invariably an individual matter, and in most cases it is preferable for regulators to deal with it by eliminating the rogue individual – preferably through a lifetime ban on any involvement in the business – rather than by withdrawing the licence of the operating company.

Requirements for management companies generally focus on:

- Capacity: as in the case of an individual, a company should demonstrate that it is competent to carry out its business, which is tested by submission of a plan of its organisational structure and a business plan. This will not only show whether the company has adequate capital for its plans, but also whether it has a realistic grasp of the demands of the business and associated costs, and whether it has put in place an appropriate management structure, procedures and systems to ensure compliance. Regulators will be particularly concerned to see that the structure provides for the clear accountability of individual managers.
- Capital adequacy: the organisation must have sufficient capital to carry on the proposed business and to accept the risks of it, and to be capable of paying some compensation to clients or regulatory fines, if required to do so.
- Ownership: the regulator will set requirements ensuring that owners of the management company are of good repute.

The amount of capital needed by a fund management company is a much-debated topic among regulators. There are three distinct approaches:

- A fixed amount of capital unrelated to the size of funds managed or to operating expenses.
- Capital expressed as a percentage of the market value of funds managed (in the case of fund management companies) or under administration (custodians, depositaries and trustees).
- A minimum fixed amount of capital plus liquid capital expressed as a fraction/multiple of operating expenses.

Where the capital requirement is based on some formula related to size or operating expenses, the regulator will typically publish an accounting format for calculating it, with attendant definitions of what may be included or defined as capital. Most regulators require that the capital required, calculated by whatever method, is in place at all times and not only at the time of the granting of the license.

Which approach to capital requirements is preferable will depend on the legislative, regulatory and management environment. The most significant relevant factors are:

- The existence of custodians, depositaries or trustees which are independent of fund management companies and which are themselves substantially capitalised.
- The availability of insurance for professional indemnity, errors and omissions, and employee fidelity bonding.
- The existence of an industry funded compensation scheme.

If none of these three features is part of the system, then it may be necessary to require fund management companies to have more substantial capital resources to underwrite potential losses to investors caused by negligence or maladministration. In this case the second approach to capital requirement, relating it to the value of funds under management, may be most prudent, although, in order to prevent the requirement for ever greater capital becoming a penalty for success, it should be capped at a realistic level.

The greater the reliance that can be placed on alternative means of compensating investors, the less capital needs to be required of a fund management company. Though regulators' instincts will tend to be to set capital requirements on the high side, such requirements can have damaging effects. They are likely to deter new market entrants, thus restricting competition, and possibly even resulting in oligopolies, which become price cartels, resulting in investors paying unnecessarily high costs. Once authorised, a fund management company will normally be required to file accounts with the regulator at regular intervals: the Securities Regulator can therefore easily spot any declining trend in capital and take any necessary action.

As far as a custodian, depositary or trustee is concerned, here there is an obvious case for a substantial capital requirement (they will act for hundreds or even thousands of funds whereas fund management companies are unlikely to act for more than tens or low hundreds) and/or a requirement for the custodian, depositary or trustee to be a particular type of company, for example a bank, which itself provides further protection through the authorisation procedures required to obtain a banking licence. Some jurisdictions require the depositary or trustee to be separately incorporated from its parent and for the subsidiary to be capitalised according to the requirement of the regulator, while others are content to rely on the substantial capital required for banks. Most systems attempt to restrict eligibility as a depositary or trustee to organisations of the highest financial standing and reputation in order to minimise risks to investor protection. The regulator sometimes also seeks to achieve clear segregation of assets and isolation of risk by requiring the custodial operation to be a company, with fully paid up capital (albeit possibly a subsidiary of a larger group) whose sole business is custody. The system also will normally define means whereby fund assets held by a depositary or trustee are to be distinguished from the depositary or trustee's own assets in the event of its insolvency.

The process of licensing and authorisation

The process of licensing is carried out by means of requiring the applicant to complete a set of standard application forms, which are designed to tell the regulator what he needs to know about the honesty, competence and solvency of the applicant. Along with the forms usual submissions include:

- Documents relating to the establishment of the enterprise – if a joint stock company, its directors and shareholders, its legal nature and status.
- Specific information relating to the product or products to be offered by the licensed company – if an investment fund, the charter or rules, the prospectus, evidence that the required capital has been paid in, and documents related to any individuals (e.g. directors), including certificates of passing of any required professional qualifications.
- Evidence that the license fee has been paid.

The regulator is usually entitled to ask for additional information from a company or individual, should he find it necessary for making a decision.

The time for considering applications is usually limited by legal and regulatory provisions. If the regulator makes a decision not to grant a license, it informs the applicant and indicates the reasons for refusal.

In the case of both fund management companies and custodians, depositaries or trustees, licences may be granted for a specific period only; or more commonly indefinitely (i.e. until revoked). Whichever is adopted, regulators usually undertake periodic formal reviews of fitness and properness that extend further than the operator's formal reports and accounts.

Need for an appeals procedure

The system should incorporate an appeals procedure so that the applicant may appeal against the regulator's refusal to grant a license or against the withdrawal of a licence or the imposition of serious penalties. The more transparent such procedures are, the easier it is for the regulator to send signals to other applicants.

Such open procedures can also play a major part in building public confidence in the system.

Supervision

Regular, ongoing supervision is undertaken through a series of activities under the headings 'monitoring' and 'inspection'.

Monitoring
After all the necessary licences and authorisations establishing the right to carry out business activities have been issued, the regulator will continue to supervise the activities of the licensed entity in order to be satisfied that it continues to comply with the law and the regulations. Exercising its supervisory functions, the regulator will require that a fund management company and each fund:

- Provides periodic reports – these will have to be filed with the regulator at regular intervals.
- Seeks the prior permission of the regulator for changes affecting authorised status. Only important changes have to be approved by the regulator – they are sometimes known as 'clearance events'.
- Notifies the regulator about changes, which have already happened. This covers less important changes which do not require a preliminary approval, but the regulator should be aware that they have happened – these are sometimes known as 'notifiable events'.
- Provides additional information on request. The regulator is entitled to ask for additional information or clarification at any time.

The regulator may require information from all parties providing services to a fund. This could include:

- Additional reports from the depositary or trustee as well as notification in certain cases where there have been breaches; the depositary or trustee is often required to sign off on fund accounts.
- Audit reports – the auditor may be required to make a report to the regulator after the annual audit and at certain other times, and is sometimes required to verify that certain regulatory procedures have been complied with during the period under review: the auditor also has to sign off the annual audit which must be filed with the regulator.

If through its routine monitoring the regulator spots minor or technical breaches, it will ensure that they are corrected. Usually the regulator establishes a deadline by which the breaches should be corrected.

If there is a suspicion that a breach is likely to have some damaging effect, this may call for further actions by the regulator – on-site inspections or special investigations to determine the extent of the problem.

Inspection visits

Routine inspections are normally carried out in a regular cycle, with each fund management company and custodian, depositary or trustee being subject to an inspection each year or at greater intervals. Frequency of inspection visits can also depend on a company's risk profile and track record with the regulator. Inspection usually involves a visit by a team to the offices of the regulated entity and a detailed examination of books and records. However, the inspection cycle is usually not too regular, so that regulated entities do not come to expect a visit in a particular month and arrange their affairs accordingly. Apart from routine inspections, inspection visits can also result from non-receipt of required reports or poor quality of reporting, when the regulator suspects that things are not in order; or from a specific complaint or referral from another regulator or from complaints made by members of public (or, not uncommonly, competitors). These may give rise to what is sometimes known as a 'for cause' or 'surprise' inspection, where no notice is given to the recipient.

Inspections may be undertaken either to check practice in a certain area, or covering all activities. The regulator will generally have a standard checklist against which it will measure quality of regulatory compliance and business practice.

Follow-up communications

As a result of both routine monitoring and inspections the regulator will communicate with a regulated entity, pointing out errors and requesting that they be rectified, which will be verified at the time of the next report or inspection visit. The regulator can issue a more generic 'management letter', pointing out in detail the errors and defects of the reporting and in the overall compliance methodology with the request to rectify errors by a certain date (when it may return to check progress).

Investigations and enforcement

Investigations

Regulation can only be effective if it is properly enforced. To be able to enforce the law and the regulations a regulator is often granted authority to investigate and impose sanctions on those who are in breach of the rules. If, as a result of monitoring and inspection visits, it is believed that the problems are greater than it is possible to resolve without decisive action, the case may be passed on to the investigations and enforcement department of the regulator.

The enforcement department will either investigate the case using its own resources or can recommend to its board that a full-scale investigation is initiated, perhaps carried out by an outside firm. The culmination of an investigation may be some kind of disciplinary action, which may take the form of a fine or even a requirement that certain individuals are dismissed and not permitted to work again in the industry. This action is usually made public.

It is worth pointing out that, given that the cost of investigation usually has to be covered by the company under investigation, and also the inevitable damage to the company's reputation arising from the need for an investigation, that investigation is in its own right one of the punishments within a wide range of sanctions used by regulators for the purposes of enforcement.

Dealing with errors

Given the scale and number of transactions undertaken by a fund management company (or custodian, depositary or trustee), there is the potential for numerous administrative errors to arise, which the regulatory system should find and require to be rectified.

The severity of an error generally is measured by the scale of actual or damage to investors. The most significant errors are ones that lead to clients suffering quantifiable actual losses or opportunity losses, where they miss out on future profit or increases in value. The actual reasons for errors are numerous, but in general they can be categorised as follows:

- Incompetence – bad or disorganised management or administration which leads to mistakes.
- Arrogance – belief by the regulated entity that regulations are an unnecessary imposition so they are disregarded.
- Deliberate fraud – a systematic attempt to steal clients' money in a variety of ways.

Sanctions

The imposition of sanctions by the regulator has several objectives:

- To compensate investors for damage caused at the expense of those who are guilty.
- To exclude from the market or to limit the future activities of companies that breach the rules.
- To make sure that the general public is aware of breaches made by a particular company.
- To penalise improper conduct.

Depending on the judgement as to the severity of the breach the regulator can, in ascending order of force:

- Issue a private reprimand, which means a black mark on the file and potentially closer vigilance in the immediate future.
- Issue a public reprimand, which makes the black mark on the company's reputation widely known.
- Demand that the individual employees are suspended or dismissed.
- Require that customers be compensated.
- Impose a fine on a company or individuals.
- Withdraw the licence – in effect putting the operation out of business.
- Inform the prosecuting authority – the regulator can recommend starting court proceedings against the entity in breach, the result of which can be the initiation of criminal proceedings against directors or managers, which might, if a guilty verdict is brought in, result in imprisonment.

INTERNAL COMPLIANCE

Fund regulation in most countries requires that regulated entities establish their own internal compliance controls, procedures and systems. This means that fund management companies, custodians, depositaries and trustees and service providers should have in place all the internal procedures and systems that are needed to demonstrate if they are in compliance or not and to enable their management to demonstrate to the regulator that their business and the funds which they manage are operated in compliance with law and regulations. The words 'procedures and systems' are taken to cover the whole complex of equipment, hard- and software, trained staff, manuals, staff contracts and clearly defined operating procedures.

Responsibility for the internal compliance function rests at a senior level, that is to say at board level in the case of a management company. Fund regulation often requires that a regulated entity has a specifically appointed and qualified person responsible for compliance controls who:

- Is sufficiently expert and well qualified.
- Reports directly to the chair of the board or a special board committee.
- Has sufficient seniority to be authoritative.

Many regulated entities complain of the burdens that such requirements impose, but any well-run business should have procedures and systems in place that ensure only authorised personnel have access to systems and that only authorised personnel can make certain decisions; that decisions are only taken advisedly and clearly recorded once taken; and that the management knows what is happening. Swift response to and correction of rapidly identified defects may help to avoid costs of reimbursement to customers, who may have been misled or inefficiently dealt with for a long time.

COMPENSATION AND REDRESS

This is the issue of recompense to investors for any failure, fraud or misman-agement on the part of fund management companies or custodians, depositaries or trustees or even sales agents or advisers, as a result of which investors have suffered losses. For regulators, compensation lies at the end of the regulatory chain and it is an important component in establishing public confidence in the regulatory system.

Use of insurance

In developed markets, it is usually possible for fund management companies, cus-todians, depositaries or trustees and other financial service providers to purchase special insurance cover called 'professional indemnity' or sometimes 'errors and omissions' insurance. Claims can be made against the insurers if the insured party becomes liable to make payments to investors as a result of its negligence, failure or omission. Insurers will only be prepared to issue such policies if they can place reasonable reliance on the effectiveness of regulation, the competence of the in-sured entity and on the legal system or other arbitration procedures to deliver independent and fair judgements. It is usually impossible to insure against fraud by the company as a whole, although the cost of theft by individual employees is sometimes insurable.

Compensation schemes and their funding

Many regulatory systems are underpinned by compensation schemes, which are intended as the ultimate safety net. These schemes may be simply funded by governments from taxpayers' money, or through a fund built up by regular con-tributions from regulated entities or levies on subscriptions to funds, or by levies on regulated entities after the event. Most government-sponsored schemes are limited and often place quite low limits on the maximum possible compensation. The dangers of unlimited taxpayer-funded compensation schemes have been well illustrated, notably by the vast cost of the rescue operation for a large number of US Savings & Loan Institutions in the early 1990s. Such unlimited schemes create a 'moral hazard' in that both operators and individual investors tend to act increasingly irresponsibly when they know they will not have to bear the costs of their own folly.

There are a number of dilemmas in deciding how to establish a compensa-tion scheme and there is no space here to rehearse all the arguments. These are complex, but the key elements are:

- What limits are there on the amount of compensation any one successful claimant may receive? Most schemes place a cap on this sufficient to cover most small investors but lower than might be needed to cover wealthy or institutional investors.
- Who pays for compensating investors? Clearly in most cases compensation should be paid by the person who has caused the damage. But, in the case that the miscreant is unable to pay the full amount and is thus declared insolvent, what should happen? This causes much debate, since honest firms may feel that they are being required to subsidise the incompetent or dishonest. Government schemes are unpopular for the reason that taxpayers as a whole are being required to fund payments to a relatively small group of fellow citizens.
- Who decides upon and adjudicates the amount of compensation to be paid in each case? This will normally be the regulator, but large cases may have to go to judicial review or to the courts, causing considerable delays.

REGULATION OF FOREIGN INVESTMENT FUNDS AND FOREIGN INVESTMENT

International (or 'offshore') locations, of which Bermuda, Hong Kong, Luxembourg and Dublin's International Financial Services Centre are the most prominent, offer sometimes lower tax and often more flexible regulation than applies to most onshore funds. Such domiciles are by no means trivial; in terms of funds domiciled Luxemburg has one of the largest fund industries in the world, despite having a population of 438 000.[6]

Traditionally such places were associated with tax avoidance or evasion. Investors simply wished to conceal assets from their domestic tax authorities or to distance wealth from a politically turbulent situation in their home country. Or there were reasons of tax shelter or deferral, since funds in many offshore centres did not have to pay tax on income or capital gains so income received without deduction of tax at source plus any capital gains could be accumulated within the fund, and the investor did not need to pay tax until he sold the shares or units and repatriated the proceeds.

However, as many countries' tax regimes have been made less onerous and, in particular, investment funds have been accorded special fiscal status in order to encourage savings, tax is a less pressing reason for domiciling funds in such jurisdictions. So nowadays, international financial service centres offer a different range of advantages:

- Investment freedoms – many jurisdictions permit investment in assets that would not be permitted for domestic funds in developed markets, and place no restrictions on borrowing and the use of derivatives. Thus the large tribe of so-called 'hedge funds' tend to be based in such places.

- Structure – many jurisdictions often do not place limitations on the types of legal or commercial structure in which funds may be created, and thus greater flexibility is available.
- Speed and convenience – many jurisdictions promote their ability to enable fast-track authorisation; an advantage for those whose home countries' regulator may be rather slow and bureaucratic.

There are also valid tax reasons for the use of offshore locations. One is that some funds are set up for institutional investors that are themselves wholly or partially exempt from domestic tax. But in many cases domestic legislation does not permit the establishment of tax-exempt funds or, if it does, imposes structural or investment restrictions on them. The result is that many funds designed for institutional investors are established in international centres.

Increasingly, also, as regional trading blocs develop, funds may be offered across borders within a certain region, provided that they meet the standards set for such funds. A well-known example of this is funds that comply with the Undertakings for Collective Investment in Transferable Securities Directive ('UCITS Directive') that can be offered across borders with the European Economic Area.

Permitting public offering of foreign funds

A question for domestic regulators is to what extent to permit the sale of non-domestic and/or offshore-based funds into their country. A number of approaches are possible:

- Ban all sales of non-domestic investment funds.
- Allow foreign management companies to offer investment funds locally only if they themselves obtain a full domestic license and comply with all domestic regulations.
- Permit sales of non-domestic funds, if operators are authorised and registered in another approved country, funds meet certain minimum standards and their marketing adheres to local marketing regulations.

Most countries impose some kind of restrictions on funds that are not domiciled in that country and not licensed by the domestic regulator, but few place any restrictions on foreign ownership of management companies that seek a full domestic licence and intend to market domestically and abide by local legislation and regulation.

While most countries wish to foster their own domestic fund industries, it can also be beneficial to involve experienced management companies from abroad. It is easy to make domestic licensing procedures so cumbersome for non-domestic institutions that none will actually enter the market (an approach partially used by Japan over many years) but in the long run, the creation of domestic cartels may result in inefficiency and poor service plus high charges for investors. The best way to foster development of a strong fund industry is competition within an effective system of regulation.

Funds and investing abroad

The ability of funds to invest abroad is often not a function of fund regulation, but of currency exchange rules, commonly set by central banks. Such controls have mostly disappeared in developed markets, but are still common in emerging markets: they often completely prevent any foreign investment by funds. It is quite common to find that funds do not invest abroad, but this may be due to reasons of tax efficiency and cost relative to investment in local assets as well as barriers presented by laws or currency controls.

This links neatly into the next chapter, which looks at what investment management of collective investment funds entails.

Those who would like to test their grasp of the contents of this chapter should turn to the self-test questions at the back of the book.

NOTES

1. Usually an Internet-based organisation enabling investors to use a single account to invest in funds offered by a wide range of fund management companies.
2. These include statistical and performance measurement organisations.
3. *Principles for the Regulation of Collective Investment Schemes*, IOSCO, October 1994.
4. The term used by IOSCO for what are described as fund management companies in this book.
5. IOSCO, September 1997.
6. *World Bank Little Data Book*, 2002.

5

Investment Management

This chapter on investment management deliberately restricts itself to giving an account of the basic principles and mechanics of managing diversified portfolios, explaining the implications of different investment styles, highlighting the impact of regulations governing the investment and borrowing powers of different funds with different objectives and outlining the demands of investment accounting. It therefore does not cover in detail areas such as:

- Techniques of economic analysis to establish the general political and economic background against which markets operate.
- The established ways of analysing companies and the securities that they issue and of establishing the credit ratings of both government and corporate bonds.
- Mathematical techniques for the control of risk and of determining ideal portfolio construction.
- The technical construction of indexed or 'tracker' portfolios.

These subjects are, of course, vital and lie at the heart of what investors expect a fund management company to do for them. However, it is not possible within the confines of a book that seeks to explain how collective investment funds operate overall to give a more exhaustive explanation of investment analysis and portfolio management and there is, in any case, an extensive academic and practical literature on the subject, which can give anyone interested a far more detailed account of the subject than could be given here.

INTRODUCTION

Investment management is the process of investing the money collected from fund investors in line with the investment objective stated in the fund's prospectus and selecting individual investments which fit that objective. The management company of a fund usually carries out this task, although part or all of it may be delegated to another appropriately authorised entity – as always the principle that, while function may be delegated, responsibility may not, applies. Delegation would be unusual in the case of most publicly offered funds, since it is the investment skill of the management company which is normally the prime selling point; however, in the case of 'multi-manager' funds delegation is the norm since it is diversification through allocation of different parts of the fund's portfolio to different managers, either by the use of funds or by direct portfolio management, that is the purpose of such a fund. The multi-manager approach is more common in the case of large institutional portfolios but not uncommon in the case of publicly offered funds.

DEFINITION AND CHARACTERISTICS OF DIFFERENT CLASSES OF ASSET

Leaving aside property (real estate), which is an asset class with its own particular characteristics and so-called alternative investments, currencies and commodities, used by hedge funds, there are essentially three main classes of asset, in which conventional funds invest, and which form the core of most portfolios. These are:

- Cash – deposits, certificates of deposit (CDs), bills and short-term paper, usually assumed to have a life or term of fewer than 90 days.
- Bonds – redeemable obligations where the issuer guarantees a certain rate of interest payable during the life of the bond and to redeem the bond on predefined terms and a specific price at the end of its life.
- Shares (also known as equities, stocks) – securities which represent a unit of ownership in a company which are entitled to the earnings of the company when they are distributed (dividends) and to a pro rata share of the remaining assets of the company in case of liquidation.

Each of these 'asset classes' has its own characteristics which describe the certainty or otherwise of receiving income or capital in the future as shown in Table 5.1.

Each asset class may be described as having different risk characteristics, which are related to the expected return from investment in it, in addition to which, within the broad classifications, different sub-sectors or individual securities may be described as having their own risk characteristics.

In investment terms risk is measured by means of volatility, based on past statistical analysis – that is to say the amplitude and unpredictability of the deviation of an individual value from a benchmark or mean. The way in which risk can be related to return is shown in Figure 5.1.

This is the basis of what is generally known as Capital Asset Pricing Model, developed by William Sharpe[1] on the basis of previous work done by Harry

Table 5.1 *Characteristics of different asset classes*

Asset	Income	Capital
Cash	Variable as interest rates rise and fall	Fixed
Bond	Fixed since the rate of interest is guaranteed during its life	Secondary market price is variable as interest rates rise and fall
Equity	Variable since dividends may rise or fall	Secondary market price is variable since share prices may rise or fall

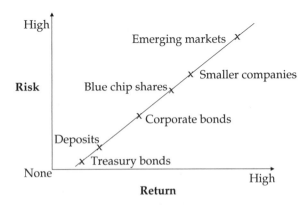

Figure 5.1 *Risk and return*

Markowitz and which forms the foundation of the 'modern portfolio theory' or the 'efficient market hypothesis'.

Thus in order to achieve significantly higher rates of return, higher risks will need to be accepted. This can be quantified as a 'risk premium' by reference to a 'risk-free rate of return' – usually defined as the current yield on a bond issued by a government whose creditworthiness is beyond question (US Treasury Bonds for example), and by reference to the volatility (or beta) of a particular security. The formula is:

$$E(R) = r + ERP \times beta$$

where r = risk-free rate of return, ERP = the expected rate of return on the asset class in question and *beta* is the expression of the volatility of the particular security.

Naturally within each broad classification shown in Figure 5.2 there will be many gradations of risk depending on the perceived creditworthiness of the issuer or credit institution in the case of bonds and deposits and on the perceived quality and profitability of the company, which has issued the shares.

This relationship between risk and return is often misunderstood by retail investors, and indeed by many professionals; and the efficient market hypothesis has many detractors. However, whatever means the investment manager uses to manage his portfolio it is his skill and judgement in understanding and controlling the risk of failing to achieve the advertised investment objectives or the benchmark that has been set that is the real test by which professional investment managers should be judged.

DIFFERENT INVESTMENT STYLES

What are termed 'investment styles' are ways of describing different approaches to the process of managing portfolios, allocating proportions of the portfolio between the different asset classes and selecting individual investments. All have the same ultimate objective – to maximise returns to the investor in a way that is consistent with minimising the risk of failure to achieve the stated objective of the fund; but the methods which the advocates of each approach or style use to try to achieve that objective can be quite different. Advocates of the different styles are, like any group that owes allegiance to a belief that is deeply held but cannot be proved, often adamant that their method is superior to all others.

The two major systems that now stand in opposition to each other are generically called 'active' and 'passive'. Of these the active approach is the oldest established (or old-fashioned according to advocates of the passive style), while the passive is a more recent introduction, being based on more quantitative techniques (or new-fangled as the traditionalists would have it). However, as will be shown later, the two systems are not completely incompatible and can be used in conjunction with one another in various useful ways.

There is a style that is a synthesis of the two, which may be described as 'enhanced passive'. This essentially uses an index benchmark but permits some deviation from it by means of altering the weightings of specific sectors or stocks from those of the index according to some pre-agreed criteria or following the manager's judgement.

Active management

Active management describes a style which attempts – by gathering and analysing economic data such as GDP growth, inflation, government finances, interest rates, currencies and corporate profits – to determine the likely future trend of relative values of different classes of asset within securities markets (this term is used hereafter to cover markets in different categories of bonds and equities and of short-term paper). The conclusion of this kind of analysis, sometimes called 'top down', will be to enable an investment manager to position the portfolio he manages according to the likely future price action of different classes of asset indicated by the forecasts. The most clear-cut decision (but not in any way the simplest) is whether the portfolio is to be invested in securities markets or not at all, given that the alternative to investment in securities is to hold the money on deposit at a credit institution or in short-term instruments equivalent to cash, such as bills and CDs, where it will earn interest but where the capital (unless the credit institution or issuer becomes insolvent) will remain intact and unchanged.

Asset allocation

In fact the process of 'asset allocation', whereby decisions are taken broadly to divide the portfolio between different asset classes, is more complex than that, given that few managers would wish to commit themselves to such a black and white decision as 'all in' or 'all out', given that the penalty for making the wrong bet would be considerable. Thus active managers, who have the choice between bonds, cash or equities, will try to construct their portfolios in such a way as to maximise returns and minimise risk, by varying the mix of several different asset classes according to their changing view of the market and according to their risk model. Managers often set themselves maximum and minimum percentages in each of the asset classes, in order to ensure that there is always a balance.

However, not all active managers have the choice of running a 'balanced' portfolio, which contains bonds, cash and equities, given that the structure of portfolios of funds is determined by the objective set in the prospectus, which is the basis on which investors have invested. Some of these stated objectives may require investment in equities only, either domestic or foreign, others in bonds, and still others in short-term money market instruments. Many funds have the specific objective of investment abroad, either in any market outside the domestic one, in which the fund is sold, or in particular regions – North America, Europe or Asia for instance – or in specific individual countries. Other portfolios have to meet guarantees, to repay the sum invested at the end of a predefined period of time, to pay pensions at a certain date or to make payments on the death of a person who has a contract of life assurance or at the maturity date of a policy, and are therefore constrained by the particular needs imposed by the guarantees.

There is also some debate about whether a portfolio which has the objective of investing in a particular type of security, rather than the objective of managing the investors' money through asset allocation, should deviate from a fully invested position at all. An investor who has invested on the promise that the fund will invest in a portfolio of, for example, domestic growth shares may have reason to complain if he finds the portfolio to be 40% in cash at a time that the market for those particular securities is rising.

Borrowing

Closed-ended funds are generally permitted to borrow without limit, subject to a decision by their directors as to the extent of the borrowing and the purposes to which it is put. Hedge funds, being unregulated, may borrow or leverage their portfolios in other ways without restraint. Both these forms of fund can use borrowing to increase their exposure to assets (it is tempting to christen this 'hyper-active management'). Borrowing by open-ended funds that are sold to the general public is usually forbidden altogether or limited to a narrow range of specifically designated purposes – meeting redemptions or purchasing securities in the event that there is a certain inflow of new money within a short period – and even then normally is limited to under 10% of the fund's net assets for a period of not longer than 90 days and similar provisions often apply to interval funds; so these funds cannot use borrowing to increase exposure to assets and hence risk.

Security or stock selection

The second part of active management, once a general allocation of available money between different broad asset classes has been made, is the process of choosing which specific bonds or which particular shares to buy.

In the case of bonds, the type of issuer and the credit rating of that issuer will to a large extent determine the bonds that will be bought. The asset allocation process, taking account of the commitment made in that part of the prospectus which sets investment objectives, will already have determined whether only bonds of the highest quality may be included or whether lower quality or even 'junk'[2] bonds may be included.

There exists in developed markets a comprehensive system of ratings calculated by such organisations as Standard & Poor's, Moody's and Fitch which enable relative risk of bonds to be assessed based on the credit ratings of their issuers, in other words the relative probability that the issuer can continue to pay the stated rate of interest each year and redeem the bond in full at maturity. This enables the total universe of thousands of different bonds to be categorised fairly tidily, for the purpose of selecting the most suitable in order to meet the portfolio objective. Other factors, such as the size and liquidity of the issue, its availability at the time of the purchase, and the remaining life of the bond until it is repaid, will also play their part. Having said that, the selection process will ultimately depend on an element of subjectivity: the personal preferences of the investment manager, based on his experience, knowledge and skill.

In the case of equities, the methods of categorising a much less homogeneous and more variable universe are less clear. The selection of which shares to buy will depend to a much greater extent on the skill of the investment manager, based on his experience, the analysis of current and future profitability and his judgement as to others' opinions and expectations of future value (always bear in mind that securities markets are a summary of people's expectations since no-one knows whether the price they pay today will turn out to be justified). It is largely in this area where quantitative techniques, often broadly described as 'modern portfolio theory', have made the greatest inroads.

Within the active management definition there fall many different subsets of style of which may be briefly categorised as:

* Value investing – seeking out neglected or undervalued securities, whose prices are likely to rise once others have recognised the undervaluation.
* Growth investing – investing in companies whose sales and profits are likely to grow much more rapidly than those of the corporate sector as a whole, and which may therefore be expected to provide higher returns.
* Investing for income – investing in shares with a high dividend yield or in high yielding bonds with a view to providing the investor with a good income return from their investment.

And many others far too numerous to list here.

Passive management and quantitative techniques

Modern portfolio theory differentiates between systemic and specific risk. Systemic risk describes the uncertainty inherent in broad political and economic events outside the control of the manager, such as changes in exchange rates, interest rates, taxation and legislation, and movements of markets measured by broad indices.

Specific risk relates to the risk inherent in the likely volatility of the price of a specific asset against other assets or against some sort of average of all assets of the same class and its expected returns (measured by the capital asset pricing model).

To say that systemic risk is outside the control of the manager is not to imply that its impact on a given portfolio cannot be minimised. This can be achieved either by reducing the weighting in any portfolio of any class of asset that is expected to be adversely impacted by any predicted changes or by the use of derivatives, which can be used to 'insure' a portfolio against unforeseen movements of currencies, interest rates and equity indices. The techniques for portfolio insurance can be usefully employed (and are) by active managers, who wish to guard or hedge against systemic risk, and who wish to deal with specific risk, inherent in price movements of individual shares, using classical analysis coupled with their skill and judgement. There is a wide variety of instruments available for this purpose – futures (agreements to buy or sell a financial instrument at a predetermined price on a predetermined date), options (where the owner of the option has the right but not the obligation to buy or sell a financial instrument at a specified price) and covered warrants (financial instruments that bestow on the holder the right, but not the obligation, to buy or sell an asset at a specified price during, or at the end of, a specified time period), each of which has a wide variety of mutations, being but a few.

In the case of most regulations governing open-ended funds that are sold to the general public, the use of derivatives is usually limited to hedging or reducing risk, sometimes called 'efficient portfolio management' – rather than increasing it, except where the fund has a specific objective to leverage or gear its portfolio. The latter are sometimes termed 'geared futures and options funds'.

Also so-called 'hedge funds' which are usually formed in a domicile which places them outside the constraints of domestic regulation can, subject to each one's own prospectus objectives, manage portfolios in a much freer and more aggressive way without having any constraints imposed on them by regulation.

It is in judging the likely outcomes that the two techniques come into conflict. Modern portfolio theorists argue that specific risk is progressively reduced towards zero as a portfolio becomes more and more diversified, and that, at the point where a portfolio exactly replicates an index (such as the American S&P 500 or the British FTSE 100, both of which aim to portray the overall movements of a market, using the prices of 500 and 100 leading shares, respectively) it has achieved the maximum desirable degree of diversification and will, obviously, then perform exactly in line with that index, leaving that portfolio exposed only to systemic risk. The theorists go on to argue that, since, in developed markets, all available information about companies is in the public domain (the efficient market hypothesis), it will be impossible for active managers, using classical analytical techniques, to beat a chosen index by identifying anomalies in the way that a market values individual shares.

Indexers also argue that large diversified portfolios managed in a conservative way are likely virtually to replicate an index anyway and thus cannot properly be described as actively managed; this can sometimes be termed 'closet indexing'. In this case proponents of the indexed style point out that customers are being charged higher fees appropriate to active management for what is in effect an indexed fund that should attract lower charges since less management is involved.

Therefore the position that carries the least risk of failure, according to the proponents of indexation, is to create what is called an 'index' or 'tracker' fund whose portfolio precisely replicates an index. An index fund can thus be certain not to underperform the index as a result of incorrect judgements but is equally certain not to outperform it either. This can either be achieved by buying shares in each company in proportion to its weighting in the index, or it can be achieved synthetically by the use of derivatives. In either case the precise methodology is subject to a number of esoteric disagreements, but the net outcome is generally understood to be a portfolio that will perform more or less in line with the chosen index.

Index funds have encountered several problems in practice:

- They may have difficulty in precisely replicating indices, since indices change constantly, needing to include new companies which have grown large enough to merit inclusion and dropping companies which have declined in size and been removed from the index; this means that portfolios will need to be constantly adjusted to take account not only of changes in the weighting of individual securities within an index but also for new entrants and leavers.
- It is uneconomic to run small indexed funds; a fund which tracked the S&P 500 would need to have 500 holdings of varying sizes, and readjusting those holdings to fit the changing profile of the index components would require buying or selling tiny amounts of shares if the fund was small, thus incurring disproportionately high transaction costs.
- It may sometimes be impossible to replicate the index in a way which complies with regulatory restrictions on fund portfolios; this is particularly acute in emerging markets, in which a major company may represent 25% of the index or more, but it is not unknown in major markets in an era of mega-mergers, where some companies may represent more than 10% of certain indices: this problem, at least in the EU, has been minimised as a result of the passage of provisions in an amending directive in 2002, entitled the UCITS product directive, which permits exemptions from certain regulatory restrictions for index funds relating to maximum percentages.
- The process of indexation drives markets in directions which are not entirely rational; in the case of indices (most) which are weighted for the size of the market capitalisation of individual companies, highly rated companies may enter an index, compelling all index funds to buy its shares, thus forcing an already highly valued company to even greater heights. This was a common problem during the technology boom of the late 1990s.
- Indices of certain countries, whose major listed companies are multinational, do not represent the economy of that country, and thus an attempt to use an index to synthesise exposure to that economy may be false – the UK is a good example of this, since many of the constituents of the FTSE 100 are, in effect, foreign companies domiciled or listed in the UK, or UK companies the majority of whose business is abroad.
- Indices may be heavily weighted towards just a few sectors in which companies tend to be large. For example, 50% of the FTSE 100 is accounted for by the shares of just 10 companies, which are mainly banks, pharmaceutical and oil companies with one telecommunications company.

An index fund, which has eliminated specific risk, can also be hedged in the same way as an actively managed fund against the impact of systemic risk.

A marriage of the two styles is increasingly commonly used in the management of large institutional portfolios. This approach, sometimes called the 'core and satellite' approach, would involve indexing a substantial percentage of the portfolio, the exact percentage to be decided by the manager or the institution whose funds have been given for management, and then using a variety of outside specialist active managers to add value in different ways. It is also possible to use this technique, traditionally the preserve of only large institutional investors, in managing the portfolios of funds, using the 'multi-manager' approach, whereby a number of different managers are appointed to manage different parts of the portfolio.

Technical or chart analysis

It is necessary to mention one other investment style, which differs from both the others described above. This is generally known as 'technical' or 'chart' analysis. Its advocates believe that, by constructing a price history of a share, bond, index, currency or commodity and showing this in a variety of graphic ways, it is possible to make predictions about likely future price movements based on historical patterns of price behaviour. Its most fervent advocates maintain that they do not even need to know what the item or asset, whose price history is represented by the chart, is, in order to be able to draw conclusions about the likely future course of the price.

As with other forms of investment style, it is possible to use charts alone as a tool for portfolio management, but it is not necessary to do so, since charts can be most useful in conjunction with more active management or fundamental analysis. Many managers make extensive use of them in this way. Many believe that charts are most useful as a tool for looking at the shares of smaller companies, whose shares are less liquid and the market in them, as a result, more imperfect; charts may well reflect better unusual movements in share prices driven by people with special knowledge. A series of charts that track the declared dealings of directors of listed companies seems to bear out this view.

This chapter does not attempt to describe all the many different ways of creating and reading charts, but a typical chart that illustrates one of the methodologies is shown in Figure 5.2.

Investment styles are not mutually exclusive

Most investment managers make use of a mix of techniques and styles, using some fundamental analysis, charts and derivatives, as well as using the

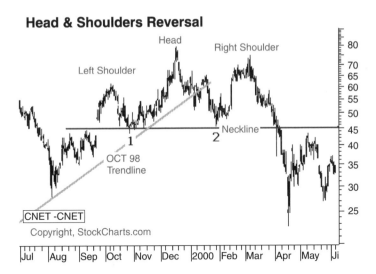

Figure 5.2 *Illustration of technical analysis*
Chart courtesy of StockCharts.com

techniques of modern portfolio theory and indexation in conjunction with active management.

THE INVESTMENT DEPARTMENT

There is no standard description of the way an investment department should be organised, structured and managed. There may be many variants depending on the regulatory environment, the type, scope and size of the funds managed, and the particular style or investment approach that the management company has chosen to follow.

Despite this, any investment department will have certain commonly recognisable components or sections. The differences from firm to firm will depend on how the components are assembled and controlled, the reporting relationships, and sometimes whether certain components are included at all.

Different parts of an investment department

Some of the most commonly recognised elements in the structure of an investment department are shown in Figure 5.3. Most of these elements will be unnecessary if the firm's investment style is 'passive' or 'indexed'. In these cases, different specialist skills will need to be applied.

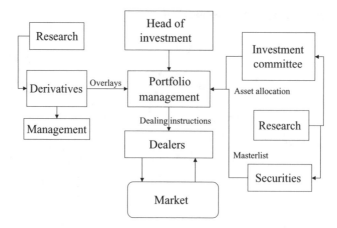

Figure 5.3 *Organisational components of an investment department*

Economic analysis

All financial markets operate within the broad context of national and, increasingly, international economies. Economic growth, currencies, interest rate policy, money supply, inflation and taxation all have a greater or lesser influence on government budgets, corporate profits, dividends and interest rates, the trend of financial markets generally and on individual bond and share prices.

The task of an economics department will be to analyse and interpret the mass of statistics that are available and to draw conclusions about likely future impact of changing economic circumstances on world markets generally, on the markets of individual countries, on different classes of asset and on particular sectors within those classes.

This kind of analysis, often called 'top down', can help investment managers, who are responsible for the management of individual portfolios, to determine broad asset allocation. The phrase 'asset allocation' is used to describe the decision process from which the overall structure of any portfolio will be determined. At its simplest it can describe the decision to be invested in securities or not. More sophisticated versions can help to give guidance as to:

- Proportions of the portfolio to be divided between bonds, equities and cash.
- In the case of an international portfolio the proportions allocated for investment in different countries and the proportions allocated to bonds, equities and cash in each country.
- In the case of certain types of portfolio the allocation of investments between different equity sectors or bond categories.

The asset allocation may be decided by an investment committee and made compulsory for all individual managers to follow or used only as a guideline.

International investment (outside the base currency of the client) is subject to the risk of currency fluctuations as well as those of the markets themselves; thus a view from the economics department on the relative future movements of currencies against one another will also be factored in, and, if desired, hedged out (neutralised) using derivatives.

Research

Research into individual companies or sectors or into the credit ratings of bonds issued by governments or corporations is usually carried on separately from the economic research described in the section above. The output of the research department will be a list of stocks or bonds whose characteristics meet the firm's criteria or style and which can be rated, according to their relative current value and estimated future prospects, as 'buys', 'holds' or 'sells'.

The research department may draw on a wide range of sources for its work; these include:

- Company reports and other announcements or information to shareholders.
- Material produced and published by broker/dealers, who have their own research departments.
- Material from independent research firms, which is sold to subscribers.
- Visits to individual companies and discussions with their senior management.
- A wide range of electronic databases which provide historic comparative data on profits, earnings, dividends and prices of equities and of yields of fixed income securities and the ratings of their issuers.

Larger firms will subdivide their research effort into regions (Europe, Asia, etc.), into individual countries or into sectors (in an increasingly global marketplace these sectors – electronics and IT, telecoms, pharmaceuticals, banks etc. – may be international in their scope comparing companies across the globe). Large firms' analysts are generally based close to the markets they cover in major centres such as New York, London, Hong Kong, Tokyo, Frankfurt, Paris and so on.

Smaller firms will often rely to a greater extent on outside research either from brokers or independent specialists, or combine research and portfolio management responsibilities in the same people.

The list of stocks or bonds which are recommended for purchase, sale or holding may be compiled into what is sometimes termed a 'master list' which individual portfolio managers are either obliged or recommended to follow.

This kind of analysis is often called 'bottom up'.

Portfolio management

Portfolio managers are the individuals designated to be decision makers in the management of specific portfolios. Individuals may often manage more than one portfolio, of which some may be those of funds and others of pension or

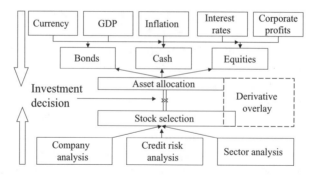

Figure 5.4 *Illustration of top down/bottom up*

insurance funds or even private individuals, or parts of larger portfolios, particularly those which invest in a wide range of different types of asset and across the world. In the case of large diversified portfolios, for example, one person may be responsible for domestic equities and others for equities of other regions, while a different person may be responsible for the fixed income portion.

The widespread use of technology – which can concentrate many sources of information and data onto a single screen on the desk of a portfolio manager, enabling him to view several different portfolios for which he is responsible in real time, even if portfolio activity is being carried out in different time zones, and to run several separate portfolios as if they were one, by allocating purchases and sales proportionately to each portfolio according to its size – enables increasing economies of scale to be achieved. There are many vendors of software designed to facilitate cascading portfolio allocation such as this.

It is at the point of portfolio management and decision making that all the techniques of managing a portfolio converge – top down, bottom up and hedging – as illustrated in Figure 5.4.

Portfolio managers need to have regard to several aspects of the management of their portfolios, apart from simply allocating assets in agreed proportions and selecting the best securities to buy and sell, including:

- The portfolio objectives as laid down in the prospectus or management agreement, and any special instructions or exclusions (for example certain clients wish to exclude investment in tobacco in the case of funds managed for medical charities, or in armaments in the case of funds managed for sects which are pacifists, such as Quakers, or, in the case of funds targeted at clients who are Muslims, alcohol and assets producing interest which that religion forbids).

- Specific objectives such as 'green' investment, which takes account of ecological factors or investment in companies which demonstrate good corporate governance and social responsibility.

- Alignment of the portfolio with internal asset allocation instructions or guidelines and with master lists of securities.
- Compliance with investment limitations laid down by laws and regulations:
  - which do not permit more than a defined percentage of the portfolio to be invested in the securities of any one issuer or more than a defined percentage of the securities issued by any issuer to be held;
  - which exclude investment in unlisted securities absolutely, or limit holdings to a certain percentage of the portfolio;
  - which exclude or limit investment in the shares or units of funds;
  - which either exclude borrowing by the fund completely, or permit it only for a defined range of specific purposes and limited to under 10% of the fund's net assets for a period usually not exceeding 90 days.
- Ensuring that the fund does not invest more than the cash it has available, which applies particularly to open-ended funds.
- Ensuring that transactions are done with approved brokers, and that 'soft' commission arrangements are honoured (this may not be necessary if all dealing is carried out through central dealers).
- Ensuring proper communication and liaison with that part of the 'back office' which is responsible for portfolio administration and valuation.

In addition to the day-to-day responsibilities for management, administration and compliance listed above, a portfolio manager will also be expected to write reports on the management of the portfolio of funds as often as the law or particular contractual arrangements requires these should be presented to clients. In the case of institutional clients, such as pension funds, the portfolio manager may also be required to attend a meeting with trustees or other representatives of the clients to answer questions or justify decisions.

Portfolio managers' time is also in demand from marketing and sales departments, particularly when units or shares of funds are sold through professional intermediaries, such as financial planners or direct sales forces. Such professional sales outlets welcome the opportunity of meeting the fund manager in person and having the opportunity to ask questions about his views on the current portfolio or the outlook for the market.

Derivative research and management
During the 1980s and 1990s the potential for use of derivatives in portfolio management has expanded enormously. Derivatives, both futures and options, have a large part to play in hedging risk or, in the case of particular funds, leveraging exposure to a certain sector, asset or currency. Thus the highly numerate and computer literate specialists, who are expert in these fields, have gained in influence within many asset management companies. The field of derivatives is complex and ever changing, and it is not within the scope of this chapter to give a full

account of all the possible uses of them in portfolio management. But it may be worth defining the two main ways in which they can be used in the context of funds, first noting that legislation and regulation in most countries forbid publicly distributed funds (unless they are in a special category of leveraged funds) from using derivatives for purposes other than reducing or containing risk. However, privately distributed 'hedge' funds will almost certainly use derivatives in a much more aggressive way.

The accepted uses of derivatives for risk reduction are in the fields of:

- portfolio protection
- anticipatory hedging
- cash flow management
- asset allocation
- portfolio insurance
- Income enhancement.

In practical terms their uses are thus:

- To reduce or eliminate systemic risk by limiting the fund's overall exposure to unexpected currency, interest rate or market fluctuations.
- To reduce the fund's exposure to unexpected falls in prices of securities which the fund holds by the use of options.
- To increase the fund's income by writing options against long-term positions.
- To protect against the risk of a high cash position in the event of an unexpected market rise.
- To synthesise the action of a market, either to achieve an indexed position or to fulfill guarantees in the case of limited life guarantee funds.
- To synthesise a temporary change in asset allocation, without buying or selling actual underlying securities.

The derivatives department usually acts independently in the case of management of fully synthetic funds (i.e. funds which do not invest in securities but use only derivatives to replicate the performance of individual securities or indices) or in the case of guarantee funds which are able to provide guarantees of returns or of minimum returns for specific future periods using portfolios of cash, bonds and derivatives.

Often it will also provide an overlay to an existing managed portfolio of securities in a way designed to limit or reduce risk. In this case the decision to hedge will frequently be one of the decisions taken by an investment committee.

In the case of hedge funds, derivatives will be extensively used to concentrate, diversify and manage risk in a whole range of instruments from currencies and commodities to equities and precious metals. Hedge funds are growing in popularity since achieving significantly differentiated performance is becoming harder, as indexing, actual or closet, becomes more and more popular and since the bearish conditions of the early 2000s have caused paper losses for most investors and have brought the concept of 'absolute return' into prominence – that is, a positive return in any market condition. Many wealthier investors are thus seeking outperformance of the norms with a small part of their wealth, and are prepared to take the sometimes real risk of losing their whole investment.

There have, however, been some notable disasters related to the misuse or the misunderstanding of the risks inherent in derivatives by the ignorant, or miscalculation of the effect of changing patterns of investor behaviour. Among these were the collapse of Barings Bank, one of Britain's oldest financial institutions, as a result of derivatives trading by a rogue dealer and that of Long Term Capital Management, an American based hedge fund.

Dealing

The process of placing deals and transacting business in securities for funds or other types of portfolio managed for clients of asset management businesses is usually a task allocated to specialists often known as dealers or traders. These people are at the front line between the asset management company and the market. Their skills are not expected to be in analysis or security selection but in the procedures of buying and selling in the market, and they can thus add value to the whole investment process by:

- Ensuring that deals are done at the best prices.
- Negotiating the purchase or sale of larger blocks in the market without excessively disturbing the market equilibrium.
- Selecting the broker or other means of transacting most appropriate to the nature of the transaction.
- Ensuring that the lowest transaction costs are paid.

Now that there are an increasing number of ways of transacting business other than on the traditional 'Stock Exchange', and since commissions are now negotiable in almost all markets (fixed commissions disappeared in the USA in the mid-1970s and in the UK in the late 1980s), where previously dealers were to a great extent reliant on brokers, the life of a dealer has become more complicated. Many electronic trading systems now permit asset management companies to circumvent the broker and deal directly with a market maker or each other.

The life of dealers has also become more complex since they often have an important role in compliance. Ensuring that dealings for clients are carried out in accordance with established norms and that individual employees of an asset management company do not, in their personal dealings, transgress either the rules for personal dealing laid down by the regulator or any internal norms for individual dealings, has become an important function of central dealers, given that most internal rules require personal dealings to be channelled through central dealers.

NEEDS AND CONSTRAINTS IMPOSED BY DIFFERENT TYPES OF FUND AND DIFFERENT STYLES

In organising and managing an investment department, there are other considerations which derive from the type of funds likely to be managed, the spread of different types of assets which will be included in portfolios and the managerial style which the particular firm adopts.

For example, asset management companies which intend to offer only passive, indexed products will not need to build the expensive and elaborate economic research and investment analytical facilities which active managers may require. They may also not need to employ classically defined portfolio managers, since the process of replicating an index lends itself to being run on a computer program or can be bought in from firms that specialise in providing indexed products, such as Exchange Traded Funds. In the case of active managers or those managers that offer different styles of management including passive, some of the most important decisions are those identified below.

Controlled or free

Given the asset allocation process and the process of creating a master list described above the management of a fund management company has the choice:

- Either of requiring that all portfolio managers follow the asset allocation process and the specific guidelines laid down by the investment committee and that they change their portfolio weightings as the asset allocation changes from time to time and that they should choose only those securities which have been through the screening process in the research department and which are thus on the master list.
- Or of allowing individual portfolio managers freedom to make their own asset allocations and to select their own securities based on any method they care to use.

The advantage of the former is that the performance of the funds managed will tend to be relatively predictable and there will be no violent or unexpected deviations from a central set of returns. Its disadvantage is that the process will be very similar to that adopted by competitors and that the conclusions reached will tend towards a consensual average, sometimes described as herding. As a result the returns of all funds of a similar type will tend to cluster round the mean, and there will be no way for the marketing department to differentiate the firm from most others in the marketplace. There are some dangers inherent in this apparently low risk approach to managing investments. If a systematic process with risk controls and close monitoring is promised it must be seen to be used. There are several cases where large clients, having been able to establish that the promised process was not adhered to, were able to bring a legal action against the managers that resulted in substantial damages being paid.

Allowing individual portfolio managers to have their freedom is, however, much riskier from a corporate point of view. It may give spectacular results if the individual is able through his own flair to achieve distinctively superior returns for investors; this in turn will attract new investors and funds managed may grow rapidly as the name of the 'star' is publicised. But this style also has risks. Star managers who can provide steady and continuous outperformance are rare and, in seeking to emulate them, individual portfolio managers are just as likely to make a mess of their portfolios with attendant bad publicity for the firm as the fund falls to the bottom of the performance league. There are some noted examples of relatively unsupervised rogue managers causing havoc and incurring substantial regulatory or compensation costs to the management company. Even if the star continues to provide results, there is a danger that he may be poached by a competitor and that the investors' money will follow him to his new company. Of course no decisions in investment management are either black or white. The degree of freedom given to or control exercised over portfolio managers will be shaded somewhere between total freedom and absolute control. Nonetheless the considerations discussed above will govern where in the spectrum they will be permitted to operate. In general large asset management businesses will tend towards the control end of the scale while small entrepreneurial firms will adopt a freer style in the hope that outstanding results will bring them to the attention of the market.

Different clients and different approaches

Most large asset managers will have and offer the capability of managing portfolios for a wide range of different types of client, including collective investment funds, pension funds, insurance companies, private clients, corporate treasurers, charities and even governments; the clients may be based in countries all over the world.

Only the very largest asset managers would be able to manage any kind of fund for any type of client in any part of the world. Medium sized managers will need to decide on their core speciality. This very often divides between the following.

The retail market
This is the market that is the main subject of this book, for which collective investment funds are generally the most suitable and commonly used vehicle. As explained in Chapters 14 and 16, funds can be sold to individuals under a number

of different guises, apart from direct purchase – these include as pension and in-surance schemes and as components in various tax-favoured vehicles, designed to stimulate savings. The investment management objectives and methods applied to the management of collective investment schemes have their own peculiarities, notably, as shown in the next section, in respect of cash inflows and outflows.

Also taxation considerations in different countries may govern such matters as:

- The value of generating and paying high dividends from equity or bond funds.
- The problem of short- and long-term capital gains levied on funds or their investors in some countries and the need to try to balance gains and losses in any given period.

Most funds are still managed in an active way, despite the growing popularity of indexed or tracker funds, and their managers strive for top performance in the league tables that are published regularly in the media. Success, which results in a fund being top or in the 'top 10' of a table of its competitors over three, six or 12 months, can have a dramatically positive impact on sales, however irrational it may be to judge a fund's results over short time periods and however much evidence there is that past performance is not a guide to future performance, something which most regulators require managers to emphasise in their publicity material. However, funds that are actively managed are coming under increasing pressure from passively managed index funds, which are cheaper to manage, thus being able to pass this on in lower charges to investors.

There is no definitive set of statistics, which enables an unquestionable state-ment to be made that either indexed funds or actively managed funds give con-sistently better returns to investors. Both sides can produce convincing historical evidence to support their respective cases.

Thus the qualities required of those who act as investment managers of actively managed funds and the disciplines imposed on them are somewhat different from those required of managers of passively managed funds.

The institutional market

The market for institutional asset management is different to the extent that, whereas managing funds for retail investors involves collecting and pooling thousands of small subscriptions, managing money for large institutions such as pension or insurance funds will involve a much more complex process of market-ing, presenting and persuasion of professional managers or trustees, who are often advised by specialised firms of actuarial or investment consultants. If successful, the sums involved in a single client portfolio can be much larger, many tens or even hundreds of millions of dollars, and thus economies of scale in management and administration can be achieved.

Institutional clients assess investment returns and performance against com-petitors much more rigorously than retail clients. However, the periods over which the judgement will be made are longer, and the expectations of the investment managers can be more realistic. Whereas retail investors expect high dividends and high capital gains all the time, those responsible for institutions accept that markets fluctuate and thus expect only relative outperformance of a benchmark (an index or a rate of interest for instance) or the competitors (better than the median for example). The investment approach required to deliver what the clients expect is rather more systematic than that for many collective investment funds; superstars are not generally welcomed in this part of the investment department, whereas, in the retail side, they can be good for sales, if not only is their performance notable but also the individuals are articulate and presentable and prepared to be quoted in the media.

While institutional money may arrive in large tranches, it may also depart in equally large amounts; periods of poor or substandard performance by asset managers who specialise in the management of institutional funds can result in a haemorrhage of business, since institutions and trustees, and the specialists who advise them, are quicker to spot and act to solve a perceived problem than the less informed retail investor. Retail business, therefore, is often regarded as more stable than institutional, since a retail asset manager may be able to survive two to three years of bad results without being too severely damaged, whereas an asset manager whose business is predominantly institutional could not.

Managing funds for foreign investors requires additional skills. Not only is the base currency in which they expect returns to be calculated perhaps different from that in which the investment manager habitually works, but also he will have to take account of accounting, taxation, linguistic and cultural factors.

Dividing portfolio responsibility

It may be beyond the capacity of a single individual to manage portfolios that are large and complex, and which cover several different asset classes in several different countries. In these cases an investment department may decide to divide the responsibility for the portfolio between several different specialists, while leaving overall control in the hands of one portfolio manager. While this makes practical sense, it can give rise to problems of coordination unless it is carefully controlled. Among the common problems are:

- Problems of coordination between different parts of the world (if regional investment teams are to be based in the region in which they are to invest); despite modern communications technology, time zones and human inertia can give rise to long distance misunderstandings.
- Conflict between individual specialists when, as a result of changing asset allocation, one person's portion is increased and another's reduced; specialists,

particularly country specialists tend to believe that their asset class, sector, country or region is 'the best' and become blind to its failings; classic cases of this were seen in the case of the Japanese asset bubble in the late 1980s and in the technology bubble of the late 1990s; this conflict will tend to slow the pace at which asset allocation is changed, often leaving a portfolio overexposed to a declining sector, region or asset class.

- Short-term cash problems, as one segment of the portfolio is increasing as another is decreasing its investment proportion; since sales and purchases cannot necessarily move perfectly in unison, investment in excess of funds available may result for a short period of time.

The capacity to cover a particular asset class or region does not necessarily have to be maintained within the investment department of a single asset management company. It is quite usual for asset managers to contract out certain specialist tasks to other asset managers. This might aggravate the problems outlined in the previous section, since an outside supplier will fight hard to keep his 'slice', and co-ordination may prove problematic.

Quite often, in the case that a relatively modest sized investment is to be made, use is made of a specialist fund, in which the fund becomes an investor. Indeed for funds that specialise in smaller or emerging markets, institutional investors that are using their investment in such a fund as a component within a larger international portfolio, are an important source of business. This is also the technique employed in managing funds and multi-manager funds.

Cash flow and liquidity constraints

One of the characteristics of funds, particularly of the predominant open-ended variety, is the way in which money flows in and out as a result of periods of strong sales or high redemptions. This may impose an unusual range of constraints on the investment manager, who will, in addition to the many other elements she must keep an eye on, have to keep informed about actual and potential sales and redemption trends, which may significantly influence the amount of cash she has to invest or money to be raised to pay redemptions. While regular inflows are a feature of pension funds and insurance funds, unexpected outflows (apart from a withdrawal of a whole portfolio from management) are not.

Strong positive cash inflow is not usually a problem if the fund's objectives are to invest in leading stocks or liquid and tradable bond issues in major markets. Such markets have ample capacity to absorb substantial amounts of money and to enable substantial sales to be made at short notice. But there have been occasions on which funds which may have become very popular have had to close to new subscriptions, if the investment manager believes that she may be swamped by the new money to the detriment of performance for existing investors. This is one of the occasions when the natural desire of any management company, which offers funds for sale to expand funds under management as quickly as possible, is tempered by investment prudence.

In the case of funds that specialise in investment in small companies or emerging markets, in which liquidity is a constraint, temporary closure of a fund for new subscriptions may be a more common occurrence.

A much more common problem faced by managers of funds is that of redemptions, if these are large and continuous and not matched by new sales. The result is a fund suffering a continuous drain on its cash reserves, and the investment manager will have to start selling investments in order to allow the fund to pay out departing investors. This may prove problematic in markets that are illiquid. Not only may it become increasingly hard to raise cash but also difficult to make sales at reasonable prices; the effect of this may be to dilute ongoing holders.

What every fund manager and regulator dreads is a 'run' on a fund. Just as a sudden surge of depositors wishing to withdraw their money from a bank can quickly result in the insolvency of a bank, so a surge of investors who wish to redeem, can cause tremendous problems for an open-ended fund and even systemic problems for the market as a whole. Most regulatory regimes allow for a moratorium to be declared by a fund that finds itself unexpectedly in this position.

One of the ways of coping with the problems of illiquidity is through the issue of funds which can be described as semi-closed or, as they are more often described 'interval' funds or 'limited' funds, which, despite being technically open-ended, may limit issue and redeem in time and by amount for liquidity reasons. Such funds are generally confined to professional investors and are not yet very commonly offered to the general public.

Generally, however, investment managers of open-ended funds will need to invest in bonds and shares that are liquid and capable of regular valuation. This will, in normal times, protect the fund against the need for extreme measures to be taken. Nonetheless a wise investment manager will keep a weather eye on cash flows.

MANAGING THE INVESTMENT PROCESS

It must be clear from the foregoing that the management of investments can be a complex business, potentially involving:

- Many different people inside and possibly outside the organisation.
- A constantly shifting background of currencies, interest rates, taxes and politics.

- A wide variety of techniques applied to the selection of investments from literally thousands of potential investments.
- Demanding clients, who expect the results that they believe they are paying for.
- A service which gives easily measurable and comparable results in a highly competitive marketplace.
- Very large sums of other people's money.
- A rigorous legal and regulatory environment.

The senior personnel of an investment management business, who are specifically responsible for portfolio management, will devote a lot of their attention to ensuring that the process runs smoothly. The penalties for failure can be considerable, since consistently poor results will result in a loss of clients and probably jobs too; major regulatory failures can result not only in loss of jobs but also possible debarment from working in the business.

There are two key areas that require attention: compliance and quality control.

Compliance

This does not just imply compliance with legal and regulatory requirements – these are important – but also with client contracts and prospectuses. There are few outcomes that are more likely to result in an angry client than a discovery that his instructions have not been obeyed (particularly if performance is poor; if it is excellent forgiveness is more likely), and few outcomes that will bring down regulatory wrath more than failure to fulfil the terms of a prospectus.

Therefore much attention is devoted to ensuring that each client is getting what he has contracted for and what he expects. This may be done by regularly revisiting original contracts and examining the portfolio in the light of them. It is also good practice to ensure that each portfolio manager is in possession of a clear brief for each portfolio under his management, including special instructions and prohibitions.

Legal and regulatory compliance will be overseen by the compliance officer or department, which will add to purely investment-based compliance a whole set of other rules relating to dealings and conflicts.

Quality control

It is increasingly common for large asset managers to have a clearly defined investment philosophy or style and detailed descriptions of how it is to be implemented covering such matters as:

- Adherence to asset allocation instructions, the permitted deviation from the norm at any time, and the time within which deviant portfolios must be brought into line.
- Use of the securities master list and the proportion of the portfolio that may be at the portfolio manager's own choice outside it.
- Extent and limitations on the use of derivatives.

In order to ensure that all is going as it should, there will be a process of regular review of all portfolios with particular attention to those which seem to be behaving oddly, either exceptionally well or exceptionally badly in relation to the generality of the other portfolios managed by the firm (or similar funds operated by competitors). There will also be the need for the portfolio manager to write regular reports to the investors of a fund or to other institutional clients, in which he will have to explain what he has done in the period under review, why he has done it and why the portfolio is invested the way it is at the reporting date; the latter is a very tough and good discipline on investment managers, who are usually some of the most highly paid employees in any asset management firm and who tend sometimes to behave like prime donne.

THE 'BACK OFFICE'

While the process of portfolio management and stock selection is the most visible of the parts of an asset management business, since investment managers are the 'stars', and their success or failure to produce good investment performances has a measurable impact on investors and on the profitability of the firm generally, the less visible parts of the business also have an important role. One of these is the department responsible for keeping the records of the investments of different funds and in other portfolios managed by the firm, and for completing the transactions that have been initiated by the investment managers and transacted by the dealing department.

Settling transactions

It is outside the scope of this book to deal in detail with the process of clearing and settlement of securities transactions, since these vary considerably from market to market, but it is sufficient to note that in markets in which there are thousands of transactions every day the scope for muddle and failure is considerable; such failures can be costly to all parties to transactions. Many firms fail through poor administration rather than poor investment results.

There are many regional variations with which the back office of an international asset management business will have to cope. Despite these, the process is tending to become more and more similar in developed countries as the investment business and securities markets become increasingly global and new techniques, such as straight-through processing, are introduced, designed to cut out almost all manual interchange, thus eliminating human error and reducing paper flows.

The placing of the deal by the dealing department is only the beginning of a complex process by which ownership is transferred to, and payment received from, a buyer; or payment made to, and ownership received from, a seller. This involves a number of different parties, which are:

- The broker acting for the fund.
- The market – whether physical or electronic – through which a counterparty, the buyer or seller, is contacted.
- The counterparty, the broker on the other side of the transaction – in the case of a broker/dealer acting as a principal, this may be the same person as the one acting for the fund.
- The fund's custodian, depositary or trustee, and the bank in whose account the fund's deposits are held, under the control of the custodian, depositary or trustee.
- The market's clearing and settlement system, through which transactions are completed.
- The registrar or central depositary, which is responsible for maintaining ownership records – the last two may be part of one and the same organisation.

Figure 5.5 illustrates the importance of the investment accounting function and of reliability that sellers deliver ownership to buyers and receive payment, and that buyers receive ownership and make payments to the sellers.

Record keeping and valuation
In addition to its responsibility for settling transactions for the portfolios of funds and other clients managed by the asset management firm, the investment accounting department will be responsible for keeping the records of the portfolios (in larger companies the responsibility for settlement of transactions will be a separate section within an overall department responsible for investment record keeping). This is important because it is upon these records that the valuation for the purposes of establishing a net asset value will be based. In this task, it is assisted by the existence of the custodian, depositary or trustee, which will itself keep parallel records of the securities that it holds for the fund; so regular reconciliations between a fund investment accounting department and the fund's custodian, depositary or trustee should help to ensure that any errors or anomalies are quickly spotted.

Very often, it will be specialists within this department who will be responsible for valuation and pricing, if these functions are kept in-house and not contracted

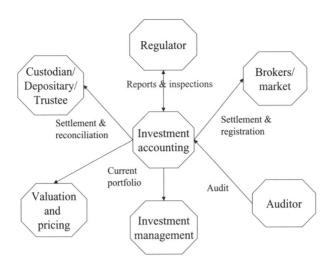

Figure 5.5 *Importance of investment accounting*

out to a third party. The price for each unit or share derived from this connects the investment accounting department with the department responsible for dealing in shares or units of the fund and for issue and redemption.

The investment accounting department is in the front line when it comes to compliance. In view of the importance that the regulator places on correct valuation and pricing it will be its responsibility to file regular reports on this to the regulator and to be available to answer questions in the event of an inspection. It will also be responsible together with the custodian, depositary, or trustee for monitoring investment limits and will be required to provide information to the auditor at the time of the annual audit of the fund.

Finally investment accounting is responsible for ensuring that the investment managers are provided with regularly updated portfolios showing the current investments and for keeping them informed of any decisions required relating to corporate actions which result from takeovers, mergers, capital increases or any other matters on which a vote is required.

LIMITATIONS IMPOSED BY INVESTMENT AND BORROWING POWERS

The type of assets that funds are permitted to hold is normally laid down by regulation, as is the maximum percentage of the portfolio that may be invested in the securities of any one issuer and the maximum percentage of any one issue or issuer that may be held. Borrowing by funds, except for closed-ended types, is usually severely curtailed.

The significance of permitted assets and borrowing rules and limitations

The type of assets that funds may hold is usually defined in legislation and regulation. Investments are normally confined to securities of different types and cash deposits. Some regulators permit real estate and other types of asset, such as precious metals, to be held, but this is unusual. Real estate is an important asset class in its own right, but is unsuitable for inclusion in open-ended fund, since it is illiquid and hard to value (no two properties are identical). The type of legal structure suitable for holding real estate is more likely to be a specialised vehicle of a closed-ended corporate type (Real Estate Investment Trusts in the USA and Property Companies in the UK). This chapter does not therefore deal with real estate in any detail.

Principal differences in investment and borrowing powers between open-ended, closed-ended and interval funds

There is an important difference between open-ended funds and closed-ended funds. Because open-ended funds are usually obliged to issue and redeem shares or units regularly at the request of investors, the ability to value the assets held in the portfolio of the fund and more importantly the ability of the manager to buy and sell those assets in order to invest new subscriptions and to meet redemptions, is a high priority. Thus the majority of the assets held by open-ended funds are usually required to be listed on a recognised exchange or regularly traded on another type of market (bonds are typically traded in interdealer markets for example). This requirement ensures that a market price can be established at the time of valuation and that there is sufficient liquidity for securities to be bought and sold in reasonable quantity at most times.

Less liquid assets, which are not regularly traded or not traded at all, are generally considered unsuitable for inclusion in the portfolios of open-ended funds and regulation usually limits the percentage of a portfolio represented by such assets to a low figure, typically 10% or less.

Closed-ended funds which have no obligation continuously to redeem shares or units, are much more suitable vehicles for holding illiquid assets, such as private equity or venture capital investments or securities in emerging markets, which, even though they may be listed, are often extremely illiquid. But even investors in closed-ended funds, whose ability to buy after the initial issue or to sell is limited to their ability to purchase from an existing investor who wishes to sell or to sell to a new investor who wishes to buy respectively, will want to be able to determine the value of their assets per share or unit from time to time in order to be able to monitor the progress of their investment and to have a guideline as to what a reasonable market price for the shares or units should be, if they wish to buy or sell.

Interval or limited funds fall somewhere between open-ended and closed-ended funds in terms of their ability to invest in relatively illiquid assets. Since they do not have to issue and redeem daily, but only at less frequent intervals of up to a year, they are able to hold less liquid assets in their portfolios. Since some such funds can limit the amount of redemption at any one dealing point, it may be argued that they only need to hold liquid assets up to the maximum percentage that they are obliged to redeem at any one dealing point.

Borrowing by funds has its dangers

Borrowing by open-ended funds is discouraged since the leverage or gearing created by the changing number of shares or units as well as the changes of the market value of the assets in the portfolio can cause unexpected damage to the share or unit value.

Even closed-ended funds' asset value per share can be seriously affected by the impact of changing market values. This is illustrated in Table 5.2.

The leverage or gearing effect of the debt is positive if the market value of the portfolio of assets rises (market value 2) but catastrophic if markets fall sharply (market value 3). The example is exaggerated in order to illustrate the point and it would be unusual for publicly offered funds, even of a closed-ended type (but not perhaps for hedge funds) to incur such high levels of debt or for market values to rise or decline by such a large amount over a short period – but it does happen: several funds have gone to the wall in the bear market of the early years of the new millennium.

In the case of an open-ended fund the net effect of changing market values will be compounded by the changing number of shares or units in issue as Table 5.3 shows.

Even though the value of the portfolio at market value 3 is the same as that at market value 1, the withdrawal of money resulting from redemptions by investors, with the level of debt unchanged, has destroyed the value for remaining investors. Hence the general rule that open-ended funds may not borrow more than 10% of the value of the fund.

Table 5.2 *Closed-ended fund: impact of market movements*

	Market value 1	Market value 2	Market value 3
Portfolio of assets	1000	1500	500
Borrowing	500	500	500
Net asset value	500	1000	0

Table 5.3 *Open-ended fund: impact of market movements and change in fund capital*

	Market value 1	Market value 2	Market value 3
Portfolio of assets	1000	1500	1000
Borrowing	500	500	500
Redemption	0	0	500
Net asset value	500	1000	0

Typical limitations for open-ended funds

Legislation and regulations usually identify the categories of asset that are suitable for inclusion in open-ended funds, particularly those that are offered to the general public. Specialised funds that are offered only to institutional investors or wealthy private individuals will not usually be subject to the limitations applied to publicly offered funds. Funds which are designed to include very esoteric assets or which do not wish to be subjected to any limitations on borrowing or their use of derivatives are usually formed as offshore funds in jurisdictions which have relatively liberal regimes, or as limited partnerships; such funds, because of the nature of the assets in which they invest, are generally regarded as too risky to be freely marketed to the general public.

The assets that are permitted to be held by publicly offered open-ended funds are selected for their characteristics of transferability and liquidity (that is, able to be bought and sold easily and quickly in reasonable quantity at any time), transparency (the terms of their issue and the rights of investors are clearly defined and there is regular disclosure of information by the issuer) and for the soundness of the issuer. Typically they would include those outlined below.

Cash and bonds
The assumption is that bonds and other types of debt instrument listed below are relatively free of risk, when issued by good quality issuers: such as sovereign debt of developed countries, deposits with top international banks, municipal debt and top quality corporate debt.

Debt issued by countries outside the top ranks, however, has proved to be anything but risk-free. Regular defaults by a number of countries in the categories 'emerging' or 'developing' have sounded warning signals that even sovereign debt needs to be carefully considered by investors, and certainly defaults on corporate bond issues are common in bad economic conditions.

Deposits made with banks, notably those of money market funds, are also not without risk unless the credit institutions with which they are placed are of top quality. Even if a bank is not insolvent, temporary difficulties may cause it to have to put a moratorium on withdrawals.

Liquidity of bonds is also a relevant topic. Many bonds trade infrequently after their initial issue, even in developed markets. This poses two problems for the managers of funds and regulators:

- The ability to ascribe a market value in the absence of frequent trades which would establish a market price.
- The inability to dispose of assets, if it becomes necessary to do so, at realistic prices.

Funds which invest predominantly in bonds and which are often sold to the public on a promise of a high return with relative security, often encounter difficulties for the above reasons.

A typical list of assets of the deposit or bond type considered suitable for publicly offered funds would be as follows:

- Deposits with banks, sometimes limited to those banks which have top credit ratings.
- Certificates of deposit, commercial paper guaranteed or accepted by banks.
- Government bonds and short-term treasury bills.
- Debt issued by agencies of government and guaranteed by government.
- Municipal or regional government debt.
- Bonds or other debt instruments issued by multinational bodies (the World Bank for example).
- Debentures and loan stocks issued by companies in any number of currencies in addition to the home currency of their country of domicile, sometimes with some limitation as to the credit rating of the issuer.
- Convertible bonds (which have both bond and equity characteristics).

Naturally there would be considerable variations in such a list from country to country, depending on the availability of particular types of deposits or debt obligations. Some countries' regulations are more restrictive than others, with the most liberal regimes leaving the problems of valuation and liquidity to the managers and their custodians, depositaries or trustees.

The types of asset described above will be used in different ways in different categories of fund. The principle which underlies the price volatility of fixed income securities is: the longer the unelapsed time until maturity, the greater the price change up or down in response to a movement down or up in interest rates.

Money market funds, which aim to behave like a substitute for a bank account, will therefore invest almost entirely in paper which has short maturities (usually fewer than 90 days) and which is issued by issuers which have impeccable risk ratings; this means that, since price changes of the underlying investments are unlikely, even in response to quite sharp interest rate movements, the price of the share or unit will remain stable at a price typically of $1 per share or unit.

The prices of funds which invest in longer term bonds will be more volatile, ranging from the most stable, which invest in the government bonds of countries with AAA ratings, to those which invest in 'junk bonds', bonds issued by domestic issuers with low ratings or even those which are in technical default, and the bonds of emerging countries.

Equities

The other main asset class in which publicly offered open-ended funds are typically permitted to invest is equity (shares or stocks in companies). Here again the criteria are those of transferability and liquidity (ability to be bought and sold easily and quickly in reasonable quantity at any time), transparency (provision of regular information to shareholders and clearly defined shareholder rights), and the status of the issuer. Again those framing the regulations face certain difficulties in defining the nature of permitted investments. The old criterion – listed on a recognised stock exchange – which passed the responsibility for supervising the quality of the companies listed, and the information that they provided, to the exchange itself, is harder to apply as trading has broken loose from traditional exchanges, which used to have a monopoly of organising trade in securities.

Despite the increased diffusion of trade in securities, it is still possible to define 'recognised trade organisers', since even so-called over-the-counter ('OTC') markets, such as NASDAQ, will not allow trade in shares of companies which have not met certain criteria. Most regulators would opt for giving a list of such trade organisers and then leaving individual stock selection to the discretion of managers.

Even with these safeguards the shares of smaller companies tend to be illiquid, and, in times of crisis, just when investors are most likely to wish to redeem, liquidity in larger companies can disappear too. Some regulators have attempted to meet this problem by requiring that funds which invest in certain types of asset should maintain a percentage of their portfolio in cash at all times, something which a prudent manager would do in any case. The danger of this approach is that the regulator may be inclined to set a high figure for the 'protection' of investors, whereas, in a rising market, such a high cash proportion will act as a drag on performance.

A much more real problem is that of valuation. Who can tell what a correct market price should be for a share which has not traded for two or three weeks or even longer? The 'synthetic' solutions, which are moderately satisfactory for bonds, cannot be used to value equities, as will be seen in Chapter 7 on valuation.

There is no neat and tidy solution to this problem, so most regulators will set broad guidelines and leave it to the good sense and business judgement of managers and custodians, depositaries and trustees to strike an appropriate balance.

Typical limitations for closed-ended funds

In general, closed-ended funds are suited to holding less liquid assets and no limit is placed on their exposure to them: some such funds hold 100% of their assets in unlisted securities (e.g. venture capital, private equity), both shares and bonds. In addition, closed-ended funds can invest in all the assets permitted to open-ended funds.

Diversification

One of the often stated advantages of funds for investors in them is diversification, that is to say portfolios which are invested in a number of different shares or bonds and which thus avoid the concentrated risk of being invested in the shares of only one company or a few companies. The question of how many different shares should be included in one portfolio to achieve optimal diversification is the subject of much academic and industry debate. The mathematically derived solution seems to suggest that around 20 different shares, provided that they represent companies in different industries, are sufficient, and that each incremental share added after that reduces risk very marginally.

Ensuring an adequate number of different holdings in any one fund
For open-ended funds a fairly standard solution, in developed markets, is to limit any one holding of shares to 5% of the total value of the portfolio – in effect requiring each fund to have at least 20 separate holdings. In practice, it would be unusual for any one fund to have as few as 20 holdings, since the business of monitoring percentages that were at the limits of what was permissible, and subsequently having to adjust the portfolio to stay in compliance, would be too time consuming.

In some less developed markets however, the 5% limitation is regarded as too low, particularly where relatively few leading shares represent a high proportion of market capitalisation; it is not unusual in some markets for the major oil and gas company or the telecom company to represent 15–30% of the capitalisation of the market. In these cases formulae can be worked out to allow, for example, 40% of the portfolio to be represented by no fewer than three shares, with no single holding accounting for more than 20%; the balance of 60% should consist of holdings which represent not more than 5% of the value of the portfolio. In this way each portfolio will have to consist of no fewer than 15 different shares.

The exception to the diversification rule is the case of investment in government bonds; since there is theoretically no specific risk involved, diversification is unnecessary. Even here, however, funds are usually required to invest no more than 35% of the fund in any one issue, since any higher percentage would invalidate the purpose of paying a fee for professional management; an investor could usually invest in one single bond without needing to pass via a fund.

Diversification rules for closed-ended funds may be similar to those for open-ended funds, or may permit greater concentration: for instance, a limit of a maximum of 10% or 15% of the value of the fund to be invested in any one issuer, rather than the 5% generally permitted to open-ended funds.

Avoiding excessive concentration in the securities of any one issuer
Equities
Classical collective investment funds aimed at the retail market are not designed to be 'holding companies' or to exercise management control functions over the companies, which they hold in their portfolios. Not only do their investment managers lack the skills to be able to manage industrial or commercial companies, but also the favourable tax environment which governments have often deliberately created to encourage savings through funds is not one which revenue services like to see abused by tax avoidance schemes designed for controlling owners of companies.

There is the additional disadvantage that large 'blocks' of shares, which represent substantial ownership of a particular company, can be extremely hard to sell in developed markets, though this is less true in emerging markets. Funds are not designed to be investment banks or vehicles for the ambitions of affiliates; the temptations for investment banks and other owners of management companies to misuse the money in funds managed by them are great, and are fully discussed elsewhere (Chapter 17).

Large holdings controlled by the same group and its affiliates may also attract the attention of the authorities responsible for policing take-overs and mergers; rules of engagement may cause holdings in excess of a certain percentage to trigger a take-over bid.

Thus limitations are placed on the percentage of any issue of voting shares of any one issuer that may be held by any fund; this percentage is often subject to aggregation of all holdings of the same security across the whole range of funds managed by any one management company. The limit will typically range from 5% to 25% or even higher. The higher limits will usually only apply in the case of closed-ended funds set up specifically for privatisation or corporate restructuring, in which cases there is a positive wish on the part of the authorities to enable the fund to exercise strong shareholder influence on companies.

Bonds
In the case of issues of bonds, there are different reasons why high percentages of an issue should not be held by any one fund or a group of funds under the same management. Clearly liquidity considerations are common to both equities

and bonds, but ownership of a high percentage of a bond issue does not confer any degree of voting control.

So the reasons in the case of bonds for not permitting a fund to hold a high percentage of an issue (or issues aggregated) by the same issuer are related more to concerns over manipulation. It would be tempting for any bank or investment bank, which advises corporate clients and helps them to raise money, to use the funds under management of its subsidiary or affiliate as 'underwriters' or buyers of last resort for a sticky issue.

Deposits

It is usual to require that not more than a certain percentage (10% might be a typical figure) of assets should be deposited with any one bank, primarily in order to minimise exposure to the bankruptcy of any one bank.

Having reviewed the implications of managing investments of collective investment funds, the next chapter looks at the net outcome of this: how investment management performance is measured.

Those who would like to test their grasp of the contents of this chapter should turn to the self-test questions at the back of the book.

NOTES

1. Capital asset prices, William F. Sharpe, *Journal of Finance*, September, 1964.
2. 'Non-investment grade bonds' or bonds where there is a reasonable chance that interest may not be paid or repayment may not be made at maturity.

6

Fund Performance

This chapter focuses on how the performance of collective investment funds is measured, why standards are set for such measurement and what these standards typically require.

INTRODUCTION

Although individual investment objectives may be different, all fund investors ideally want to get the highest possible return on their investment either in the form of capital, or income or a combination of both. All other things being equal, an investment that returns more is more attractive. But how can a return be measured in relative terms so as to make comparisons possible?

This is best done through measurement of performance. Performance of open-ended, interval and closed-ended funds is expressed as a percentage change – rise or fall – in a fund unit or share's net asset value (NAV)[1] over a certain period (though for closed-ended funds percentage rises and falls in the share price may be measured as well as the NAV, see later). Fund performance is usually expressed as the 'total return',which takes account of both the increase or decrease of the net asset value of the fund's shares or units and of distributions (that is, income paid to fund investors). It may be presented as a figure in a table, or a line on a graph; it may be found in a great variety of sources.

The principal formula for performance calculation, based only on the percentage increase or decrease in the NAV of shares or units over a given period (note: without including the effect of distributions) is very simple. It is as follows:

$$P = (B - A)/A \times 100$$

Where:

- P = performance in percentage terms
- B = the net asset value per share or unit on the last day of the period over which it is wished to calculate the performance
- A = the net asset value per share or unit on the first day of the period.

Table 6.1 *Fund performance over the period 01.01.02–30.06.02*

Fund	NAV 01.01.02	NAV 30.06.02	Performance
Fund D	125	136	+8.8%
Fund E	150	136	−9.3%
Fund F	324	398	+22.8%

Table 6.1 illustrates a typical use of such figures, showing that fund D has risen by 8.8%, while fund E has fallen by 9.3% and fund F has done best with a rise of 22.8%.

Historic nature of performance

There is one very important thing to understand about figures that show performance: they are a historic indicator. This means that they only describe how well or badly the investment has done over a defined period in the past. There is much debate as to whether past performance is any guide to future performance. Some findings indicate a degree of persistence of both good and bad performance but others contend that this is not supported by any sound statistical evidence. In the future the performance of the investment may follow a different pattern from the past, and it is very difficult to predict how it is going to change, owing to a great number of factors that may affect it, most of which are not predictable. Investment through funds is different from investment into fixed income instruments like bonds, which guarantee a fixed rate of income and repayment of the principal at a certain date, or bank deposits, which guarantee that the sum deposited can be withdrawn without gain or loss, unless the fund is of a fully guaranteed type (and these are not common). In general funds do not guarantee any amount of regular income payments or repayment of principal; and the share or unitholder accepts the full market risk.

Therefore past performance:

- Should not be expected to be repeated in the future.
- Is not a reliable guide to future performance.
- Must only be based on actual past (and not extrapolated past) performance.
- Should not be mathematically extrapolated into the future.

WHY PERFORMANCE IS SO IMPORTANT

Fund operators worldwide tend to focus on competing by showing superior performance (though many regulators would like to see greater competition in other areas such as cost). Therefore they:

- Use past performance as a primary marketing tool: particularly in advertising but also in prospectuses and other disclosure documents; in many markets it is a regulatory requirement to disclose performance information in funds' prospectuses and annual financial statements.
- Use performance information for communication with investors: through direct mail, personal meetings, and Internet, television, radio and press coverage.
- Often set themselves the specific task of achieving a certain level of performance or beating a certain benchmark (a reference point against which performance measurement is compared such as a stock market index for an equity fund).

On the other hand fund investors:

- Track the performance of their investments to see whether and how well they meet their investment objective, and make decisions about holding or selling.
- Compare their investments with investments in other funds or with other financial products or benchmarks.
- Consider performance a very important factor when choosing a fund (sometimes not giving enough attention to other characteristics of the fund such as risk and despite warnings about the historic nature of the performance).

Performance information, as well as the underlying price data, is also used for:

- Calculating performance fees for funds where operators may charge such fees (refer to Chapter 8).
- Detecting statistically significant deviations from an average or from a benchmark by compliance departments of management companies and by regulators, which could be an indication of pricing errors or manipulation. If there are errors or manipulation the regulatory consequences may be severe.

REQUIREMENTS FOR PERFORMANCE PRESENTATION

There are two facts to be borne in mind:

- Performance is a statistical indicator and therefore can be calculated, presented and interpreted in a variety of ways.
- Performance is such an important factor in defining investors' decisions, that there is a temptation to manipulate or misrepresent it.

It is crucial therefore that fund performance is calculated and presented in a way that is:

- Accurate.
- Fair.

- Comprehensive.
- And not misleading to investors.

Any presentation that does not conform to these principles can mislead an investor by showing exaggerated results or by raising unrealistic expectations. Investment decisions made on the basis of misleading performance presentation inevitably lead to disappointment with a specific fund, and sometimes disillusionment with investment funds in general.

Performance presentation and investor protection

In order to prevent bad practice and to achieve comparability of performance, regulators in most countries establish requirements for performance presentation. IOSCO[2] has established key principles governing representation of fund performance, which are:

- Advertising containing performance information should not contain any untrue statement or fact or omit any fact needed in order to prevent performance information given being misleading.
- Performance information should be calculated and presented from the point of view of a typical fund investor.
- Advertised performance should be calculated according to a standardised formula.
- Where advertised performance is not calculated according to a standardised formula such calculations must be done upon a consistent basis.
- Performance information should be presented for standardised time periods.
- Performance information should be as recent as possible: where it is no longer current, there should be prominent warning of the fact that performance may since have become lower.
- Performance information should be accompanied by a relevant benchmark.
- Performance information should be accompanied by prominent warnings that performance changes over time and that past performance is not a guide to future performance.
- A fund should provide relevant information about its performance to any investor.

Depending on the particular regulatory regime these requirements may be set up in the form of:

- General prohibitions on use of misleading or inaccurate statements, or omissions in advertisements, including advertisements which do not contain fund performance information, and/or:

- Introduction of specific Performance Presentation Standards (PPS), which state how performance shall and shall not be presented. PPS tend to standardise performance presentation in order to make it meaningful, accurate and easily comparable. In some countries PPS are set up by fund trade associations rather than regulators.

If performance is to be used in fund disclosure and advertising documents, it is not uncommon for regulators to require that:

- Figures are prepared by an independent and objective performance specialist or performance tracker or rating agency (famous names include Standard & Poor's Fund Services and Lipper – a Reuters company).
- Reference is made to the source of performance information in a fund's disclosure and marketing documentation.

The best standards of performance presentation, whether they are a part of officially established rules or not, also suggest that any presentation should be accompanied with explanations as to how the figures were derived, so an investor can draw the correct conclusions and make meaningful comparisons. The rules relating to performance presentation and the prohibition of the use of false and misleading statements and compliance with PPS, if they exist, are usually enforced by regulators by means of:

- Reviewing funds' disclosure and advertising materials.
- Inspecting funds to determine correctness of calculation and achievement of performance (records must be kept).
- Dealing with investors' complaints about advertisements or other materials in which performance is used.

There are many issues related to performance presentation, each of which carries certain risks of misleading investors. The following sections explain what these issues are and how to deal with them in order to prevent misrepresentation.

COMMON MEASUREMENTS OF FUND PERFORMANCE

Total return

The simple performance calculation in Table 6.1 assumed that none of the funds made any distributions – that is, paid out income. However, if a fund had paid out any income during the specified period, fund investors would have had two different sources of return – distribution of income and capital gains (increase in value of shares or units) – both of which should be taken into account when performance is measured. A measure of performance universally used by independent

Table 6.2 *Comparative NAV performance*

Fund	NAV 01.01.02	NAV 30.06.02	Performance
Fund D	12.5	13.6	+8.8%
Fund G	32.4	35.4	+9.3%

analysts for the purposes of making performance comparisons is that of 'total return', which encompasses both changes in NAV resulting from appreciation or depreciation of the underlying portfolio (capital gain/loss) and the payment of any distributions of income (or capital gains if these are required to be distributed).

According to Table 6.2 fund G performed better. However, how would the two funds be judged if fund D had made a distribution of 0.4 per share on 31.3.02 and fund G had not made a distribution at all? The result for fund D has been reduced by the value of distribution paid out (refer to Chapters 7 and 15 for an explanation of this) and if it had not been paid out, the outcome would have been different.

In order to calculate total return it is assumed that any dividend that has been paid out to investors during the performance measurement period is theoretically reinvested in shares or units of the fund. The investor therefore ends up owning more shares in fund D at the end of this period. To calculate how many more shares the investor obtains, it is necessary to know the price of the shares of the fund that has paid the dividend on the day after the dividend has been declared. The calculation for fund D would then be as in Table 6.3.

In this case the computation shown in Table 6.3 establishes that, contrary to the figures shown in Table 6.2, fund D actually gave a better total return to its shareholders (11.8% for the period) than fund G (9.3% in the same period) after distributions are taken into account.

Treatment of income

For the reasons given above, most PPS require the reinvestment of income to be taken into account and treated consistently, in that income should be deemed to be reinvested:

• On a particular day (PPS in different countries deem this day differently).
• Either gross or net of income tax.

PPS also require that the basis of calculation of such reinvestment must be clearly stated.

Table 6.3 *Calculating total return for fund D (assuming no market movement between 31.03.02 and 1.04.02 and no tax payable on distribution)*

Date	Number of shares/units owned	Price per share/unit	Distribution amount	Value	Increase/decrease in value over period
01.01.02	1000	12.5		12500	
31.03.02	1000	14.7		14700	
31.03.02 Distribution			400 (0.4 per share/unit)		
1.04.02	1027.97[1]	14.3			
30.06.02	1027.97	13.6		13980	+11.8% Total return

[1]Original 1000 units plus 27.97 units (400/14.3) where 14.3 is the price paid per share or unit purchased with the dividend on 1.04.02.

Presentation of yield

Total return is a key indicator of performance of any investment fund, in particular performance of funds investing in shares naturally is compared with performance of shares, which usually both pay out dividends (giving an income) and generate capital gain – thus funds investing primarily in shares should (and may be required by rules to) show their total return. However, investment funds investing in bonds and comparing their performance with the performance of bonds may wish (and may be required by rules) to present their yields separately.

Yields also are quoted for equity funds: but because future dividends are uncertain, these are usually calculated on the basis of dividends actually paid to investors in the last year, divided by the current price (so if income in the period is 1.00 and the fund share or unit price is 10.00, the yield is 10%). The yield will be quoted either net or gross of tax – which of these should be clearly stated.

In the case of bond funds two forms of yield are quoted:

- Running (or current) yield: this is an estimation of the income an investor in a particular fund is likely to receive in a year, divided by the current price of the fund share or unit. Estimation of what will happen to income in that year is possible since coupons on bonds will be paid at a known rate of interest and on a known date (assuming that the issuer does not default) so is more certain than future dividends. This yield figure also may be quoted gross or net of tax and the basis clearly stated.

- Redemption yield: this is an estimation of the total return of a fund, usually over a 10-year period, taking into account predicted income and any potential reduction or gain in capital, in addition to charges. This may be quoted gross of tax or net, which should be stated.

Many funds that aim to pay a high income decide to levy all charges against the capital, rather than the income, of the fund. If a fund only quotes a running yield, investors will have no idea of the potential impact of charges on capital returns: so it is becoming common for regulators to require that both running and redemption yield figures are quoted, and that differences between the two are explained.

Reliability of underlying data

Performance can be calculated on the basis of:

- NAV per share at the beginning and at the end of the specified period
  or
- Prices at the beginning and the end of the specified period.

In order to be meaningful, comparable and not misleading, such prices and NAVs must be reliably available and must be calculated on a consistent basis. This implies that:

- Reliable market prices of fund assets must be available, or, if market prices are not available, asset prices are established according to specific valuation procedures (refer to Chapter 7).
- The figures for NAV per share or unit are calculated according to a consistent methodology usually established by the regulator.
- In cases when prices of fund shares or units are used, prices are established in accordance with standardised fund pricing rules for open-ended and interval funds (or in the case of closed-ended funds, derive from a regulated and transparent market).

TREATMENT OF ENTRY AND EXIT FEES

However, should NAV, or offer to bid prices (for more information on what these prices are, refer to Chapter 9) – which take entry and exit costs into account – be used in performance calculations? Table 6.4 and further illustrations show how the selected method may make an impact on performance.

It is clear that on the basis of comparison of NAVs the return is $(1000 - 500)/500 \times 100 = 100\%$. On the basis of offer to bid the return is only $(950 - 525)/525 \times 100 = 81\%$.

Table 6.4 *NAV basis versus offer to bid basis*

01.01.02	NAV	500
	Offer price	525
	Bid price	475
30.12.02	NAV	1000
	Offer price	1050
	Bid price	950

What basis is used – NAV per share or a price, and what kind of price (offer or bid) – depends on:

- The objective of performance measurement:
  - to investors the key concern is what money they would have made if they bought at the beginning of the period and sold at the end of it – thus they would compare the offer price at the beginning, which they would pay to enter the fund, with the bid price at the end because this is what they would get if they redeemed from the fund (the round-trip cost);
  - however, to judge the success of investment management activity the key measure is the rise or fall in NAV in the period.
- The nature of the benchmark with which the fund is being compared: for instance, if fund offer to bid prices are used for comparison, these include charges for entering and exiting the fund as well as other costs paid by the fund in the relevant period. Comparing this figure with an index will not be fair because an index does not include costs of entry and exit. Offer to offer figures are therefore used for index comparisons – in the case of Table 6.4, $(1050 - 525)/525 \times 100 = 100\%$ (though this does not address the problem that funds also have annual operational costs which indices do not).
- By contrast, comparing a fund on an offer to bid basis with returns on a deposit account in the same period will be fair, because the interest paid on the account will have been net of charges (even if these are not visible).
- The type of fund – investors in closed-ended funds, where fund shares are traded on a stock market, can only buy and sell their investments at a market price (unless shares are bought at the time of the primary offer[3] or redeemed upon liquidation of the fund). They would compare market offer price and bid prices for fund shares over the period because they reflect the costs of their 'round trip' in and out of the fund; though they will also look at NAV to see how fund share prices relate to these.

If fund performance is quoted 'offer to offer', 'bid to bid' or 'NAV to NAV' charges will not have been included in the calculation.

Table 6.5 *Required explanations*

Element of disclosure	Required explanation
Formula	Whether it is total return or another indicator
Treatment of income	Whether income is taken into account or not, if yes whether net or gross income
Prices, fees and charges	Whether performance is measured on the basis of prices or on the basis of NAV What pricing basis is used What the currency of prices is Whether fees and charges are included and on what basis Amount of fees or charges

Performance presentation standards: formula

Some jurisdictions create standardised formulas for calculating and presenting performance. This standardisation enhances the investor's ability to compare funds' performance. It also aims to prevent manipulation of data in order to distort the performance figures to the advantage of the fund management company.

For instance, in the USA, where entry charges applied to shares in the same fund may be different, depending on the amount invested (larger investments might be charged a lower entry charge) rules require the deduction of the maximum sales charge that could be applicable.

The formula-related explanations shown in Table 6.5 should be given whenever performance figures are quoted.

TIME PERIODS

Different returns over different time periods

Returns over different time periods are very likely to be different. A long period of time over which the performance was, in aggregate, excellent might include shorter periods of worse and even negative returns.

Misrepresenting performance

A fund management company wishing to show itself in the best light may present only performance calculated for the periods when it was at its best and ignore periods of poor performance. It may wish to quote the longer rather than the

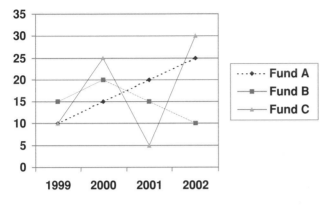

	1999	2000	2001	2002
Fund A	10	15	20	25
Fund B	15	20	15	10
Fund C	10	25	5	30

Figure 6.1 *Volatility*

shorter period to hide volatility, or it may only wish to quote the shorter period if that shows the best performance.

Fund C publishes an advertisement which shows that its price from the middle of 2001 until the middle of 2002 rose from 5 to 30, an increase of 500%, whereas the price of fund A rose in the same period from 20 to 25, an increase of only 25% (these figures cannot be taken to represent reality but are exaggerated to illustrate the point). These statements conceal the fact that, as Figure 6.1 shows, the price of fund A has increased steadily over a long period, while the price of fund C has been extremely volatile. An investor who bought fund C at mid-1999 would have lost half of her money by mid-2001. Giving year-on-year performance figures or showing performance by a line graph will illustrate volatility where simply giving a cumulative performance figure over a period will not.

Distortions of performance caused by misapplication of time periods may send the wrong signal to investors and make it impossible for them to make fair comparisons between funds.

Performance presentation standards: time periods

Most countries have rules related to time periods for the presentation of fund performance. The most common of them are:

- All funds should quote performance using the same periods of time: the most commonly used time periods are one, three, six and nine months and one, three, five and 10 years.
- All funds should quote performance to specific dates – the last day of the month or quarter, for example, rather than to some arbitrarily chosen dates. The dates between which the performance is measured have to be specified, whenever performance figures are quoted.
- If figures for short periods are quoted, than a figure for a longer period should also be given. Usually this is for a minimum of five years or since inception of the fund, whichever is the shorter.
- Performance figures should not be given for periods of shorter than one month and should be current.
- Performance figures should be as up to date as possible.
- Fund returns should not be annualised (except in the case of bond fund yields), because that conveys the impression to an investor, that an investment return that has been achieved in a past period can be repeated in the future. Annualisation 'backwards', for instance calculating an annual average return on the basis of an actual return over three or five years, is also unfair because actual performances over each of the years may differ significantly from the average. Annualisation may thus be used to camouflage volatility.
- A relatively new requirement, whereby if cumulative performance figures are shown over any period, then the performance of the fund for each separate year of the period shown also must be quoted.

DISCLAIMERS AND WARNINGS

Disclaimers and warnings are used to prevent investors from being misled by fund performance data. The most commonly used warning directly related to performance indicators is to the effect that: 'past performance is not necessarily a guide to future performance' and the 'value of money invested in a fund and the income deriving from it may go down as well as up'. The purpose of this disclaimer is to prevent investors expecting the same performance that the fund achieved in the past.

Although risk warnings that explain the risks of investment in general and in particular the risk of investment in specific funds are not directly related to performance presentation, they also prevent an investor from perceiving fund performance information as a guide to the future because they warn about the possibility of negative investment returns and impossibility of predicting the future value of an investment.

In order to be effective disclaimers and warnings have to be clearly worded and noticeable (for instance, not minimised through use of small print).

BENCHMARKS

A benchmark is a reference point against which measurement is made. The suitability of use of a particular benchmark will vary according to the comparison being made.

Making comparisons

While knowing the performance of their investment is clearly of interest, investors will wish also to compare it with the performance of other financial products or the performance of other funds, i.e. a benchmark. In comparing an investment with a benchmark investors will wish to assess:

* Whether the investment objective is being achieved and whether it would have been achieved better elsewhere.
* Whether added value has been provided by the investment manager of a portfolio as opposed to the market as a whole.

Fund management companies' performance targets are frequently related to a chosen benchmark: common examples of these are summarised in Table 6.6. In general, funds can be compared either against a figure representing all other funds – an 'industry' benchmark; or against funds in the same 'sector'. The term 'sector' will usually refer to funds which fall into a certain category according to a definition set down either by regulators or by fund trade associations, usually done by reference to fund investment objectives (growth, income, mixture), the asset classes in which funds invest (equity, bond, money market) and specialisation (for instance, geographic or sector such as healthcare or energy) – examples of these are given in Table 14.1.

PPS usually require that, whenever performance is quoted and compared with a benchmark, the benchmark must be specified and must be an objective and generally accepted one, which is regularly calculated by a recognised body. (The cynic will note that some benchmarks are easier to beat than others; indices, in particular, being more difficult to beat than other averages of other funds.)

Comparing a fund to other funds

Comparing one fund to another fund

The more similar the investment objectives of the funds with which comparisons are made, the more visible is the difference of the impact of investment management and the effect of fees and charges. To make comparisons relevant,

Table 6.6 *Summary of common benchmarks*

Type of comparison	Benchmark
Comparing a fund to other funds	Another similar fund's performance Industry or sector average Industry or sector median[1]
Comparing a fund to another financial product	Returns on that financial product
Comparing a fund to 'the market' in which it invests	Securities or bond market indices
Comparing a fund to an economic indicator	Economic indicators, e.g. inflation indices, interest rates

[1]Middle performing fund – i.e. 50 of 100.

performance figures must be calculated on a similar basis: the same formula, the same treatment of fees and charges, the same time periods, etc.

Comparison between two funds can be made not only through direct comparison of respective performances, but also through comparing the respective performances with another benchmark (e.g. a sector or a more general index).

Comparing a fund with an industry average
Performance of a fund can be compared with an average (depending on the construction principle – arithmetic or geometric, simple or weighted) of performance of all funds or a group of funds sharing the same features ('in the same sector'), for instance funds investing only in domestic corporate bonds or only in European 'blue chip'[4] equities.

Availability of prices of all funds for a period of time makes it possible to construct an index showing the average performance of all funds. Then a performance of an individual fund can be compared with the relevant fund index.

Comparing a fund with an industry or sector median
The principle here is the same as the above, i.e. comparing with an average; but in this case the comparison is with the median fund: the middle-performing fund (i.e. the fund ranked 50 out of 100). A median is by its nature slightly harder to beat than an average but has the merit of being a real fund, which 'the average' fund is not. Thus it will have a specific performance record.

Comparing funds with other financial products

While it is natural to compare a money market fund to a bank deposit, since they both aim to pay back the sum originally invested, performance of equity or bond funds is also often compared with bank deposits since banks commonly compete with funds to attract money.

Also since people may be taking money off deposit in order to invest in such funds, they want to know if this is likely to prove worthwhile by comparing their performance.

Comparing funds with 'the market'

Investors also may be interested to see how well or badly their fund investment has done by comparison with 'the market'. In fact this means a comparison of a fund's performance with the change of an average price of a particular market sector over a certain period of time. Such a comparison is best done through comparing fund performance with the change in a market index. Of course it is important that the chosen index is a fair benchmark against which to judge the performance of the fund: comparing a sector specialist fund with the relevant sector index for example.

An index is a statistical composite that measures changes, usually in percentage terms, from a base period. Securities indices show the change of the average price (different types of average can be used – e.g. arithmetic or geometrical average, simple or weighted) of the securities included in the index (known as index constituents) by comparison with the average price of the constituents of the index at the base date (this price is known as 'base value'). For instance the well-known 'Footsie' (FTSE 100 or Financial Times Stock Exchange 100 Index) is a capitalisation weighted arithmetical index of the prices of the 100 companies listed on the London Stock Exchange that have the largest market capitalisations (so the constituents change over time). It has a base value of 1000 as at the base date of 31 December 1983. In the UK the whole family of FTSE indices is used; each index of the family assesses the performance of a different market segment: FTSE Smallcap, for example, includes companies with relatively small capitalisation (GB£20m to GB£150m). There is also a range of international indices (e.g. FTSE All-World Index, MSCI World Index, FTSE Eurotop 100 cover many companies in many different countries) that can be used. In the USA the main indices are the Dow Jones Industrial Average (DJIA) and Standard & Poor's (S&P) 500, and the NASDAQ Composite, which also have a large number of sub-sectoral indices derived from them. Most countries with developed stock markets offer a range of indices and investors will often see references to the DAX (Germany); the CAC 40 (France); the BCI (Italy); the Nikkei (Japan); the Hang Seng (Hong Kong); the TSX (Canada); and many others. Indices continuously change to reflect changes in the value of companies and new indices are constantly added to meet the demands of investors or to recognise the emergence of new markets.

Comparison with economic indicators – inflation indices

Investors may also be interested to see whether their investment in a fund provides a real rate of return (i.e. over and above inflation) – that is, effectively preserves the buying power of their money over time. Inflation – which is a process of continuously rising prices, or put another way, of a continuously falling value of money – is measured by different indices in different countries, the 'Retail Price Index' (RPI) being the most prominent in the UK. In the USA various indices have been devised to measure different aspects of inflation. The CPI (Consumer Price Index), for instance, measures inflation as experienced by consumers in their day-to-day living expenses.

Every country has its own set of indicators measuring inflation, but the underlying principle is the same – a price of a standard set of goods on a given date is compared with the price of the same 'basket' on the base date. The comparison of fund performance with inflation indicators is particularly important for investors in countries with high rates of inflation (it is important that such countries take inflation into account when taxing capital gains).

Performance presentation standards: comparators

Objectivity of comparators
In order for comparisons to be statistically sound, PPS say that the figure for each comparator must be calculated in the same way in every case and over the same period of time and must be seen as objective – that is, not capable of being manipulated to someone's advantage. Objectively and consistently calculated fund performance indicators are ones which are calculated according to the rules by an independent organisation, i.e. not a fund management company, on the basis of correct and up-to-date NAV or price information.

As far as the benchmarks are concerned, the rates for bank deposits and for inflation are freely available. However, since there are a number of possible statistical methods of calculating these (the most obvious being whether to take a simple or a compound rate), it is best if an index of each can be published by an independent source.

Financial indices used for comparisons should meet a number of criteria. For instance constituents of such indices should not be subjective and there should be a set of publicly available rules on the basis of which this or that constituent is included in or excluded from a particular index. Full information on index composition should be easily available, as well as other characteristics: such as construction principle, base date, base value and interval of calculation.

Relevance of benchmarks

Comparing apples with apples...
In order to make a comparison fair and not misleading, a relevant benchmark should be selected which tracks the markets in which the fund invests or of investments similar in nature to the ones in which the fund invests. For instance it is natural to compare performance of a fund whose investment strategy is investment in British small companies with a relevant index, for instance the FTSE Smallcap. Or if the fund's objective is to provide a high current income from investment in equities it can be compared with the FTSE 350 Higher Yield. A fund investing in bonds can be compared with a relevant bond index and a deposit rate. Funds with the investment objective of maintaining the real value of capital can be compared with an inflation index. If a fund's portfolio is represented by different classes of assets, it may be interesting to compare each part of the portfolio with a relevant index and to see how performance of every part influenced the total performance.

If a chosen benchmark is relevant to the nature of fund's investments and the investment objective, it is easy to assess the skills of portfolio managers and to monitor the progress of the investment strategy based on the fund's stated objective. For instance performance of a fund, whose policy is to invest in Spanish equities can theoretically be compared either with a very relevant Spanish shares index (the Madrid SE) or the less relevant world index. If the fund outperforms the Spanish shares index, it is more likely because of a good choice of shares by the fund manager. If the fund outperformed the world index this may have been achieved due to the fact that all Spanish enterprises did better than the enterprises in the world in general (that is, the Spanish index outperformed the world index) and thus the outperformance was due to market forces and not the skills of the manager. However, if a fund's investment objective was not restricted to investment in Spanish companies, but was investment in shares internationally, but it outperformed the world index by allocating assets to the Spanish market, this would be a measure of investment skill.

...and apples with pears?
Comparing a fund's performance with an irrelevant benchmark may be at best uninformative and at worst misleading but it is tempting to do, since it may make the fund look more attractive to investors. Another temptation is to use a benchmark that is relevant – but is not the most relevant one (done to make the fund look better). For instance, when comparing the 5-, 10- and 15-year performance of a fund with a deposit someone might choose to use figures for a short-term deposit, which pays a lower rate of interest, rather than a longer-term deposit

which pays a higher rate of interest which is clearly more relevant to investments held over 5, 10 or 15 years.

While on this subject, it is worth looking at an example of seeking to mislead by omission of facts. A claim from a fund that it is 'in the top four funds in the Korean smaller companies sector' sounds as if the fund manager knows what he is doing – particularly if you are an ordinary investor who has no idea how many funds there may be in that sector. However, if the unvarnished truth was stated that 'our fund is fourth of the only four funds that invest in Korean smaller companies a much clearer idea of the expertise of the fund manager emerges. Regrettably tactics such as these are not uncommon: to the degree that they have even been humorously celebrated in song by Robin Angus, a well-known investment trust (closed-ended corporate fund) analyst and performance measurement specialist. The last verse of his 'Rentanindex Song' (written with apologies to Gilbert & Sullivan's song 'I Am the Very Model of the Modern Major-General' from *Pirates of Penzance*) goes as follows:

'There's outperformance waiting: I'll make you sure you get your share of it,
For you've been outperforming too, although you're unaware of it.
The Goddess Truth she need not blush (I haven't quite forgotten her),
Your figures may be rotten, but I'll find an index rottener.
Your dreadful US holdings may have driven you to mania –
I'm sure they've outperformed the Tramways Index in Albania,
So don't forget this wise advice – for trust men always treasure it –
It isn't what you measure – but the way in which you measure it.'[5]

PERFORMANCE REPRESENTATION

There are many ways to make performance information user friendly, understandable and comparable. The most common ways of portraying relative performance are explored in this section.

Rankings

These are tables showing the performance of all funds in descending order of return with medians and upper and lower quartiles marked (see Table 6.8). The number of a fund in such a table is known as its 'rank'. The median is the middle-performing fund. A quartile is a group of funds, which occupy one-quarter – top, second, third or bottom – of the whole list of ranked funds. A quintile, which is sometimes always used, refers to fifths.

Quartiles, also, can camouflage the truth.

Table 6.7 *Best performing funds of Stellar Fund Management Company*

	Quartile 1 year	Quartile 3 years	Quartile 5 years	Quartile 10 years
American Small Cap	1	2	1	1
Far East Equity	2	2	1	1
Asean Growth	1	1	1	2
UK Blue Chip	2	1	2	1

Look at Table 6.7. First of all, an ordinary investor probably only sees the '1' and '2' and thinks that these mean first and second in fund performance, not first quartile (in the top 25%) and second quartile (between 25% and 50% in performance terms). Secondly, if a fund was consistently the best performing fund in its sector (that is, number one) then its performance would certainly be used – so it is unlikely that the funds shown were right at the top of the performance tree, as it were; even though all those '1' and '2' figures might make investors think otherwise. Thirdly, the use of quartiles possibly makes performance look less volatile than it is – bearing in mind that a move between quartiles one and two, if there were 100 funds in the sector, could mean a move from number two in the sector to number 50. Also, what this table does not tell you is that Stellar Fund Management Company has a total of 50 funds under management: the four shown here could be the only ones with respectable performance; it may also have four or five quite similar funds to the ones shown here, whose performance is very much worse. Indeed, it is possible that all the other 46 funds operated by Stellar were persistently fourth quartile over the same periods as shown in the table: if this was also shown in this table, it might give a fairer idea – but not one that was attractive to investors.

Last, but not least, quartiles can be deceptive in that they show only ranking relative to other funds. They do not show actual performance – that is, percentage rise or fall in value. A fund may be in the top quartile but still have negative performance: it may only be down 5% where most other funds are down more than 5%. Equally, a fund may be in the bottom quartile but still show a positive return.

Simply to give quartile rankings, therefore, is potentially misleading: a fund's percentage rise or fall in value, at the least, should be shown; preferably against a sector average also. Table 6.8 shows an example of fund ranking, with quartile borders (demarcating the quartiles of performance of the funds shown) marked in bold lines; while Table 6.9 shows a more complete representation of an individual fund's year-on-year performance as typically shown in an annual report with both position in sector or ranking (e.g. in 1998 fourth out of 47 funds) and quartiles.

Table 6.8 *Example of ranking*

Rank Fund Name	Group name	Bid price	Offer price	Yield	1y% Perf	3y% Perf	5y% Perf
1 MERRILL GOLD & GENERAL (INC)	MERRILL	264.30	281.90	0.57	+49.2	+79.8	+68.4
2 SCHRODER SEOUL (INC)	SCHRODER	32.93	35.00	0.00	+32.0	−19.5	+26.9
3 BARING KOREA (INC)	BARINGS	78.67	83.77	0.00	+30.4	+21.2	+83.7
4 JPMF NEW EUROPE A (INC)	JPMF	43.86		0.00	+25.4	+24.6	n/a
5 JPMF KOREA (INC)	JPMF	45.79	48.46	0.00	+22.8	+8.0	+50.9
6 OLD MUTUAL THAILAND (INC)	OLD MUTUAL	39.45	42.06	0.00	+22.4	−20.1	−18.4
7* BWD RENSBURG AGGRESSIVE GTH (INC)	BWD RENSBURG	119.98	129.61	1.51	+22.3	n/a	n/a
8 CR SUISSE EURO FRONTIERS CLS R (INC)	CREDIT SUISSE	71.18		0.00	+20.2	n/a	n/a
9 NEW ST DELTA (INC)	NEW ST	104.60	115.10	1.85	+15.8	+1.7	n/a
10 DWS ASIAN GROWTH (ACC)	DWS	145.90		0.00	+14.8	−3.2	−2.7
11 BARING EASTERN (ACC)	BARINGS	172.30	183.30	0.20	+14.4	−8.0	−16.2
12 FR PROV RET ASIAN EQUITY (INC)	FRIENDS PROV	91.56		1.19	+14.3	−16.7	−19.3
13 EXETER PACIFIC GROWTH (INC)	EXETER	29.89	31.53	0.00	+14.0	+12.6	+26.0

Source: Trustnet. Reproduced by permission of TrustNet Limited, subsidiary of Financial Express
*Median performance.
_____ – quartile borders

Graphs and charts

Line graphs show price movement over time, sometimes compared with other comparable funds or an index, as shown in Figure 6.2. A line graph is a very effective and graphic form of performance representation, since it is an analogue and because it allows assessment of investment volatility within the time period: a graph shows a price or value at any time point within a specified period and allows a user to see the performance between any two points in time within the period. Even here, however, time periods can be chosen advisedly.

Table 6.9 *Example of rankings and quartiles*

Calendar year performance	Corporate bond fund total return	Position in sector	Quartile rank	Sectoral average
1998	+9.3%	4/47	1	+6%
1999	+16%	8/52	1	+13%
2000	+12%	44/58	4	+13.5%
2001	+3.1%	4/65	1	−2%
2002*	+4.1%	33/77	2	+3.6%

*As at 31 October.

All above figures include net reinvested income. Unit trust performance figures are on a buying price to buying price basis and are in the graph as at the end of the relevant month unless stated otherwise.

The source of this data would also be quoted usually by an independent data provider.

Bar charts are commonly used to show results of a sum invested over, say, one, three, five, seven and 10 years in a fund compared with the result of the same sum invested in a bank or an index or the average of other funds. An example is shown in Figure 6.3.

Ratings

Funds can also be rated – i.e. ascribed a certain mark of quality. Ratings can be expressed in different ways: for instance, similarly to bonds – AAA etc. (Standard & Poor's) or by using 'star' ratings (Morningstar). The basis of ratings will vary but must be clearly disclosed to be of value (it is worth noting that in some cases the fund management company or fund will have to pay to have the rating done).

The *Financial Times* provides three fund ratings as to performance: 'measured relative to a fund's risk profile and adjusted for risk'[6] (1 = very low through to 5 = very high); risk 'measured by volatility'[7] (1 = very low through to 5 = very high); and charges (1 = very low through to 5 = very high).[8]

Every supplier of ratings has its own unique rating methodology. As a rule it is based on comparison of quantitative indicators: performance (sometimes risk-adjusted performance), volatility and costs. Usually consistency of results is taken into account. Some rating agencies also make assessments of qualitative factors, such as quality of management, investment process, corporate status. Although fund ratings are made by experienced analysts on the basis of sound methodology, they are based on past performance and in some instances express the opinion of the analyst. Therefore no one rating should be perceived as a single reliable indicator as to fund selection.

Morningstar Category"	UK Equity Large Cap	Morningstar Rating"	★★★★
IMA Sector	UK Equity Income	Total Net Assets (mil)	569.79
Latest NAV	41.04	Currency	Pence
Bid	-	1 Day Change	0.0
Offer	-	YTD Return	3.1

Morningstar Rating" out of 496 funds in the Morningstar Category": UK Equity Large Cap, as of 2003-03-31 | Read more about Morningstar Rating"

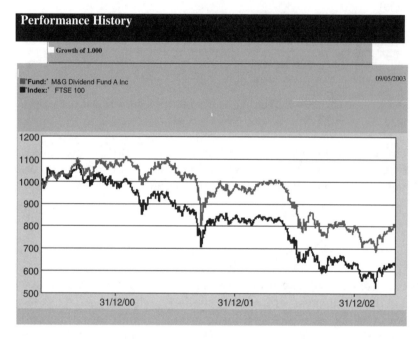

Figure 6.2 *Linear performance graph and star rating. Reproduced by permission of Morningstar*

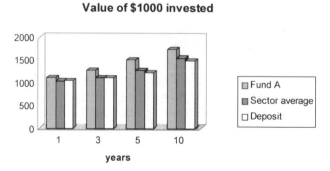

Figure 6.3 *Typical performance bar chart*

PUBLICISING PRICE DATA AND PERFORMANCE INFORMATION

In most markets a view is taken that a diversity of sources of performance information and wide distribution is good, as it provides better opportunities for investors to assess the success or the failure of their investments and make informed decisions and intelligent choices. A summary of typical sources of performance information is given below.

- Newspapers – normally regulation requires fund management companies to publish open-ended and interval fund prices in one or more newspapers with a national circulation. Some newspapers publish not only prices, but also performance figures and ratings. In some instances the newspaper itself makes these calculations, but often this is done by specialist firms – performance trackers and rating agencies (see below). On-line versions of newspapers are frequently linked to specialised financial websites, which quote prices and performance figures for funds.
- Data providers – in some developed markets financial data collectors like Bloomberg, Reuters and Extel obtain prices directly from fund operators or from newspapers. Their websites offer a set of simple mathematical calculations across different time periods based on the fund prices at the beginning and end of each period.
- Specialist companies and rating agencies – specialist companies, such as Lipper, Standard & Poor's and Morningstar use basic price information from data providers to calculate performance over different periods of time and present it in a variety of meaningful ways, helping to make comparisons. They sometimes offer a more qualitative assessment of funds' performance, based on factors such as price volatility, an assessment of the skill and experience of the manager of the fund, portfolio turnover, consistency, success in achieving specific target returns and so on. Rating agencies and fund performance trackers sell analysis, for example to newspapers and magazines who wish to publish performance tables as a service to their readers; and to fund managers who wish to have the figures analysed in a particular way.
- Financial advisers and other fund distributors – these are usually well equipped with fund performance information contained in fund disclosure documents, provided by fund management companies. They also use performance-tracking products and services of rating agencies, as well as fund-related information from newspapers, magazines and the Internet. This information helps financial advisers to offer the most suitable investments to their clients and to illustrate fund performance to them.

- Regulators – normally regulators neither collect fund prices, nor calculate and present performance figures. Price and performance information comes to regulators' attention inasmuch as it is a part of mandatory reporting and disclosure. In a few countries regulators publicise on their sites fund performance information provided by specialist companies.
- Trade associations – these may provide price data and performance information related to their members. In some countries they collect the data and compile performance information themselves and in other countries they use services of specialist companies.
- The Internet – fund operators that publish performance of their funds on their corporate websites as well as fund trackers, rating agencies and newspapers, use the Internet extensively for the purposes of fund performance presentation. There are also specialist financial websites, fully or partially dedicated to funds, where fund performance presentation can be found. Internet tools enable representation of performance in a variety of user-friendly ways. Many websites offer:
  - current prices and performance figures over varying periods of time;
  - 'searchable databases' and 'finders', which help to identify funds that meet chosen criteria such as performance, or risk, or charges;
  - lists of best and worst performing funds ('tops and flops');
  - facilities enabling comparison of a fund's performance with an index of choice or with the performance of another fund.

Performance information is often presented in a user-friendly forms, for instance as graphs and charts.

The key information upon which all performance measurement of funds is based is the fund's net asset value, to which charges are added, which creates the prices at which dealing then takes place. The next few chapters of the book cover these areas, starting with valuation.

Those who would like to test their grasp of the contents of this chapter should turn to the self-test questions at the back of the book.

NOTES

1. For an explanation of net asset value, see Chapter 7.
2. *Performance Presentation Standards for Collective Investment Schemes*, IOSCO, February, 2003.
3. A primary offer is the offer for sale of a new issue of securities; the secondary market is where ownership of previously issued securities is transferred (stock market).

4. 'Blue chip' refers to shares of companies with national strong reputations and a long history of profit growth and dividend payment and quality management: the reference is to the game of roulette where blue chips have the highest value.
5. NatWest Securities, *1996–1997 Investment Trust Annual* (reprinted from Wood Mackenzie, *Investment Trust Annual 1984*).
6. FT Fund Ratings.
7. FT Fund Ratings.
8. FT Fund Ratings.

7

Valuation

The next four chapters of this book focus on the key elements of fund administration: the tasks usually carried out by that Cinderella of the fund management world, 'the back office'. This chapter looks at how valuation is done, with the next chapter outlining the charges that can be levied on funds, which in turn affects pricing of funds, which is described in the next chapter. The final administration-related chapter describes what issue and redemption is, how dealing is done and how fund investors are serviced.

INTRODUCTION

Valuation is the process whereby the net asset value of a fund, and of a unit or share in that fund, is calculated. Essentially the current value of all long-term and all current assets held, and the current value of all current and long-term liabilities due, are calculated. The total value of all fund liabilities is then deducted from the total value of all fund assets, resulting in a figure called the 'net asset value' or 'NAV' of the fund. This figure, when divided by the number of shares or units currently in issue in the fund, is the 'net asset value per share (or unit)'. The formula for net asset value per share or unit is thus: $A - L/N$ where $A = $ assets, $L = $ liabilities and $N = $ number of shares or units in issue in the fund.

For open-ended and interval funds, this calculation creates the basis for the calculation of the price at which the share or unit is then sold to or redeemed from the investor (see Chapter 9).

THE IMPORTANCE OF VALUATION

Correct valuation is particularly important for open-ended and interval funds because it determines the basis of the price at which investors will buy or sell shares or units; this price must be fair to all fund participants whether they are incoming, outgoing or ongoing. Broadly, each unit or share in issue in a fund has rights to an equal proportionate part of each of all the assets of the fund.

So, in principle, the money that a new investor pays per unit or share should be sufficient to go into the market to buy an equivalent proportion of each of the fund's existing assets at current prices. Equally, the money that a redeeming investor takes out of the fund in principle arises from the sale of an equivalent proportion of all the fund's assets at current prices. This is why fund assets are required to be 'marked to market' for valuation purposes – that is, that their most recent market price must be used for valuation: otherwise investors will enter or exit the fund at the wrong price and ongoing holders may be 'diluted' (have their assets reduced, since incoming investors have paid too little or outgoing investors have been paid too much) or 'concentrated' (have their assets increased since incoming investors have paid too much or outgoing investors have been paid too little): a fuller explanation of this is given in Chapter 9.

Regulators pay particular attention to valuation, since it is capable of being manipulated to give a falsely good impression of fund returns, which can thus act as a lure to new investors.

Valuation of fund assets and pricing of fund shares or units are central to the operation of funds. If investors are to entrust their money to a common pool, they must have confidence that the way in which the investments owned by that pool are valued and priced is fair and does not disadvantage them. Though this may seem obvious, the facts of market practice and behaviour mean that unless great care is taken in constructing and regulating valuation and pricing systems, investors can easily be disadvantaged either to the benefit of other investors or – more seriously – to the benefit of the fund management company, which may be able to gain in a number of different ways. In addition, since the net asset value of a fund is the sole means by which investors can judge the performance of a fund manager, any error in valuation or manipulation of fund asset prices, on which valuations are based, may cause existing or potential investors to take investment decisions based on misleading or even fraudulent information.

It is therefore normal for regulators, in addition to specifying the type of investment considered appropriate for different types of fund, to make specific rules covering the methodology of both valuation and pricing of funds, and the procedures for carrying them out.

In most cases, valuation and pricing are undertaken by either the fund management company or by a specialist third-party administrator; in certain countries it is the responsibility of the depositary or trustee. In the case of open-ended funds of a contractual or trust type, which do not, like corporate funds, have directors to look after investors' interests, regulators often make the depositary or trustee responsible for ensuring that the fund management company properly applies the valuation and pricing rules, and for checking valuations. In addition regulators may require that the auditor, in the course of the audit, takes samples of the valuation and pricing calculations and verifies that these have been correctly and properly carried out. Some regulatory regimes also require independent valuation of certain assets, most commonly property (real estate) though sometimes also of unlisted securities.

Accurate valuation of assets is also important in ensuring compliance with investment and borrowing limitations on funds; fluctuations in the prices of individual assets held in the portfolio may, for example, mean that limits set for maximum holdings in any one issuer or asset class can be exceeded inadvertently, which may cause a regulatory breach for which penalties may be suffered.

FACTORS IN VALUATION

Frequency of valuation

All funds value their assets at regular intervals. Usually a minimum frequency is established by regulation, which also establishes that open-ended and interval funds are not permitted to set prices for selling and redeeming shares or units unless an up-to-date valuation has been undertaken. In the case of open-ended funds which have to invest in liquid assets, such valuations are normally undertaken every day or at the very least once every other week. Closed-ended funds normally value their assets less frequently and may do so only every month, or at intervals of three or six months. Interval funds may only be required to value their assets immediately prior to a pricing and dealing point but not less than once a year. The central assumption, however, in this chapter, is that daily valuation is the rule.

For open-ended funds, the basic principle is that the more volatile the prices of assets in which the fund invests, and/or the greater the volume of ongoing buying and selling of shares in a fund, the more frequent valuations should be. In the case of closed-ended funds, the calculation of NAV provides essential information for investors, who will want to compare the price at which the fund shares or units trade in the secondary market to their NAV. But since fund management companies of these funds do not generate revenue on an ongoing basis from sales of new shares or units in closed-ended funds and are not generally required to value frequently by law, they do not have much incentive to spend money on frequent valuations – particularly if they hold illiquid assets, which are more expensive to value. Usually they will therefore undertake periodic valuations at specific dates and will publish an NAV at those dates. In between these valuations, investors can estimate the fund's NAV by knowing what the fund's actual investment portfolio was on the previous valuation date and adjusting for the changes in the market prices of the assets in the portfolio. Sometimes brokers create models of closed-ended fund portfolios and publish their own estimates of their NAVs on a daily basis as a guide for investors. However, closed-ended funds that invest primarily in liquid, listed securities may be able to do valuations cheaply and easily and may choose to undertake this daily.

Availability of current and reliable asset prices

Where a fund invests only in securities which are frequently traded on an active and regulated stock exchange or on a dealer market which has a system for regular disclosure of prices and volumes of trades, which is immediately accessible in physical or electronic form, valuation is relatively simple since current prices for fund assets will be accessible and reliable. But many funds hold assets, for which an up-to-date market price does not exist or cannot be relied upon. Accordingly, definite principles for the valuation of various types of asset are required. These may be set by regulators, or rulebooks may leave it to depositaries, custodians or trustees or fund directors to agree such principles with fund management companies.

Examples of valuation problems frequently encountered in both developed and developing markets (but more frequently in the latter) are:

- Bonds which trade infrequently or not at all.
- Shares or bonds, which have traded in the past, but in which trade dries up.
- Unlisted securities of all sorts, if permitted.
- Trades which take place 'off market' and which are not reported.

Liquidity is the key factor in determining which valuation method should be applied. The greater the liquidity – that is, the greater the regular volume of unconnected transactions in an asset – the greater the confidence that can be placed in being able to sell or buy the asset at that price. The less the liquidity, the less confidence can be placed in the ability to buy or sell at that price and the greater the adjustment that needs to be made for this uncertainty in the valuation process.

Scope for manipulation and abuse

The less liquid the asset, the more important the principle of independent valuation becomes. Unlisted and unquoted securities are a prime example since their prices are fairly open to manipulation. For example, a fund manager can make small, repeated, purchases of such securities which will have the effect of pushing up the price of those securities over time. Others may notice the rising price, and decide to buy too, so they don't miss out; so the price will keep rising. This rising price will be included in the fund valuation, so the fund value will go up, and the manager's fee will go up. Alternatively, the fund manager may buy an unlisted company's shares through a broker, who wants to do more business with the manager; so if the broker is asked to give a quote for the current price he would pay to buy those shares from the manager for use in valuation, he may inflate their real value in order to be helpful. If this quote is then used in the valuation, again the valuation will rise and so will the manager's fee. Valuation of such assets therefore requires special care. There are several steps that a regulator can take:

- Ensuring that the methodology and process of valuing non-traded or infrequently traded assets is standardised and allows as little scope as possible for individual variation.
- In the case of both equities and bonds, requiring that assets which have not been traded, and for which no realistic brokers' quotations can be obtained are written down to a price, which represents a discount to the traded equivalent, over a period of time (but not to zero).
- Trying to ensure that all trades, on or off market, are reported to a central point and price and volume information are disseminated (developed markets have achieved some success in the case of bond trade, which takes place on an interdealer market, in encouraging dealers to report trades).
- Requiring that if brokers' quotes are used for valuation, an average of three quotes must be used and that brokers must be prepared to deal at the prices that they quote.

In the case of open-ended and interval funds, depositaries, custodians or trustees or fund directors or the regulator may require valuations of unquoted securities to be independently verified. With closed-ended and with most open-ended funds of the corporate type, the directors collectively take responsibility for such valuations and, even if the rules do not require this, they may often choose to take independent advice.

Where less liquid assets form part of a fund portfolio, its reports to investors should make this clear and also state clearly the basis that has been used in the valuation of such assets. But it may also be noted that the margin of error in valuations of unquoted investments is potentially large.

A summary of the typical valuation bases that might be established by a regulator for both liquid and illiquid assets is given in Table 7.1.

Consistency and clarity

Whichever type of valuation system is chosen from the wide variety of options, the two principles that all regulators will insist on being applied are consistency and clarity.

Consistency means that the chosen valuation and pricing method must be applied in the same way at every valuation and pricing point, and that there is no possibility of varying it to suit the interests of the fund management company or a particular group of holders, while clarity means that the method should be fully disclosed to holders and potential purchasers. Changes in the valuation methodology are required to be notified to holders, who may have the opportunity to vote on this in certain jurisdictions or be given time to redeem or sell if they do not like the proposals.

Table 7.1 *Summary of typical valuation basis*

Type of asset	Valuation method
Cash and short-term deposits	At face value
Bonds traded on a recognised market	At the day's closing market price, or the market price available immediately prior to the valuation point
Equities traded regularly on a recognised market	At the day's closing market price, or the market price available immediately prior to the valuation point
Derivatives traded on a recognised market	At the day's closing market price, or the market price available immediately prior to the valuation point
Equities traded irregularly or traded on an unofficial market	Cost (price paid by the fund) OR the most recent traded price, provided this was a genuine price resulting from several unconnected deals and not simply one trade or several trades by connected parties OR quotes from brokers. Possible write down provision
Short-term paper (bills or CDs)	Straight line to redemption, unless there are violent fluctuations in interest rates
Bonds, not traded	Comparative basis: taking the price of a comparable traded bond, and discounting for less liquidity; OR a methodology designed to attribute a discounted present value to future income receipts and redemption proceeds
Equities, not traded	Cost OR estimated value. Estimation methods are (1) using a fixed multiple of earnings (the P/E ratio) and discounting; (2) comparing with a traded share and applying a discount; (3) the company's net asset value (e.g. in the case of property companies)
Property (real estate)	Cost OR independently estimated market value

VALUATION CALCULATION

The concept of a valuation is simple. It is the aggregate of the market values of all the fund's holdings plus cash on deposit, plus any net current assets less any current liabilities and any longer term liabilities; accruals are made for income received from investments and for expenses (for more on accruals, see Chapter 15). The resulting figure, the net asset value, is then divided by the number of share or units in issue to derive a net asset value per share or unit.

Table 7.2   *Example of a fund net asset value calculation*

Investment[1]	Number of shares/bonds	Bid price – $	Ask price – $	Middle price – $	Market value at middle price – $	% of NAV
Goofy Films	29 300	2.35	2.37	2.36	69 148	2.4
Arctic Trading	14 500	4.56	4.68	4.62	66 990	2.3
Bank of Antarctica	15 550	3.17	3.20	3.185	49 526.75	1.7
Greathawk Securities	125 600	0.15	0.16	0.155	19 468	0.7
Borracho Wines	56 720	1.78	1.84	1.81	1 02 663.2	3.5
Disconnected Telecoms	12 750	4.97	5.10	5.035	64 196.25	2.2
Sysfalco	1 000	15	15.5	15.25	15 250	0.5
Geek Software	65 452	1.45	1.55	1.50	98 178	3.4
Mainline Drug Co	21 980	3.16	3.30	3.23	70 995.4	2.4
Articled Towel Group	78 956	1.25	1.39	1.32	1 04 221.92	3.6
Becalmed Shipping	105 675	0.65	0.72	0.685	72 387.375	2.5
Chalk and Cheese Chemicals	35 478	1.92	2	1.96	69 536.88	2.4
Delta Oil	56 790	1.87	1.96	1.915	1 08 752.85	3.7
Elephant Housing	35 000	2.85	2.99	2.92	102 200	3.5
Frankenstein Securities	60 000	2.15	2.20	2.175	1 30 500	4.5
Graveyard Insurance	34 678	5.23	5.37	5.30	1 83 793.4	6.3
Mongolian Mining	89 000	1.16	1.20	1.18	1 05 020	3.6
Inorganic Foods	78 945	1.98	2.20	2.09	1 64 995.05	5.6
Perilous Construction	21 455	4.58	4.63	4.605	98 800.275	3.4
Last Year Fashions	78 900	2.67	2.86	2.765	2 18 158.5	7.5
Total shares					19 14 781.85	65.4
Sky Corp 5% Loan Stock 2006	1 23 400	0.81	0.82	0.815	1 00 571	3.4
Treasury 8% Stock 2020	10 75 000	0.72	0.725	0.7225	7 76 687.5	26.5
Total bonds					8 77 258.5	
Current assets						
			Cash	109 879		
			Debtors	45 678		
			Brokers	43 567		
			Acc. Inc	35 442		
				234 566		
Current liabilities						
			Due to	87 893		
			Tax	1 567		
			Acc. Exps	9 876		
				99 336		
Net current assets					1 35 230	4.6
Net asset value					29 27 270.35	100.0

[1] The names of the companies are imaginary. Some of them are derived from those used by Oliver Stutchbury in his book *The Management of Unit Trusts* published by Thomas Skinner in 1964 and are intended as a small tribute to this excellent work.

If the fund shown in Table 7.2 has 250 000 shares or units in issue the NAV per share or unit for the fund would be:

$$29\ 27\ 270.35/250\ 000 = 11.70908$$

This will probably be rounded for dealing purposes to 11.71.

To arrive at the calculation shown in Table 7.2 the normal procedure in valuing a fund is for the fund management company, the depositary, custodian or trustee, or a third-party specialist who is contracted to carry out administrative and accounting functions, to obtain a current set of prices or a valuation of listed securities from a specialist service provider or from electronic feeds directly from exchanges. It will add to this its own valuations (independently verified if necessary) of unlisted securities, and the current balance of cash and the income account (the fund will maintain an income account for all dividends and interest) and deduct accrued expenses (the annual charge payable to the fund management company and other costs of operation) and any other liabilities are deducted also.

Among the points arising from this valuation are:

- Investments denominated in foreign currencies are translated at the exchange rate ruling on the valuation date.
- Amounts defined as current assets include amounts the fund is due to receive for sales of assets contracted for but not yet completed and for sales of shares or units made but for which payment has not yet been received.
- Amounts defined as current liabilities include amounts the fund is due to pay for purchases of assets which have been contracted for but not yet paid and for redemptions of shares or units accepted but not yet paid.
- Income is that received by the fund or accrued since the last distribution made by the fund. The definition of income received will vary depending on the degree of certainty that can be placed on the date that the payment is expected to be received, and on the bank payment system. In many countries, whose systems are not reliable, income will not be booked until it is actually in the fund's bank account.
- Expenses are those accrued at an appropriate fraction of the contracted annual rate since the last payment.

COMMON VALUATION ERRORS AND PROBLEMS

Incorrect fund share or unit valuation, which results in an incorrect price for dealing, is one of the most common problems in management of funds and one of the most potentially damaging to the interests of shareholders or unitholders. This means that regulators will give verification and supervision of valuation and pricing a high priority within their supervisory duties.

There are many ways in which a valuation and calculation of a share or unit price can go wrong. Most of these are due to human error. Some of them are:

- Using the wrong price for assets: this may either be due to deliberate manipulation, or, more commonly to incorrect transcription or data entry. For instance, governments issue dozens of different bonds with different lives and interest rates – a 5% bond redeemable in 2005 will have a very different value from an 8% bond redeemable in 2020; companies issue many classes of share – preferred, voting, non-voting – all have different prices. It is quite easy to record the wrong price.
- Mathematical errors.
- Failing to include a recently purchased security or continuing to include a security which has been sold.
- Incorrect cash balance.
- Incorrect accruals of income and/or expenses.
- Using the wrong number of shares or units in issue as the divisor to establish NAV per share or unit.

As will be seen later, even small inaccuracies in a resulting share or unit price can have seriously damaging outcomes for share or unitholders, and can be very costly for the management company, when they are detected and it is compelled to put them right. This may involve reconstructing a price history over several months and compensating any incoming, outgoing or ongoing investors, who have suffered damage, loss, or opportunity cost.

RELEVANCE TO EXCHANGES, MERGERS AND TAKE-OVERS AND CONVERSIONS

Correct NAVs are also crucial to protecting investors' interests in situations other than buying, selling or holding fund shares or units.

Share exchange

Investors may be invited to subscribe for fund shares or units not in cash but by offering securities in exchange, though some regulators only permit cash subscription for funds. The fund management company may choose to transfer the exchanged securities into the fund portfolio (assuming the asset is an eligible investment) or sell them and subscribe the resulting proceeds for the investor in the normal way. Where securities are accepted into the fund, an accurate valuation is vital. This is easy with liquid securities but problems could arise if exchange of illiquid securities into the fund is permitted.

Mergers and take-overs

A merger is where two funds amalgamate to form a single fund – a take-over is when one fund – as with a company – makes a successful bid to acquire the other fund.

Accurate calculations of NAV are vital preceding any merger or take-over between funds. Though take-overs are not usual in open-ended funds, they do occur with closed-ended corporate funds. If shares or units in a closed-ended fund trade at a large discount to NAV, this creates an incentive for outsiders to make a bid at somewhat less than NAV or for arbitrageurs to purchase stakes and attempt to encourage take-over bids or other restructuring moves that reduce the level of the discount. They may even try to force conversion of a closed-ended fund to an open-ended fund, to enable them to redeem their holding at net asset value; or to liquidate the entire fund, in which case they will also receive NAV. As an example, if a fund has an NAV of 100, but the arbitrageur buys at 80, if the fund is liquidated or converted to an open-ended fund, the arbitrageur can take a profit of 20.

A merger, in international terms, generally involves the exchange of shares or units in one merging fund for shares or units in a second merging fund or by means of the creation of a fund over the top of the two entities to be merged, which will issue its shares or units to the share or unitholders of each of the two

---

Opening position

Fund A has a NAV of 200 per share and 100 000 shares in issue

= total net assets of 20 000 000

Fund B has a NAV of 100 per share and 400 000 shares in issue

= total net assets of 40 000 000

Merger terms

Fund A wishes to merge with Fund B and issues one of its own shares for

each two shares of Fund B

Result

Fund A will, after the issue of shares to the shareholders of Fund B have a

total number of shares in issue of 300 000 and total net assets of 60 000 000

Figure 7.1 *Illustration of a merger of two funds*

funds in proportion to their size. Figure 7.1 shows an example of a merger. Clearly share or unitholders in these funds will not vote for such a merger unless they feel that the proposed rate of exchange offers them a fair deal.

The new net asset value per share will be 60 000 000/300 000 = 200 per share. This means that the holder of 10 shares in fund B, each worth 100, with a total value of 1000, will now hold 5 shares in fund A, each worth 200, with a total value of 1000. The merger has achieved exchange of equal value.

Accurate NAVs assist share or unitholders to evaluate such proposals. Clearly the holders of a closed-ended fund whose shares or units stand at a premium to net asset value will not be happy to issue those shares or units in exchange for shares or units in another fund whose shares or units stand at a discount.

Conversions

Funds may be established in one legal or operational structure and later seek to change this (e.g. move from a trust form to a corporate form or a closed-ended fund to open-ended fund). This also may apply where legislation has created specific types of fund (such as privatisation or restructuring funds) which later wish to become normal open-ended investment funds. If the conversion is effected by means of a share exchange into another fund, any inaccuracy in the NAV calculations for either fund could create substantial dilution for one group of investors.

The next chapter looks at the charges and costs that normally can be levied on funds by management companies and service providers and the implications that these can have for fund investors.

Those who would like to test their grasp of the contents of this chapter should turn to the self-test questions at the back of the book.

8

Charges

INTRODUCTION

Charging is the levying of fees and expenses on funds by fund management companies and other service providers. These charges range from the fees levied on a fund by a management company to operational costs as varied as regulatory fees and printing of annual reports.

Few things in life are free and the services provided by financial companies and investment fund managers are certainly not one of them. Management companies and the other firms that provide services to them and to the funds themselves are in business to make a profit and will expect to earn revenues, which represent the best possible return on their investment of capital and effort. Their instinct therefore is to charge as much as a competitive market will bear for the services they provide to investors. There is a fundamental conflict of interest here, since investors clearly have the opposite wish, to pay as little as possible for the service they are buying (higher costs result in lower investment returns).

Much of the discussion about charges, fees and commissions therefore revolves around the way in which this conflict may be best managed and resolved. The key issues facing regulators and the market are:

- What types of charges and expenses should be permitted and how should they be levied and accounted for?
- What expenses of operation of a fund should be paid out of which charge?
- How should charges be disclosed and their effect on investment returns be presented?
- Should there be a cap placed on charges by regulation?

TYPES OF CHARGES AND EXPENSES

The fees and expenses charged to funds for various management and administrative services fall into two main categories: those that are paid only by investors entering or leaving the fund (but do not affect the fund) and those costs that are levied on the fund. These are summarised in Table 8.1 and explored in more detail below.

Table 8.1 *Summary of fund charges and expenses that may be payable*

Types of charges and expenses	Definition
Charges levied upon investors upon entering or leaving the fund	
Initial charge[1]	Fee paid to the management company upon subscription to an open-ended or interval fund, based on a percentage of NAV per share or unit
Redemption charge	Fee paid to management company upon redemption from an open-ended or interval fund, based on a percentage of NAV per share or unit
Rounding	Rounding up of a share or unit price to a convenient value for dealing
Dilution levy	Levy made either on entering or redeeming investors to compensate ongoing investors for dilution that would otherwise be caused, based on NAV per share or unit
Charges or expenses levied on the fund	
Annual management fee	Fee paid annually to management company primarily for investment management and administration of a fund, based on a percentage of average annual net assets of the fund
Performance fee	Fee payable to a management company upon outperformance against a stated benchmark; usually based on a percentage of such outperformance
Directors	Fees and expenses paid to board directors of corporate form funds
Custodian, depositary or trustee	Fees (often based on a percentage of average annual NAV) and expenses payable to the custodian, depositary or trustee of a fund
Share or unitholder servicing	Costs of registration, administration, payment of dividends, issuance of reports and accounts, etc.
Audit	Fees and expenses of the fund audit
Valuer	Fees and expenses of independent valuers or appraisers
Regulatory fees	Authorisation fees payable to the regulator
Borrowing	Charges and interest payable on fund borrowing
Taxes and duties	Any taxes or duties payable by the fund
Holders' meetings	Cost of such meetings where convened by holders
Legal fees	Associated with fund founding documents and their amendment; sometimes on transactions in fund assets
Brokerage	Cost of transactions in fund assets
Establishment costs	Usually only for corporate funds, cost of creation of the fund (prospectus, legal fees, regulatory costs, etc.) and sometimes of its marketing also (closed-ended funds only)

[1] The costs of the launch of a closed-ended fund, including promotional costs, are usually borne by the fund (see 'establishment costs' section of Table 8.1).

Broadly the management company of open-ended and interval funds establishes initial and redemption charges according to its own commercial judgement, though within any upper limits that may be established by regulation. Equally, the ongoing costs of operation paid by a fund of the contractual or trust type are usually negotiated and contracted by the management company. The exception is funds of a corporate type, where generally the board of directors of the fund negotiates and contracts for services to the fund though it may delegate this task to the management company.

Application and limitation of charges

Not all the charges outlined in Table 8.1 are made to all funds in the same way. Different regimes and funds that are constructed in different legal forms will use different permutations of these charges and fees (for instance, the cost not only of establishing a fund but also of the marketing of the initial public offering is payable by a closed-ended corporate fund – this does not usually apply to any other form of fund).

Many regulatory systems define the type of permissible charges and may exclude certain types of charge such as performance fees. They may also define which expenses must be borne by the management company out of its fee and which may be charged directly to the fund: or they may also forbid certain types of charge to be made.

It is not uncommon for regulators to set limits to charges. This can be done either by setting a limit for specific charges (e.g. initial and redemption charges and annual management fees); or by limiting the total annual cost of operation of a fund; or by imposing a limit for the total charges levied over some period of time.

A common regulatory principle is that no charge or expense is payable by a fund or investor unless it has been clearly disclosed in the prospectus. Charges are also required to be consistently applied and to be levied at stated regular intervals and may not vary from those given in fund prospectuses and other offering or contractual documents – for instance, by being levied in some months and not in others in order to massage performance. Certain types of charge (primarily initial, annual and redemption) usually may not be increased without the assent of the depositary or trustee and/or the regulator and may also require the assent of investors expressed at an extraordinary general meeting.

In general, in developing markets with unsophisticated investors, relatively poor disclosure and lack of competition, a system of control or capping of charges may be necessary, though the danger is that everyone will simply charge the maximum possible. In a more mature industry where there is extensive competition and clear disclosure, there is less reason to impose such controls.

Competition with other financial services also has an impact; for instance, it is hard to levy any initial charges on money market type funds, since banks and other deposit takers do not levy such charges on deposits, and therefore such charges would make the funds uncompetitive.

One-off charges made at the time of purchase or redemption

Initial charges

Typical levels of initial charge (also called 'entry fee', 'front-end load' or 'sales charge' or 'sales load') will vary according to the type of fund and according to the marketplace in which it is being offered. In general, a range from zero up to 8.5% is common.

In markets where 'load' funds (those that have initial charges) compete with 'no-load' funds (those with no initial charges) it is worth bearing in mind that the higher the initial charge of the 'load' fund, the greater the investment return that fund needs to earn in order to compete with a 'no-load' fund. Where an investor invests 100 when buying one share or unit in a fund, and there is no initial charge ('no load'), then all her 100 gets invested and earns returns from day one. If she invests 100 but there is an initial charge of 7%, only 93 of her money will be invested and will have to earn 7% before it can even compete against the no-load fund.

Typically fund management companies will seek to maintain initial charges on the sale of open-ended or interval fund shares or units if possible. Their aim will be to cover all their marketing expenses out of these initial charges, prefer-ably also retaining a part, which may be added to the management company's revenues. Also fund management companies commonly may pay part of these initial charges in the form of commissions to sales agents or distributors who make sales on their behalf.

As markets develop and more fund management companies are established, competition gradually grows and lower initial charges may become used as a competitive tool. The result is usually an overall fall in the level of initial charges, which settle at a lower level of 2–6%. Pressure on initial charges has resulted in an increasing trend towards funds operating on a 'no-load' basis, in which case there is no initial charge at all and managers hope to achieve profits by attracting substantial volumes of funds on which they can earn annual management fees for a long period. In some cases this can be compensated for by higher annual charges or even, in the USA, by a special additional marketing charge to the fund, known by the number of the section of the legislation that permits it as a '12b–1' charge; but this is subject to certain constraints including a cap of a total of 1% of a fund's average annual net assets, of which up to 0.25% may be used to remunerate sales agents.

Table 8.2 *Volume reduction trigger points (or 'breakpoints')*

Investment	Sales charge (%)
Under $25 000	5.75
$25 001–$50 000	5.50
$50 001–$100 000	4.75
$100 001–$250 000	3.75
$250 001–$500 000	2.50
$500 001–$1 million	2.00
Over $1 million	none

Many management companies, if their funds are subject to an initial charge, will operate a system of discounts for volume. This may take the form of a tapering charge, where only smaller investments attract the full charge and larger investments are subject to a reducing level of charge, which will sometimes reach zero for very large investments. Fund management companies may sometimes aggregate volumes over a defined period and reduce charges based on a number of transactions during that period.

There is sometimes controversy over the way discounts on initial charges are granted. Wishing to attract a new and possibly large investor, management companies may make a special, on-off reduction in initial charge or pay an extra commission in order to attract him to the fund, but may not offer the same deal to others. This is patently unfair. Ideally, regulators should ensure that prospectuses include a table of volume reductions that applies evenly to all investors and is non-negotiable. An example of such an approach is given in Table 8.2.

Conflict between commission and charges
Clearly an investor is better off paying a low, or no, initial charge. But, given that shares or units of funds are often distributed through brokers, financial advisers or salespeople, a no-load or low load fund is unattractive to advisers if there is no commission payment to remunerate them for their work and advice. There may be a tendency, therefore, for advisers to select a fund with an initial charge sufficient to pay commission even though there exists a comparable fund with lower or no initial charges.

No-load funds and trail commissions
This could be solved by management companies of no- or low load funds by the payment of a renewal (or 'trail' or 'service') commission or fee to an adviser, commonly payable out of the management company's annual management fee or sometimes out of the fund. This approach may work if advisers can find another

way of being paid for their initial advice, for instance by charging a professional fee, something that many regulators would like to see, since it would, according to this view, remove a bias towards recommendation by advisers of funds with higher initial charges and hence higher commissions for them. Payment of renewal fees means that the adviser, while receiving no immediate commission, would receive an annual trail fee as long as the investor remains in the fund. This is regarded as both good for the fund management company, since there is an incentive for the adviser to keep the investor invested in the fund, and for the adviser who can thus build up a regular annual income rather than being solely dependent on clients making new investments or on 'switching' existing clients from one fund to another in order to generate commissions.

The alternative would be for a management company to finance the payment of an initial commission on a low or no-load fund. This would initially need to come out of its own pocket, since there is no front-end load to compensate.

The argument for charging marketing costs to the fund as opposed to the investor is a complex one. In cases when an initial charge is made, new investors are essentially being billed for the marketing and commission expenditure required to bring them into the fund, since the management company hopes that these will be at least covered by the amount of initial charges. In theory an existing investor does not benefit from further sales and therefore has no interest in paying for ongoing marketing out of the returns expected from the investment. Only the management company will benefit from the additional revenue derived from a larger fund, resulting from new sales.

Those who persuaded the US Securities and Exchange Commission to accept the additional marketing charge termed 12b-1, paid by the fund, did so by advancing the argument that an expanding fund was easier to manage and that this together with the benefit of not paying an initial charge would give superior returns of an annual amount at least equal to the cost of the 12b-1 charge. If this was true then an existing investor could see a benefit from paying this additional amount. It may be worth noting that some Investment Company Institute research in 1999[1] showed that 63% of 12b-1 fees was used to cover the cost of compensating broker-dealers for the sale of fund shares against 32% used for administrative expenses and 5% used for advertising and sales promotion.

Trail commissions, whether paid to financial advisers or to other sales agents, create administrative complexity, since individual investments will need to be precisely tracked in order to determine the level of charge payable and to whom the payment is to be made. In the case of trail commission paid to an intermediary either instead of or in addition to an initial commission, the management company will wish to establish that the investor whose investment is the subject of the commission payment remains in the fund; otherwise the intermediary will be receiving a loyalty payment for disloyalty.

Redemption charges (or 'back-end loads' or 'deferred sales charges')

If a fund management company levies a low initial charge and the investor sells within a short time of purchase, the initial charge received may be less than the costs of processing the purchase and sale transactions, in which case the management company will make a loss. The same will apply if there is no initial charge ('no load'), and a commission has been paid to an intermediary. Also, if the management company does not receive the annual charge for a long enough period to compensate it for the cost of marketing to attract the new investor, it will be out of pocket. For this reason some fund management companies impose a straightforward redemption charge, usually expressed as a percentage of share or unit NAV, which is designed to disincentivise early redemption.

However, a flat redemption fee (say 2% if an investor redeems in under five years) can be off-putting to investors, however worthy an attempt it might be to persuade them to hold on for the long term. An alternative is a gradually reducing back-end load or, more technically, a 'contingent deferred sales charge', whereby the redemption charge will be highest in the first year and then reduce in each succeeding year until, after a defined number of years, usually six, no redemption charge is levied. Redemption fees are usually only used by no-load or low load funds: basically it can be regarded as a way of protecting the 'investment' made in attracting new investors to the fund.

It can be presented to holders that this type of redemption charge rewards the long-term investor and deters short-term traders and that it is therefore preferable to have a system that includes redemption charges if the effect is to reduce or even eliminate initial charges. However, investors always object to charges that are not clearly stated at the outset, so clear disclosure of such charges is important. Also, many investors coming to sell their shares or units after a year or two will have forgotten the existence of a redemption charge even if this was clearly disclosed at the outset, so that this can be the cause of complaints by investors.

Disclosure of 'shareholder (or unitholder) fees'

In order to minimise the potential for misunderstanding the cost of entering and exiting a fund, some regulators require disclosure in the fund prospectus of maximum figures for 'shareholder (or unitholder) fees', i.e. the maximum cost that may be incurred in entering and exiting the fund (illustrated in Table 8.3), separately from the annual operational cost of the fund (see 'total expense ratio' below) and from 'total shareholder cost' (or total unitholder cost), which is the cost of entering a fund, plus the annual cost of operation of a fund, over a specified period (an illustration of how total expense ratio and total shareholder cost are shown is given in Table 13.3 as part of the illustration of typical prospectus contents).

Table 8.3 *Shareholder or unitholder fee disclosure (US style)*

Fee	Rate
Maximum entry fee	4.5%
Maximum redemption fee	None
Maximum tapering redemption fee	None
Maximum sales charge on reinvested dividends	None
Switching fee[1]	None
Account maintenance fee[2]	None

[1]Charge which may be levied when an investor redeems shares from one fund managed by a fund management company and reinvests in shares in another fund managed by the same firm, which is known as 'switching'.

[2]Fee which some management companies charge if an investor's account with that firm has less than a certain minimum in it.

Rounding up

When share or unit prices in open-ended funds are calculated, the precise NAV may run to many decimal places. The correct price might, for example, be 55.83579. In most systems, the NAV is rounded to arrive at a convenient dealing price, for example to 55.84. Where the fund management company acts as a principal (refer to Chapter 10) in dealing in shares or units, the management company will retain such rounding adjustments and careful framing of the rules will be required to prevent abuses. For example, if the rules permit rounding to a tenth of the currency unit, the rounding of a unit from 555.366 to 555.37 creates a rounding adjustment of .004. But if the units were subdivided tenfold, the rounding of 55.5366 to 55.54 would create a rounding adjustment of .004 multiplied by 10, or .04, on units with the same value as the original higher priced unit. Under such a system management companies will have an incentive to keep share or unit prices low, which they can easily achieve by subdividing shares or units.

It is preferable for regulation to require that any permitted rounding adjustments are retained by the custodian, depositary or trustee and paid into the fund.

Dilution levy

Where a fund is priced at a single price based on a middle market price for both sale and redemption (refer to Chapter 9) there may be some element of dilution of the interests of ongoing investors resulting from redemptions. This derives from the fact that the price paid to the outgoing investor may be higher than the price for which fund assets can be sold in the market to meet the redemption; and the fact that this price also does not take account of the costs of selling these assets, which will affect ongoing investors in the fund. A 'dilution levy' is thus made on the redeeming investor of an amount sufficient to eliminate any dilution. This charge is paid back into the fund to compensate investors and cannot be retained by the management company. As a general rule, this levy has tended only to apply to large redemptions; regulation may or may not require such a levy to be made where funds are single priced (refer to Chapter 9).

Switching fee

A management company may wish to incentivise investors to keep their money invested in the funds operated by that company, rather than see investors disinvest from their funds and go to another management firm or another financial institution instead. In theory, an investor moving from fund A of a management company to fund B of the same company would have to pay the initial charge on entering fund B; but the company may choose only to levy a reduced, or no, initial charge on such transactions ('switches'), or to levy a simple flat administrative fee instead rather than lose business.

Recurring or annual charges

Fixed annual management charges

Under some systems, management companies may levy on funds an annual charge of a fixed predetermined amount, which is determined in relation to the theoretical annual costs of operation. However, this way of compensating a management company is very rare.

Another – also unusual – variant on this found within some funds and limited partnerships is the allocation of a proportion of the assets in the fund to the management company in lieu of the annual management fee; presumably on the basis that this gives them an incentive to make the fund perform well.

Management charges based on a percentage of assets

The most common system is for the fund management company to levy an annual fee based on, and expressed as, a percentage of the net asset value of the fund under management. This aligns the interest of the management company with investors, since both benefit from a rise in the value of the assets, and, if the value falls, the amount of the management fee is proportionately reduced.

Normally this charge is accrued daily within the NAV at a rate of 1/365th of the stated annual rate and may be taken out of the fund and paid to the management company fortnightly or monthly. This method is regarded as fairer to investors, since it spreads the cost over a whole year. The alternative of making the charge once a year based on the net asset value at the year-end could create an advantage for an investor who redeemed immediately before that date and thus was able to escape paying the fee. It would also be a gamble for a management company, which would be handsomely compensated if the assets of the fund as a result of a rising stock market happened to be at their high point on the day of calculation, but would lose out if the day of calculation coincided with the bottom of a bear market. In the case of money market funds, which investors use as a substitute for a bank deposit, and who thus enter and exit frequently, the accrual principle is particularly important.

Annual fees vary widely. In some systems, the fund management company pays for all expenses, including the custodian, depositary or trustee and auditor, out of the annual fee: in others all these costs are paid directly by the fund.

Table 8.1 shows a list of ongoing costs that may or not be borne out of the stated annual management fee. As far as the fund management company is concerned, the more of these that can be charged directly to the fund, rather than being paid for out of the management fee (as was traditionally the case in some countries), the more of this fee is retained by the management company and the greater its profitability is likely to be.

There are no absolute norms for determining what costs must be borne by the management company and practice varies according to the legal nature of the fund, also – corporate-type funds have tended to have more costs charged directly to them than trust or contractual funds. But in very general terms, the management company is usually responsible for providing investment management, portfolio accounting and valuation and calculation of the share or unit price at the least and in many countries they also pay for any advertising, publicity, commissions or other marketing costs also from within their annual management fee. The fund may pay directly, in addition to the annual management fee, for the following:

- custodian, depositary or trustee fees and expenses
- registration and shareholder or unitholder servicing
- directors' fees and expenses
- audits
- cost of appraisers or valuers
- costs of transactions in fund assets
- taxes and duties
- legal costs directly associated with the fund
- costs of borrowing
- regulatory costs related to the fund itself
- production, printing and circulation of periodic reports
- in limited circumstances, some initial start up and subsequent marketing costs of open-ended and interval funds (closed-ended funds bear all the cost of their initial public offering, as a rule).

Table 8.4 *Total expense ratio illustration*

	Stated annual fee only £	All expenses included £
Management fee	500 000	500 000
Custodian		40 000
Other		200 000
Total	500 000	740 000
Value of fund	50 000 000	50 000 000
Expense ratio	0.01	0.0148
	1%	1.48%

Clearly therefore, the annual cost to investors of maintaining their investment is likely to be higher than just the headline annual management charge.

It is for this reason that many regulators now require that the total cost of operating the fund, including both the headline management charge and all other costs of operation, be disclosed in a meaningful way. The figure that results from this calculation is referred to as the 'total expense ratio'. The cost of the management fee is added to the total of all other costs charged directly to the fund in the most recent accounting year and expressed as a percentage of the average net asset value of the fund during the year. An example of differences this calculation highlights is shown in Table 8.4 – though this fund might state that its annual management fee is 1%, which an investor could take to be its total operating cost, its actual operating cost per annum is nearly half as much again, at 1.48%.

In general, the level of annual management fees will vary according to the nature of the fund's investment objective and the assets it holds. The lowest annual fees are payable on money market funds, higher fees are payable on fixed income or bond funds, still higher fees on equity funds and the highest fees are levied on more esoteric funds such as hedge funds. Typical fees (for developed markets) might be in the range shown in Table 8.5.

In less developed markets, annual charges of 3–5% and total expense ratios of up to 10% are not unknown; but the higher the charge, the more performance can be reduced, which is unattractive to investors.

There are two variants on annual management fees, which have the effect of reducing the level of fees paid once certain volumes of funds under management are exceeded. The first relates to the size of an individual fund: a sliding scale may be applied, saying that, for instance, while the total value of the fund is less than say $250 million, the annual fee will be 1%, whereas once it is between $250 million and $500 million, this would reduce to 0.90%, and so on. The second establishes a similarly sliding scale that reduces the level of the management fee

Table 8.5 *Typical annual management fee ranges for funds investing in different asset classes*

Type of fund by asset class	Annual management fee – percentage fee range
Money market	0.20–1.25
Fixed income or bond	0.5–1.5
Equity (domestic)	0.75–1.5
Equity (international)	1–2
Indexed[1]	0.25–1.5
Fixed portfolio[2]	0

[1] An index fund is one that is passively managed (refer to Chapter 5) – often being computerised – and therefore costs less to manage.
[2] These are funds such as US Unit Investment Trusts that have a fixed portfolio so there is no investment management fee though the fund will bear annual operating costs.

charged across all the funds operated by a particular management company as its total funds under management increase.

Usually, a vote of shareholders or unitholders is required before an increase in the annual fee above the maximum stated in a fund's prospectus can be made. However, some systems permit the establishment of open-ended or interval funds where the prospectus states that fund management firm may increase the fee upon giving a term of notice to investors, in order to enable those who object to redeem their shares or units before the new charges take effect (no redemption fees are payable in this period).

Performance fees

Essentially annual management fees relate to performance anyway, in that since they are based on a percentage of net asset value, if that value rises, then the fee will also rise. A relatively recent variant, which relates the *level* of the annual management fee not only to fund value, but also to a fund's performance against a benchmark, is found amongst some equity-invested open-ended funds in the USA. For example, Fidelity Investments® measures some of its equity funds' performance on a three-year rolling basis against a benchmark: when these funds' performance beats their benchmark the annual management fee which can be levied is higher and when it lags the benchmark the fee is lower.

The complication in charging performance fees for open-ended funds – that is a fee that is levied in addition to an annual management fee, which specifically relates to a fund's performance – is that these funds have a constantly shifting population of share or unitholders and that therefore it is very difficult to define a time period, over which performance is measured, that is fair to all.

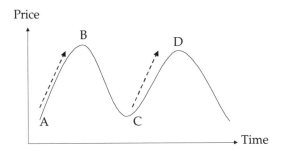

Figure 8.1 *Complexity of applying performance fees to open-ended funds*

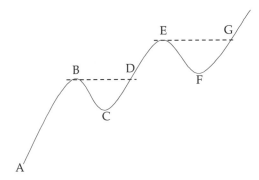

Figure 8.2 *Performance fees levied only on passing 'high water marks'*

Figure 8.1 illustrates the point: the investor who buys at point A and sells at point C will have made no profit but will have paid a performance fee for period A–B. The investor who buys at point A and sells at point D will have paid a performance fee twice for the same gain, between points A and B and again between points C and D.

The norm with performance fees is to set a benchmark and for the performance fee to be levied on returns achieved in excess of the benchmark. For example, a fund might set its benchmark as an annual return of 15%, with a performance fee of 15% of any increase in excess of this figure; alternatively, outperformance of a specific index by a specified percentage may be used. This type of performance fee is not usually permitted for publicly offered funds.

Many privately offered hedge funds are subject to performance fees, where a method of calculation is used to ensure that fees are not charged twice. The result is that fees only become chargeable once a fund price has passed its previous peak or 'high water mark' as in shown in Figure 8.2.

Essentially this means that a performance fee may only be charged when pre-vious 'high water marks' of performance have been surpassed: that is, between points A and B but not between points C and D and once again from D (at which point the price has reached its previous peak) to E and so on.

Accounting for charges

Annual charges and costs are normally deducted from the income received by the fund from its investments in the form of interest and dividends, which has the effect of reducing the amount of distribution or dividend paid on to share or unitholders. However, these costs may be paid out of the capital of the fund or some from both income and capital in the event that there is insufficient income to cover the costs. The principle of consistency is applied. The prospectus must state clearly which practice is to be followed and management companies cannot vary practice to suit their particular purposes.

Typically, management companies that offer high income funds may prefer to take the charges out of capital in order to boost the apparent yield on the funds, but it should be made clear to share or unitholders that their capital is thus being eroded.

There may also be a tax dimension to the decision as to how to account for an-nual management charges, for instance whether the tax regime permits deduction of the costs of management from the gross income received or not.

TRENDS IN COSTS AND CHARGES

Chapter 1 highlighted the fact that collective investment funds are popular in part because they offer small investors cost benefits deriving from economies of scale. It is interesting to note that while there has been a general tendency in the USA for mutual fund total shareholder costs to fall (that is, the cost including both entry and annual operating charges) it is estimated that those in Europe have been rising. For instance, US data[2] shows that total shareholder costs for equity funds fell from 226 basis points (2.26%) in 1980 to 128 basis points (1.28%) in 2001, while similar figures for bond funds were 153 basis points in 1980 and 90 basis points in 2001 and for money market funds were 55 basis points in 1980 and 36 basis points in 2001. These falls were attributed to two main sources – falls in front-end loads (which may in addition be affected by the fact that the larger the volume of the sale, the greater the discount on the front-end load); and falls in annual operating costs (which may be affected by the sliding scales that reduce management fees as volumes of funds under management increase). During mutual funds' heyday in the late 1990s sales volumes were large and funds under management were expanding strongly, so these sliding scales will have caused costs to reduce as a proportion of volumes; however, falling sales and recent contraction in funds under management have reversed this trend. A recent study noted that the median total expense ratio of US mutual funds rose from 1.249% in 2001 to 1.266% in 2002.[3]

Which leads into a key factor to be remembered when comparing levels of charges and costs between European-based funds and US-based funds: economies of scale. As a recent study[4] has noted, the US mutual fund industry at the beginning of 2003 was around twice the size of the European one; but whereas there were around 8200 funds in the USA there were around 25 600 in Europe, resulting in an average fund size of $887 million in the USA but only $136 million in Europe. The two sets of figures are not, of course, directly comparable – Europe is not (despite the European Commission's efforts) a single market, as the USA is; and the European statistics include countries which vary from the developed through to the newly emerging – the latter group tend to have a relatively large number of funds with relatively small amounts of money under management – whereas the USA can only be described as a fully developed market.

Having first explored how a net asset value per share is reached (Chapter 7), and then what initial or redemption charges may be added to these (this chapter), the next chapter looks at how these two components are used to create the dealing prices at which transactions in fund shares or units take place.

Those who would like to test their grasp of the contents of this chapter should turn to the self-test questions at the back of the book.

NOTES

1. *Fundamentals*, 9(1), ICI, Washington, April 2000.
2. Investment Company Institute, *Fundamentals*, Vol 11(4), September 2002.
3. *Global Themes in the Mutual Fund Industry 2002*, Lipper Research Study, © Reuters, 2003.
4. *Discriminatory Tax Barriers Facing the EU Funds Industry: A Progress Report*, Pricewaterhouse-Coopers and FEFSI, 2003.

9

Pricing

INTRODUCTION

This chapter looks at the different ways that fund share or unit prices may be calculated; the implications of using these different methods and how the resulting prices are disclosed. While this chapter explores all the various methods that are in use it is normal that individual fund regulatory regimes establish the pricing methods that are permitted, or required, to be used; and set rules for the content and frequency of disclosure of resulting share or unit prices.

Pricing is the process by which the price (or prices) at which shares or units in a fund can be bought or sold on any one day is (or are) created. Usually pricing regulations establish:

- The basis of the market prices to be used for the calculation of net asset value per share or unit of a fund ('dual' or 'single' pricing).
- Whether the purchase or sale is fulfilled at an existing or a future share or unit price ('historic' versus 'forward' price).
- The inclusion or exclusion of initial and redemption charges from such prices.

IMPORTANCE OF THE CALCULATION OF A CORRECT PRICE

The prices at which dealing in shares or units of closed-ended funds takes place are formed in a different way from the way that the prices at which dealing in open-ended or interval fund shares or units takes place are formed. Since shares or units in a closed-ended fund can only be sold if a buyer can be found, the price at which the sale is made will be that agreed between the buyer and the seller through a stock exchange or trading system and may be either more or less than the net asset value of those shares or units. Closed-ended fund share or unit prices are therefore an outcome of levels of demand and supply.

However, the price at which shares or units of open-ended and interval funds will be sold to new investors and redeemed from existing investors is required by regulation to be based on the net asset value derived from the portfolio valuation

Table 9.1 *Dilution of ongoing holders' value through mispricing (assumes) no market movement)*

	Net assets	Units in issue	Number of units purchased	Price of purchase	Amount invested	NAV per unit
Opening position	100	10				10
New investment			10	5	50	
Closing position	150	20				7.5

(refer to Chapter 7). This chapter deals mainly with the way in which a net asset value per share or unit is transformed into a price for dealing in open-ended or interval fund shares or units.

Many regard the creation of a dealing price or prices as the most important part of the operational procedure of an open-ended or interval fund. Certainly most regulators pay a great deal of attention to the calculation of the price and will always wish to reassure themselves that the operation has been carried out in accordance with the established method laid down by regulation.

Maintaining fairness between different classes of share or unitholder

The main purpose of using current market values as the basis for carrying out the valuation and creating the price for dealing in shares or units is to maintain the balance between the interests of three distinct categories of share or unitholders. These are:

- Incoming – new purchasers.
- Outgoing – those wishing to redeem.
- Ongoing – those who are already share or unitholders and who are continuing to hold.

Each will have different interests, which conflict with the interests of others. Incoming purchasers will wish to pay the lowest price possible, while outgoing redeemers will wish to be paid the highest price possible. The ongoing holders want to ensure that the prices respectively paid by the incomer and to the outgoer do not reduce the value of (or 'dilute') their continuing interest. A simplified example of the way this dilution can occur is illustrated in Table 9.1.

This example given in Table 9.1 is grossly exaggerated and simplified (since it assumes no market movement amongst other factors) in order to make the point simply and clearly. From it one can see that an existing share or unitholder who, prior to the new transaction, enjoyed a unit value of 10 (i.e. net asset value of 100 divided by the 10 units in issue) shown at the 'opening position' would have had a unit value of only 7.5, at the 'closing position' (i.e. net asset value of 150 divided by 20). This is quite simply because the new investor paid too low a price (5 per unit–shown as new investment) when he should have paid the market net asset value based price (10). The incoming investor has 'diluted' the ongoing investor–that is, reduced the value of the assets owned by that investor. If the incoming investor had paid too much–say 15 per unit–however, the ongoing holder's value instead would have been 'concentrated' or increased. The fund value would have become 250, which divided by 20 would be 12.5 per unit and the ongoing holder would have gained 2.5 from the injection of a higher value into the fund than that required by the market-based net asset value.

Without wishing to labour this point, one can easily see that dilution and concentration would also result from applying a similar calculation to the cases in which an outgoing share or unitholder was paid out too much or too little.

Table 9.1 shows an extreme case of under valuation for illustrative purposes. In reality pricing errors are much smaller than these, but the effect is exactly the same, and can be amplified if the error continues to be repeated over a long period.

The whole theoretical basis and practical application of pricing shares or units of open-ended and interval funds derives from the simple need to maintain a fair balance between the interests of all three categories of fund investor.

The nature of the securities markets can also give rise to potential inequity

Adherence to a carefully constructed set of valuation and pricing principles can enable gross errors and abuses to be avoided. But the very nature of market trading practices also creates scope for inequity.

The market price of a security will depend on the dealing system prevailing in a particular market. In markets which use a 'price-driven' system, that is where market makers or dealers are present (who buy securities with their firm's own money, hoping to make a profit on resale), such as the London Stock Exchange, NASDAQ or the New York Stock Exchange specialists, there will be a 'bid-ask' (or 'bid-offer') spread for any security, representing the prices at which the market maker is prepared either to bid to buy or to offer to sell that security respectively. The difference between the two prices is called the 'spread' and represents the profit of the market maker.

The size of the spread between bid and ask (also known as 'offer') prices will depend on the nature of the security, the volume of trading and the practices in the market where the security is traded. In highly liquid securities of big companies in major markets, the spread can be as low as 0.1%; but this can widen for medium sized companies to 4%–6% and for small illiquid companies to 10%–12%.

By contrast, in so-called 'order-driven' markets, in which buyers and sellers are matched without the intermediation of market makers there are only single prices, which represent the price at which the last transaction was done.

The existence of a price spread in the securities in which a fund invests raises the question: when valuing the fund's portfolio, what should be taken as the 'market value' of each holding: the bid price, the ask price, the latest transaction price or some other price based on these? Which is fair to all three categories of fund investor?

DUAL VERSUS SINGLE PRICING

'Dual pricing' system

Theoretically, in order to avoid dilution when operating in a 'price-driven' market, a fund should quote two prices (hence the term 'dual pricing'): one – the ask or 'offer' price – for incoming share or unitholders, which reflects the cost of buying into the securities that comprise the portfolio of the fund at the ask price in the market and the other – the 'bid' price – for outgoing share or unitholders, that reflects the proceeds that would be received from selling the securities that comprise the portfolio of the fund when selling at the bid price in the market.

Therefore, in effect, each day two valuations would need to be done, one at market ask prices and one at market bid prices. Since the fund price spread will depend on the actual market price spreads in the shares in the fund portfolio, spreads will vary between funds depending on the nature of their portfolios. The price spread of a fund investing in the shares of smaller companies will be much wider than the spread of a fund investing only in the largest 'blue chips'. Also the theoretical costs associated with making the transactions needed to buy or sell shares to accommodate incomers or outgoers should be added or deducted from the prices.

Figure 9.1 shows how a 12% spread can arise, using a simplistic basis of the offer and bid price of a single share (102 and 98 respectively). To calculate the offer price for the unit, the offer price of the share is taken, plus the transaction cost[1] of buying the shares for the fund's portfolio (1%) and the initial charge (6%), resulting in a unit offer price of 109 rounded to the nearest whole number. To calculate the bid price for the unit, the bid price of the share is taken, and dealing costs (1%) have to be subtracted, resulting in a unit bid price of 97 rounded to the nearest whole number. Though this 'offer to bid' or 'dual' pricing is a good theoretical solution to the pricing problem, it does result in wide share or unit price spreads, which, once the initial charge is included, can be as high as 12%. It is hard to explain to potential customers that, if they were to buy shares at 100 today they could only sell the shares back at 88 the same day: and that the

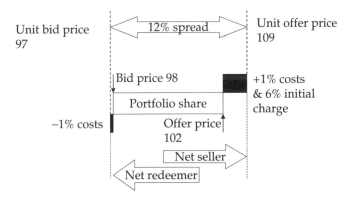

Figure 9.1 *Dual pricing model*

share price would have to increase by over 12% before they would make a profit when they sold their shares. In practice, in dual pricing systems what tends to happen is that the fund will be priced within the 12% spread: when it is selling more shares or units than it is redeeming (i.e. it is 'net seller') it will move its price up to the top of the 'offer' price, since it is having to consistently go into the market to buy more securities at the offer price. Conversely, when the fund is buying back more shares or units than it is selling, it will move its price down to the bottom of the 'bid' price range, since it is consistently having to go into the market to sell securities to meet redemptions. Thus in the example of Figure 9.1, on the full offer basis it would be offering units for sale at 109, with a bid price of around 7% below that at around 102 (the difference being charges and transaction costs); and on the full bid price it would be redeeming units at 97 and offering units at around 7% above that, i.e. an offer price of around 104.

The complexity of dual pricing and the size of the spread can be offputting to investors and it is for this reason that most countries, including the UK, which still permits dual pricing in certain cases, have moved or are moving towards a system of 'single' pricing.

'Single pricing' system

Straightforward single pricing
The concept of single pricing is straightforward. The solution is to ignore the spread on the securities in the fund's portfolio and the transaction costs involved in buying and selling fund assets and to take the 'middle market price' as the basis for valuation in all cases. This would mean that where the price spread of a security in the market is 98–102, it would be valued in the portfolio of the fund at 100, the middle price between the bid and ask as shown in Figure 9.2. As a

Figure 9.2 *Straightforward single pricing*

consequence the fund itself will have just one price at which investors buy and sell – hence the term 'single pricing'. Charges may be added to or deducted from this price.

This system was developed in the USA in the 1970s and is used by US mutual funds. It is now in common use in the UK and much of Europe as well. It is simple and easy for the public to understand. It works well in markets where securities are freely traded in large volumes and spreads on underlying securities in the portfolio are small, where transaction costs are modest and the funds themselves are large. In these circumstances, the system is unlikely to produce significant inequity between different classes of investor. Regulators who have adopted this approach have accepted that the system cannot be mathematically perfect, but take the view that over a long period of time and across thousands of transactions both in portfolio securities and in shares or units of the fund, the process will be self-balancing.

However, in markets where spreads are wide, where transaction costs are high or where a substantial part of fund portfolios is held in infrequently traded assets, this system is very likely to produce a significant degree of disadvantage for some investors most of the time, particularly in the case of a fund which is subject to many redemptions, where it will be paying out a higher amount per share or unit redeemed (at mid market) than it will receive on sales of fund assets at the 'bid' price, causing ongoing holders to be diluted to the point at which there might theoretically be no assets left to pay out the last remaining investors.

Dilution levy

One solution to this is the 'dilution levy', which is designed to eliminate this inequity and tends to be used when very large redemptions are being made. This is the deduction from the redemption value of the share or unit of an amount that compensates the ongoing holders in the fund for the costs of the redemption-related transactions[2] and the difference between the mid market and bid prices of the securities being sold. This levy is then paid back into the fund. Regulation may or may not require that such levies are applied but if they are levied, they must be levied fairly across all investors and may not be levied twice; that is, both on subscription and on redemption of any one fund share or unit.

The levy is realistic, in that in most circumstances, where there is regular trade in roughly equal amounts of sales and redemptions, there is no need for it to be applied. It is flexible, in that there are usually guidelines specifying the circumstances when a levy should be applied. The drawback is that investors do not know whether or when the levy will be applied. In practice, this may not matter since it is only in the most extreme circumstances that the levy would be more than a very small percentage.

Swinging and semi-swinging single pricing (or 'dilution adjustment')
An alternative to the simple single price or that price with a dilution levy would be to have a single price, but for the valuation to be based on the offer basis when the fund had a surplus of sales over redemptions and on the bid basis when it had a surplus of redemptions over sales (hence the term 'swinging'). However, the pattern of sales and redemptions can often be erratic, so with this system the fund price could swing frequently from one basis to the other. The effect could be to add price volatility of some 6–10%, which would certainly deter investors. This system, termed 'dilution adjustment', may be used according to UK regulations. However, since in the UK a management company is able to act as a principal in fund shares or units (an explanation of this, and its implications, are given at the end of this chapter), rules state that it may not use the swing to benefit itself if it owns shares or units in the fund (this is to prevent, for example, a fund management company buying at today's bid-based price of 55 and deliberately moving to an offer basis the next day and selling its holding to new investors at the higher price of 58, enabling itself to make a profit of 3 per share or unit at its own discretion).

Some offshore funds have been established with a variation of this system, where the price moves part way towards the ask basis when the fund is expanding and part way to the bid basis when the fund is contracting: a system known as 'semi-swinging single pricing'. Figure 9.3 illustrates swinging single prices.

HISTORIC VERSUS FORWARD PRICING BASIS

A separate issue concerning pricing is whether dealing in open-ended or interval funds is on a 'historic' or 'forward' basis (see Figure 9.4). With the historic system, the fund values at a certain point, known as the pricing point, during the day

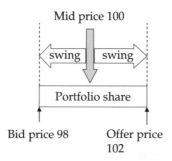

Figure 9.3 *Swinging single price*

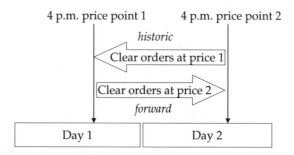

Figure 9.4 *Forward versus historic pricing*

and publishes a price; this price remains valid for investors for dealings, both purchases and redemptions, until the next price is calculated at the next pricing point. For instance, when a fund investing in domestic securities values daily, the valuation will normally be undertaken at the close of the market, the price will be published the following morning and that day's dealings will all be done at that published price. In the case of a fund investing internationally the pricing point may be at any convenient time taking into account the closing times of the markets in which the fund invests.

Using the forward pricing system, the fund accepts orders from investors during the day but does not fulfil them until the *next* pricing point. It then processes all those orders at that price. Only orders received prior to the pricing point are fulfilled at the price. Any order received even a moment after the pricing point has to be carried forward, to be executed at the next pricing point.

Drawbacks of historic pricing

Though the historic pricing system is far easier for investors to understand, since they know a price at which they can deal, it has very considerable drawbacks, which is why most countries have adopted forward pricing. Essentially the historic pricing system allows investors – particularly insiders – to profit from events known to them but not necessarily to others. If the market in which a fund invests rises sharply, investors can still buy shares or units at yesterday's price, knowing that when the fund is next valued the price will rise and they can sell for a profit. Or if the market falls sharply, investors can still sell at the higher price derived from a valuation based on yesterday's market prices. If the regulations permit fund management companies to buy shares in their own funds, dealing as principals, they have an unhealthy incentive to profit in this way. The profits of incoming and outgoing investors of the fund are of course at the expense of ongoing investors, who are being diluted, constituting a massive conflict of interest for fund management firms. Where valuations are more widely spaced – weekly or even monthly – the scope for profiting at the expense of existing investors, if a historic pricing system is in use, is far greater. It is for this reason that, where regulators permit historic pricing, there are usually rules requiring that if markets have moved by more than a certain percentage (e.g. 2%), or if management companies have reason to believe that markets have moved, that the fund must re-price or move to a forward price.

Drawbacks of forward pricing

Though it might seem difficult to ask investors to deal at an unknown (forward) price, in reality most investors do not intend to buy a fixed number of shares or units but intend to invest a fixed sum of money, so the specific price at which they buy is not necessarily a concern to them. It is because most investors invest a sum of money that fractions of shares or units, known as decimalisation, can be issued to make it possible to invest all of a sum of money in the cases where a round number of whole shares or units cannot be made to match the sum of money.

It is also a fact that units or shares in funds are primarily designed for long-term savers and investors and not for short-term speculators; the fact that the forward, unknown price may be marginally higher than expected, which is to their disadvantage, or lower than expected, which is to their advantage, will become immaterial in the context of the return that they hope to make over a five- or 10-year period. So long as investors understand this and know they will receive rapid notification of the price, and can verify this against the published price, investors are likely to be content.

The price itself

It is unlikely that any price for fund shares or units that is the result of dividing a net asset value by the large number of units in issue will come out at a conveniently round number. Therefore most regimes permit a price to be rounded to, for example, two places of decimals.

In general, in a dual priced system, the initial charge will be included within the offer to bid spread, though again as a general rule, the charge expressed as a percentage of the net asset value per share or unit will also be quoted alongside the offer and bid prices. In a single priced system, the price will not include any initial or redemption charges, which are required to be disclosed separately and are respectively added to, or deducted from, the net asset value per share or unit upon subscription or redemption.

EFFECT OF ACTING AS PRINCIPAL

The distinction between acting as a 'principal' and as an 'agent' in the sale and redemption of open-ended and interval fund shares or units is an important one to understand. Acting as a principal means that the management company, or another person, actually becomes the owner of the fund shares or units by buying them back from one investor and then reselling them to another (in effect it is the market maker or dealer). The management company can also require the depositary or trustee to create new fund shares or units and buy those shares or units from the depositary or trustee for its own account and can also require the depositary or trustee to buy back shares or units from it, for liquidation.

This privilege is clearly open to abuse, since a management company is in possession of information that outside investors cannot access, and can make decisions about pricing, particularly if the fund is operated on a dual price or a swinging single price basis, in its own interests rather than in the interests of fund investors. The fund management company is in complete control of the situation as a dealer, being able to trade with investors and with the depositary or trustee. It not only knows the likely future trend of the fund share or unit price but also can influence it.

By contrast, in acting only as an agent, the management company, or any other person, simply facilitates transactions in shares or units, but never actually owns them. The same distinction is made between principal and agent in the case of broker-dealers. A dealer (or market maker) will act as a principal, in that the shares he buys are for his own account and the shares that he offers for sale are actually owned by him; he hopes to make a capital gain from the transactions that he does. A broker acting as an agent will facilitate transactions by arranging the purchase or sale of securities with a counterpart and will make her money by charging a commission for doing so.

If the management company is permitted to own shares or units in a fund managed by it, and is permitted to buy shares or units directly from investors and resell them to other investors or is permitted to require the depositary or trustee to create shares or units for sale to it or to buy back and liquidate shares or units owned by it, it must be made clear to the investor that the management company is acting as a principal either in buying shares or units from the investors or selling them. In this way the investor may be made aware of the potential conflict.

If the management company is permitted to act as a principal in a historic pricing system, the company can cause large numbers of shares or units to be created on days when the market rises, knowing the share or unit price will rise the following day and it will then be able to re-sell those shares or units at a profit. But in doing so, it will have diluted the potential profits of existing investors in the fund. In certain circumstances the management company may also be able to sell short (that is, sell fund shares or units that it does not own) if it knows that it can create or buy back the shares or units at a lower price on the next or subsequent days.

The justification for permitting the management company to act as a principal has traditionally been that, like all dealers or market makers, it can thus create liquidity for redeeming investors without having to require the investment managers to sell underlying securities to raise cash to pay out the redemptions; it is argued that otherwise this might have to be done at disadvantageous prices or might destabilise the market.

Many jurisdictions absolutely forbid the management company to act as a principal in dealing in fund shares or units under any circumstances in order to prevent conflicts of interest arising. Some jurisdictions permit the management company to act as a principal only in certain conditions, for example where the management company is required to act as the redeemer of last resort in cases where assets cannot be sold quickly enough to meet requests for redemption.

For further information on disclosure of fund prices turn to Chapter 13; examples of such disclosure appear in Tables 13.5 (single priced open-ended and interval funds), 13.6 (dual priced open-ended and interval funds) and 13.7 (closed-ended funds).

The next – and final – chapter on fund administration moves on to look at how issue and redemption of fund shares or units is undertaken, how transactions are recorded and how fund investors are serviced.

Those who would like to test their grasp of the contents of this chapter should turn to the self-test questions at the back of the book.

NOTES

1. Brokers' commissions and any transaction duties (taxes) payable.
2. Brokers' commissions and transaction duties.

10

Issue and Redemption

The sale of shares or units to and redemption of shares or units from investors follows on from the process of valuation and pricing; this chapter looks at how issue and redemption of fund shares or units are undertaken, how ownership of fund shares or units is recorded and how fund investors are serviced.

INTRODUCTION

It is important to recognise that in some countries there is a distinction between the process of sale of shares or units to investors, known as 'issue' and the repurchasing of shares or units from them, known as 'redemption', and the process of creating new shares or units, known as 'creation' and the liquidation of redeemed shares or units, known as 'cancellation'. This is because in the process of issue and redemption the management company may intermediate either as a principal (where it buys shares or units for its own account – that is, using its own money – and reissues them to new investors) or as an agent (where the management company simply facilitates the process of selling new shares or units and repurchasing existing ones). In the case that a management company acts as a principal, shares or units do not necessarily need to be created in order to satisfy buyers, since the management company may already hold a supply of these; and shares or units do not necessarily have to be cancelled when they are repurchased, because the management company may choose to buy and hold them itself. Therefore, in the case where the management company acts as a principal, 'issue' may be separate from 'creation' and 'redemption' may be separate from 'cancellation'.

However, where the management company does not act as a principal, only as an agent, it is likely that all shares or units that are sold will need to be created, so 'issue' and 'creation' will be the same thing, and all shares or units that are redeemed will need to be cancelled so 'redemption' and 'cancellation' will be the same thing.

Open-ended funds and interval funds, whether in trust, contractual or corporate form, are subject to specific regulations governing the creation and issue and the redemption and cancellation of shares or units. The form of these regulations varies but there are common features that have been arrived at by trial and error over the 80 or so years that such funds have operated in developed markets.

The demands of dealing with issue and redemption for open- and closed-ended funds are quite different. The former have to issue and redeem daily – or at a minimum once every other week – whereas the latter will only issue for a limited period, and hardly redeem at all. There may also be technical differences between issuing and redeeming shares in a corporate-type fund, since a public offering of shares is usually covered by securities laws; issuing and redeeming units in a trust-type fund, which may or may not be defined as securities by domestic laws; and issuing and redeeming participations in contractual funds, which are usually but not always defined as securities.

However, the public offer for sale – whether of a fund share or unit in a corporate fund, trust fund or contractual fund – is always subject to the terms of an offering document that is usually called a prospectus, which has to be registered with the regulator, which generally also regulates the minimum content of the document (refer to Chapter 13). Amendments to the prospectus generally are also required to be registered with the regulator and notification of such amendments may have to be published in mass media before taking effect. Regulators may also require that other documents – such as the fund rules – are made available to potential investors on their request; and that forms for application for subscription or redemption contain certain specified information.

This chapter largely deals with the process of issue and redemption of shares or units of open-ended and interval funds since closed-ended funds are normally created in the form of joint stock companies, which will have to follow the procedures laid down by company law.

CLOSED-ENDED FUNDS

Corporate closed-ended funds

Initial issue

Since the procedure for the initial issue of shares in a closed-ended fund of a corporate type is usually very similar to that for issuing securities in joint stock companies generally, it is not dealt with in detail here. There will need to be the usual process of registration of the company with the relevant authorities, and in many countries a specific permission of the regulator for the formation of the company as an investment fund.

Thereafter a prospectus will be approved and issued and subscriptions collected usually over a period whose extent is capped by regulation (commonly at 21 days).

Some regulators require that if the target for the amount of the issue is not reached the money must be returned to subscribers without any charge (this provision is often applied to open or interval funds too).

Further issues

Under most legal systems, limited companies may make new issues of shares only if authorised to do so by their shareholders. In the case of closed-ended corporate investment funds, this is because in many circumstances the interests of existing shareholders could be damaged (diluted) by additional share issues to a new set of shareholders, particularly if the shares are issued at a discount to NAV. Most regimes require for this reason that new shares in such funds are offered to existing shareholders in proportion to their existing holdings to which they have an absolute right to subscribe (known as 'pre-emption rights'); only after this, if all shares offered have not been taken up by existing shareholders, may the shares be offered to new shareholders.

There are some situations in which it may be advantageous for existing share-holders in a closed-ended fund if new shares are issued. If the shares in the fund consistently trade in the market at a premium to their NAV, this is of ad-vantage to any existing shareholder who wishes to sell. But it is not advanta-geous for existing shareholders who wish to buy more shares. If many existing shareholders wish to do this – perhaps by regular subscription – then the direc-tors of the fund may seek authority to make small regular issues of new shares to satisfy the demands of such shareholders. Such issues will prevent any fur-ther rise in the premium to NAV at which the shares trade and may help to reduce it.

If the shares in one closed-ended fund trade at above their NAV while shares in a second closed-ended fund trade at below their NAV, it would be worthwhile for the first fund to acquire the second, assuming it could secure agreement to a deal at below the second fund's NAV. This would be achieved by an exchange of new shares in the 'premium' fund for existing shares of the 'discount' fund, which valued the discounted fund shares at less than NAV. The difference between the acquisition price of the shares and the NAV of the acquired fund would add to the NAV of the acquiring fund.

Such situations are rare and the majority of closed-ended corporate funds make only one issue of shares, when they are originally formed. Often there is no ter-mination date for a closed-ended fund, but if a fund is constituted with several different share classes, each of which has different rights within a common pool of assets, then establishment of a redemption date when the fund is to be liquidated and the assets distributed to shareholders will be essential (refer to Chapter 3). Where a redemption date is announced in a fund's prospectus, it will stand unless it is subsequently altered by a majority vote of shareholders.

Buy backs

In some legal systems, limited companies may, with the agreement of their general meeting of shareholders, apply for permission to purchase back their own shares from investors. Where this is the case, closed-ended funds in the form of limited companies may also apply for such permission. In the case of closed-ended funds, this would only be proposed if the shares were trading at below their NAV. Usually, buy backs are not in the interests of the fund management company (which probably will have significant representation among the fund's directors) because they reduce the pool of assets on which the management company earns fees. So such buy backs are usually proposed only when a fund's shares stand at a large discount to NAV and often only when the fund is under threat from external proposals for restructuring. In this event the management company may fear the loss of the management contract that would result from a restructuring sufficiently to propose that the company repurchase some of its shares from investors. Such a move will usually result in a reduction of the discount to NAV at which the shares trade in the market, which benefits those investors who wish to exit the fund.

While some countries' regulations require that a company buying back its shares may only do so for cancellation, others permit or require the shares to be held 'in treasury' for subsequent resale. This approach is less disadvantageous to fund management companies, so is increasing in popularity.

Non-corporate closed-ended funds

Legal systems sometimes permit the creation of closed-ended contractual or trust funds, though these are not common. They issue a limited number of participations or units in a single offer, as with closed-ended investment companies, but may or may not be listed on stock exchanges. They often have a fixed term of existence and some have a fixed portfolio also. If fixed term, fixed portfolio funds invest in bonds, this enables them to offer guaranteed income and guaranteed redemption value, which can be popular with investors.

These funds are formed either by trust or by contract and are licensed or authorised by approval of the regulator. The principles governing issue and liquidation of these funds would be similar to those outlined above for corporate closed-ended funds, but the specifics will be governed by fund law and regulation and not by company law.

INTERVAL FUNDS

Interval funds are a sort of half-way house between and open-ended and closed-ended funds. While they are technically open-ended funds in that they issue and redeem shares or units, they only do so at limited intervals, usually at least once a year. While regulations set the parameters within which this can be done, the funds themselves may in addition (and provided this is permitted) limit not only the times at which they are 'open' for issue and redemption, but also may limit the number or value of shares or units that may be issued or redeemed during any one opening. In addition, some interval funds may require advance prior notification of any purchase or redemption requests.

Having accumulated requests from potential purchasers and from those existing holders who wish to redeem, an interval fund will value and price at the dealing point and satisfy both purchasers and redeemers to the extent that its rules permit. In the event that it is unable to satisfy all such requests, because it will only accept net redemptions up to a certain percentage of the fund's value for instance, its rules may indicate what action should be taken. This might either be on a 'first come first served' basis or by scaling down all requests in the same proportion.

The mechanics of issue and redemption for such funds are precisely the same, however, as those described under 'open-ended funds' below.

OPEN-ENDED FUNDS

Open-ended funds, whether in trust, contractual or limited company form, are subject to specific regulations governing the issue and redemption of shares, units or participations. The form of these regulations varies but there are common features that are summarised below.

The prospectus

Prospectuses offering open-ended funds will, broadly, contain the same basic information as closed-ended funds, but will have additional information as required by regulation (refer to Chapter 13). What is worth mentioning here, since it is relevant to the process and mechanics of issue and redemption, is that most regulators require that all prospective investors are at least offered – or in some cases must be given – a copy of the prospectus, and sometimes the founding document (that is, the articles of a company, the rules of a contractual fund or the trust deed of a trust fund) of the fund as well. This must usually be done either before any purchase is made or at the time that the purchase is made.

The process of subscription and issue of shares or units

An individual's investment in an open-ended fund may arrive by a number of routes, since there is an increasing number of intermediaries that stand between

177

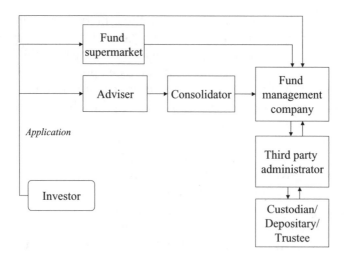

Figure 10.1 *Illustration of possible application routes*

the management company and the ultimate client. Some of these have speeded up and facilitated the process, although not without some additional cost to the management company. Figure 10.1 illustrates some of the various routes through which orders to purchase shares or units in a fund may be received, depending on the distribution channels used (refer to Chapter 12).

The term 'consolidator' is used for any organisation that collects and channels orders from intermediaries; this type of organisation acts like a central clearing and settlement agency, enabling intermediaries to settle a wide variety of transactions with different fund management companies by means of a single payment to the consolidator, and management companies or their administrators similarly to receive one payment in settlement of a large number of transactions from different sources via the consolidator. There are a number of such organisations in developed markets, each of which operates slightly differently, but each of which will make a charge to the fund management company (or less often the intermediary) for its services. These organisations are not usually accessible by the general public, who may use fund supermarkets (refer to Chapter 12) in much the same way instead; these too will charge the fund management company for their services.

The activities involved in issuing shares or units in open-ended funds are outlined in Figure 10.2. Before looking at them in more detail, it is worth noting that if a management company uses an outside administrator or registrar (or in the USA a 'transfer agent'), to carry out what is generically called either shareholder or unitholder servicing or 'third-party administration', this organisation will carry out the following functions associated with issue and redemption, which would

Dealing	Receipt of orders to purchase from various sources
Contract	Dispatch of contract and request for payment
Payment	Receipt of payment
Registration	Set up a register entry
Advice	Confirm completion of transaction
Certificate	Issue certificates where relevant

Figure 10.2 *Activities involved in issue*

otherwise be carried out by the management company. Such service providers may be part of a depositary or custodian or trustee organisation or may be independent from it.

The list given in Figure 10.2 summarises the most extended process, when transactions are done remotely (e.g. by phone), so involving more steps than may be required where an order is placed and payment is made for fund shares or units simultaneously over the counter at a bank. However an order is received, it will be necessary also to receive payment and set up a register entry for the new holder.

The steps outlined in Figure 10.2 can be explained in greater detail as follows:

1. The investor completes an application form and sends it to the management company or to his appointed service supplier with or without payment; as shown above this may arrive via a variety of routes. At this stage many management companies require that the investor completes a declaration to the effect that he has received, read and understood the prospectus and its terms. The application will include not only the investor's personal address (and sometimes a unique identity number) and choice of fund and sum to be invested or number of shares or units to be purchased but may also include instructions regarding dividends (whether they are to be paid to the investor or reinvested) and a dividend mandate section, where the investor may choose to mandate the payment of dividends direct to a bank account. It is worth noting that even in technologically advanced countries, physical delivery of a signed application and payment by post or to an office may be needed to open an account, though electronic or telephone dealing may be possible subsequently; electronic signatures are now permitted in some countries, but their practical use is not yet widespread amongst retail investors.

2. The dealing department of the management company or its service supplier will prepare and issue a contract note confirming the deal: this is sent to the investor with a request for payment if this has not already been received. The contract note specifies the date of the deal; the date of the contract note; the name of the fund; the number, possibly in fractions of shares or units if a round sum of money has been invested (see later), and price of shares or units sold to the investor; any sales charges added to the price of shares or units; the total amount paid or payable and the account or client reference number.

3. The management company notifies the custodian, depositary or trustee of the deal. When the investor's payment is received it is passed to the custodian, depositary or trustee for the account of the fund. The custodian, depositary or trustee confirms receipt of this payment to the management company and also to the registrar and authorises the creation of new shares or units. Setting up the system so that the registrar needs to have confirmation of purchases by investors from the management company and confirmation of receipt of payment from the custodian, depositary or trustee is another safeguard against fraud.

4. The registrar enters the investor's details on the fund's register and issues a certificate of ownership to the investor where a certificate is required or requested. In most systems, it is the entry on the fund's register that is definitive proof of ownership; the certificate or advice is merely evidence of this. In some countries, an 'excerpt from the register' is issued as confirmation. Alterations to the register must therefore also be subject to strictly controlled procedures.

Regulators may set time limits within which certain functions must be completed, and a maximum period for entry onto the register following receipt of a valid application and payment and for the issue of certificates is often specified. Experience shows that even what seems an undemanding target – say six weeks from the date of the deal – can become impossible to meet in practice if a huge flood of purchases overwhelms the capacity of the systems being used or the capacity of authorised security printers if a certificate is to be the proof of ownership. Realistic estimation of an administration system's capacity is therefore essential for the fund management company. One advantage of a dematerialised system (that is, one where the electronic register is proof of ownership) is that it eliminates the need for issuing certificates.

Where the management company is acting as a principal in fund dealing, new shares or units will not necessarily need to be created to satisfy sales, since the management company may resell shares or units in its possession. However, these will need to be re-registered to the new owner.

Dealing	Receipt of orders to redeem
Contract	Despatch of contract and request for renounced certificate where relevant
Certificate	Receipt of renounced certificate where relevant or check of validity of ownership
Registration	Removal of holders' names from register
Payment	Issue of payment

Figure 10.3 *Activities involved in redemption*

The process of redemption and cancellation

The various possible steps in this process are summarised in Figure 10.3.

Here again these steps are associated with a remote transaction; where a transaction is over a bank counter all these steps may be completed on a single day. The most important issue is the validation of ownership by the person who initiates the redemption since it is possible that the person making the request for redemption is not legally the owner of those shares or units.

Where the fund is certificated the simplest procedure is for the certificates to carry a form of renunciation on their reverse. By signing this, the investor renounces ownership and requests redemption. The investor sends the renounced certificate to the management company or third-party administrator, which enters the deal on the system, passes the certificate to the registrar for confirmation that the deal is in order and then to the custodian, depositary or trustee (who will require confirmation from the registrar) to authorise the release of the cash redemption which the management company then transfers to the investor and cancellation (or liquidation) of the shares or units. In the case of non-certificated shares or units, increasingly the norm under dematerialised systems, no certificate exists to be returned, and only the investor's authorisation needs to be received either in written form, or by telephone or in electronic form if the investor has a security PIN number or agreed code word.

If the management company acts as principal, then ownership of the shares or units being redeemed passes to it instead of the shares or units being cancelled. It will still need to check the validity of the redemption with the registrar before making payment but will not need authorisation from the custodian, depositary or trustee to make such payment since it will pay for the redemption from its own resources, and will hope to resell the shares or units to a new investor at a profit. In the meantime, the management company becomes the registered owner of those shares or units. Regulators usually set a time limit for the settlement of redemptions. A normal requirement in a daily valued fund would be for the dispatch of redemption proceeds to the investor within four to 10 working days of receipt of a valid application for redemption.

Practical steps that management companies can take to reduce problems with fraudulent redemptions, where no established security procedure exists, include checking that the redeeming investors are who they say they are by contacting the addresses or phone numbers on the register to check that it is the holder who is applying for the redemption.

COMMON PROBLEMS

In newer markets regulators and management companies are likely to encounter a number of practical problems in the process of issue and redemption. These mainly concern the timeliness and security of the transaction.

Timing of a transaction

There is sometimes doubt as to the date on which a sale or redemption transaction is actually effected. There can also be delays at the level of a sales agent between the time he receives the order and the time he transmits it to the management company. The common practice in developed markets is that a transaction is effective on the date on which the transaction is accepted and the contract or confirmation issued by the management company, in some cases whether or not payment has been received at that time. Alternatively, management companies may empower their accredited agents to accept transactions and issue contracts on their behalf, in which case the effective date will be that on which the agent issues the contract or confirmation.

It is important to remember that the new investor will enjoy full ownership rights (including rights to capital growth, dividends or distributions, special offers, rights issues, mergers and take-overs and any other rights attaching to the ownership of those particular shares or units) from the date of the contract, this being equivalent to the practice in securities markets generally.

Some jurisdictions allow payment to be made by the new purchaser of shares or units at a later date than that on which the contract is made; others will not permit a contract to be issued until payment has been received. In the event of payment at a date later than the contract date, the NAV calculation of the fund will need to show the amounts due for later payment in current assets, as debtors, since the shares or units are regarded as having been technically issued at the date of the contract. Once payment is received the amount of the payment will be shown as cash and removed from debtors by a contra entry.

If payment is permitted at a later date, and the investor is in effect buying on credit, non-receipt of payment within the period defined in the prospectus will invalidate the deal and shares or units will have to be cancelled. In no circumstances should management companies allow a purchase to be reversed by a redemption until payment has been received for the purchase; otherwise an investor could speculate without risk, simply by redeeming only if the market rose and refusing payment if it fell. It is for this reason that in many countries the practice is that the effective date for the commencement of ownership of shares or units is that on which payment is received, if different from the date on which the application from an investor for a purchase is lodged.

Delays at the level of the sales agent, which may be slow in transmitting orders from clients, are dealt with as a problem between the agent and his customer, since the management company cannot take any action if it has received no instructions.

Handling payments

The main set of problems in the issue and redemption processes, not unsurprisingly, concerns the movement of cash and payments made by and to the investors. Payment could be made by an investor directly to a management company or to a fund's custodian, depositary or trustee or by an investor through an adviser (or adviser via a consolidator) or supermarket to a management company. Of these, clearly the most reliable will be directly to the custodian, depositary or trustee, which, as a major bank or other financial institution with a reputation to preserve, could be judged as unlikely to steal cash in transit. It is customary, however, to allow the payment to be made to the management company or its sales agent, who should then pass it on to the custodian, depositary or trustee promptly.

Then there is also the question of redemptions and who should be responsible for paying the investor. While generally only the custodian, depositary or trustee is authorised to draw cash directly from the fund's bank account, it may be convenient for the custodian, depositary or trustee to pass redemption money to the management company for onward transmission to the redeeming investor.

The custom of permitting the management company to deal directly with the investor in receiving and making payments has given rise to a system whereby the management company can keep money received from and due to an investor in a specially designated bank account controlled by it, details of which are also accessible to the custodian, depositary or trustee. In this way it can calculate daily the net amount due to or from the custodian, depositary or trustee depending on whether there is a net surplus of sales or a net surplus of redemptions, when the daily dealings are closed.

All that is then required is for the management company to give documentary evidence of the deals done and to request the custodian, depositary or trustee either to authorise a net payment for a surplus of redemptions or to pay to the custodian, depositary or trustee any amount of surplus of sales over redemptions. The account is thus balanced to zero at the end of each trading day and movements into and out of the fund account are controlled and authorised by the custodian, depositary or trustee without the need for the custodian, depositary or trustee to receive and make individual payments for each transaction.

The greatest risk in cash handling lies at the level of the agent. Sales agents are sometimes either incompetent or dishonest and the frequency of loss at this level always causes concern. For instance, an analysis of payments by the UK Investors Compensation Scheme[1] for claims since 1988 showed over 85% of settled claims as having been where there has been the involvement of an agent.

There are really only two ways of dealing with the problem of agents and cash. One is simply not to permit them to handle cash, but for payments only to be made by cheque or bank transfer directly to the fund or fund management company or to the custodian, depositary or trustee and to inform investors never to give physical cash to agents or to make cheques or bank transfers payable to them. The other is to require such agents to be licensed, and to require them to follow the rules for handling of client money set for other similarly licensed financial advisers such as stockbrokers. This requires client money to be placed in separate accounts from that of the adviser or agent concerned and may require a custodian to hold such money on clients' behalf.

'Cooling off' and cancellation of transactions

Some jurisdictions allow investors to withdraw from or cancel transactions in fund units or shares provided that this is done within certain deadlines (usually in the region of 7–14 days from the transaction). Provisions such as these are made in order to enable people who feel that they have made an incorrect investment decision (either for themselves or upon the advice of an adviser who may perhaps have applied undue pressure in order to make a sale or to get a higher commission) to withdraw from or cancel the transaction. The ability to withdraw pre-sale in effect means that the sale is not implemented until the 'right to withdraw' period is over – so the management company notifies the client that the purchase order will not be fulfilled until the 'right to withdraw' period has passed.

Alternatively under the right to cancel the management company accepts the order and allocates the shares or units at the current price or NAV to the investor, advising them of their right to cancel within the specified term and of the requirement to pay. If the transaction is cancelled, the investor will only receive back the relevant current price or NAV on the cancellation date (so the investor's money is at risk over the period), together with any initial charge. This is designed to prevent cancellation rights being a one-way option against the fund, which otherwise could be used by a purchaser to cancel if the price of the shares or units he had ordered had declined. Forbidding an unpaid sale to be reversed by a redemption, if there is a profit, is based on the same principle.

Dealing with big redemptions

It is not uncommon for an investor – often a financial institution – to have holdings in excess of 5% of the issued capital of an investment fund. When such investors wish to redeem, the impact of selling a substantial slice of a fund's portfolio to meet the redemption can reduce the prices of those assets in the market, and thus reduce the value of the assets of the ongoing investors in the fund.

A solution to this is to offer what is known as 'in specie' redemption, whereby the exiting investor, instead of receiving a cash redemption, receives a part of each of the fund's assets in proportion to the size of his holding to the total value of the fund (e.g. in the case of an investor holding 10% of a fund, 10% of each of the holdings of the fund). The advantage is that the fund is not having to reduce the value of its own assets by selling, thus disadvantaging ongoing investors, and the exiting investor can then choose to sell these assets at its own convenience.

Such redemption is only ever applied to large investments and is only usually permitted by regulators if provision is made in the fund's prospectus for such redemption.

'In specie' subscription to a fund by way of an exchange of an equal value of shares or units in a fund for an eligible portfolio of securities – that is, one that meets the fund's investment objective – may also be possible (refer to 'share exchange' in Chapter 7) and is commonly done by institutional investors when creating exchange traded funds (refer to Chapter 14).

REGISTRATION

Registration can be described as the task of creating and maintaining the records of fund share or unitholders. There is little difference between the activity of registering the holders of funds and of joint stock companies (for a closed-ended corporate fund it is exactly the same); although as a general rule, registers of open-ended and interval funds will change more frequently than registers of closed-ended funds because new shares or units are constantly being created or cancelled.

Registers of share or unitholders are essentially lists of names and addresses of fund investors that also record the dates of purchase or sale and the numbers of shares or units held by each registered holder. It is necessary for the register to be maintained and kept up to date for a variety of reasons:

- To validate ownership claims – inclusion on a register is the ultimate proof of ownership: unless bearer certificates are issued, in which case physical possession of the bearer (see more below) certificate is the proof of ownership.
- To enable communications to be sent to share or unitholders – reports, notices of meetings and any other information.
- To pay dividends or distributions only to fund investors at the relevant date (see more below).
- To be able to calculate regularly the total number of shares or units in issue – which is integral to all funds' ability to calculate a correct net asset value per share or unit.

Registers are also highly valued by management companies as mailing lists for selling their new products or services. This, and the introduction of new technology, has changed the nature of share or unitholder registers in developed markets.

Responsibility for keeping the register of fund holders

There are two key issues when creating regulatory frameworks governing the keeping of fund registers:

- Which organisation is responsible for the maintenance of the register of share or unitholders.
- To whom may the actual day-to-day work be delegated (refer to Chapter 4 for the principle of delegation).

There are several possible variants on the theme of responsibility and delegation, as there are for most administrative functions connected with the management of a fund: these are summarised in Table 10.1.

It is worth noting that in some countries, however, all registration – including that of funds – has to be undertaken by a central securities depositary, which is delegated to undertake the task by the responsible entity.

Bearer

Many countries permit the issue of bearer certificates as evidence of ownership for both securities and investment funds. A bearer certificate carries no name, and possession of it is proof of ownership, just like currency. This means that transporting it represents a security risk. Bearer shares of investment funds are not

Table 10.1   *Responsibility for register and delegation*

Legal form of fund	Responsibility for register	Can delegate to
Corporate	Directors	Management company, custodian, depositary, registrar, third-party administrator
Trust	Trustee	Management company, registrar, third-party administrator
Contractual	Management company	Depositary, registrar, third-party administrator

common for this reason; also because they enable tax evasion, and so are disliked by tax authorities. They are now uncommon in the case of publicly offered funds.

Registered and certificated systems

It used to be common both to have a register and to issue share or unit certificates ('materialised' securities), and most registrars, even those which have moved to a non-certificated or dematerialised system, will still issue certificates on request (sometimes only at an additional charge) if they are particularly required. Share or unit certificates are sequentially numbered and contain the name of the holder and the number of shares or units held, the name of the fund and the date of issue; those representing shares or units in an open-ended or interval fund sometimes have a form on the back to enable a holder to renounce his ownership in the event of his redemption.

Certificated systems are cumbersome, requiring the issue of additional certificates if further purchases are made or the reissue of a fresh certificate for a smaller number of shares or units if a partial redemption was made, as a substitute for the certificate that had been returned to support the redemption. Also under this system fund name changes, mergers, splits or consolidations all require the issue of further or new certificates. Finally share or unitholders frequently lose or mislay their certificates and thus are not able to complete redemptions without great delay and the need to issue replacement certificates.

There are, however, some advantages to a certificated system, particularly in newer markets. A certificate, although it is not the final proof of ownership (as is a bearer share), physically exists, looks significant and can thus indicate a sense of value to the unsophisticated investor, who is unaccustomed to the concept of dematerialised ownership. Moreover, dematerialised systems need very sophisticated and reliable IT systems; a certificated system does not need such 'high tech' solutions and carries with it its own built-in control mechanism. In addition, as the issue of each certificate is recorded and a certificate physically created and issued, and – in the case of open-ended or interval funds – destroyed or defaced after redemption, duplication of entries or incorrect entries may be less likely, and thus reconciliation of the register total of shares or units in issue with the total of shares or units in issue as per the certificate records may be more reliable and can be carried out manually, albeit with some effort. It may also legitimately be asked whether it is economic for new markets to place a high IT cost on management companies, when simpler, albeit more primitive, systems will serve just as well until a critical size is reached.

It is quite common in the case of a certificated system for an indemnity to be required from the investor before a lost certificate can be replaced. This protects the registrar from the possibility that, at some time in the future, the original certificate will be found and a double redemption occur on both the original and on the new certificate. However, such indemnification usually requires the investor to pay for an element of insurance against this eventuality, which is not popular.

Dematerialised systems

More modern registration systems, which rely almost entirely on electronic resources, bring many advantages. There is no need to issue certificates as such; share or unitholders will simply receive a 'statement of account' that shows the record of their holding as held on the electronic register ('dematerialised' system). Such a statement can carry a great deal more information than a certificate, since it can cover all holdings in funds of a single management company, with a history of transactions in the period, with numbers, dates and prices, and payment or reinvestment of dividends, and an up-to-date value of the total holding at current market prices. There will thus be no need to issue balancing certificates for partial redemptions, or new certificates in the event of name changes, mergers etc. A dematerialised system, in effect, permits the use of an open-ended fund almost like a bank account. In fact, money market funds are virtually bank accounts, the development of which would have been impossible in a fully certificated environment.

Dematerialised systems also permit the issue of fractional shares or units, often known as decimalised shares or units. As Table 10.2 shows, this is useful in making it possible to allocate units precisely matching a sum of money to be invested, in a case where it would be impossible to allocate a round number of whole shares or units sufficiently precisely. It is also useful in the case that distributions are reinvested, once again enabling relatively small amounts of money to be fully invested without the need for balancing sums to be dealt with.

Dematerialised systems enable much more effective use of the register as a marketing tool. It is now common to keep registers by individual client names on

Table 10.2 *Example of decimalisation*

	Sum to be invested	Share/unit price	Number of shares/units allocated	Uninvested balance
No fractions	1000	3.28	304	2.88
Decimalised system	1000	3.28	304.878	0

a single relational database, rather than keep a register for each fund. Formerly a register was kept separately for each fund: as a result, each register had to be gone through when clients forgot which fund they had invested in. Also, it used to be difficult to de-duplicate a share or unitholder's interest if he held shares or units in more than one fund when using registers as a mailing list for promotional offerings; as a result, for example, a holder of six different funds within the same management group would receive six general mailings rather than one. This was wasteful for the management company and irritating for the client. By creating 'client-facing' systems, which can also record responses to mailings or offers, preferences, etc. more targeted and effective marketing is possible.

Dematerialised systems also bring greater convenience to the active investor. Once an account is established, which may require a physical signature if electronic signatures are not yet permitted, an investor may buy and redeem, switch to a different fund (that is, redeem an existing fund investment and reinvest in another fund of the same management company) or change standing instructions by telephone or on the Internet, using appropriate PIN numbers or security codes.

Payments for redemptions can be dealt with, either by sending out a cheque, a solution which allows for the possibility of fraud or theft, or by electronic transfer to a specifically designated bank account, for which transaction the investor accepts liability in the event that he changes his banking arrangements without notifying the fund management company.

Holding of sub-registers

There is an increasing tendency for advisers and investors to purchase and redeem fund shares or units through consolidators and fund supermarkets. These organisations basically package all the orders placed through them during a day into a single set of transactions, resulting in a daily consolidated net issue or redemption order per fund on behalf of all their users to each management company who subscribes to their services. Only the consolidator or the supermarket therefore will know on whose behalf these orders are placed. For this reason, its name will go on the register of the fund as the holder of units and the supermarket or consolidator will then hold a sub-register for each fund identifying who its customers are and what their holdings are. The consolidator or supermarket will also hold its own customer-facing set of accounts, where it records all the holdings of the clients of a financial adviser, or all the holdings of an individual investor.

Legal aspects of registration and transfer of securities

Ownership rights of holders of securities and transfer of ownership will be subject to a wide variety of different legislative requirements, depending on the country in which the fund is based and the type of legal system that it has and also the countries into which the fund is sold. Whatever the legal requirements are, there are certain technical and practical matters, which any registrar will need to address which include:

- Changes of name of registered holders (e.g. marriage or divorce or gift).
- Deaths and probate.
- Powers of attorney.
- Changes of address.
- Shares or units pledged as security by their holders.
- Share or unitholders whose contact details are lost.
- Lost certificates if certificated.

How these are dealt with will vary within each jurisdiction; usually they will be common to all securities registration in that country. Where a management company or third-party administrator services funds sold into a series of countries, it will need to be able to service fund investors in each of the requisite languages.

Transferability of shares or units

One problem that may arise is that of the freedom of holders to transfer ownership of shares or units of investment fund, if they are regarded by national legislation as securities. There is no question that this right must exist in the case of closed-ended investment funds formed as joint stock companies, since these are usually listed on a stock exchange and their shares can only be bought and sold in the secondary market. It must also exist in the case of exchange traded funds (refer to Chapter 14). There may be a number of reasons why some may wish to extend this right to include open-ended and interval funds. Leaving aside the legal problem of whether units of contractual funds or trusts are classified as transferable securities, which may affect the issue, the reasons for enabling such transferability are sometimes given as:

- Permitting individuals to transfer shares or units by way of gift.
- Permitting transactions in a secondary market.

- Permitting distributors to make wholesale purchases of shares or units from the management company in their own name with a view to retailing these to small investors.

In the first case, it is relatively logical to permit such transfers to be made but only providing that the management company or third-party administrator is notified of such transfer free of payment; in this way the new owner is properly recorded and distributions and information will be sent to the new owner.

The other two cases amount to the creation of a secondary market in open-ended funds where none needs exist. Given that the shares or units of most open-ended funds can be purchased or redeemed on any day from the management company at a net asset value based on current market prices and calculated in the way required by the regulations, it would be highly undesirable if shares or units were to be traded in a secondary market at prices other than those that are thus calculated and officially published since incoming investors would be likely to paying too much or too little for their units and outgoing investors would be likely to be receiving too much or too little.

The fact that shares or units of open-ended funds are sometimes listed on stock exchanges does not imply that this creates a secondary market. Excepting exchange traded funds, these listings usually are purely technical, designed to permit investment by institutions whose regulatory status allows investment only in listed securities.

It is conceivable that secondary markets in shares or units of interval funds might serve a purpose where they only open once per year; however, these are likely to trade at a discount during the year (so there will not be much incentive to exit) and then move back to NAV as the dealing period draws nigh.

DEALING WITH FUND DIVIDENDS OR DISTRIBUTIONS

For simplicity this section refers to both dividends issued by corporate funds to holders, and distributions by trust and contractual funds to holders, as 'distributions' (the principle of what is distributed – i.e. only income or capital – is dealt with in Chapter 15). This section discusses the options for making distributions of income, whatever its composition or source.

Frequency of payment

The frequency with which distributions are paid will be determined by the type of fund that is paying them, but as a general rule reflects the practice of listed companies: commonly this is half yearly or yearly. Funds whose advertised purpose is to pay a high income often try to pay distributions more frequently than this – some pay dividends monthly to coincide with a typical investor's expenditure cycle, while others pay quarterly. The frequency of payment may also be determined by the efficiency and cost of making frequent small payments; in countries without a highly developed banking system such payments may be expensive, or even impossible to make.

Accumulation or income shares or units

There are two forms of shares or units of open-ended or interval funds – 'income' and 'accumulation'. Only shares or units known as 'income' shares or units pay out distributions to their holders. 'Accumulation' shares or units instead retain all the income, this retention being reflected in an increasing share or unit price as the income is compounded over time. There are frequently tax reasons for this retention, since some countries seek to encourage saving through funds by granting tax privileges to them only if income is not paid out, or by taxing distributions if they are paid out but not if they are reinvested. In such cases investors who need to take an income may do so by redeeming shares or units on a regular basis; some fund management companies will offer automatic facilities for this.

On the other hand other tax regimes, the UK and USA for example, require funds by law to distribute either the vast majority or all their income as a distribution to share or unitholders and the USA requires capital gains to be distributed too. This means that distributions will be taxed as if they had been received even if they are not paid out, but are reinvested (see below).

In the case of some funds under certain types of taxation regime, it may be effective for funds to make distributions in the form of additional shares (known as a 'scrip dividend') rather than cash.

Reinvestment of income

Where distributions are paid out on income shares or units, particularly if they are paid out gross (untaxed) and only taxed in the hands of individual investors at their appropriate rate (in the USA for example) fund management companies may offer a facility to reinvest distributions by the purchase of more shares or units. This facility is particularly useful and relevant if the shares or units of the fund are held in a tax-free environment like a pension plan or other tax-privileged savings plan. The effect of this is to increase steadily the number of shares or units held over time as distributions are reinvested at each dividend date in more shares or units, in contrast to the accumulation system where the reinvestment of income within the fund is reflected in an increase in the price of the share or unit.

Mandating distributions

Not all investors wish to receive their distributions directly by cheque. Most find it convenient for dividends to be paid directly into a designated bank account and only to receive notification at the time of payment. Fund management companies also prefer to pay distributions this way, since it is much cheaper to transfer money in bulk than to generate and send out individual cheques, though this will apply only in countries with developed banking systems.

Dividends on bearer shares

The exception to the general rules about payment of distributions will be bearer shares, to which are attached coupons, which need to be cut and presented to a paying agent for receipt of distributions. Most banks will offer the facility of keeping a client's bearer shares and undertaking distribution collection on their behalf. Bearer shares of funds are becoming less and less common. If they exist, often their existence is only technical, and the bearer shares are immobilised in the vault of a bank, and what is in effect a register of owners is kept in dematerialised form.

Entitlement to distributions and payment

Most funds operate a distribution entitlement system similar to that used in securities markets generally as to entitlement to distributions or dividends. Ownership rights start at the date on which the contract is made, and a new purchaser is thus entitled to receive any distributions or dividends declared after that date. Immediately after the declaration of the dividend the shares or units will be priced 'ex dividend' (or 'xd'), that is to say any new purchasers of shares or units on or after the date that the shares or unit are quoted 'xd' will not be entitled to receive the recently declared dividend but will be entitled to the next one. The payment date, on which cheques will be sent out or bank transfers made, will be some days or weeks later than the 'xd' date.

When fund shares or units become xd, the share or unit price, which had included accrued income (or was 'cum dividend' or 'with dividend'), will decrease by the amount of the dividend per share or unit that has been declared to reflect the fact that a new purchaser will not receive it.

Unclaimed distributions

It is not uncommon for investors to fail to claim their distributions – cheques may be sent but never cashed, or bank accounts to which payments may have been sent may have been closed and the payment returned. It is generally considered good practice to keep such money in a special account and meanwhile to make an effort to track down the recipients. Should no-one claim such distributions after a specified period of time (usually linked to statutes of limitations) then they would usually be paid back into the fund.

The subject of the last four chapters of this book has been administration. The next few chapters are focused on another area of fund management activity: the way funds are marketed.

Those who would like to test their grasp of the contents of this chapter should turn to the self-test questions at the back of the book.

NOTES

1. *Annual Report*, 2001.

11

Marketing Activities

INTRODUCTION

This and the next three chapters of the book cover the marketing of investment funds. These subjects are simply too extensive to cover in a single chapter so they have been divided into: the process of creating a fund (covered in Chapter 14 on product development); how its existence is publicised (covered in this chapter), how shares or units in the fund are sold (known as 'distribution' and covered in Chapter 12); and how fund investors are communicated with (covered in Chapter 13). This first marketing chapter reviews influences on fund marketing, including regulation and the overall activities that a fund management company's marketing department undertakes, setting distribution, product development and investor communication in context.

A fund management business clearly must have customers – without investors in its funds, it has no business. In order to have a successful business, it must first attract customers, and then retain them: the key role of marketing. However, attracting new customers to any business can be expensive and if they are needed to replace customers that are continually leaving, then the business is unlikely to develop profitably. It is worth remembering that existing customers are usually the cheapest source from which to acquire further new business. If people are already investors in a fund, their contact details are known and they can be contacted through the post or email, which is usually far more cost-effective than having to advertise in print or broadcast media. What is more, if they are already investors, they know the management company involved, and provided that they have some spare money, may well invest again with the same group if their previous experience has been satisfactory. So it is important not only to attract customers, but also to retain them.

Marketing is defined in dictionaries as 'moving goods or services from a provider to a consumer'. Some definitions add the words 'at a profit' to the end of this phrase; regrettably, this is not always the case in relation to investment funds – as anyone who has been in charge of marketing of funds during a prolonged recession or stock market downturn will know. There is a fundamental contradiction in the marketing of equity-invested funds in particular, since

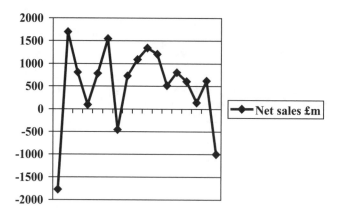

Figure 11.1 *Sales rollercoaster – monthly net sales June 2001 – November 2002*
Source: IMA. Reproduced by permission of the Investment Management Association.

investors should buy such funds when stock markets are low, and sell when they are high; unfortunately they rarely do invest when markets are low, usually because they have lost confidence during the downturn, and have an unfortunate tendency to pile into the market when it is nearly at its peak. This means that marketing when stock markets are low tends to be less productive than marketing when markets are high and investor sentiment is more positive. Sales of funds can also be volatile, as Figure 11.1 shows, and do not always repay marketing effort.

Fund marketing (and advertising in particular) therefore generally tends to focus on the products that are likely to sell:

- Due to having a present competitive edge – during periods of low interest rates, for instance, funds offering higher income through investing in bonds or equities are often popular. There can be dangers in such strategies: it seems likely, in the case of higher income bond funds, that many investors dissatisfied with bank interest rates do not appreciate that benefiting from the higher interest rates offered by bond fund products also involves higher levels of risk to their capital.
- Due to having a tax advantage – often related to a 'wrapper' that enables people to save a certain amount of money each year into a tax-advantaged product (e.g. the UK Individual Savings Account or ISA and the French Employees' Savings Plans). Governments often use such tax reliefs to incentivise investment, usually into mainstream asset classes but sometimes into specialist ones such as venture capital.
- Or due to being 'hot' – that is, in fashion. 'Hot' funds can be a self-fulfilling prophecy, particularly when the market in which they invest is small and there

is a limited supply of assets. The early new fund performs well, so copycat funds are created by other management companies to invest in the same assets, increasing demand for the assets and thus raising their prices, which in turn improves fund performance, and in turn makes these funds even 'hotter' so more people invest and the funds buy more of the same assets so prices go up again and so does fund performance. The 'dot.com' boom was a classic example of this.

The marketing division of a fund management firm should focus its activities on attracting the maximum amount of business for the minimum amount of marketing spend, in order to make its contribution to the business as profitable as possible. In order to do this, its activities will include:

- Management: setting and controlling targets and budgets, co-ordinating activities, allocating tasks and monitoring results.
- Researching and defining target markets: this saves time and money since it will prevent the firm marketing to people who are unlikely to become customers, or using inappropriate media to reach the target market, or marketing at times when potential customers are unreceptive.
- Developing the brand: that is, defining and maintaining the style and the qualities associated with the fund management company's name. This often reflects the pricing of services provided by the company – the branding and style of a company which focuses on offering low-cost services will be different from that of one offering a premium service.
- Developing the products: designing funds to meet customers' needs.
- Advertising the fund management company and its products: this will be done by creating advertising messages and paying to place them in the media that will most cost-effectively reach the target market, making this market aware of the company and its products.
- Promoting the company and its products: this is done through public relations and promotions designed to make opinion formers aware of the company and its products and to encourage them to communicate a favourable impression of these to potential customers (e.g. getting a journalist to write a complimentary review of a new product), the difference with advertising being that this communication is indirect and there is no direct payment for 'placing' of such comment.
- Creating and maintaining investor communications systems and marketing databases.

Marketing financial services such as funds is complicated: the result of the 'purchase' may not be experienced for many years (e.g. pension-related savings) and people in general find financial planning intimidating. This has given rise to the adage that 'life insurance is sold and not bought' which broadly applies to funds too: the vast majority of fund sales are intermediated by an adviser or sales agent, often because people need human contact – perhaps to try to reassure themselves that they are doing the right thing.

MARKETING CONTEXT

Three factors will have a strong impact on marketing-related decisions. The first is the nature of the fund management company itself, the second is how consumers make financial services choices and the third is regulation governing marketing and sales activities, which is usually governed both by specific fund legislation as well as general legislation.

The impact of the nature of the fund management company

There are a number of factors here, which will affect the marketing strategy of a fund management company. These include:

- The ownership of the management company, and related objectives and style: the owners could be individuals, financial institutions or other companies such as retailers. They may have an existing brand or strength, or distribution channels in place, which the management company can use; or the company may be being started from ground zero. The brand image and style of the owners will also influence the management company; a deeply conservative bank will probably sit ill with a subsidiary fund management company that focuses on high-risk emerging markets equity, for example.
- The need for profitability: do the owners of the company need it to make profits within a couple of years? Or can they afford to wait for five or 10 years? This will affect a fund management company's ability to pursue different strategies: for instance, a need for short-term profits will reduce ability to pay high commissions to sales agents or to offer low-cost products, both of which would reduce short-term profitability; while a longer term horizon will permit short-term profit sacrifice.
- The resources available: the financing available to the company will affect the ability of the marketing division to pursue different strategies: for instance, to sustain the higher fixed costs of employing a salaried or part-salaried salesforce compared with the lower variable cost of paying commissions to advisers on sales made; it could also indicate a need to focus on servicing a small number of large clients (institutional-type business) rather than a large number of small clients (retail-type business).

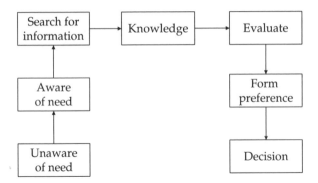

Figure 11.2 *The buying process*

These in turn will indicate whether the company will aim to have a specialist product range, aimed at a niche market; or a wide product range to meet general consumer needs.

Essentially, the two extremes of approach to the consumer market that can be defined are a 'leader' strategy, where the company sets out to be consistently and highly visible over the long term, steadily building a business – this requires long term commitment and deep pockets; or an 'opportunist' strategy, whereby a company simply seeks to create products and exploit them effectively, as the opportunity arises, which is a short-term strategy that may not require deep pockets.

The nature of consumer decision taking

Another factor to be borne in mind when developing a marketing strategy is how people make financial services choices and the factors that influence them in making such choices. Before making a purchase, they will go through a set of processes illustrated in Figure 11.2.

It is very important that fund management companies are able to influence potential investors at every stage of this process, and to quickly and efficiently provide the information that will predispose investors towards their fund or funds, rather than a competitor's. A fund management company also must think through how it wishes to be able to influence potential customers at each stage of the process, and what is needed to get them to move towards a decision to purchase shares or units in their particular fund or product, instead of someone else's.

People's choices (see Figure 11.3) will also depend on external factors such as the culture from which they derive, and their social reference group, family, role and status; and on internal factors which are both psychological – their motivation and perceptions, attitudes and beliefs – and personal – what life-cycle

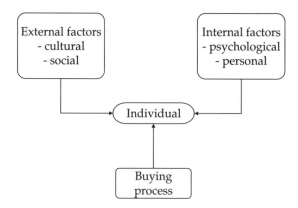

Figure 11.3 *Factors affecting financial services choices*

stage they are at, their position, age, employment, lifestyle and personality. Products can be designed specifically to attract a certain market: a relatively recent development has been Islamic products that meet Shari'ah requirements,[1] for instance.

A fund management company needs to help people to reach a decision to buy their products through ensuring that information and guidance is available to them to justify this decision. Personal recommendation ('word of mouth') from previous purchasers is nearly always a strong influence on decision making; thus it is important that fund management companies keep existing customers satisfied. Ensuring that a decision, once taken, can be quickly and simply and easily implemented is also important; if it cannot, the customer may go elsewhere. People are increasingly intolerant of transaction complexity: if one provider makes life easy and the other does not, even if the former is more expensive, they may be chosen on the grounds of saving of time. The more steps consumers have to go through to buy a fund, the less likely they are to complete all of them and the sale will be lost.

Consumer attitudes to risk are also very important. The way that this is characterised varies. One form of risk is that of losing the money invested: there is some evidence that some cultures bother more about losing money that they do have than they bother about the opportunity cost of not making money that they could have made in a different investment. They are likely to prefer products where the value of their capital is preserved – basically lower risk investments such as deposits or government bonds: the risk here is that these may not preserve the buying power of that money due to inflation. At the other end are those who seek out high risk products, hoping for high returns.

Other consumer attitudes that are also relevant are openness to new products (some people are much happier to experiment with investing in something new than others, who will wait until it is tried and tested) and openness to use of technology.

The impact of regulation

Marketing of financial services in general is usually heavily regulated, since decisions about mortgages, pensions and savings have a substantial impact on people's lives. While most household purchases are used or consumed within days or weeks, so their satisfactoriness can be judged almost immediately, the outcome of household financial decisions may not be known for years, or even decades, in the future: so there is much greater uncertainty about outcomes.

This means that fund marketeers have to pay due regard to the variety of legislation that governs marketing and sales of services and products in general, which relates to matters such as contracts, descriptions of goods or services, content of advertising ('legal, decent and truthful' is a common requirement – readers of this book will not, perhaps, be surprised to be told that the most common complaints about fund management advertising to advertising regulatory authorities derive from competitors rather than customers), telephone sales and electronic commerce, to name a few.

However, marketing also has to comply with fund-specific – and sometimes financial services-specific – law and regulation too. This regulation is usually designed to protect the ordinary consumer from being misled or deceived by a fund management company, or by salespeople working for such companies, and generally applies only to publicly offered funds. Many countries exempt the private offering of funds from requirements placed on publicly offered funds on the basis that such funds can only be offered to professional or expert investors or companies that are assumed to have sufficient expertise to form their own judgements about funds and their relevance to their needs. Thus the marketing of privately offered funds will be different to that of publicly offered funds.

Where funds are to be sold in several countries – for instance, under the EU UCITS Directive – matters become even more complex: a different set of marketing regulations is likely to apply in each country, though they may have many common factors. The international nature of the Internet can further complicate the picture; a website established to promote the funds of a management firm in its home domicile is potentially accessible by anyone worldwide, but is created only under home domicile regulation. Some countries require websites to have entry passwords specifically designed to ensure that only permitted investors can participate in funds through such sites (this is designed to ensure that their citizens are effectively protected by only permitting investment in eligible funds); others are more relaxed.

The complexities of marketing funds in different countries can begin to be understood by studying publications such as the *European Fund Market Yearbook*[2] or the *International Guide to Marketing Investment Funds*.[3]

In general, the newer funds are to a market, the more personal contact will be required to make sales: 'looking someone in the eye' remains a key part of financial decision taking for many people, despite the increasing use of the Internet.

THE MECHANICS OF MARKETING

Management of marketing

Most of the functions of marketing can be undertaken either internally or externally from the management company. The most common structure would be to have an internal department responsible for the function, reporting to the Board: the department will call on external service providers as needed.

It is normal for specific targets to be set which marketing is required to achieve in any given year, and for performance to be measured regularly both against these targets and in terms of results achieved against money spent (i.e. cost-effectiveness). Targets are usually expressed in terms of sales of funds to be achieved within a defined period, and are usually specific to countries or regions, or to different marketing or sales teams (e.g. institutional sales versus retail sales, sales through financial advisers versus direct sales). Name awareness is another measure: that is, how many people recognise the name of the company (industry folklore tells of a company which discovered after some name awareness research amongst its investors that well over 10% of its investors had never heard of it – and, no, it had not changed its name or merged with another company).

Tracking performance against targets is important, since failure to attain targets has revenue and capacity implications for the management company; if sales are lower than targeted, revenues will be below target; if they are higher than targeted, administration systems and personnel may not be able to cope. As market conditions improve or worsen, targets will need to be adjusted accordingly.

A marketing plan and budget should be created for each financial year, against the targets set, and progress against it should be monitored weekly or at least monthly in terms of:

- Cost – budgets spent versus budgets allocated, and reasons for discrepancies.
- Timing – whether the schedule has been achieved, and if not, why not and the consequences that this will have for the budget.
- Target – whether target sales have been achieved, and if not, why not: this should include tracking sales per distribution channel and/or per sales team against targets and against each other, to assess effectiveness.

Usually separate budgets will be agreed for different activities and for particular projects such as the launch of a new fund, with pre-agreed expenditure limits and deadlines for each activity.

Progress should also be assessed in terms of results achieved for money spent. This is done in several ways, including:

- Tracking the number of responses to each advertisement or to each mailing campaign (which necessitates having coding and tracking systems in place to check such response), and comparing the results by dividing the cost of each advertisement or campaign by the number of responses received (known as cost per response).
- Tracking the amount of money invested as a result of each advertisement or mailing campaign, and dividing the cost by the amount of money raised, which can be compared for each advertisement or mailing to assess effectiveness (known as cost per conversion).
- Tracking the amount of money invested as a result of each distribution channel against the cost of servicing that channel to see where best results are occurring and trying to assess why.

Fund managers in each country will establish their own acceptable cost per 100 or 1000 of currency units attracted and may, if such data is available, be able to compare their results with other managers, to give a further measure of effectiveness.

Cost control is a vital element of marketing and is important when using external contractors, who should operate under clear reporting and budgetary conditions.

Researching the different markets

Identifying the market to be targeted by a management company, whether for the company overall, or for a particular fund, is a key task of a marketing department.

Institutional or retail
The first question is whether the market to be targeted is 'institutional' or 'retail': that is, whether the company is seeking to attract investments from financial institutions, such as pension, charitable, insurance or other investment funds; or from individuals – or both. Some fund management companies target only the institutional market, selling specialised investment expertise such as emerging markets, which the institutions either do not have in-house themselves or can be supplied more cost-effectively by third parties. Some fund management companies target only the retail investor, offering a range of products to meet ordinary people's

Table 11.1 *Differences between institutional and retail clients*

	Institutional	Retail
Number of such investors	Tens or hundreds of thousands internationally	Hundreds of millions internationally
Amount invested	Generally $100000 or more per investment	Generally $1000 or more per investment
Level of initial charge acceptable	Generally 0–2%	Generally 0–8%
Level of annual charge acceptable	Usually 0.25–1.25%	Usually 2% or less
Fund investment objective	Have specific investment need which investment objective of fund must meet accurately	Have general investment need and risk profile which investment objective of fund must meet
Fund portfolio	Require detailed information on content and changes	Require general information on content and changes
Fund performance analysis and reports	Usually monthly or weekly	Usually six-monthly
Service	Usually require personal service with named liaison person	Do not usually expect named liaison person

needs. Many companies target both markets, with different sections within the marketing or sales divisions focussing on these two groups, since their needs are different. Table 11.1 summarises the key differences in dealing with institutional and retail clients.

As a general rule, the level of information required by an institutional investor, both prior to and after investing, will be much more frequent and detailed than for a retail investor. Special reports are sometimes prepared for institutional investors, which may be individually generated to meet their specific needs (e.g. demonstration of compliance with certain portfolio limitations, or avoidance of investment in tobacco products for a lung cancer charity, for instance).

Marketing departments may develop privately offered funds that are targeted specifically at institutional investors only, with the possible addition of professional investors or rich individuals who may also be permitted by regulation to invest in such funds, since they are judged to be sufficiently expert or to have expert advisers. These funds are often located in low tax domiciles (also referred to as 'offshore' domiciles) that permit greater portfolio flexibility and a wider range of legal and operating structures.

Obtaining data

Details of potential institutional investors are best derived from professional directories, handbooks or yearbooks or specialist databases. It will be necessary to build up an in-house database, which should be constantly maintained and reviewed for changes in address, personnel, etc. Sometimes such databases can be bought in; sometimes they are built from scratch.

Data used to identify potential retail target markets is a more complicated area. It can focus on two different aspects: one is essentially demographic and the other attitudinal.

In many countries demographic information is available from a government statistical office. This characteristically covers:

- age and gender
- income structure
- occupation
- social structure (households)
- asset ownership
- savings from income
- location
- ethnic or religious group.

Such data can be used to assess trends which may have significance for fund managers: for instance, in Europe generally an ageing population is placing increasing strain on state pension systems whose costs are met by current taxpayers (known as 'pay as you go' systems). Numbers of workers are reducing as numbers of pensioners are increasing due to greater longevity. This is likely to lead to greater need for governments to encourage individuals to save personally for their retirement and to place less reliance on state pensions, which could create more demand for funds (an example of what this sort of stimulus can do can be seen by looking at the Swedish fund market in the last decade).

Traditionally in developed markets the people who have had money available to save or invest have been the older managerial or professional male whose children have left home, so has reduced expenses, and who needs to put money aside for retirement. Another group has developed in recent years: the 25–35-year-old male or female manager or professional, often living in a two-income household, who has money left over to save.

The key is to find a group that has money available to save, and then to find out what will be the most cost-effective way to reach them by checking, amongst other factors:

- Where they live (if it is all in the same area, posting literature through doors or local posters might work).
- What programmes they watch or publications they read.
- What are their hobbies and interests.
- What communication methods they use – phone, Internet, etc.

This sort of information helps to target marketing effort: at certain sports for sponsorship, for instance (is the reason why so many fund management companies sponsor upmarket sporting events that they like that sport but normally could not afford to attend in sufficient style, or that their clients like the sport? Perhaps there is a happy coincidence). If statistical data of this type is not available, common sense will have to substitute.

Qualitative data is based on research that is usually undertaken by specialist firms, to assist in effective targeting. In the case of the financial sector, attitudes to saving generally, to risk and to decision taking are all important. Different research groups create different labels for groups with different characteristics. In general, these refer to:

- Attitude to risk: potential loss of capital as well as opportunity for gain.
- Sensitivity to price: i.e. levels of different types of charges.
- Ability to take decisions independently, or need for advice.
- Attitude to saving – passive or active.
- Savings need – for capital growth or a rising income.
- Attitudes to use of technology.

All these will influence how the fund management company will need to adjust its marketing and sales techniques to meet the target customer's need, in order to make the desired sale. As an example, those who like taking their own financial decisions, and are confident researching for themselves, are price sensitive and like using technology, could be ideal customers for Internet-based services; whereas those who need personal advice and who do not like technology may be best persuaded by a salesperson who fills in the necessary applications for them, provided that they are not price sensitive.

Monitoring the competition

Most management companies will spend time researching and monitoring the activities of competitors either formally or informally and will monitor both other types of financial products and other funds. This is done to ensure that they are aware of potential threats to the attractiveness of their own products, and to enable them to respond effectively to such threats. If a management company has a particular strength – for instance, the lowest cost provider – then it will need to constantly check that this position is not under threat, and identify either what adjustments it is capable of making if a competitor should undercut it, or cases it can make to justify a decision not to move to lower costs. An example might be that it could not then provide some of the services its investors wanted, which the 'undercutter' did not provide and was thus able to charge less.

Surprisingly little distinguishes the vast majority of funds with a similar investment objective from each other though in theory fees and performance, as well as portfolio composition, should do so; a successful launch of one fund by one firm tends to lead to a series of 'me too' funds from competitors. Creating funds or a management company that are distinctive is difficult, though not impossible. A good example is the leading 'no-load' fund provider of the USA, the Vanguard Group®, whose unusual ownership structure (the funds own the management company) and obsession with offering value has resulted in funds with the lowest average total expense ratio for a management company that the authors are aware of: 27 basis points or 0.27% (or $2.70 per $1000 managed – a quarter of the US average of $13.20 per $1000 managed[4]).

Branding

Branding is essentially ensuring that people associate certain qualities or values with a particular name, which influences attitudes towards that name. Sometimes a brand is associated with a particular product – let us say, a detergent – and sometimes with a company which offers a range of products. The latter is usually the case in relation to funds – it is the management company (or its parents') name that is the focus of the brand though if the management company is a subsidiary, it may damage the parent brand if its style contradicts it or if it gets into regulatory trouble.

The sorts of qualities or values which fund management companies might wish to associate with their names could range from: 'value for money' through to 'expensively exclusive'; from 'conservative' through to 'aggressive risk taking'; from 'scientific' to 'gut instinct'. Perhaps the increasing internationalisation and scale of fund management is enhancing the tendency that the authors perceive towards increasing vapidity and lack of effective differentiation in the sector; though this could be partly a result of regulation and consumer concerns – managers are less willing, for instance, to take higher investment risks because this can mean a greater chance of lower returns, preferring instead be near the median (sometimes referred to – unkindly? – as 'planned mediocrity').

If a strong brand name is to be achieved, consistent effort over many years will be needed, with all supporting promotional activity and materials being consistent with the brand image. Mailing very glossy brochures, for instance, is inconsistent with a 'value for money' brand.

Advertising

Advertising is used to inform and to persuade, and to alert people to opportunities. It can be used to develop awareness of a management company's name and qualities, or to promote a specific fund or range of funds.

Influences on the method of advertising selected will be:

- The target market and its characteristics.
- Budgets available.
- The message to be conveyed and its suitability to different media: television is good for creating awareness, but poor at conveying large amounts of detail, which is often required for financial product advertising due to regulation. Putting a lot of detail on screen is costly; unless people record the advertisement, the information is difficult to retain, and response has to be separately through a phone call or other contact. Print media are excellent for conveying detail, though, and are relatively cheap. Choice of media can also affect perceptions of potential customers: some have more confidence in financial groups which advertise on television because – in their view – this is expensive, so it shows they are big and able to finance such expenditure. Advertising the existence of a website is an increasingly popular method of enabling people to access information.
- What competitors are doing.

There are essentially three types of fund advertising:

- Brand or image advertising, promoting the qualities of the management company (unsurprisingly, usually along the lines of 'we are the greatest' though these days regulators require evidence to support this).
- 'One-step' product advertising which includes subscription information so an investor can subscribe immediately: however, this is very expensive as regulations require usually publishing the prospectus in the advertisement in order to provide the basis for an informed investment decision.
- 'Two-step' product advertising, which encourages investors to apply for detailed subscription information about the product or product advertised, which they can then use to subscribe if they so decide.

Advertising also supports the work of advisers and salespeople: it is much easier to sell a product from a known provider than from someone the potential investor has never heard of; it can also be used to promote Internet-dealing facilities.

The results from different advertisements should be constantly monitored, not only in terms of cost-effectiveness, as outlined above, but also in terms of:

- Which advertisements work better than others – for instance, if different advertisements are placed in the same media on the same page, which gets the highest response and conversion rates.

- Advertising within which publications or during which programmes works best – that is, which achieve the highest response and conversion rates, at which times or in which positions (for instance, financial pages versus general news pages).
- What timing works best – that is, whether advertising around holidays achieves a higher response or conversion, or not; or over weekends or on weekdays, etc.; and different times of day for broadcast programmes.

It is very important to keep file copies of all marketing materials, including all advertising placed, together with details of its placement and support for any claims or facts given in it that are required to be capable of substantiation. This is both for regulatory reasons, and for reasons of self-defence – in case customers subsequently complain about inaccurate or misleading advertising.

Investment performance, which is an important component of fund advertising, is covered in Chapter 6. It is worth noting that whenever reference is made to performance in fund advertising, regulation will require accompanying statements that:

- Past performance is not a guide to future performance.
- The price of units or shares and the income from them can go down as well as up.
- Investors may not get back what they invested.

Public relations

Public relations focuses on the creation and maintenance of favourable perceptions about a management company and its funds. This is usually done through informing and persuading opinion formers, whose views then influence a wider range of people.

Characteristically, opinion formers include:

- Journalists and commentators.
- Subject specialists.
- Members of parliament and of political parties.
- Regional, national and foreign government officials.
- Community or religious leaders.
- Consumer organisations.

Most management companies will have an internal department responsible for the public relations function and may hire external advisers also. Their primary function will be to ensure effective communication of messages about the company to the selected opinion formers, maintaining the visibility and good reputation of the company. For a public relations officer being articulate is a pre-requisite; being photogenic is also preferable. They will be expected to promote the launch of new funds, creating a favourable environment for sales of shares or units, possibly with events such as press conferences or visits to relevant organisations (a favourite is foreign trips for journalists to visit countries in which new funds will invest, particularly where breweries are involved).

Public relations departments must also keep up-to-date information on all the company's products and key facts about the company, ready to answer queries; and must respond effectively and promptly to questions about relevant issues. They, and external agencies, should *facilitate* effective communication, not impede it. It is also important that somebody who is technically competent and an able public speaker should act as a spokesperson for the company, and build relationships with relevant opinion formers.

A particularly effective use of public relations is to ensure a favourable mention of a fund on the same page as an advertisement for the same fund appears. Where journalists are regarded as expert and unbiased, this effectively endorses the fund and carries weight with potential investors. This helps to form the 'preference' highlighted in Figure 11.12 above.

Public relations departments are also expected to anticipate and plan for any damage limitation exercises that may be needed if, for instance, a market is suspended so issue and redemption of funds investing in that market are also suspended. Indeed, public relations is all about anticipation of events, positive or negative, and planning to minimise the damage and maximise the benefit for the company concerned.

A key factor in public relations is credibility; opinion formers tend to have good antennae for stories and any weaknesses in them; and competitors will always help them to seek such weaknesses out. It is very important that public relations departments and company spokespeople should be authoritative and credible on a continuing basis; backing all publicity with succinct and relevant supporting data is always worthwhile.

Promotion

Promotion can include anything from giving out free branded gifts, to appearing at financial or other exhibitions or sponsoring sporting, hobby or artistic events. It is a range of activities designed to keep the management company's name in front of the target audience. Promotion should be consistent with the brand of the promoter and be directed at the company's target market. Sponsoring sporting or other events is popular because institutional customers, advisers and sales teams can be invited to attend the event, as well as putting the company's name in front of the audience at the event.

Management companies can also stage 'roadshows', visiting towns and cities where they have clients or potential clients, or financial advisers or sales teams, and making presentations on new or existing products and taking questions. Many people value the opportunity to meet fund managers and representatives of fund management companies and to ask questions. If institutional investors are to be attracted to a particular fund, it is quite common to stage a special series of formal presentations with detailed information support in major cities internationally where such investors are based, to explain the proposed fund to the target market. Funds wishing to attract international institutions would normally do roadshows in New York, Frankfurt, London, Hong Kong and Tokyo at a minimum.

In emerging markets, promoting funds to individual investors can be very expensive and relatively unrewarding. An alternative strategy whereby management companies contact companies with employees who have savings or pensions needs and arrange to make a presentation to them at their place of work, and set up particular schemes on their behalf can prove more effective.

Investor communications systems

Marketing departments are usually responsible for putting together investor communications materials and for the creation and maintenance of marketing databases of existing and potential customers. Regular, good quality communications are an important part of building customers' confidence in a management company's abilities. A schedule and budget is usually created to cover those investor communications that are required by regulation to be issued, to ensure that deadlines are not missed (refer to Chapter 13 for more about such communications). There will usually be a designated person who will be responsible for their correctness and timely issue and liaison with the compliance department (refer to Chapter 4) is necessary to ensure regulatory requirements have been met.

Good quality databases that process data quickly are also vital to maintaining customers' confidence in the competence and efficiency of the management company. Traditionally fund registers were held fund by fund, and an investor with holdings in three funds would have three different register entries; today it is more common to have a customer account per individual, which lists all their transactions with the management company and in its funds. These databases should be capable of yielding information on: investors in a certain area (to invite to a roadshow, for instance); investors of a certain age group (those due to retire, for instance, who could be sent details of a new retirement product) or by other common characteristics in addition to their buying and selling patterns.

It is advisable that such databases should also record details of how sales came about, in order to track the type of approach most likely to appeal to that individual (e.g. direct mail rather than personal call). Management groups that distribute their products through different sales channels will need to be able to identify which customer was reached by which channel, and which adviser or salesperson, in order to correctly track and pay commissions due. Financial advisers, in particular, can be sensitive if management companies send marketing materials direct to their client, in case the client buys direct and the adviser gets no commission; whereas, if the mailing information is sent to the adviser for him to send on to his clients, he can ensure that any purchases resulting from his mailing bring him commission income.

The different methods of distributing fund shares or units, and their implications, are reviewed in the next chapter.

Those who would like to test their grasp of the contents of this chapter should turn to the self-test questions at the back of the book.

NOTES

1. *Islamic Finance*, Philip Moore, Euromoney Books, London, 1997.
2. *European Fund Market Yearbook*, Feri Fund Market Information Ltd, London, 2003.
3. *The International Guide to Marketing Investment Funds*, Editor Tim Cornick, Finance and Investment Research Ltd, London, 2001.
4. The Vanguard Group® for the year 2001.

12

Fund Distribution

This chapter describes what fund distribution is, reviews the channels through which fund distribution can be done and the implications of using these different channels.

INTRODUCTION

Distribution is the means by which the product (i.e. fund shares or units) reaches the customer and describes the process by which the potential customers convert interest into an actual transaction – that is, how a sale is made. This is a vital process, since all the expenditure that may be made on advertising and marketing can be wasted if the potential customer finds the process of making a transaction difficult and time consuming and gives up. Much of the effort devoted to distribution is therefore designed to make the process of choice and transaction as easy as possible.

'Distribution channels' are the different routes that can be used by fund management companies to reach potential and existing customers. These channels can be broadly divided into 'direct' and 'indirect' as shown in Figure 12.1. Essentially direct distribution is where sales by the fund management company or its affiliates are made directly to the investor whereas indirect distribution occurs when distribution is done through a third, external, party.

Methods of direct distribution include using a team of salespeople employed by the management company or its parent or affiliate (for instance, an insurance company); selling through branch networks belonging to a parent or affiliated company such as a bank (very common in many countries) and direct marketing – the placing of advertisements to which investors respond, or use of Internet sites, for instance. Methods of indirect distribution include selling through financial advisers (e.g. stockbrokers, qualified financial advisers), through sales networks that are available for hire, or through fund supermarkets, discount brokers and introducers (see later). Table 12.1 summarises these.

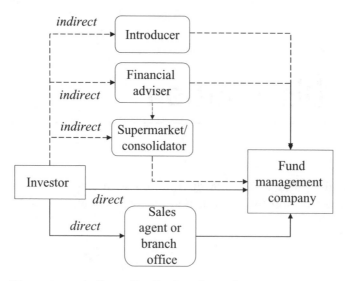

Figure 12.1 *Direct versus indirect distribution channels*

Table 12.1 *Summary of direct versus indirect distribution channels*

	Direct	Indirect
Type of distribution channel	Own or affiliated sales force Own or affiliated branch network Direct marketing	Independent financial advisers including stockbrokers, accountants, lawyers, private client bankers Sales networks Fund supermarkets Discount brokers Introducers

DIRECT SALES CHANNELS

The direct sales route establishes a direct relationship between the management company (often as an affiliated entity of a member of a larger group, e.g. a bank or insurance company) as promoter of the funds it manages and the customer. Direct routes to the customer have several advantages:

- They are within the control of the management company, which may be able to build a total picture of the customer's financial status.
- Quality control can be more readily ensured.

- They enable a continuous two-way relationship to be built with the customer, building customer loyalty.
- Cross-selling of new products may be easier.

There are three main variants of the direct distribution channel, which may be used in combination with each other, or indeed with indirect channels.

Salespeople

If the management company is part of an organisation that sells through a sales force, typically an insurance company, or if, less likely, it has its own dedicated sales force, then using this route may be a successful strategy. The advantages of control over the process of sales and the ability to determine to some extent the type of products being sold at any time in the cycle can be considerable. Also given that the sales force is often 'tied' to the management company and can only sell its products, without the need to mention competitive ones, the environment for sales is less sensitive to performance factors. The main disadvantage is that, unless the sales force is very large, the outreach and coverage that can be achieved may be limited.

Use of sales forces also carries some risk. There is the problem of high pressure selling which is particularly likely to arise if the sales force is remunerated only by commissions on sales: this can result in salespeople attempting to force people into buying, selling them unsuitable products or being driven to make exaggerated claims if they are desperate to make commission on a sale. There is also the possibility of fraud and theft by an individual salesperson, if they persuade the client to make payments directly to them personally. Lastly, funds will be competing with other products (for instance, life policies) for sales through the same channel and, where they pay lower commissions than other products, may not be sufficiently competitive to sell successfully.

The ability to distribute funds in this way may also be affected by law and regulations governing the practice of 'cold calling' – that is, telephoning or turning up in an office or home in person to sell fund shares or units without a prior invitation. This may be part of fund law and regulations but is more usually part of wider ranging laws.

Branches

Distribution through branch networks is typically the way that many 'universal' banks, which are involved in wider financial services, will distribute their fund and other products. Clearly a bank starts with the great advantage that it already 'owns' the branch customer and may have some considerable knowledge about the client's financial affairs (though data protection legislation may restrict cross-use of this). Furthermore most people place a fair amount of trust in their bank, believing it to be a solid and safe financial institution.

The disadvantage as far as the management company of a bank is concerned is that, unless that bank has a well thought out approach to the sale of wider financial services, staff at branches are not necessarily knowledgeable about non-banking products and may be nervous of encouraging customers to take money off deposit and of the risk of selling a customer a product which subsequently turns out to be unprofitable. Also, the expertise typically required of bank branch tellers does not include salesmanship, therefore specially designated and specially trained staff may be needed.

Given that customers may not wish to place all their financial affairs in the hands of one institution, some banks adopt a more open approach (known as 'open architecture') to their offering of non-banking financial products to their customers. Rather than offering only the non-bank products of the bank's own asset management or life assurance subsidiaries or associates, banks may offer their customers a range of competitors' products that they have researched and judged suitable.

Direct marketing and the Internet

Direct marketing is usually done through the placement of advertisements in print or broadcast media, the mailing of brochures advertising a fund or range of funds and offering of information on funds on fund management company Internet sites, with the buyer subscribing directly to the fund management company in response. In some countries it is possible to make sales 'off the page' by placing advertisements for funds with a coupon which can be clipped and sent to the fund management company with a subscription. However, many regulators now insist that any such sales must be made only on the basis of full prospectus information: this would mean including the prospectus content in the advertisement, which is usually considered too expensive. It is for this reason that most advertisements in printed media ask the reader to request a prospectus by mail or phone or via an Internet site from which it may be downloaded, rather than attempting to solicit an immediate direct purchase by sending in a coupon or making a telephone call.

The Internet is clearly a potentially valuable sales tool. Potential clients may be offered a large amount of information about the management company and its products, as well as a full prospectus to be downloaded and an application form to be completed. However, a potential purchaser using the Internet will need to be knowledgeable, confident, self-motivated and feel that he does not need to seek advice. Even in the most developed financial markets, relatively small percentages of financial transactions take place in this way (for example, of people buying equity funds in the USA between June 2000 and May 2001, only 24% bought on-line[1]). Electronic signatures are now possible in some countries, but the potential for unregulated transnational advertising and transactions continues to cause concern to regulators: many fund management websites have mechanisms to filter out applicants from ineligible countries.

INDIRECT SALES CHANNELS

The indirect route to the customer has many advantages for a management company, among which are:

- Lower – and variable – cost, since the remuneration of the sales agent will be based only on successfully completed sales and there is no need to maintain costly salaried branch or sales force structures.
- A potentially very wide and diversified distribution base.
- The ability of the customer to seek independent advice can theoretically enable the adviser to select the most suitable investment from the whole range of products available in the market.

However, there are plainly some disadvantages:

- There is much less control over what is sold and how, since there is likely to be less loyalty and advisers may be obliged to offer the best product.
- The question of who 'owns' the customer – that is, the management company or the intermediary (the intermediary will certainly think that it is him or her). This is particularly true in the case of sales channelled through fund supermarkets or consolidators, which hold sub-registers, as a result of which the management company may not have a record of the name of the end customer at all.
- A much more performance and service conscious environment, since all competitors will be targeting the same range of outlets, which are professional and therefore more demanding.
- The cost of servicing and paying commissions to the agents.

The three main channels of indirect distribution are outlined below.

Independent financial advisers

These are firms or individuals who advise their clients on how to invest their money and who may recommend the products of a management company only amongst a range of other investment products. They are differentiated from sales forces, which are tied to the management company or the bank or insurance company that owns them and which can generally only offer a single proprietary range of products, in that they advise on making a choice from a wide range of products and product providers. They generally work with their clients to put together a total financial plan, which may include mortgages, pensions, life assurance and investments; thus their purchases of funds are made in the context of a portfolio of products.

Clients of financial advisers are often wealthy and thus the average size of their purchases may be larger. Some advisers also offer managed portfolios, using collective investment funds as the base, and therefore are able to place substantial sums with the management company or fund of their choice.

Within the general category of these advisers one may include stockbrokers who offer services to private clients; private banks, which offer management services to wealthy individuals and lawyers and accountants that offer financial advisory services. These advisers are often remunerated by commission on fund sales paid to them by the management company concerned, rather than by a fee paid by the client to the adviser for their services.

Most management companies would expect the cost of paying commissions to these advisers to be covered by the initial charge; however, many management companies are now prepared to pay a continuing commission (known as 'trail' or 'renewal' commission) to advisers so long as their clients remain invested. In some countries, the cost of paying this trail commission is borne by the management company out of its annual management fee, while in others it may be possible to charge this to the fund. In some regimes, if a management company is prepared to pay a commission on a fund when there is no initial charge then the regulator may permit a management company to recoup the cost of this over time by making a charge to the fund on the basis that it is in the interests of share or unitholders generally for the fund to remain an expanding fund, so there is some justification for charging the cost of the continuing commission to the fund. If the regulator does not permit this, then the cost will need to be borne by the management company out of its own revenues.

In either case the payment will need to be terminated once the share or unit holding to which it refers has been redeemed, since neither would it be regarded as fair for the fund to continue to bear the cost of maintaining a holding which was no longer present, nor would a management company wish to continue to pay for a loyalty which no longer holds. This creates added complexity and cost for any administration system.

Not only does the cost of paying and administering commission to intermediaries tend to increase and become more complex, as discussed above, but also the payment of commission leads often to accusations of potential bias in favour of those funds or management companies that are prepared to pay the highest commissions. This commission bias is perhaps the greatest disadvantage of this sales route when compared with direct channels of distribution.

There are some strong arguments in favour of a financial adviser charging his client a fee for both initial and ongoing advice just as any other professional such as a lawyer or an accountant would. While this clearly removes the potential for a commission bias, and might even be popular with some clients, there are indications that people may not be prepared to pay a realistic level of fees: research from the UK indicates that investors would be willing to pay only between around $15 and $300 per hour, with the average at $105, when actual costs are in the range of $180 to $375.[2] Some advisers offer their clients the choice: they can either pay a fee or allow the adviser to be remunerated by commission.

It is worth noting that financial advisers increasingly deal in funds through consolidators (refer to Chapter 10) or fund supermarkets (see below) which offer the advantage of greatly simplifying transactions both for financial advisers and management companies – in the UK it is thought that around 15% of fund sales through independent financial advisers are transacted through supermarkets currently. These supermarkets are Internet-based services offering their clients information on and dealing in the funds that subscribe to their services, through a single Internet-based customer account. In the case of advisers, the supermarket will in effect hold a sub-register for each adviser of all the holdings of that adviser's clients transacted through them, which means that fund management companies increasingly have no knowledge of the 'end client'. Supermarkets also have the advantage that they 'net out' all buy and sell transactions each day so only a single clearing transaction is needed from or to the financial adviser and from and to the management company; they also calculate and advise management companies of commissions due to advisers on their supermarket-based transactions. Interestingly, however, the cost of provision of the supermarket's services is often met not by the adviser or the client but by the management company, which pays trail commissions to the supermarket or consolidator and to the adviser too. This can mean that up to 50% of the annual fund management fee may be paid out to these distribution channels in fees.

Sales networks

These may be described as similar to direct sales forces, but they are sales forces which are not tied to any one provider and which are therefore for rent. They share some of the characteristics of direct sales forces but also some of those of independent advisers. Consisting of a large force of often self-employed salespeople paid by commission only, their organisers may choose to market and sell a selected range of products directly to individuals. If these products are chosen by reason of their suitability and value for the customers of the direct sales organisation then they have the characteristics of an independently advised product, but the dangers of commission bias are also present, since clearly it may be highly advantageous for a management company to ensure that its product is included in the range of products available to a large sales force with national coverage and capable of generating substantial sales. Here again the problem of competitiveness of commission rates payable on different products may affect sales.

Fund supermarkets

Fund supermarkets offer clients, through a single Internet-based client account, information on and dealing in a selection of funds from different fund management companies (who subscribe to their service), showing comparable prices across the range, and using a centralised uniform administration system. Essentially fund supermarkets can be divided into those which enable transactions only on 'business-to-business' terms (known as 'B2B' – that is, dealing between financial advisers or sales networks and fund management companies) or on 'business-to-consumer' terms (known as 'B2C' – that is, dealing between fund management companies and retail customers) or both. Where the supermarket is B2C, the funds offered to the public are often no-load, or sometimes low load, with the supermarket taking an initial as well as a trail commission on the low load funds.

Such supermarkets often offer their own 'wrappers', that is tax-privileged envelopes within which shares or units in funds can be held (such as Individual Savings Accounts or 'ISAs' in the UK, refer to Chapter 16), which may be useful both to advisers and to direct retail customers.

The way supermarkets charge for their services varies in different countries, but they may:

- Charge the retail clients a set fee for operating an account for them, often scaled by the amount invested through that account.
- Charge a flat fee per transaction by a retail customer.
- Take an initial and/or a trail commission from the fund management company.

Discount brokers

Discount brokers originated in the USA. They mostly facilitate transactions for self-directed investors (that is, non-advised sales) and, as such, compete with B2C supermarkets. They give a wide range of information about the funds in which they offer dealing, as well as offering dealing facilities.

Most discount brokerages are Internet-based and permit investors to buy funds with no initial charges (no load) or at low commission rates that they have negotiated with fund management companies; they may also take trail commissions from fund management firms.

It is something of a mystery why – as happens in the UK, for instance – retail customers persist in buying funds with high initial charges directly from management companies when they could buy them more cheaply through fund supermarkets or discount brokers.

Introducers

The other way through which funds can be distributed is using so-called 'introducers'. These are people or organisations that 'introduce' business to a fund management company, but who do not act as advisers on the resulting transaction and are not usually involved in the transaction either. These introducers are often paid a commission (usually a smaller one than that paid to salespeople or financial advisers, who are involved in more work) for successfully bringing business to a firm. Examples of these introducers include 'affinity groups' such as clubs or societies, who may send mailings to their members introducing a fund management firm or a fund, for instance. Introducers are not usually required to be licensed or authorised by a regulator since they have no advisory role and the potential subscriber and the fund management company take responsibility for decision making.

Use of multiple distribution channels

Few fund management companies distribute their products through only one sales channel, though many may distribute preponderantly through one. A key factor will be the ownership of such companies – where the owner has existing distribution, it is likely that this will be the predominant channel to be used.

In general, 'independent' fund management firms (that is, those that are not part of diversified financial group) have tended to sell more through financial advisers or through direct marketing since often they lack access to the major distribution networks, which tend to be controlled by banks or insurers (this was a common early problem for foreign fund management companies entering Continental European markets, where distribution was until the 1990s almost totally bank dominated). This is something that may well change if 'open architecture' becomes more common: such management companies could then sell more through banks, for instance.

Some fund management companies may be established simply to enhance exploitation of an existing distribution system – for instance, those created by retailers or supermarkets with pre-existing branch networks and established brands – so largely exploit this route. Traditionally bank and insurance owned management companies tended to sell their products through their branches or sales forces; however, in recent years they have increasingly been selecting products from a panel of providers that they offer either in competition with their own products, or alongside those products in order to offer a more complete range ('open architecture').

There are complexities to servicing more than one distribution channel, particularly where a management company sells through financial advisers but also wishes to sell direct to the public. In the former case, an initial charge will be needed to motivate advisers; but in the latter case, offering funds with no (or a low) initial charge would be more attractive. The adviser will rarely be happy to find a management company undermining his potential commission-earning capacity by advertising to encourage investors to apply more cheaply direct to the management company and may threaten to take his business elsewhere.

TRENDS IN DISTRIBUTION

It might be expected that as consumers become more sophisticated in financial matters and as financial education increases, that the need for advice as to which product to choose might reduce, and that sales direct to consumers might therefore increase. However, this does not appear to hold true: possibly because the proliferation of products, whose complexity is also increasing, is making choice more rather than less difficult for consumers – or perhaps simply because people value personal contact and advice. For example, a study of the trends in mutual funds in the USA in the 1990s[3] shows that new sales direct to investors of long-term funds[4] fell from 23% in 1990 to 18% in 1999, with new sales made through a third party or intermediary rising from 77% to 82% in the same period. The same study notes that during this period many direct marketed funds turned from traditional direct marketing (representing 62% of new sales in 1990 but only 43% of new sales in 1999) towards third-party distribution channels (intermediaries of various kinds) instead. However, they tended to use the 'non-traditional' third-party channels which expanded during the 1990s: that is, employer-sponsored pension plans (in 1999 more than three-fifths of all fund owners held fund shares in defined contribution plans[5]); fund supermarkets, which started in 1992 in the USA; mutual fund 'wrap programmes', where advice and assistance is provided for an individual on an asset-based rather than front-end load fee, fee-based advisers and variable annuities.

Advised retail sales of funds in the UK have also been increasing as a percentage of total retail sales in recent years, reaching 89% in 2002[6]; however, it is worth noting that direct sales often are stronger when equity markets are performing well and fall off when markets are depressed.

The trend towards electronic rather than paper-based dealing in funds, is strengthening: in the UK it is estimated that this could cut costs substantially where a centralised system is used – but the cost of developing systems to accept such orders can be high if done on an individual company basis and if links are needed between an electronic system at a supermarket and an electronic system at the fund management company or its third-party service provider.

REGULATORY ASPECTS

The degree to which distribution of funds is regulated varies from country to country. The most common principles of such regulation are that:

- The entity which is the originator and primary distributor of the funds (that is, the fund management company) should be licensed before it markets any funds.
- Those who sell funds or advise which ones to select should have appropriate competence, be honest and possibly specifically licensed.
- The issuers of fund marketing materials (the fund directors or management company) must take responsibility for their completeness, accuracy and content.
- The employers of employed or tied sales agents must take responsibility for their conduct.
- The content of sales and marketing materials should be accurate and not misleading.
- Investors should receive sufficient information about a fund to make an informed choice.
- The way salespeople or advisers represent a fund or funds should not be inaccurate or misleading.
- The status of the person selling or advising on a fund should be clear (that is, they are commissioned salespersons or representatives promoting certain products only, or are competent to give financial advice across a range of products); some regimes also require a statement of the amount of commission payable to the advisers or salesperson to be made to the client prior to the transaction.
- Where advice is given as to which fund or funds to invest in, that the advice should be based on knowledge of the customers' financial position and appropriateness of the fund or funds for their needs.

- The basis of fund performance should be made clear and only fair and relevant comparisons with other funds or investments should be made (see Chapter 6).
- Any right to withdraw from or cancel a transaction should be made clear.

Regulatory aspects – selling direct

There are a number of regulatory issues that arise from direct sales. The first and most important is the responsibility for the conduct of employed or commissioned salespeople, whether they are part of a dedicated sales force or are located in a branch. Here most regulators require the management company to accept full responsibility for all the actions of those who have direct contact with customers, who give them advice or accept orders to make transactions on their behalf. Sometimes there is a requirement that training is given or that salespeople are required to pass an external or an internal examination to establish their knowledge and competence. In order to be able to identify individuals for regulatory purposes, often the regulator will require the names of accredited salespeople to be supplied to it, so that it can track those who may have been censured or dismissed by one management company if and when they reappear in another one. This does not imply that the regulator needs to license such individuals, since that would shift responsibility for their misbehaviour from the company that employs them to the regulator itself, a responsibility many regulators might not wish to assume.

Another set of issues arises from the timeliness, content, quality and extent of information that must be provided to a potential customer before purchase of shares or units of a fund directly from an advertisement in the media or across the Internet. The Internet in particular, given its global reach, will need to be the subject of co-operation between regulators worldwide. As an example, the EU has taken a pragmatic line and has ruled that advertising of funds on the Internet is subject to the advertising regulation of the country in which the management company holds its primary license, with the home country regulator taking responsibility for its compliance with domestic rules, even if the other EU countries, in which clients may reside, have different or additional rules relating to advertising and distribution.

In order to ensure that purchasers have had all the necessary information to enable them to make an informed decision, many regulators require that an application form is bound into a prospectus and can thus only be used if it is physically detached from it; this ensures that any purchasers have held a copy of the prospectus even if they have not read it. Some management companies will go further and require purchasers to sign a statement that they have read and understood the terms of the offer as contained in the prospectus. In the case of direct sales, when the customer may have been subject to some heavy persuasion, some regulators require a period of 'cooling off' during which investors are entitled to withdraw from the transaction or a 'cancellation period' during which they can exit the fund (refer to Chapter 10).

Regulatory aspects – indirect distribution

In the case that a professional intermediary or sales network is interposed between the management company and the customer, it will be the intermediary or network which is licensed and regulated; the management company will not have to take responsibility therefore for the way in which the business is conducted, as it will if the transaction is carried out by a direct employee or by a sales force employed by or solely contracted to it. The intermediary in this case is the agent of the client for whom the agent should be obliged to try to do the best deal.

The intermediaries of the type that typically advise clients to buy collective investment funds and undertake transactions on their behalf, described above, will be licensed either under the regime which applies to broker-dealers or, sometimes, a regime which specifically covers advisers on investments and financial planning; some may be members of professional bodies that regulate their conduct, such as chartered accountants or lawyers. The following aspects of their activities in relation to the distribution of collective investment funds are usually of interest to regulators:

- The competence of their managers and staff.
- The quality and impartiality of their advice.
- The timeliness, quality and clarity of the information they give to clients.
- If permitted to handle client money, the arrangements for ensuring that it is kept clearly separate from the advisers' own.

SUPPORTING DISTRIBUTION CHANNELS

It is important to remember that each distribution channel will require support from the fund management company. Financial advisers, salespeople, fund supermarkets and discount brokers all will essentially be 'customers' of the fund management company (as are direct investors) in terms of their need to be serviced with information, enquiry facilities, publications, transaction documentation, transaction support, etc. – and of course efficient calculation and payment of commission due will also be important for these channels.

There will usually be separate teams supporting work with different distribution channels – for instance, a team working with financial advisers, probably divided into geographic regions; a team servicing the sales force, probably also divided into geographic regions; and another group working with direct retail customers, often supported through a national customer service call-centre; etc. A separate team will also support sales to the institutional market (refer to Chapter 11).

Each team will have targets for new sales for each year or maybe per fund launch. The efficiency of such teams and their communication with other parts of the management company is crucial – the launch of a good product can be badly affected by problems such as the lack of literature availability; inability to deal on a supermarket due to failure to sign the new fund up; the failure to process an avalanche of applications by the closing date for an initial offer; or the failure to answer questions about commissions payable on differential subscriptions.

It cannot be stressed enough that each distribution channel needs advertising support too. All other things being equal, an investor, whether investing via an adviser, a fund supermarket or a salesperson, is more predisposed to buy a fund if it is from a provider that they have heard of than if it is from one that they have never heard of (which does not inspire confidence, as a general rule – 'If they're so good how come I haven't heard of them?').

The next chapter moves on to look at typical communications with fund investors, both before and after they enter the fund, and why regulation establishes certain basic requirements.

Those who would like to test their grasp of the contents of this chapter should turn to the self-test questions at the back of the book.

NOTES

1. *Mutual Fund Fact Book 2002*, ICI, Washington, 2002.
2. *Polarisation: Consumer Research*, Financial Services Authority, London, January 2002.
3. *Perspective*, **61**(3), ICI, Washington, July 2000.
4. Equity, bond and hybrid funds.
5. *Perspective*, **61**(3), ICI, Washington, July 2000.
6. December 2002 statistics, IMA, London.

13

Fund-related Communication

INTRODUCTION

Having looked at typical marketing activities and the distribution channels through which funds are sold, this chapter moves on to look at how fund management companies typically communicate with potential and existing fund investors and at the regulatory requirements that often are imposed upon such communications.

It is easy for people to lose confidence in fund management firms or funds if information they receive is incomplete, unreliable or late; equally, unsophisticated investors can be lulled into a false sense of security by fund management companies making misleading claims or being economical with the truth – and there is a potential incentive for them to do this if it will attract more money under management from which more fees will be earned. The whole area of communication between fund management firms and potential or existing investors therefore is one to which regulators pay a lot of attention.

There are a wide variety of forms of communication between fund management companies and fund investors, which can be broken down into four different categories:

- Mandatory communications required by regulation: these are established in order to ensure that investors are given sufficient reliable and accurate information to make an informed investment choice, and having made that choice, are given timely information about the results of their investment.
- Voluntary communications designed to keep customers informed.
- Dealing with customer enquiries and complaints.
- Sales and promotional messages, which are covered in Chapter 11.

The first three categories are addressed in this chapter. All these communications – even those that are not mandatory – are affected by requirements of fund law and regulation; whose key aim is to ensure that materials are accurate and not misleading and to maximise comparability, in order to facilitate informed choices.

In developed fund markets, investors can also obtain a wide variety of other information and opinions about funds and their management companies from newspapers, newsletters, magazines, books, programmes and websites; trade associations of funds also offer generic explanatory literature and provide statistics; and regulators may also provide generic information and guidance about what funds are and how to select a fund to meet specific needs. Such information is, in general, harder to find and more expensive to obtain in emerging markets where access to information may be jealously guarded, regulatory disclosure requirements relatively weak and access to the public through the media may be restricted or biased by vested interests. This is a considerable barrier to fund development, since quick, cheap and easy access to reliable and clear information helps to build investor confidence.

There are some general principles that should be applied to all customer communications in relation to funds:

- Always assume the reader is someone who knows nothing about financial matters – never use jargon, or if it must be used, explain each term it or provide a glossary.
- All communications should be clear and simple – if necessary, test them on friends or relations who do not work in the financial sector to see if they are comprehensible.
- All materials should be consistent with the relevant brand; a style should be set for each communication (e.g. annual report, newsletter) and consistently followed.
- Maximum use should be made of graphics, which many people find communicate more, more accessibly, than paper than pages of prose.
- The contact details of the fund and the management company should always be included and easy to find.
- Materials should always be clearly dated.
- Samples should always be maintained for the files for future reference, as should evidence supporting information given.
- As fund investors tend to be older and their sight is more likely to be impaired, use reasonably large and clear typefaces which strongly contrast with the background (reversed out typefaces on pale grounds may be artistic but they are not easy to read).

RESPONSIBILITY FOR COMMUNICATIONS

Responsibility for the correctness of documents – such as prospectuses or annual reports and accounts – and their compliance with regulation will lie with different organisations and individuals, depending upon the legal structure of the fund. Usually responsibility will lie with the directors of a corporate fund or with the fund management company or even a combination of the two.

It is usual to appoint a person to be responsible for overseeing production of investor communications on behalf of the management company; that person may also be required to check that such communications comply with regulatory requirements, to sign off to this effect and to ensure that the document has been cleared by the regulator where this is required. Co-ordination will be required between this person and the administration department or registrar who deals with despatch of mandatory information to fund investors and careful attention will be needed to ensure that regulatory deadlines for despatch of such data are met.

MANDATORY COMMUNICATIONS

The precise nature and content of documents required by regulation to be provided to investors will vary from country to country. Table 13.1 summarises those communications usually required by regulation, the general principles as to their content and timing of provision or publication and the general nature of responsibility for such communications.

Table 13.1 *Mandatory communications and associated requirements*

Type	Content	Timing	Responsibility for content
Prospectus (or 'key features' or 'scheme particulars' or 'short form prospectus' document)	To be accurate and complete and not misleading All information needed to make an informed investment choice Risk warnings Subscription and contact details	Required to be offered (or actually given, in some regimes) to investor prior to investing Required to be updated annually for open-ended funds; or if material change occurs	Corporate fund: directors of the fund Trust fund: management company or management company and trustee Contractual fund: management company or management company with depositary

(continues overleaf)

229

Table 13.1 (*Continued*)

Type	Content	Timing	Responsibility for content
Annual report and accounts	Audited accounts giving true and fair view of gains, losses, expenses and income Fund performance Distributions made Reports of board (corporate fund only), manager, trustee or depositary and auditor Current portfolio and changes in period Outlook for fund Contact details Previous year's comparative figures	Required to be published in mass media or mailed to investors each year usually within four months of financial year end	Corporate fund: directors of the fund Trust fund: management company or management company and trustee Contractual fund: management company or management company and depositary
Semi-annual report and accounts	Covers first six months of financial year Similar to annual report but briefer Accounts are unaudited	Required to be published in mass media or mailed to investors each year usually within two or three months of end of first half of financial year	As for annual report
Net asset value or price per share or unit	Fund contact details plus share or unit prices and/or NAV and charges	Required to be published daily for open-ended funds, whenever NAV is calculated for interval funds, and weekly, monthly or quarterly for closed-ended funds	Corporate fund: directors of the fund Trust fund: usually management company Contractual fund: usually management company

Prospectus requirements

A prospectus is primarily a legal document and as such is both restricted as to its content and expensive to amend. Many fund management companies therefore produce additional fund marketing literature, separately from the prospectus, because this allows greater freedom of expression (perhaps an unduly tactful way of saying a stronger sales pitch!) and can be updated more quickly and less expensively.

Regulation usually states that the prospectus:

- Must be accurate, complete and not misleading.
- Must contain a certain amount of required minimum information and may not omit any of that information.
- Must not contain other matters than those required by regulation.
- Must either be approved by the regulator prior to use or must be filed with the regulator; as must any adjustments to it.
- Must be made available free of charge.
- Must be offered or given to the potential investor before a sale is made.

A summary of typical required contents for fund prospectuses is given in Table 13.2. Sometimes regulation also establishes liability on the board of directors for corporate funds, and the fund management company or the fund management company and trustee for trust funds and the management company or management company or depositary of contractual funds for any damage caused to investors by inaccurate or misleading statements or omissions.

In the case of open-ended or interval funds where sale of shares or units is ongoing, regulations usually require that the prospectus be updated at least annually (taking into account the previous year's audited results) or if any material change occurs or any new matter arises that affects existing or future investors in the fund. Some amendments may only be able to be made following a vote of fund investors (see later section on general meetings).

Risk disclosure in the prospectus

Risk disclosure increasingly is seen as a key element of prospectuses. Many attempts have been made to represent risk numerically (star ratings from one to five being an example), but it is very difficult to adequately convey the range and impact of the risk factors involved, which include the following:

- Potential fluctuations in the value of capital invested and/or in the amount of income earned, associated with the relevant asset classes.
- Foreign currency risk where a fund invests abroad.
- The impact of taxation or changes in taxation policy on the fund, fund assets or fund investors.

Table 13.2 *Summary of characteristic prospectus requirements*

	Closed-ended	Interval	Open-ended
Date of prospectus	✓	✓	✓
Name of fund[1] and its legal nature and authorisation	✓	✓	✓
Investment objective of fund and investment policy to achieve objective	✓	✓	✓
Permitted investments and borrowing powers, use of derivatives	✓	✓	✓
Risks associated with the nature of the fund and its investments and use of borrowing powers and derivatives	✓	✓	✓
Capital being offered, price, minimum investment, minimum and maximum sum to be raised	✓	✓	✓
Capital structure and life of fund, if limited; currency/currencies of issue	✓	✓	✓
Annual fees and costs payable by the fund, any caps on these, how and when these are to be levied (date or frequency, if levied on income or capital or both and the impact that this will have)	✓	✓	✓
Disclosure of interests of directors of corporate funds	✓	✓	✓
Statement that investors' liability is limited to their contribution to the fund	✓	✓	✓
Rights of investors to information and in relation to voting (for each share class in issue, if relevant)	✓	✓	✓
Circumstances in which the fund may be wound up	✓	✓	✓
The dates of the accounting year and any interim accounting periods and dates for distributions to be made	✓	✓	✓
For the management company: date of foundation, legal form, authorisation, country of incorporation, ownership, names of directors, issued capital, management of other funds, address, and details of contract including remuneration and reasons for termination	✓	✓	✓

Table 13.2 (*Continued*)

	Closed-ended	Interval	Open-ended
For the custodian, depositary or trustee: date of foundation, legal form, authorisation, country of incorporation, ownership and details of contract including remuneration and reasons for termination	✓	✓	✓
For the investment adviser if relevant: name, legal form, authorisation, connections with fund or management company, details of contract including remuneration and reasons for termination	✓	✓	✓
For the auditor: name and address	✓	✓	✓
For the registrar: name and address, details where register held and access to it	✓	✓	✓
Frequency and timing of fund valuation; basis to be used	✓	✓	✓
Impact of taxation on investors	✓	✓	✓
Amortisation of fund launch expenses	✓		
Pricing basis and how the share or unit price is calculated		✓	✓
How to subscribe for shares or units	✓	✓	✓
How to redeem shares or units or part of a holding		✓	✓
Application of any dilution levy		✓	✓
Entry and exit charges and any other sales-related charges, any maxima that apply, and how these are levied		✓	✓
Performance of the fund over a five-year period or since inception, whichever is shorter: including highest and lowest share or unit price per year		✓	✓

[1] Regulatory regimes may require that the name of a fund must be accurate and not misleading.

- The liquidity of assets which the fund will hold, which may be low when investing in small companies, for instance.
- The risks associated with investing in specific countries, e.g. the sustainability of legal rights.
- The volatility of markets or sectors or individual shares in which a fund invests.

- The use of derivatives that may reduce or enhance risk.
- The amount and method of borrowing the fund intends to utilise (this risk is usually associated with non-publicly offered funds and closed-ended funds which may have unlimited borrowing powers).
- The risks inherent in the structure of the capital of the fund, where this is complex (rights of different share classes over income or capital, etc.) or where there are sub-funds.

As a result, risk disclosure in prospectuses remains largely descriptive rather than graphic, though graphs are useful in illustrating volatility of the fund itself over stated periods.

Cost disclosure

In recent years there has been increasing focus on required regulatory disclosure of the cost of investing in a fund, which focuses upon:

- The total cost of a 'round trip' investment in a fund over a specified period (that is, including entry fee and cost of operation of fund over period and any exit fee): this is known in the USA as 'total shareholder cost' and in the UK is referred to as 'effect of expenses' and is illustrated in Table 13.3.
- The cost of remaining an investor in a fund for a year – that, is the fees paid for management and all other expenses paid by the fund in the period: this is usually referred to as a 'total expense ratio' or 'annual fund operating expenses' also illustrated in Table 13.3.
- The costs of entering or exiting a fund, also known as 'shareholder fees', also illustrated in Table 13.3.

These calculations are designed to enable investors to compare relative cost effectiveness of different funds. Essentially, the regulator requires an assumed rate of return to be used by all funds of the same type, and the most recent audited costs of the fund to be applied to each year of the calculation, over a specified period. (In the authors' view, it would be preferable for figures simply to be given over the last audited year's operation since firstly this is a real figure and secondly it does not entail any element of forecasting of both unknown future performance and unknown future cost.)

Short-form prospectus

Recognising that prospectuses have become very long and investors may be put off reading them (anecdotal evidence indicates that few investors ever actually read all of a prospectus), some regulators have started to permit use of an abbreviated prospectus, known as a 'short-form prospectus' or 'mini-prospectus', which must be consistent with the full prospectus and also must include information on how to obtain a copy of it.

Table 13.3 *Example of prospectus disclosure of 'total shareholder cost'*[1]

Let us say hypothetically that the fund's annual return is 5% and that the fund shareholder fees and annual operating expenses are as shown below. For every $10 000 invested, the table says how much would be payable in expenses over the period assuming the investment was made at the beginning, and redeemed at the end, of the period. Although actual costs may be higher or lower, based on these assumptions the investor's estimated expenses would be:

Period	Effect of all charges, fees and expenses
1 year	$547
3 years	$754
5 years	$977
10 years	$1617
Shareholder fees	
Entry fee (front-end load, initial charge)	Maximum 4.5%
Maximum deferred sales charge	None
Maximum sales charge on reinvested dividends	None
Redemption fee (back-end load, exit charge)	None
Total expense ratio (annual operating expenses)	
Annual management fee	0.52%
Other expenses	0.45%
Total annual operating cost	0.97%

[1] Loosely based on the US model illustrated in *A Guide to Understanding Mutual Funds*, Investment Company Institute, Washington.

In some countries models of prospectuses and mini-prospectuses are created by the regulator and must be used; within Europe a standard model mini-prospectus for funds investing in different asset classes has been created and can be found on FEFSI's website (www.fefsi.org).

Requirements for annual reports and accounts

The annual report and accounts is the fund's document of record as to its progress over the accounting period, as it is for any business. While there are many regulatory requirements governing its content, it is also the document of record as to how the fund manager has performed, so merits due attention. Investors' confidence can be much improved if the reasons for good or bad performance and investment policy in the future are clearly and succinctly explained – fund managers who can communicate effectively as well as performing well have a double value!

The essence of an annual report is that it should tell the fund investor (exactly as it would tell a shareholder in a company) what has been happening over the previous year – how the money they have invested has been used, and what results it has achieved. It must include audited accounts for the fund, which usually have to comply with a fund-specific set of accounting rules (see Chapter 15 for more details). As a general rule, a fund's annual report and accounts has to include the information laid out in Table 13.4.

Explanations and examples of the annual report sections identified in italics in Table 13.4 can be found in Chapter 15 on accounting.

The regulator will usually establish requirements for how the performance of the fund over the last five years of the fund is shown – most commonly, as the percentage rise or fall in the value of a share or unit in the annual financial accounting period – and how the table of distributions is shown (this varies enormously from country to country largely due to different taxation requirements).

Table 13.4 seeks to highlight the main components of fund reports and accounts, but each regulatory regime will have its own requirements: for instance, in some jurisdictions a fund may have to show what percentage of its transactions by value were undertaken through each of its major brokers.

The report and accounts is required to be signed off by the directors of a fund, if present, or one or more directors of the management company.

Requirements for semi-annual report and accounts
The half-yearly report and accounts contains broadly the same information as that given in the annual report and accounts, with less detail in some areas, but only covers the first six months of the financial year with a comparison with the same period of the previous year: it is not required to be audited.

Use of the report and accounts
Regulation generally requires that a copy of the annual and semi-annual report and accounts:

- Is filed with the regulator.
- Is sent to every investor in the fund.
- Is sent to any potential investor who requests it.
- Is offered to those who request a copy of the prospectus of the same fund.

In recent years, regulators have started to permit the production of 'short-form' accounts, which are summaries of the main report and accounts, since – again – evidence indicates that few investors will slog through full reports and accounts. The short form of accounts is particularly useful where a fund has many sub-funds or sub-portfolios which each have to be accounted for.

Table 13.4 *Required contents of a fund's annual report and accounts*

	Closed-ended	Interval	Open-ended
Name of fund, authorised status, investment objective	✓	✓	✓
Names and contact details of fund management company; custodian, trustee or depositary; investment adviser; auditor; lawyer; registrar and their authorised status where relevant	✓	✓	✓
Investment report from management company (commentary on the past year and investment outlook, how investment objective was fulfilled)	✓	✓	✓
Statement of responsibilities of directors, management company, auditor and depositary or trustee	✓	✓	✓
Report of auditor and depositary or trustee	✓	✓	✓
Statement of total return	✓	✓	✓
Statement of movement of shareholders' or unitholders' funds[1]		✓	✓
Portfolio statement[2]	✓	✓	✓
Balance sheet	✓	✓	✓
Total expense ratio	✓	✓	✓
Summary of portfolio changes[3]	✓	✓	✓
Statement of accounting policies[4]	✓	✓	✓
Detailed notes giving the figures underlying items in italics above	✓	✓	✓
Distribution table	✓	✓	✓
Statement of net asset value per share or unit and number of shares or units in issue at the beginning and end of the accounting period	✓	✓	✓
Performance of the fund in each of the last five calendar years or since inception, whichever is earlier	✓	✓	✓
Highest and lowest price per unit or share in each of the last five calendar years or since inception, whichever is earlier, and distributions paid in each year	✓	✓	✓

[1] Closed-ended funds' capital is fixed so there is no movement in holders' funds.

[2] List of each asset held by the fund usually categorised by asset class, region, country or sector and sometimes by liquidity (listed and traded versus non-listed and untraded), giving the percentage of the total portfolio each represents.

[3] Usually shown as a list of sales, with value per asset sold and a list of purchases, with value per asset bought; often reflects only larger (rather than all) transactions.

[4] This will refer to the requirements of the accounting standards governing the accounts.

Anyone with a professional interest in fund reports and accounts who does go through the entire document can derive a lot of interesting information from them, however: for example the portfolio turnover of a fund can be calculated if the total value of asset sales and purchases is given.

Requirements for the disclosure of net asset value or price per share or unit

This disclosure is required in order that investors can easily check either the current value or price of their shares or units, or obtain guidance on what price they are likely to have to pay if they want to buy shares or units. These values and prices are also tracked by fund performance measurement houses and used in their calculations. Usually they are printed in newspapers, in a special section and they are often displayed on websites of fund management houses, fund data providers and supermarkets.

Whether a fund discloses net asset value per unit or share, or price per unit or share, or net asset value and price per unit or share will depend on what type of fund it is and how it prices. A closed-ended fund will calculate net asset value per share, and its market price per share will also be disclosed, usually through the stock exchange on which it is listed. An interval or open-ended fund will calculate its net asset value per share or unit: if it is dual priced, it will add its charges to the net asset value and disclose its buying and selling prices, giving its entry charges separately as a percentage. If it is single priced, it will disclose a single price – in effect its NAV – with its entry charge disclosed separately, again as a percentage.

As a general principle, the net asset value or price of a fund share or unit is required to be published as often as it is calculated, as soon as possible after it has been calculated. An example of the disclosure of NAV and price disclosure for various types of funds is shown in Tables 13.5.–13.7.

Table 13.5 *Net asset value/price disclosure for single-priced open-ended or interval funds*

Fund	Basis	Time[1]	Initial charge	Single price	+/− on previous price
A	F[2]	12.00	3.5%	67.59 c	+3.64
B	F	16.00	3.5%	276.9 c	+10.60

[1] Time of valuation point.
[2] Forward price.

Table 13.6 *Net asset value/price disclosure for dual-priced open-ended or interval funds*

Fund	Basis	Time	Initial charge	Offer price	Bid price	+/− on previous price
A	F	12.00	5.25%	85.06 c	89.78 c	+2.57
B	H[1]	16.00	5.25%	68.31 c	72.10 c	+2.28

[1] Historic price.

Table 13.7 *Net asset value/price disclosure for a closed-ended fund*

Fund	Price[1]	+/− on previous price	52-week high price	52-week low price	Net asset value	Discount or premium (+)[2]
A	165.5 c	+1.5	235 c	148 c	184.9 c	10.5%
B	279.5 c	+0.5	409 c	244 c	318.5 c	12.2%

[1] Closing mid-price.
[2] Premium is the difference between the market price and the NAV expressed as a % of NAV where the price is higher than NAV, discount is the difference between the market price and NAV where the price is lower than NAV.

VOLUNTARY COMMUNICATIONS

An enormously wide variety of sales and promotional communications are used in relation to investment funds. A few are summarised here (advertising is covered in Chapter 11).

Newsletters

Management companies may choose to send out newsletters (or more rarely magazines) covering current investment issues and other information that they think will be of interest to investors, at regular intervals: these are increasingly being issued by email rather than by post (saving on post, paper and printing). These can also be used to advertise new products to existing investors.

Newsletters particularly tend to be used for communicating with financial advisers. Increasingly such information is being made available on closed-user groups within fund management company Internet sites or posted on websites with notifications being sent of such postings to interested users.

Yearbooks

This name is slightly misleading in that it implies that it is a status report or summary on a year. In fact, these publications are essentially annually produced mini-prospectuses for each and every (usually open-ended) fund in a fund management company's range, also covering performance, and including application forms and all information needed by a potential investor all bound into a single publication. These are particularly useful when the management company does not wish to advise investors which of their funds they should select: it can simply give them the yearbook for them to read and make their choice. For this reason, it is quite common to include decision-trees in such publications, which help investors to identify whether they need income, or growth, or both; what term they wish to invest for; and what level of risk they wish to accept, in order to find out which funds are most likely to be suited to their needs.

Websites

Websites are increasingly used by management companies not only to display information and enable comparisons between funds, but also to provide dealing in the funds offered by that company either on their own site, or through fund supermarkets (refer to Chapter 12): the latter appears to be more popular, probably because investors can handle all their investments and transactions through a single supermarket account and have access to a wider range of product information and choice. Actual dealing over the Internet may also be offered in some countries but will depend both on the level of security and on the ability to use electronic or digital signatures, which partly depends upon enabling legislation. It is quite common for an investor to have to open an account with a management company using a paper-based application and signature, but to be able to deal electronically or by phone thereafter subject to security precautions.

Factsheets

Many fund management companies' websites feature 'factsheets' on funds that are also available in printed form, which summarise key information about a single fund on a single page. These are useful references both for potential retail customers and for financial advisers.

Statements of account

Customer-facing databases enable fund management firms to send statements of account to their clients, usually half-yearly, which record the opening balance of funds held, all the transactions undertaken in the period (purchases, sales, payment of dividends, etc.) and the closing balance (similar to a bank statement). Including promotional literature on new funds within such mailings can be effective when customers are pleased with current results.

QUERIES AND COMPLAINTS

Dealing with queries

All fund management companies have to deal with a range of queries and complaints. As a general rule ordinary queries are dealt with by customer services divisions. These will cover a wide range of issues from whether people can invest for their children and how, to queries about taxation that may be levied and when dividends are payable. These queries can broadly be classed as administrative and can be dealt with separately to more serious complaints. It is good practice, however, to have deadlines within such queries should be answered; indeed, some companies set a series of standard response deadlines including the maximum number of rings on a telephone within which it should be answered.

One way of dealing with frequently asked questions is to prepare a standard list of the most common questions and their answers and print them so they can be sent out to all potential investors (known as 'FAQs'). It is generally worth logging common queries and their nature so that new materials or systems or procedures can include answers to them, or so that clear pointers are given as to where to find answers, to avoid such questions in future.

Keeping a log of queries also indicates, over time, whether certain queries are persistent, indicating that systems or procedural adjustments are needed to current practice or that more or clearer information is needed.

Dealing with complaints

Complaints are a complex area. Very broadly, these break down into two areas – complaints due to those errors or omissions or inefficiencies or deliberate malpractices which cause loss or damage; and complaints about similar problems, where no loss or damage has arisen. It is worth bearing in mind that regulators may be concerned about both: the first, because investors' interests have been damaged; the second because they are indicative of failings in management, systems or procedures.

At the very least, complaints should be seen as a form of feedback about the quality of the management company concerned and as an indication that systems, procedures or information provision could be improved. Bear in mind that time and effort taken to resolve complaints is costly and relatively unproductive; though there is some evidence that customers whose complaints are resolved satisfactorily are likely to be more loyal customers.

Some regulatory regimes set out procedures and deadlines for handling complaints, while others do not, so in practice dealing with complaints varies enormously. Where rules do exist, it is often a regulatory requirement that a complaints ledger must be established and each complaint, and how it was dealt with, by whom and by when must be entered into the ledger. The regulator may also require that the ledger is to be made available to it for inspection upon request. In addition, regulation may also establish a requirement that a person who has sufficient seniority to resolve complaints is put in charge, rather than junior personnel who lack the necessary authority to sort problems out or raise their implications at board level.

Regulators usually require that fund management companies identify the body responsible for regulating them on printed materials and letterheads, so that complaints about the management company (or other regulated service provider) can be addressed to the relevant organisation. It is usually a principle that a complaint should first be addressed to the organisation concerned; only if that firm fails to respond to the complainant's satisfaction within a reasonable period should the matter then be referred to the appropriate regulator or ombudsman (an ombudsman being an independent adjudicator that ombudsman scheme members pay for, and whose judgement they accept as binding). Regulators or ombudsmen may themselves provide public information advising people what they should expect from a regulated entity such as a fund management company and how to complain if things go wrong.

While many complaints may be administrative – failure to amend addresses, incorrect details on contracts, etc. – some will be more serious, where customers may have suffered a loss as a result of an error or omission. This can easily happen if an error has occurred in fund pricing, and investors have received too little upon redemption or paid too much upon subscription. Where such errors have minor impact – less than a half of 1% of the price, for instance – it is generally accepted that the cost of correcting the error is too high by comparison with the benefit of correcting it. However, errors of a larger amount than this will give rise to compensation being due to those who have suffered loss or damage. Other complaints may also give rise to compensation being payable: for instance, a misleading prospectus.

It is sensible for any fund management company to build into its procedures a series of cross-checks to try and avoid such errors arising: for instance, in common-sense terms, it should never be left to a single individual – who however good, may be off colour one day – to oversee all aspects of valuation and pricing.

WHO MANAGEMENT COMPANIES COMMUNICATE WITH

The distribution channels used by a fund management company will affect whom that company communicates with. Essentially, where the distribution is indirect (particularly when a financial adviser or supermarket or discount broker is involved – refer to Chapter 12) then the management company may not hold the personal details of the investor in the fund and communications will have to be channelled through the relevant financial adviser, supermarket or discount broker. From the management company's point of view, this reduces the work involved in communications with investors: although it is likely to be paying a trail fee to the financial adviser or supermarket to do this work instead. In general, financial advisers in particular are sensitive if fund management companies communicate directly with their clients (for instance, sending a special offer on a fund which is included in an annual report mailing) since this may be seen as 'going behind the adviser's back' in order to avoid paying out commissions on any resulting transactions.

Essentially, as far as financial advisers are concerned, they are the 'customer' of the fund management company; and their clients of course being to them, the financial adviser, and not to the management company.

Where communication is directly between the management company and the investor, then any correspondence will be despatched directly to the investor at the contact address recorded on the register. It is increasingly the norm to offer Internet-based rather than paper-based correspondence and documentation.

In the next chapter, the last on marketing-related issues, the considerations involved in meeting consumer needs for funds and fund-related services and products are elaborated.

Those who would like to test their grasp of the contents of this chapter should turn to the self-test questions at the back of the book.

14

Product Development

INTRODUCTION

This chapter looks at the considerations that have to be taken into account in creating new funds, or fund-related services, that management companies then market and distribute to potential investors, as covered in previous chapters.

The objective in creating the new product may be:

- To offer a fuller range of products to their clients.
- To meet a particular need that it is perceived exists or may exist.
- To exploit a new opportunity (for instance, a change in taxation).
- To ensure that they compete effectively with other fund management firms.

At rock bottom, the reason for product development is usually to earn more fees from attracting and managing more money, and therefore potentially enhance the profitability of the fund management company. Of course, a fund management company may choose to offer a new product that is unlikely to make a profit, because if they fail to offer it, business may go to competitors instead; but this should be a conscious decision rather than an unintentional outcome.

Traditionally product development in the investment fund sector is said to be either 'investment led' or 'marketing led'. 'Investment-led' development is where a new investment opportunity arises – for instance, in a new asset class or sector or country – and leads the product development process; whereas 'marketing-led' development seeks to identify investors' needs (for instance, for a high income) and create a product to meet it.

PRODUCT DEVELOPMENT IS DYNAMIC

Development of products takes place within a constantly changing environment. The main factors here are:

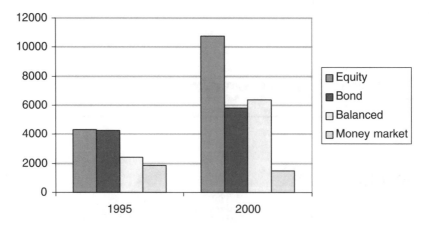

Figure 14.1 *Number of funds by type of assets: UCITS in Europe 1995–2000*
Reproduced by permission of FEFSI (the European Federation of Investment Funds and Companies).

- Consumer preferences that change with market movements, economic outlook, age and income.
- Legislative and regulatory policy where changes may affect not only funds, but also competitor products, how funds are sold (e.g. E-commerce) and who can sell them.
- Fiscal policy that may change the attractiveness of funds, fund 'wrappers' or potential fund assets as well as products which compete with funds.
- Competitive pressures which may derive from the public sector (where budgetary demands may drive governments into offering low-risk National Savings products paying high interest, for instance) as well as the private sector.

This changing picture can be made even more complex when a product is created with the objective of selling it across borders, since a wider variety of preferences and legal and fiscal frameworks will affect the potential for success. Figure 1.3 illustrates, for instance, the very different asset preferences that exist within the six largest domestic fund markets worldwide: these, it should be noted, are likely to be an outcome of fiscal regimes as well as relative risk tolerance, which in itself changes over time. As illustrated in Figure 14.1, a FEFSI[1] survey of the period 1995–2000 also illustrates rapid change that can take place in asset preferences as reflected in the funds being offered, with a 149% increase in the number of equity funds, a 36% increase in the number of balanced funds, a 122% increase in the number of bond funds and a 19% fall in the number of money market funds.

FUND INVESTMENT OBJECTIVES AND THEIR IMPLICATIONS

The investment objective of the fund and the assets that have to be bought to fulfil this objective will have a substantial influence on the way a fund product is structured. In general terms, there are three possible broad investment objectives:

- Providing income.
- Providing capital growth.
- Providing a mixture of the two.

However, over the years a vast number of broad and narrow subsets of these objectives have developed, each of which are described slightly differently from country to country. Table 14.1 seeks to summarise key examples of these broad categories.

'Capital protection' funds that are not money market funds usually offer investors a defined return in terms of capital; or possibly of capital and of income. In order to offer a defined return, the management company has to know for what specific period the money is to be invested, in order to identify which assets with matching maturities (i.e. bonds or derivatives) can be bought and what return can be offered. Such funds therefore have to be able to accept money and pay it out only at defined times, if they are to be able to offer certainty. This is impossible with an open-ended fund where investors can enter and exit every day, so these funds are usually formed as interval or limited or closed-ended funds (in the USA 'unit investment trusts' are used for this purpose, for instance, being fixed term, fixed portfolio funds).

Table 14.1 *Fund objectives and categories*

Objective	Broad categories
Income	Immediate income – usually investing in government (lower risk to capital, lower income) or corporate bonds from high grade (medium risk to capital, medium income) to junk (potentially high risk to capital, high income) Growing income – usually investing in equities
Growth	Capital protection – usually investing in money market instruments, or combinations of bonds and derivatives Capital growth – usually investing in equities; may aim for cautious (lower risk to capital, lower growth potential) through to aggressive growth (high risk to capital, high growth potential)
Balanced	Income and capital growth – usually investing in a mixture of government or corporate bonds and equities

There is a great debate about the use of terms such as 'guaranteed' or 'capital protected' in relation to funds. Regulatory interpretations may vary, but if a fund is said to be 'guaranteed' it is generally construed that at a minimum the amount invested is guaranteed to be repaid or that a defined level of income will be paid during the life of the fund. Usually any such guarantee is required to be given by a third party other than the fund management company. A variant of a guarantee is where a guarantee of capital or income is linked to the performance of a benchmark, such as a stock market index: investors may not understand, however, that if the benchmark fails to meet predefined targets this will modify or invalidate the guarantee, so this needs careful explanation.

Beyond the broad categories outlined in Table 14.1, there are further subsets of fund categories, most of which fall within the 'growth' objective. These include:

- Indexed funds: where the assets of the fund are invested in a portfolio of shares which seeks to replicate a stated stock (or bond) market index; or the fund buys derivatives based on a stated stock market index (note: these are not the same as exchange traded funds or 'ETFs', see below).
- Regional funds: these invest in a specific continent such as Asia or Europe, or a region within a continent, such as Central Europe.
- Country funds: these invest in a specific country such as Japan or South Africa.
- Themed funds: these are funds which invest within a certain sector, such as energy or healthcare, for instance; or only in large, or medium, or small companies; or in emerging markets; or in environmentally friendly companies or in companies with high ethical standards of business (investing in these last two groups is sometimes characterised as 'socially responsible investment' or 'SRI': whereby investment management policy takes into account the impact on society of the issuers in whose securities funds invest).
- Funds of funds: these are funds which invest only in other funds, which may be managed by the same management company or by different management companies (a point to watch is that regulators may ban or limit the potential for double charging at the overlying or underlying fund level for entry, annual and redemption fees). Multimanager funds are a variant on these whereby investment is not made in other funds, but portions of the fund's assets are handed over to different (usually external) managers to manage.
- Property or real estate funds: these are funds which invest either in the shares of companies involved in the property market; or in real estate itself (residential or commercial land or buildings), although some countries have separate legal and regulatory frameworks for the latter (for instance, American Real Estate Investment Trusts or 'REITs').

Considerations in developing fund ranges

Different fund management firms will take different views of the variety of funds that they should offer. A major financial institution that has many branches serving the mainstream retail market may well focus on a few, large funds (which have the benefit of maximising economies of scale for investors) with broad investment objectives: for instance, a money market fund and a bond and derivative-based fund for capital protection; a government bond fund for secure but lower income and low risk to capital; a corporate bond fund for higher income with more risk to capital; an equity income fund for higher income and higher risk to capital; a domestic equity tracker (index) fund for growth and a global equity tracker (index) fund, also for growth.

An independent fund management firm that sells its products primarily through financial advisers may feel the need to offer a larger number of funds that focus more narrowly – for instance, including regional or country funds or themed funds such as biotechnology – with a constant stream of new funds to keep these advisers interested. Alternatively, it may focus on offering funds within a specialist niche such as corporate bond funds worldwide.

At the other end of the scale is the fund management house that seeks only to attract institutional or professional investors, and therefore has to offer something that they are unlikely to be able to produce cost-effectively and successfully for themselves. Their focus might be emerging markets, for instance; or investing in a specific country or sector; or venture capital or private equity (see below).

It is worth bearing in mind that given that a high percentage of sales are likely to be of mainstream funds, the cost and benefit of developing specialised funds need to be considered carefully.

While mainstream retail funds are likely to be formed as open-ended funds, since these are easy to invest in and so appeal most to the public, more specialist funds may be formed as interval or closed-ended funds; while funds for the professional investor are commonly formed as partnerships (refer to Chapter three).

Some more esoteric fund types

A range of other funds also can be created which sometimes – but not always – can be made available to the general public, including those reviewed below. Their characteristics are summarised in Table 14.2.

Exchange traded funds ('ETFs')
ETFs are open-ended investment funds whose shares or units – unusually – trade like stocks, on an exchange. Therefore, like closed-ended funds, their shares or

Table 14.2 *Summary of main characteristics of more esoteric funds*

Fund	Legal structure	Operational structure	Exit route from fund
Exchange traded fund	Company or trust, listed on exchange	Open-ended	Sell on exchange or in specie redemption
Private equity	Limited partnership, limited liability company, may be listed	Closed-ended or interval	At end of fixed life, or at stated intervals, with notice: may have a 'lock in' period
Venture capital	Limited partnership, limited liability company, listed on exchange	Closed-ended	At end of fixed life or at stated intervals, with notice: may have a 'lock in' period
Hedge fund	Often limited partnership, not listed	Interval or closed-ended	Usually only at stated intervals, with notice: may have a 'lock in' period

units may trade at a premium or discount to net asset value though this is usually only small since new blocks of shares or units can be created or redeemed any day at net asset value also so differences are usually arbitraged out. These funds replicate domestic or international equity or bond indices, after which they are often named (e.g. SPDRS or 'spiders' which track the S&P 500). Their advantage is that since they are traded like stocks, they can be bought and sold at any time of the trading day and are subject to normal market orders (e.g. limit). They do not have initial charges (though brokerage is usually payable on purchases and sales) and as indexed funds their annual management costs are low.

Private equity funds
This term covers funds that invest in unlisted and untraded companies and may also invest in public companies that are going private. Characteristically these funds take larger stakes in companies than ordinary funds do, usually have a seat on investee companies' boards and are actively involved in the business decision taking of the companies in which they invest. There are a range of more specialist sub-categories into which such funds fall, the best known of which is possibly 'venture capital funds', which tend to focus on putting money into new – that is, start up – companies from which they hope to make high returns. Tax incentives

may be given to these funds to incentivise people to take on the high risk of financing 'the companies of tomorrow'.

It is common for managers of such funds to have a stake in the funds that they manage, and to be incentivised through performance fees or carried interests (whereby if certain performance targets are achieved, managers are awarded additional holdings in the fund).

Hedge funds

The term 'hedge fund' essentially refers to any investment vehicle that can exploit wider investment and borrowing powers than those permitted to on-shore publicly offered funds (refer to Chapter 5). Hedge funds' only restrictions on their investment strategies are those set out in their prospectuses so potentially in investment and borrowing terms they can:

- Invest in alternative assets such as currencies and commodities.
- Gear through unrestricted borrowing (borrowing of 10 times net assets is not uncommon).
- Use derivatives in any way they like.
- Have large exposures to single issuers.
- Go short (sell investments they don't own), which classical investment funds are not permitted to do.

Commonly they also have performance fees (based on a percentage of profits, often), managers may invest alongside investors, and investors are only able to exit at stated intervals (e.g. monthly or quarterly or annually).

Their greater investment flexibility can offer a greater probability that they will achieve their return targets: some are referred to as 'absolute return' vehicles in that they aim to give a specific annual return regardless of market indices, e.g. a target absolute return of 15%.

There has been much discussion about whether hedge funds should be permitted to be publicly offered, since they have been performing better than many classical investment funds during recent bear markets. However, this debate seems to lose sight of some salient points: firstly, that it is estimated by Tremont Advisers, hedge fund consultants, that 700 of the estimated 6000 hedge funds worldwide closed in 2002 and that 800 will close in 2003, which does not inspire confidence. Secondly, a recent study by Capco[2], a US services and technology solutions provider, of 100 such closures over a 20-year period indicated that 50% of hedge funds failed due to operational risk alone, rather than bad investment decisions (38% failed as a result of investment risk alone). The report also notes:

'Even more alarming was that of 'operational failures', misrepresentation (reports and valuations with false or misleading information), misappropriation of funds (fraud) and unauthorised trading were implicit in 85% of cases.'

Historically, only institutional investors and rich individuals have been exposed to these risks, where the level of exposure to hedge funds is probably low relative to their total portfolio. But is this an appropriate level of risk to which to expose ordinary investors, whose portfolios are smaller so more of their wealth is at risk and whose chances of understanding the risks involved are also rather less than those of institutional investors with legions of advisers at their heels?

Also, whereas ETFs, private equity and venture capital funds have similarly high disclosure standards to other publicly offered funds, hedge funds are not subject to any disclosure requirements other than those set by their prospectus, and are usually reluctant to disclose their portfolio positions. The requirements that serve to protect investors in publicly offered funds simply do not exist for hedge funds. If they are more widely offered, without being subject to at least some of the requirements imposed on publicly offered funds, it seems likely that disasters and loss of confidence could ensue.

This is not to say that there are not some very good, professionally managed hedge funds: there are. But how is the investing public to separate the sheep from the goats when disclosure is poor?

A recent IOSCO report[3] concluded that while there were various problems that would need to be dealt with (one of which being how to define a hedge fund), that if such funds were to be publicly offered – in this case, through funds of hedge funds – then improved disclosure and competence of management would be key.

FUND STRUCTURAL CHOICES

The legal and operational structures (refer to Chapter 3) and categories of fund that are able to be created in any one domicile will be dependent upon the legal framework of that country and the countries in which the fund is also to be sold. It is quite common for the widest variety of choice of structures to be available in the so-called 'offshore' domiciles such as Dublin, Luxembourg, Bermuda, Channel Islands, Cayman Islands, etc. However, if the fund is to be offered publicly the regulation of the chosen domicile will usually need to offer broadly equivalent investor protection to the market or markets in which the fund is to be sold. Despite the large numbers of funds domiciled in such 'offshore' centres, the majority of funds created for sale in a single domestic market are usually still domiciled in that country (this partly may be due to preferential tax treatment of domestic funds over foreign funds).

Legal and operational structures

Table 14.3 summarises the general range of fund structures that may be available though it would be unusual for all of these to be available in any one country

Table 14.3 *Possible fund legal and operational structures*

Legal structure	Operational structure		
Corporate	Closed-ended	Interval	Open-ended
Contractual	Closed-ended	Interval	Open-ended
Trust	Closed-ended	Interval	Open-ended
Partnership	Closed-ended	Interval	[1]

[1] Usually partnerships cannot be sold without the consent of the general partner – or sometimes all partners – so these cannot function as open-ended funds.

(since, for example, contractual and trust funds do not usually exist in parallel and open-ended corporate funds are impossible to operate in some countries).

The closed-ended structure is generally less popular with investors (refer to Chapter 3 for reasons) so is likely only to be chosen where it offers a specific advantage: for instance, where the ability to terminate the fund at a fixed date enables specific benefits to be offered to investors, or where the proposed portfolio is illiquid.

Other structural considerations

When designing a fund product, another consideration is whether the following structural variants on funds are possible or relevant:

- An 'umbrella' fund – this is a single fund which contains within it a number of sub-funds, which are essentially different portfolios (the name derives from a golf umbrella that has different coloured panels – representing the different portfolios). An investor can choose to buy units or shares in any of the underlying portfolios, and (if the taxman allows) may be able to exploit the advantage of being able to switch between two portfolios – for instance, from UK equities into US equities – without a realisation occurring for capital gains purposes. More commonly, this 'switch' is a taxable event – although the management company can allow switches between the sub-funds on more attractive charging levels than might be possible for a switch between one fund and another.
- The issue of different forms of unit or share in a fund – commonly for open-ended and interval funds these are either 'income' shares or units or 'accumulation' shares or units, as described in Chapter 10.
- A multi-unit or multi-share class fund permits a variety of unit or share classes to be issued, each of which may be in a different currency in order to be sold

Table 14.4 *Example of multi-share class fund and charging structure*

Share class	Entry/initial charge	Annual management charge	Redemption charge
A: Institutional	0%	1%	0%
B: Advisory[1]	6%	1%	0%
C: Direct[2]	0%	1%	2% if redeem within 1 year

[1] Shares sold through financial advisers who are remunerated by commission.
[2] Sold directly to investors through advertising and in-house website.

into different countries, or have a different charging structure designed for different distribution channels. An example of how this might work is illustrated in Table 14.4.

The authors have seen examples of multi-class funds where even the annual fee varies according to the type of share purchased – specifically, where those investing large sums are charged lower annual management fees than those investing smaller sums. Given that a few larger investors are cheaper to service than a large number of smaller investors, where such costs are met by the management company through its fee this charging structure might appear rational – the management company is in effect rebating its charge. However, there is an increasing trend for all costs of operation of the fund to be paid by the fund: in such a case in effect the annual management fee pays only for asset management, so using the differentiated annual charging structure appears to imply that one investor's $1000 costs more to manage than another investor's $1000 – when they are both part of the same pool managed to the same mandate.

It is, however, common practice – for instance, in the USA, where funds can be enormous (the value of the Fidelity® Magellan® Fund at the end of October 2002 was $58 billion[4]) – to reduce the percentage annual fee level as the fund expands in size: but this is applied to the total size of the fund and to all investors equally. In such a case it is stated in the prospectus that management fees will ratchet down as the scale of the fund increases, with specific sizes and fee rates given – see Table 8.2 (it is worth noting that in falling markets, fund fees can rise as the fund contracts in size, as a result).

Multi-class umbrella funds can become unimaginably complicated: imagine an umbrella fund with 30 sub-funds, each offered in four currencies, each of which offers three different classes of share and also offers an accumulation or an income variant of each of these (a total of 720 variants). The systems implications of these structures therefore are considerable.

Additional services

Potential for sales of investment fund products can be improved through offering ancillary services, which may include:

- Reinvestment of distributions – that is, the ability to buy more shares or units in the same fund with any distributions payable (there is some debate over whether it is fair to charge initial or entry fees on such reinvestment, or not).
- Savings plans – these permit people to invest a stated minimum amount every month or every quarter in shares or units of a fund. This periodic acquisition has the benefit of what is known as 'cost averaging': if unit or share prices are high, the money will buy fewer shares or units, but will buy more shares or units if share or unit prices are low – overall, the cost is likely to be lower than if they were all purchased at one time. These services are difficult and costly to operate unless an efficient direct debit banking service is available.
- 'Wrappers' – these are essentially accounts within which eligible individuals can hold certain assets (including shares or units of funds) on tax-privileged terms, provided certain rules are complied with. Management companies – or their subsidiary or affiliate companies – may be permitted to offer such accounts, which will commonly invest into their funds; but are likely to need to be approved by taxation authorities as meeting certain requirements before they can do so. In-house operation of such accounts may involve substantial systems investments, but third-party providers are usually available as an alternative. Indeed, management companies themselves may operate such wrappers on behalf of clients: for instance operating defined contribution pension plans for employers (e.g. 401k plans in the USA). In the UK these 'wrappers' include Individual Savings Accounts and personal pensions.

FACTORS IN PRODUCT DEVELOPMENT

These fall into four key areas:

- competitiveness
- profitability
- constraints on management
- funds which are past their 'sell by' date.

Competitive considerations

It will be important when developing a product to bear competitive considerations in mind, such as:

- Levels of initial, annual and exit fees.
- Level of annual expenses (total expense ratio).
- Relative risk compared to other funds or products (loss of capital, fall in income, etc.).
- Relative tax efficiency compared to other products: another product that invests in the same assets but with a better tax treatment is likely to outperform the one that suffers more tax.
- Relative performance in terms of capital growth or income, looking at other funds or competing products: outpacing inflation can be an attractive feature in inflationary environments.
- Ability to make and fulfil guarantees.
- Brand image – does the new product fit the fund management company's image?

Profitability

The different fund operational structures have some implications for profitability of a fund and therefore have an impact on product development. The main factors are:

- Whether the fund launch costs are payable by the fund (in which case they may be amortised, usually for up to five years) or by the management company, which will reduce potential profitability of the management company. In general, a closed-ended fund bears all the cost of its fund raising, just as any ordinary company does: equally generally interval and open-ended funds tend to pay only their own legal and regulatory costs but not marketing costs, which are borne by the management company. Even where closed-ended funds are concerned, limits may be placed in the prospectus on the proportion of the fund which may be used to pay launch costs, with the management company bearing any excess over this: this is designed to limit the consequences of any miscalculation of the fund's appeal by the management company.
- The volatility of potential management fees: fees from a fixed capital closed-ended fund will be less volatile, since they vary only by performance, than fees from an open-ended or interval fund whose capital will fluctuate as a result of sales and redemptions as well as investment performance.
- Whether initial charges, which are payable to the management company and therefore contribute to profitability, are payable: these are usually only levied on interval and open-ended funds and not on closed-ended funds (where amortisation of launch expenses to the fund is more normal, refer above). These charges usually cover costs such as advertising and payment of commissions to salespeople (refer to Chapter 8 for more on charges).

- The level of annual management charges that is payable to the management company (or to an investment adviser retained by the fund) and which contribute to fund management company profitability. These are payable whether the fund is closed-ended, interval or open-ended: usually levels of charges relate to the cost of managing the fund portfolio: the more exotic the portfolio, as a general rule, the higher the charge (refer to Table 8.5); the more computerised the management of the portfolio, the cheaper the management.
- Whether performance-related fees, which may be payable to the management company (or investment adviser, if different) and can enhance profitability, can be levied. These are rarely permitted to be levied on open-ended or interval funds, often because regulation bans this, but can be levied on closed-ended funds since their fixed capital enables fairness to be achieved (refer to Chapter 8).
- Whether redemption charges, which may be payable either to the management company or to the fund, depending on which bore the cost of marketing the fund, can be levied. Only the former will therefore affect management company profitability. Redemption charges are usually designed to ensure that the acquisition cost of a client of a no-load fund is recovered before that client can exit the fund and therefore to reduce the potential to fail to cover marketing costs.
- The life of the fund – the shorter the life of a fund, the shorter the period over which the management company will derive management fees from it. As a general rule, open-ended and interval funds have indeterminate lives, as do some closed-ended funds; but any closed-ended fund with a complex capital structure will have a fixed life. Such periods generally vary from five to 50 years.
- The ability to charge operational expenses to the fund can be very important to management company profitability. In some countries, the annual management fee paid to the management company has to cover all the costs of operation of the fund other than brokerage on transactions, taxes and audit (this has tended to be the case with trust and contractual funds rather than corporate funds). This means that the fees and expenses of the custodian (or depositary or trustee) and the registrar, regulatory fees, cost of reporting and of meetings, etc. all have to be paid by the management company from its fee, thus reducing its potential profitability. However, in recent years, regulators have allowed more and more costs to be charged directly to funds, subject to disclosure, so management companies have retained more and more of their fee and potentially become more and more profitable.
- The risk of conversion of a fund, which usually only applies to closed-ended funds. A risk in creating closed-ended funds is that the investors will become disaffected by the fund standing at a discount and vote to convert the fund to open-ended status, enabling their exit at net asset value. This is likely to

lead to a contraction in the size of the fund, and a resulting loss of fees to the management company (sometimes management companies suggest reduction of their fees on the closed-ended fund to avoid having to convert the fund). Liquidity of fund assets is key to convertibility – if they are not sufficiently liquid, an open-ended fund will be impossible to operate.

- Loss of management contracts for funds can also give rise to reduction in profitability: this tends to happen more with corporate or trust funds, whose investors have votes, than with contractual funds; and is potentially more common where fund boards are required to have a majority of independent directors (see Chapter 17 for Warren Buffett's pithy comment on this).
- The ability to offer purchase of fund shares or units through tax-privileged 'wrappers' can enhance profitability of management companies by enabling dual charging (at the 'wrapper' and 'fund' level – though the ability to do this is often restricted by regulation) or because it may be possible to levy higher charges on the 'wrapper' than on the fund.
- Duration of holdings: in general, the longer investors remain in a fund the more likely the fund management company is to make a profit on their holding.
- Size of holding: this is not relevant where investor servicing is charged directly to a fund – but where these costs are paid out of the management company's pocket, if there are 1000 holdings of 1000 each they will clearly be more expensive to service than a single holding of 1 000 000 – so larger fund holdings would be more profitable to the management company.

The factors listed above apply variably to closed, interval and open-ended funds, as summarised in Table 14.5.

Constraints on management

A number of investment management factors also can constrain fund product development:

- There may be a lack of assets in which the fund can invest – in other words, there may be more money available to invest than assets available to be purchased.
- This can lead to another problem – if a fund is not fully invested, in a rising market its performance will lag behind that of fully invested competitor funds.
- Alternatively, if the fund is fully invested, it can have liquidity problems if a wave of redemptions arises and it has difficulty selling assets, particularly if it invests in a specialist and narrow market.
- Funds can become so large that their investment decisions 'move markets' so the fund's ability to change its investments can become problematic (this was said to have been true of the Fidelity® Magellan® Fund mentioned above).

Table 14.5 *Summary of profitability factors for closed-ended versus interval and open-ended publicly offered[1] funds*

	Closed-ended	Interval	Open-ended
Ability to amortise launch costs	Yes	Limited	Limited
Variability of fund capital	Lower	Higher	Higher
Initial charges	Unusual	Usual	Usual
Annual management charges	Usual	Usual	Usual
Performance-related fees	Common	Rare	Rare
Redemption charges	Not applicable	Possible	Possible
Life of fund	Limited or unlimited	Limited or unlimited	Unlimited
Ability to charge fund operational expenses to the fund	Usual	Usual	Usual
Conversion of fund	Common	Rare	Rare
Loss of management contract	Occasional	Rare	Rare
Ability to offer funds through 'wrappers'	Common	Common	Common

[1] Privately offered funds are not governed by regulation so may have very different cost and fee structures.

The problems of specialist funds that are past their 'sell by' date

A further problem arises from funds that are past their 'sell by' date: that is, the fashion for them is over, so the funds are suffering steady redemptions and are reducing in size, and the market in which they invest is falling also, since there are more sellers than buyers. It is very difficult to 'turn around' such a fund since there is no new money to invest in more exciting new assets; and the fund's best assets, which are the most saleable ones, have probably been sold off first.

The most common strategy to deal with this problem is to merge the unsuccessful fund with another, more successful, fund (and ensure the successful fund's performance track record is used thereafter). Usually this means merging a narrower specialist fund into a more generalist fund (e.g. Japanese smaller companies into a Japanese fund or an Asian smaller companies fund). There can be times, however, when the existing fund has been such a disaster that even to merge it proves impossible and the fund has to be liquidated (nobly mentioning no names).

This chapter completes the coverage of marketing-related issues. In the next few chapters, aspects of the fiscal and legal operation of funds – i.e. accounting, taxation and fund governance – are explored and their significance examined.

Those who would like to test their grasp of the contents of this chapter should turn to the self-test questions at the back of the book.

NOTES

1. *The State of the European Investment Funds Industry*, The European Federation of Investment Funds and Companies, 2001.
2. www.capco.com.
3. *Regulatory and Investor Protection Issues Arising from the Participation by Retail Investors in (Funds of) Hedge Funds*, IOSCO, February, 2003.
4. Fidelity Investments®website: www.fidelity.com.

15

Fund Accounting Standards

INTRODUCTION

The next three chapters focus on technical issues that potentially have a strong impact on the success of collective investment funds. This chapter looks at accounting, the next at taxation and the following at fund governance.

This chapter deals with the technical accounting principles relating to the way the statutory financial accounts of funds are constructed and presented to share or unitholders. However, there are other aspects that relate to the operation and administration of funds, which would normally be covered under the general description 'accounting'. In this book these may be found in the following places:

- Portfolio valuation and pricing of shares or units for issue and redemption: this is dealt with in detail in Chapters 7 and 9, respectively.
- The characteristic content of reports and accounts required to be submitted to share or unitholders, which is covered in Chapter 13.
- The accounts of the management company, which will much more closely resemble those of a normal commercial company, which are dealt with in Chapter 18.
- The additional reports to regulators which may be required (e.g. submission of daily net asset values, figures for issue and redemption, and portfolio transactions) some of which may be based on fund accounts and some of which may be audited. The frequency and format of these will vary enormously according to local regulations and are not discussed in detail in this book.

WHY FUNDS HAVE SPECIAL ACCOUNTING STANDARDS

Accounting is essentially the activity of creating and maintaining the financial records of a fund: these are usually required to be audited at least once per annum by a professional independent auditor.

A special approach to fund accounting is needed because, even though many of these funds are constituted as companies, they do not behave in the same way as trading companies. Unlike normal companies, a fund usually has no full-time employees, no office or factory, and no plant and equipment. Instead, it is basically like a box containing certificates representing ownership of assets, with a group of people (the fund board, the custodian, depositary or trustee and the fund management company) who control access to the box and what is inside it.

This is the reason that developed financial markets have created special accounting standards for funds, referred to as 'Statements of Recommended Principles' or 'SORPs' or 'Generally Accepted Accounting Principles' or 'GAAPs'. These standards may be produced by regulators or by the industry (usually the trade association), in consultation with accounting bodies: for instance, the UK SORPs for open-ended funds[1] are published by the Investment Management Association while the SORP for closed-ended funds[2] is produced by the Association of Investment Trust Companies, which is the trade association of closed-ended funds. In general, different standards will be needed for companies versus trusts versus contractual funds (their legal nature being different) and for open-ended and interval versus closed-ended funds.

Fund accounting standards also have to take into account the application of the long list of standards published by both the Federal Accounting Standards Board ('FASB') in the USA and the International Accounting Standards Board ('IASB' – which replaced the International Accounting Standards Committee in 2001), based in London, particularly those which relate to accounting for securities and derivatives. It should be pointed out that certain of the International Accounting Standards – IAS 32 (Financial Instruments: Disclosure and Presentation) and IAS 39 (Financial Instruments: Recognition and Measurement) for example, may not be entirely applicable to investment funds. The IASB has reputedly been developing standards for funds and other investment institutions, although they have not as yet published these.

USERS OF FUND ACCOUNTS

Fund accounts are of interest to the following parties, for the reasons given:

- Existing and potential investors who want to know about the investments held by the fund, their capital value, the income from them and the costs of achieving performance.
- The management company, since the accounts showcase the returns that it has achieved for investors and form the basis for levying its fees.

- The depositary or trustee, which is usually required to state that the fund has complied with certain requirements as part of the report and accounts (a custodian does not have a regulatory duty to make such reports simply being a safekeeper of assets without oversight capacity).
- The regulator, which wishes to validate that the fund is being managed in compliance with the law and regulations.
- The taxation authorities, which will regard the accounts as the basis for validating that the fund complies with requirements for eligibility for fiscal treatment as a fund.
- Creditors and potential creditors of funds that have the power to borrow, who can use the accounts to validate ability to pay interest and repay capital.

Given the above, it is clearly vital that fund accounts are accurate and not misleading; also that they disclose information on a clear, consistent and comparable basis. This is another reason for establishing accounting standards for funds.

STANDARDISATION OF FUND ACCOUNTING

Funds are usually required to produce an annual audited report and a six-monthly unaudited report. These must be sent to or made available to all investors in the fund and to the regulator. In some countries, the annual report must be made up to the end of a mandatory accounting year (for countries which have a year-end fixed by law usually to 31 December), even if a fund has only been operating for only part of it; in others, the accounting year may start from the date of inception of the fund.

Often, neither existing accounting rules nor the regulations made by regulators provide precisely detailed rules for the presentation of financial statements by funds. This can lead to different management companies presenting information in quite different ways and using a different accounting basis. This will not only produce different figures, possibly misleading investors into thinking that one fund is performing better than another; but will mean that no one fund can be compared directly with another fund, which is unhelpful to all users of fund accounts.

This is another key reason for the establishment of accounting standards for funds – to ensure clarity and consistency in the basis and content of these documents, as well as because a specialised approach is needed for these investment vehicles.

In many countries accounts are required to be completed in formats whose length, complexity and obscurity makes them almost impenetrable to the ordinary investor. For this reason, regulators may permit special standardised 'short-form' accounts to be sent to holders, which are shorter and clearer than those required to be submitted to regulators, tax authorities or other government departments. The purpose of these short-form accounts is to show investment return, and the costs of achieving it – they are, therefore, a statement of information underlying the net asset value. Such accounts are required to include a statement of total return, a statement of movement of holders' funds (open-ended and interval funds only), a statement of assets and a distribution table, where applicable. These are explored further below.

KEY PRINCIPLES OF FUND ACCOUNTING

Key principles of fund accounting are:

- Income and capital of the fund must be accounted for separately: this means that while accounts must clearly show the total return achieved on the fund's investments, they must also identify what returns relate to income (dividends and interest earned by fund assets) and what returns relate to capital (rise or fall in value of the assets owned by the fund). The key reason for this separation is requirements established by taxation authorities, who usually differentiate taxation of income from taxation of gains and therefore need to know the derivation of the total return. In addition, taxation rules often require either that funds distribute all, or most, or none of their income to investors; or may ban distribution of capital gains or require distribution of capital gains – and fund accounts must demonstrate compliance with any such requirements in order to qualify for tax treatment as a fund.
- Open-ended and interval funds also must account separately for the movements in holders' money associated with purchase and redemption of holdings, which has an impact on fund capital, from movements caused by investment performance.
- Taxes due to be paid on income and on capital either by the fund or the holder must be clearly and separately identifiable; it is the possible difference in tax treatment of capital and income highlighted above that is one of the main reasons it is imperative to be able clearly to distinguish the two (refer to Chapter 16 for more on taxation).
- The operating expenses of the fund and fees paid to contracted service providers to the fund must be clearly identifiable and clearly attributed either to capital or to income, or to both.
- The derivation of distributions to investors must be clearly identifiable as being from income or from capital or both, again for tax reasons.
- The basis on which the investments within the portfolio are valued must be clearly stated and must be consistent both within the accounts and year on year unless good reason for change can be demonstrated.

- The basis on which accounting is done – usually historical cost convention[3] – should be clearly stated and should be consistent throughout the accounts and year on year (this basis is usually mandated by the tax authorities or the regulator or the accounting standard).
- Whether investments are accounted for at trade date (that is the date on which the transaction was agreed, or entered into) or at settlement date (that is the date on which the transaction is completed) should be clearly stated and consistently applied; reason for any change should be recorded.
- The accounts should clearly and consistently apply the accruals concept (that is, the accounting method by which income and expenditure are recognised as they are earned and incurred even though they may not have been received or paid, as against the cash accounting basis where income and expenditure is only recognised upon receipt or payment): when this is not applied, reasons should be clearly recorded.
- The custodian, depositary or trustee should keep in respect of each fund parallel accounts to the fund management company, and these accounts should be reconciled at stated intervals.
- Comparative figures from the previous year's audited accounts are always given.

ACCOUNTING FOR OPEN-ENDED AND INTERVAL FUNDS VERSUS CLOSED-ENDED FUNDS

Despite the fact that closed-ended funds are generally constituted as joint-stock companies with a fixed capital and open-ended or interval funds (whether in the corporate, contractual or trust form) have variable capital, there are elements which are common to the accounts of both types. Open-ended, interval and closed-ended funds are usually required to include in their accounts:

- A balance sheet, or in the case of an open-ended or interval fund, a statement of net asset value, which is in effect a balance sheet, showing assets and liabilities on the closing date of the financial reporting year.
- A statement of total return – that is, the fund's investment performance – which shows the net gains and losses on investments in that period; other gains and losses (usually due to currency movements); net income and expenses after taxation also showing separately gross income, total expenses and the tax charge; total return for the period; distributions; and the net increase or decrease in share or unitholders' funds in the period.
- A portfolio statement, showing the securities and cash held on the last day of the reporting year and highlighting the main portfolio changes during the period under review.

- Notes to the accounts, detailing their basis.
- The net asset value of the share or unit at the beginning and end of the accounting period, with comparative figures for the previous year.
- The amount of the dividend or distribution for the reporting year and from the previous year.
- The auditor's report and signature.

In addition, open-ended and interval fund accounts must include:

- A statement of movement of shareholders' or unitholders' funds: this shows increases or decreases in the size of the fund resulting from sales and redemptions of shares or units (as opposed to increase or decrease in fund assets from investment performance) so does not apply to closed-ended funds.

Closed-ended corporate funds will also have to comply with any other requirements of joint-stock company law, securities law, the civil or commercial codes, and corporate taxation law from which they lack an exemption.

TWO KEY COMPONENTS OF FUND ACCOUNTS

Figures 15.1 and 15.2 show examples drawn from a UK-based unit trust fund, which illustrate a statement of total return and a statement of movement of unitholders' funds respectively. Apart from the balance sheet (or statement of net asset value, basically, which is illustrated in Table 7.2) these are the two key components of fund accounts.

The statement of total return, shown in Figure 15.1, with its accompanying notes describes how:

- The increase or decrease in capital values has affected the total portfolio value. Note that realised and unrealised gains are distinguished from one another. In some cases, the USA for example where gains need to be distributed, this may affect the tax position of the fund or its share or unitholders.
- The income from the fund is made up from interest and dividends from both domestic and foreign sources. In many countries income from dividends and income from bank or bond interest is taxed differently.
- The expenses and costs of managing the fund are shown and also aggregated to form the total expense ratio.

The movement in share or unitholders' funds statement, shown in Figure 15.2, required for open-ended and interval funds only, is designed to show the effect of issue of new shares or units and redemption of existing shares or units during the period under review, combined with the effect of total return on investments derived from the statement of total return shown in Figure 15.1.

STATEMENT OF TOTAL RETURN
for the year ended 28th February 2003

	Notes	**2003** £'000	£'000	*2002* *£'000*	*£'000*
Net losses on investments during the year	2		(220,179)		*(56,337)*
Other gains/(losses)	3		304		*(242)*
Income	4	21,241		*32,303*	
Expenses	5	(9,857)		*(12,483)*	
Net income before taxation		11,384		*19,820*	
Taxation	6	—		—	
Net income after taxation for the year			11,384		*19,820*
Total return for the year			(208,491)		*(36,759)*
Distributions	7		(11,399)		*(19,828)*
Net decrease in unitholders' funds from investment activities			**(219,890)**		**(56,587)**

---

2. Net losses on investments

	2003 £'000	2002 £'000
Proceeds from sales of investments during the year	761,743	*602,239*
Original cost of investments sold during the year	(812,477)	*(541,441)*
(Losses)/gains realised on investments sold during the year	(50,734)	*60,798*
Net depreciation/(appreciation) thereon already recognised in earlier years	10,593	*(57,986)*
	(40,141)	*2,812*
Net unrealised depreciation for the year	(180,038)	*(59,149)*
Net losses on investments	(220,179)	*(56,337)*

---

3. Other gains/(losses)

	2003 £'000	2002 £'000
Foreign currency gains/(losses)	304	*(242)*

---

4. Income

	2003 £'000	2002 £'000
Dividends from UK companies	20,914	*31,654*
Dividends from overseas companies	118	*425*
Underwriting commission	92	*42*
Bank interest	117	*182*
	21,241	*32,303*

(cont).

5. Expenses

	2003 £'000	2002 £'000
Payable to the Manager, associates of the Manager and agents of either of them:		
Manager's periodic charge	8,369	11,010
Registration fees	939	915
	9,308	11,925
Payable to the Trustee, associates of the Trustee and agents of either of them:		
Trustee's fees	74	232
Interest payable	434	279
Safe custody fees	20	31
Security charges	15	8
	543	550
Other expenses:		
Audit fee	6	6
FSA fee	—	1
Registration expenses	—	1
	6	8
Total expenses	9,857	12,483
Average fund size during the year	669,516	880,813
Total Expense Ratio (TER)	1.41%	1.38%

The TER is the total expenses of the fund (excluding interest payable and security charges) expressed as a percentage of the average size of the fund during the period. Fund expenses are inclusive of VAT where appropriate.

6. Taxation

a) Analysis of charge for the year

There is no corporation tax charge for the year *(2002 - nil)*.

b) Factors affecting the tax charge for the year

The tax assessed for the period is lower than the standard rate of corporation tax in the UK for an authorised unit trust scheme. The differences are explained below:

	2003 £'000	2002 £'000
Net income before taxation	11,384	19,820
Corporation tax at 20% *(2002 - 20%)*	2,277	3,964
Effects of:		
UK dividends not subject to corporation tax	(4,183)	(6,331)
Expense not deductible for tax purposes	3	2
Movement in taxable income accruals on receipt	3	11
Movement in excess expenses	1,900	2,354
	—	—

Authorised unit trust schemes are exempt from tax on capital gains. Therefore any capital return is not included in the above reconciliation.

c) Deferred tax

After claiming relief against accrued income taxable on receipt, the fund has unrelieved excess expenses of £65,192,000 *(2002 - £55,677,000)*. It is unlikely that the fund will generate sufficient taxable profits in the future to utilise these expenses and therefore no deferred tax asset has been recognised.

7. Distributions

The amount shown in the Statement of Total Return on page 6 takes account of income received on the creation of units and income deducted on the cancellation of units and comprises:

	2003 £'000	2002 £'000
Final distribution payable 28th April 2003	11,558	15,675
Add: Income deducted on cancellation of units	346	4,688
Deduct: Income received on creation of units	(505)	(535)
	11,399	19,828

This amount has been calculated as follows:

	2003 £'000	2002 £'000
Net income after taxation	11,384	19,820
Security charges	15	8
	11,399	19,828

Details of the distribution for the year are shown on page 21.

Figure 15.1 *Statement of total return*
Source: 2003 report and accounts for the Invesco Perpetual UK Growth Fund. Reproduced by permission of INVESCO PERPETUAL

This is useful information since it illustrates that there were two factors in the value of the total fund shown for the year ended in February 2003: the increase in the size of the fund resulting from an excess of sales over redemptions of 250 51 000 and the decrease in size resulting from investment returns (both capital and income) of 219 890 000 which outweighed the sales. In the year to February 2002 by contrast, the fund suffered substantial redemptions of 402 046 000 as well as a decrease in value resulting from negative investment returns of 56 587 000.

An informed study of fund accounts yields a lot of interesting information.

ACCOUNTING BASES

Accounting for income

In developed markets, funds normally use the accruals basis for accounting for income. This means that the income from certain securities, particularly fixed

STATEMENT OF MOVEMENTS IN UNITHOLDERS' FUNDS

for the year ended 28th February 2003

	2003	2003	2002	2002
	£'000	£'000	£'000	£'000
Net Assets at 28th February 2002		724,104		1,169,040
Movement due to sales and repurchases of units				
Amounts received on creation of units	46,742		37,723	
Less: Amounts paid on cancellation of units	(21,691)		(439,769)	
		25,051		(402,046)
Net decrease in unitholders' funds from investment activities		(219,890)		(56,587)
Stamp Duty Reserve Tax		(239)		(259)
Unclaimed distribution monies		1		1
Income accumulation		10,335		13,955
Net Assets at 28th February 2003		**539,362**		**724,104**

Figure 15.2   *Statement of movements in unitholders' funds*
Source: 2003 report and accounts for the Invesco Perpetual UK Growth Fund. Reproduced by permission of INVESCO PERPETUAL

interest securities, is apportioned evenly over the relevant period within which it is due. For example, if a fund owns a bond that pays interest six-monthly and the fund values its assets weekly, then the appropriate fraction (7/182.5) of the next income payment will be added to the accrued income account at each weekly valuation.

Dividends on shares are not usually accrued, since they vary in amount, and are not totally predictable. They are usually recognised for accounting purposes at the date on which the shares become ex-dividend (the date after which a new purchaser will not be entitled to receive the dividend just declared) on the understanding that the dividend will be received on a known date in the near future.

This method of accounting for income is, however, unsatisfactory when there is a high risk of default on interest payments, or delays in payment and receipt, or the date of payment of a declared dividend is uncertain. This may well apply in emerging markets both in respect of equity dividends and bond interest. For this

Table 15.1 *Accounting basis*

Type of asset	Accounting basis
Debt securities not subject to abnormal risk of default (e.g. government bonds)	Accrual
Debt securities subject to serious risk of default	Cash
'Blue chip' equities (low risk of failure to pay dividends as stated)	Accrual
Other equities	Cash

reason a mixture of accruals and cash accounting (when dividends or interest are only entered into the accounts upon receipt) for income may be more appropriate in these markets, as shown in Table 15.1.

Accounting for expenditure

Expenditure should be accounted for on an accruals basis. This means items are recorded as incurred and not at the time of settlement. Fees for fund management companies, investment advisers, auditors or custodians, depositaries or trustees should be accounted for on an accruals basis. In the case of an open-ended or interval fund, it is clearly inequitable to wait to the end of the year to charge the annual management fee, since investors who sell before the year-end escape paying their share. Likewise it is inequitable to charge the fee only at the start of the year.

Management companies also prefer to receive a regular stream of payments rather than gamble on one payment in a year, which, since it is based on the net asset value of the fund, might be significantly higher or lower than expected because of market conditions on the date of deduction.

Modern practice with open-ended funds is for one-twelfth of the annual fee to be charged each month; fees are accrued at daily or weekly valuation points up to the date of each monthly payment.

Accounting for securities transactions

In accounting for securities transactions, normal practice in developed markets is to account for purchases and sales at the date of the trade, not at the date of settlement. The reason is that the fund is exposed to the capital gain or loss resulting from the trade from the date of the trade when the contract is made and not from the settlement date. It also acquires any rights to dividends or other events such as rights issues, share splits or take-overs from that date.

However, where there is a real risk of non-settlement of trades, particularly where there is no effective legal remedy for such a failure, then it may be appropriate to adopt settlement date accounting for securities transactions. The problem with this approach is that, if settlement takes a long time, then the valuations may be significantly distorted during the period between transaction and settlement of a large purchase or sale: its use therefore is only recommended in extreme situations. Regardless of this, the accounts should always show separately those transactions that have been settled and those that have not.

POTENTIAL ACCOUNTING PROBLEMS IN DEVELOPING MARKETS

In some developing markets, the adaptation of existing accounting frameworks has often produced systems that are quite inadequate and unsuitable for funds. Over time, reforms are likely to bring them closer into line with the systems in use in developed markets.

The main problems associated with accounting for funds in developing markets are associated with corporate funds, which are usually ill-served by ordinary company accounting rules which do not allow for two features of funds:

- Their fixed assets' value, which will change constantly and sometimes sharply, unlike most ordinary companies' assets which are carried at cost or depreciated cost.
- In the case of open-ended or interval funds, their issued capital will also change constantly.

Contractual open-ended or interval funds, since they are not legal entities as such, can usually have a self-standing accounting regime designed specially to accommodate their unique features, so they are generally less of a problem. Corporate-type funds, particularly of the closed-ended type, however, will have to address a range of issues. Such closed-ended corporate-style funds have been used in cases of privatisation or corporate reconstruction, and are often created without adequate attention having been paid to the format of their accounts, since to the accounting profession and, more important to the tax authorities, they are technically companies and bear more than a superficial resemblance to an ordinary commercial enterprise. As a result their financial reports may have to be squeezed into an accounting format for which their business is ill-suited and which will consequently deliver a set of accounts devoid of meaning. Accounting in this way may also give rise to certain taxation problems to the disadvantage of shareholders. In the next sections some of these problems that relate to the balance sheet items summarised in Table 15.2 that are found in the accounts of a closed-ended corporate fund are discussed.

Table 15.2 *Summary of items found on the balance sheet of a closed-ended fund*

Balance sheet item	Comments
Assets	
Fixed assets	There are unlikely to be any fixed assets other than investments, unless the fund is internally managed, in which case there may be some property and equipment
Investments	The investments will normally be marketable securities; there is no need to categorise these in detail on the face of the accounts. It will be more normal to show the portfolio by way of note. The key point is whether these investments are shown at cost or at market value - see above
Current assets	
Cash and short term investments	It is usual to include under this heading any investments with a life of less than twelve months, including bank deposits and short term paper. It is possible that some of these investments may be shown at market value rather than face or cash value
Debtors	The majority of these will be for amounts due from the market (brokers) for securities for which a sale has been contracted but not completed
Dividends receivable	Dividends declared or interest due but not received
Liabilities	
Issued capital	The amount of capital issued and paid; authorised but unissued capital can be shown by way of note
Ordinary shares	This figure will be the product of the number of shares in issue multiplied by their nominal value
Reserves	
Share premium reserve	The aggregate amount of premiums over the nominal value at which shares have been issued
Capital reserves	The balancing figure for any profit (loss) on sale of assets at a figure different from book value or from revaluation of assets to market value
Retained profits	Profits retained and not paid out as dividends
Long term liabilities	Debts which are due in more than 12 months
Current liabilities	
Creditors	The majority are likely to be for payment due to the market (brokers) for purchases of securities contracted but not settled
Bank overdraft	Debts due in less than 12 months
Taxation due	Taxation due but not paid

Accounting for varying fixed asset values – the nominal value problem

The required allocation of a nominal value (or par value – a stated amount of cash value such as one dollar) to shares in funds of a closed-ended corporate-type fund can give rise to a range of problems. Under many countries' company law, a fund may have problems when the value of its nominal capital needs to be adjusted to take account of increases or decreases in the value of fixed assets (the securities held in the portfolio) on the balance sheet. Shares or units in open-ended funds of all types do not usually have a nominal value, since they are continuously issued and redeemed at varying prices, and since open-ended funds do not have to show what would be conventionally regarded as a balance sheet.

Examples of problems that may arise in the case of nominal value of closed-ended funds of the corporate type include:

- Being required to call shareholder meetings if the company's value falls to less than a certain proportion of nominal value – say 50%.
- A company being regarded as insolvent if the value of assets falls to below the nominal value of the shares.
- Being required to issue new share capital to bring the total nominal value of shares in issue in line with a higher value of fixed assets, which involves time-consuming and expensive shareholder meetings and registration.

There are a number of solutions to this:

- Not requiring a nominal value to be placed on shares (shares of no par value are permitted in the USA for example).
- Making any allocated nominal value per share very low (one cent rather than one dollar).
- Allocating the nominal value of shares to issued share capital and the difference between the nominal value and the price at which the shares have been issued to a share premium account on the passive side of the balance sheet (which does not solve the second problem above).

How to adjust liabilities (passive side) if the value of fixed assets changes

The last solution, which is commonly used, gives rise to another accounting problem, however:

- When sales of fixed assets shown on the balance sheet at cost are made at a profit, this has to be reflected on the balance sheet since it is not a theoretical profit (as is that thrown up by a current market value higher than cost) but a real one.
- When assets are revalued and the increase or decrease is shown by an adjustment to the value of fixed assets then an adjustment may be required to nominal capital.

Portraying market value of securities

The most significant accounting policy decision is how and where to show the market values of securities held as investments. There are two choices:

- To require the investments to be revalued at the balance sheet date.
- To require that investments shown at cost on the balance sheet, with market value dealt with in a note.

In the case of closed-ended funds there may, however, be reasons why it is difficult or inappropriate to use market values:

- The fund may hold a high proportion of its assets in illiquid investments that are not traded on a stock exchange and whose market value is hard to assess.
- The sale of assets at market prices may produce capital gains tax liabilities for the fund (in the case where the fund is not tax-neutral); an adjustment may have to be made in respect of potential tax liabilities.
- Revaluation of assets to market values (even where no sale takes place) may, in certain tax regimes, produce a capital gains tax liability.

Besides that, the disadvantage of showing the market value in the balance sheet is that it will only be accurate once a year. Unlike other typical commercial assets (land, buildings and machinery) the market value of securities will fluctuate daily. It is therefore more meaningful for the market value of assets to be shown on a non-statutory schedule or note attached to the accounts. This gives some scope for directors to give estimates of current values of securities that are not listed or traded with suitable warnings that these are estimates.

These reasons should never apply to open-ended funds for which regular valuations of assets at market value are mandatory in order to derive an NAV at which investors buy and sell. Open-ended funds should always include their assets, which are required to be of a more liquid character than those held in closed-ended funds, in their accounts at market values. Indeed open-ended funds, when they calculate an NAV are in effect showing a balance sheet every day, in which the fixed assets are valued at market value.

However, even if the market values of the portfolio of securities of closed-ended funds are shown separately from the balance sheet as suggested above, there will still need to be adjustments to cover the situation when securities are sold at a profit (or loss) from the balance sheet value. This will need to be reflected in the balance sheet since it is a 'real' rather than a 'theoretical' event.

These increases or decreases on the asset (active) side of the balance sheet resulting from sales at prices higher or lower than cost are usually accounted for by setting up 'reserves' on the liability (passive) side of the balance sheet. These reserves may include:

Table 15.3 *Realised and unrealised reserves (assuming no market movement)*

	Unrealised capital gain reserve – 000's	Realised capital gain reserve – 000's
As at 01.01.02	11120	15160
Realised gains	(1120)	1120
As at 31.12.02	10000	16280

- Capital reserves reflecting realised or unrealised profits (less losses).
- Revenue (or income) reserves reflecting income received but not paid out by way of dividend.

This approach to accounting for realised and unrealised gains is now generally accepted practice in most developed markets, whereby fixed assets are shown on the active side of the balance sheet at current market value, with corresponding entries on the passive side of the balance sheet for capital reserves, realised and unrealised. These are shown under capital and reserves and are included in 'total shareholders' funds', since the gains, realised or unrealised, and the income not paid out belongs to shareholders. If this accounting methodology is adopted, then 'total shareholders' funds', less any long-term liabilities, divided by the number of shares in issue will produce a figure for net asset value per share.

The statement of total shareholders' funds will show a transfer from one entry to the other when an asset is realised, in the following way. When a sale is made and a gain (loss) realised, the associated unrealised gain (loss) figure is deducted from the 'unrealised capital reserve' and the realised gain (loss) is added to the 'realised capital reserve' as shown in Table 15.3.

Effectively the unrealised gain reserve simply reflects the variation between the market value of assets and cost of assets. But when an investment is sold at a profit or loss, this is a real event and must be permanently reflected in the balance sheet, which is done through the realised gain reserve.

Accounting for varying capital
An open-ended or interval fund does not have a balance sheet as such, all the necessary information being conveyed by the statement of net asset value. But a way needs to be found to account for the issued shares or units whose number varies continuously.

This can be achieved, as mentioned above, by accounting separately for the inflow and outflow of money resulting from purchases and sales, as shown in the statement of movements in holders' funds.

Every country has its own peculiarities with regard to company and contract law as well as different taxation and accounting: so while the principles outlined above generally apply, there are a wide variety of constraints which may affect the accounting outcome.

RELATIONSHIP BETWEEN TAX AND ACCOUNTING

The taxation of funds and the accounting methods they use are intimately connected. The way in which capital and income are accounted for and shown will depend on the way in which each is taxed in the hands of the fund and in the hands of the holders and on prohibitions or requirements for distribution of income or capital. Depending on the tax treatment accounts may need to show:

- Net capital gains realised of a taxable nature in the hands either of the fund or the holder.
- Net capital gains realised which are exempt from tax either in the hands of the fund or the holder.
- Income received of a taxable nature (different types of income – interest and dividends for instance – may attract different rates of tax).
- Any tax credits resulting from tax already paid and offsettable against liabilities.

The accounting system will have to be set up in such a way that all these different items can easily be recognised for the purpose of compiling tax returns. Different types of income and realised gains need to be presented to holders, and the certificate or statement which accompanies a dividend can be complex; it will have to show these items in a way which can be used by the holder to calculate his own tax liability, if any.

A detailed description of how income from different sources suffers different tax rates can be found in the next chapter, which focuses on taxation of funds.

Those who would like to test their grasp of the contents of this chapter should turn to the self-test questions at the back of the book.

NOTES

1. *Statement of Recommended Practice for Unit Trusts*, Financial Services Authority, January 1997; *Statement of Recommended Practice for Financial Statements of Authorised Open-Ended*

Investment Companies, Financial Services Authority, November 2000, which are in the process of being replaced by SORPS issued by the Investment Management Association.

2. *Statement of Recommended Practice for Financial Statements of Investment Trust Companies*, Association of Investment Trust Companies, January 2003.

3. An accounting principle requiring all financial statement items be based on original or acquisition cost: in the case of investment funds, this is usually required to be adjusted for current market values.

16

Fund Taxation

INTRODUCTION

The way in which collective investment funds are taxed – primarily on their income and capital gains – is inevitably, like all aspects of taxation, complex and varies greatly from country to country. This chapter does not seek to be an exhaustive guide to taxation in any particular country, but rather explores the issues and problems, their implications for funds and fund management companies, and looks at some different solutions in different countries. Any reader wishing to obtain specific guidance on the taxation of investment funds in any particular country should consult a specialist in that country: though there are some useful surveys[1] of country taxation that may be of help.

Taxes are compulsory financial contributions imposed by governments in order to raise revenue, which may be levied on income, capital, property or services so they may affect funds in different ways.

TAXATION OF FUNDS IS KEY TO THEIR SUCCESS

The taxation of funds is a key issue for funds and their management companies. Taxation affects both the attractiveness of funds compared with other investments, and also the systems that may have to be designed and implemented in order for funds to operate efficiently and cost-effectively and to be capable of providing the necessary tax liability information to their investors. Accounting practice will affect taxation strategy; for instance, if accounting standards do not require the capital and income of a fund to be distinguished, it will be difficult to apply taxation separately to these elements. Taxation and accounting considerations relating to funds are often, therefore, inextricably intertwined.

Since most people will always try to avoid paying more tax than is absolutely necessary funds need to be at least tax-neutral by comparison with direct investment in securities and ideally even have a tax advantage. In developed markets, use of particular fund structures is often a direct result of past and current taxation regimes, since their management companies have had to design vehicles to minimise tax liability and maximise returns in order to attract investors. Hence the use of the trust or contractual fund forms which in some countries have been more effective in minimising tax liabilities than the corporate form. It is often quite possible to form funds in corporate as well as trust or contractual form, but none come into existence: commonly because their tax position is too unattractive.

The existence of any tax incentive does not have to be within the fund itself, provided that the fund is neutral from the taxation perspective (or at least not disadvantaged), but may lie within a complementary product or 'wrapper', as is usually the case with a pension or savings plan (basically a wrapper is a tax-privileged 'wrapping' within which assets including fund shares or units may be held). Such tax-advantaged wrappers are a most important determinant of investor behaviour. For example:

- In Australia 80% of fund investment is related to retirement provision.[2]
- In the USA in 2001 it was estimated that around a quarter of net new cash flows to mutual funds was related to retirement provision[3] which is tax incentivised.
- In France nearly two-thirds of French investment funds are held in tax-favoured accounts.[4]

Governments sometimes deliberately seek to use taxation incentives as levers to influence the behaviour of individuals or corporations. While the motivation for introducing such incentives is understandable, the consequences are rarely as straightforward or beneficial as anticipated. In general tax incentives work when they encourage people to do what they want to do but do not work when they try to motivate people to do things they do not want to do. Fund management companies in virtually every market in the world lobby governments hard either to remove tax disadvantages or to achieve favourable treatment.

It is also perhaps worth noting that tax incentives do not always work: there are countries where there are substantial tax incentives to invest in funds, but people do not do so. One key reason being that where countries have primarily cash economies and where many people work in the 'grey' market, everyone avoids tax – so they do not want anyone to know that they have money which might be taxable, which would become obvious if they put money into a fund.

Political and social factors in fund taxation policy

It is worth considering why governments should consider that funds merit favourable treatment as a taxable group. Fundamentally, it is because free market economies need to attract individuals' savings to finance their future development. Most people do not have sufficient capital to be able to achieve a good spread of risk in direct investments; do not have the expertise to choose them;

and if they did, would find the cost of investing their small amount of money to be disproportionately high in relation to the benefits achieved. Funds provide a solution to this problem, offering spread of risk, expert management and economies of scale that make them cost-effective. Therefore they are able to raise money for investment in capital markets which otherwise might be less productively kept on deposit or even 'under the mattress'. It is this role in mobilising savings that justifies favourable tax treatment, though funds are hedged around with operating and tax regulations designed to prevent abuse of this status.

A factor that can substantially affect taxation policy on funds – particularly in developing markets – is the tax collection system available to the government concerned. It is clearly much easier to collect tax at the enterprise or fund level, where there may only be tens or hundreds of entities (which have their own accounting personnel and tax advisers), than at the individual level, where there will be millions of people who are not experienced in dealing with tax and accounting issues. Many countries simply do not have the capacity, as yet, to deal with individuals' taxation, which imposes restraints on fund taxation strategy.

Last, but not least, it is worth pointing out that in today's global markets many investors have access to neighbouring countries' funds. There are two separate issues here, tax evasion and tax avoidance. Leaving aside the evasion aspect which involves breaking the law, investors are likely to try and avoid paying more tax than they have to by choosing funds, where they are permitted to do so, where the overall impact of taxation is less. A notable feature of Western Europe's markets is the gradual convergence of the tax regimes applying to funds, which has been driven by investors' ability to opt for lower taxed funds domiciled outside their own country, for example in Luxemburg. Tax legislation that makes domestic funds unattractive will in the long run simply drive capital towards other countries' funds. Despite this convergence, however, there are still disparities, which tend to discriminate against foreign domiciled funds in favour of domestic ones. However, recent attempts to tax foreign domiciled investment funds at rates higher than those applicable to domestic funds in both Spain and Germany have been defeated by pressure from the funds industry, maintaining that this was inconsistent with the Treaty of Rome (the Treaty that established the European Union).

MAIN TAXES AFFECTING FUNDS

The main forms of tax payable by funds internationally are:

- Taxes on income – payable on any income of the fund whether from interest on deposits or bonds, dividends from equities, or rental from real estate (referred to hereafter as 'income tax' though this tax may technically be classed as 'corporation tax').

- Taxes on capital gains – levied on any profit made on the sale of assets held by the fund.

Many countries that are new to the business of investment funds make inadequate distinctions between capital and income, and do not differentiate between them, taxing both income and capital gains as 'profits'. Most developed countries make a distinction between the two.

Where both forms of tax outlined above exist, but are levied at different levels – say 35% on income but only 25% on capital gains – there will be an incentive to 'convert' income into capital in order to minimise tax; and if these rates were reversed, to 'convert' capital to income. These differences can give rise to a variety of innovatory fund structures designed to avoid or minimise the overall level of tax paid by an investor. If these funds become too attractive and damage taxation revenues substantially – or if the fund structure is used by entities which are not really savings vehicles – taxation authorities will have to change the rules, thus giving rise to the ever more complex taxation regulations applying to funds in most countries.

Funds may also be liable to a large variety of other taxes – for instance, *ad valorem*[5] duties relating to securities transactions or value added tax on the fees paid to service providers – but are likely to have the same liability as any other entity transacting business in the securities market. Provided all competing products share the same tax liabilities, these taxes will not usually substantially affect the competitiveness of the fund form.

Possible elements of fund taxation

Table 16.1 shows how taxation may theoretically have an impact on the income and capital gains received by a fund and paid out to its share or unitholders at different levels. It must be emphasised that no regimes tax funds at all possible levels – that would be intolerable and ensure that funds were not bought by anyone; Table 16.1 simply illustrates the general permutations.

The table shows that a fund may be liable to pay tax on income or gains received from its investments, which may already have been taxed in the hands of the company in which investment is made or credit institution in which deposits are held; and on distribution of income or gains to their investors. In addition, investors themselves may have taxation liabilities on their fund returns, particularly if their tax rates are higher than any taxes paid by the fund. In theory, therefore there may be four levels of taxation applied on returns received by fund investors, whereas only two at the most would usually apply to a person holding shares directly in a company instead of through a fund.

Table 16.1 *Possible fund taxation*

Level at which tax may be levied	Capital gains	Income
1 Issuer of securities (in which fund invests)	Possible but very rare	Tax withheld on interest or dividend payments
2 Fund	Tax as profits, whether or not distributed	Tax as profits, whether or not distributed
3 Fund payment to individual share or unitholder	If distributed as dividends, subject to withholding tax	If distributed as dividends, subject to withholding tax
4 Individual	Tax as income or capital gains	Tax as income

Table 16.2 *Double taxation problems for funds – dividend paid via a fund*

	Dividend amount	Less withholding tax	Dividend received by fund Y	Dividend received by fund investor Z
Dividend paid by investee company X to fund Y	100	20	80	
Dividend paid by fund Y to investor Z	80	20		60

Ability to offset tax liabilities is key

A key factor in fund taxation is whether funds are permitted to offset their own tax liabilities against tax already paid at source on income or gains that they have received. If they cannot, they are likely to suffer something like the problem shown in Table 16.2. In this case the investor buying company X shares through a fund will have paid 20 more in tax than the direct investor in company X shown in Table 16.3; so the fund would have to produce a dividend that was at least 20% higher than company X in order to attract investment.

In the two cases shown it is clear that an investor via the fund is worse off, since he is in effect having to pay what is described as 'withholding tax' twice, whereas the direct investor only pays it once.

Table 16.3 *Double taxation problems for funds – dividend received directly by the investor*

	Dividend amount	Less withholding Tax	Dividend received by investor Z
Dividend paid by investee company X	100	20	80

Funds should be at least 'tax neutral' or 'fiscally transparent'

The principle which has become generally accepted internationally is that funds, whether corporate, trust or contractual, open-ended, interval or closed-ended, should be 'neutral' or 'transparent' in tax terms: that is, they should leave the individual investor in the position of paying the same amount of tax as if he had purchased the underlying assets of the fund directly. The general idea is that the fund itself suffers no tax, since this would interpose an additional level of taxation between the assets held by the fund and the returns the investor in the fund receives from them, compared to a direct holder of those assets. Some countries adopt a tax-neutral stance on income, but by allowing capital gains to accumulate inside the fund without suffering tax, introduce an element of tax privilege – essentially by permitting investors to defer their personal tax liability.

However, in countries where funds are in the early stages of development, existing tax regimes often fail to take any account of the distinction between a corporate fund and any other company. This can impose several layers of tax burdens on such funds and their investors, notably when there is no distinction between capital gains and income, which are both aggregated and taxed as 'profit'.

The situation may be aggravated by the fact that until a solid framework of law is established and enforced, business owners are often suspected of exploiting all possible means of avoiding the payment of taxes, so tax codes for business are often complex and exacting. Changes to existing legislation may be driven by the perceived need to prevent tax avoidance, often with unintended and unwelcome consequences for funds. Legislators and regulators need to work together to ensure that tax laws do not thus penalise fund investors.

The aim of transparency or fiscal neutrality is entirely logical if the position of the individual investor is considered. He may purchase securities himself through the medium of the stock exchange, or he may buy shares via a fund. In both cases he owns the same securities. Why should his tax treatment differ?

TAX INCENTIVES AND FUNDS

In most countries where funds play a significant role in drawing individual investors' money into securities markets as a source of long-term capital, there is a possible counter-argument: that the fund investor should enjoy a tax advantage relative to the direct investor in securities, as is the case in some European countries. If this argument is accepted, however, then it is more efficient and equitable to create a special class of tax-privileged plans or 'wrappers' than to give funds themselves a tax advantage. This leaves funds as 'tax-neutral' while the tax-privileged plans themselves – which are associated with specific individuals, subject to whatever limits the government decides – may invest in funds. This is the approach used in the USA, the UK and in several countries of Continental Europe, in which special plans designed to encourage long-term savings or provision for retirement enable investors to hold their investments in an environment which is free from taxes.

Essentially there are three potential elements of tax incentives for such 'wrappers'. Put very simply, these can be characterised as shown in Table 16.4.

That is, the contribution to the wrapper may be from gross (untaxed) or net (taxed) income; while within the wrapper income or gains may be taxed or untaxed; and upon exit from the fund, income or gains may be taxed or untaxed. It is rare that tax exemptions are given at all three stages; most usually a combination of the first two or last two, or part thereof is used. This representation gives rise to the description of a wrapper as 'EET' (exempt on entry, exempt inside, taxed on exit), for instance.

Preventing abuses of fund status

Any special tax treatment for funds should be limited to suitably qualifying funds: usually these are required to have regulatory approval and to meet specific tax authority requirements. Regulatory approval seeks to prevent undesirables from exploiting investors attracted by 'tax-free' labels, while tax authorities seek to prevent misuse of 'tax-free' fund status by securities traders, trading companies and others.

Table 16.4 *Possible tax treatments of wrappers*

Upon entry	While within	Upon exit
Exempt or taxable	Exempt or taxable	Exempt or taxable

When dealing with closed-ended corporate funds it may be difficult taxwise to distinguish a fund from a normal limited company. Giving special tax treatment to closed-ended funds could encourage the proprietors of ordinary limited companies to adapt the structure of their own companies to try to secure the more favourable tax treatment: if they succeeded, a government could lose substantial tax revenues. Tight definitions of what are often known as 'qualifying companies' are therefore required.

An example is the definition of 'investment trust companies' in UK tax legislation. These are closed-ended investment companies that can benefit from certain tax alleviations if they fulfil the following criteria set by the taxation authorities:

- The company is not a 'close' company (broadly under the control of five or fewer investors).
- The company must be resident in the UK.
- The company's income must be derived wholly or mainly from investment in securities (over 65% of total income) or rental from eligible properties.
- No more than 15% of the company's assets may be invested in the any one issuer.
- The company may not retain more than 15% of the income it receives from investments (that is, it must pay out 85% or more of dividends and interest received).
- The company may not distribute as dividends surpluses arising from realisation of investments.
- The company's ordinary shares must be listed on the London Stock Exchange.

The company has to submit its annual report and accounts to the tax authorities. If these show that the company is not in compliance with the above requirements the tax authorities will levy tax as if it were a normal company.

Policy on taxation of fund income

In theory the taxation of fund income should be simple, but in practice it is not, due to the varying sources of income that a fund may have, and the different levels of tax that may, or may not, be payable on them.

Examples of different approaches: USA and Europe
There are essentially two ways of approaching the application of tax to fund income. One is that of the USA, which is known as the 'pass-through' system. Whatever income the fund receives is simply passed on to fund investors with no tax intervention. The investor receives a statement annually from the fund, which identifies dividends distributed for the period (which includes short-term gains as well, see below). The investor must then declare these dividends on his tax return.

Table 16.5 *Example of tax credit applying to basic rate tax payer (assuming notional basic rate of tax of 20% withheld)*

	Fund			Direct		
	Tax	Credit	Amount	Tax	Credit	Amount
Dividend paid			100			100
Tax withheld	20			20		
Received by fund		20	80			
Tax to pay	0					
Dividend to investor		20	80			
Received by holder		20	80		20	80
Tax to pay	0			0		
Net			80			80

This probably is the most transparent approach to fund taxation; but it demands a taxation system that can deal with millions of individual tax returns, and a degree of sophistication on the part of the investor who will have to deal with dividend statements which show several different sources of distributed income and gains each of which may attract a different tax rate.

Another approach is exemplified by the UK and most of Europe and is essentially based on 'tax credits', sometimes called the 'imputation' system. This means that companies deduct (or withhold) tax at a certain rate from dividends, before distributing them with a note to the effect of the tax already paid. The fund that receives such a dividend net of tax passes on this 'tax credit' to its investor, who will then only pay more tax if his tax rate is higher than the basic rate of tax applicable to dividends. Table 16.5 shows how this works, giving the comparison with direct investment to demonstrate resulting equity of treatment of direct and fund (indirect) investment in securities.

These are some variations on this theme:

- Different countries may tax interest on bonds or interest on bank deposits at different rates from dividends on shares.
- If dividends or interest are received from abroad, a fund may or may not be able to claim double tax relief (this will depend on bilateral tax treaties).
- If recipients' personal rate of tax is higher than 20% then they must pay the difference between their rate and the 20% paid.
- Some countries allow a person whose tax rate is zero to reclaim the amount of the tax credit. These may be individuals or exempted persons, like pension funds or charities.

Unfortunately for the 'tax credit' system, funds are unlikely only to receive income that has borne tax at source. It is possible that tax is not deducted from interest paid to the fund on domestic government bonds or bank deposits, or from any domestic real estate rental income which the fund receives; or that any such tax is payable at a different rate on each. The picture becomes even more complicated when the fund owns a variety of foreign assets, potentially in a range of countries, each with their own, varying, tax regime that may mean that the fund is unable to claim excess tax paid or may need to pay domestic tax on their receipt. Where investment abroad is concerned, the availability of international double tax treaties is therefore an important consideration in establishing the returns that funds may be able to make.

These differences in tax rates on various types of income may require complex accounting adjustments and tax calculations and will certainly require careful records to be kept. Individuals completing their tax returns frequently expect funds to be able to give them detailed information on tax liabilities that they may have; providing such information is one of the services provided by fund management companies to their investors.

Complexity of accounting for different sources of income

Whatever the general framework of tax legislation, funds will have certain defined liabilities to tax on their income (and capital gains). In different jurisdictions, funds may receive gross income or income taxed at different rates at source. A variety of methods are therefore needed to account for the fund's taxation liabilities.

For example, take the case of a fund in a jurisdiction that has a relatively transparent system. The fund receives dividends and interest payments from domestic listed securities net of income tax at a rate that corresponds to the basic rate of income tax for individual investors. The fund has a liability to the basic rate of tax on this income but this liability is met by the tax credits passed to it by the issuers of the securities it owns. Such income therefore flows though the fund with no actual tax being deducted or paid.

But this is not the end of the story. The fund also keeps some money on deposit with banks where it earns interest, which is paid without any deduction of tax. It also invests in some foreign shares; here dividends are received net of the relevant countries' withholding taxes, which may be higher or lower than the domestic rate. It also holds some Eurobonds[5] whose interest is paid gross.

Assuming tax legislation defines the fund's tax liability as the basic rate of tax, and taking this rate of tax as 20%, the fund's tax liability would be calculated along the lines of those shown in Table 16.6.

It is assumed (as is usually the case) that the management expenses of the fund are a valid deduction from its gross income in computing its tax liability. Where sufficient gross income (from sources such as bank deposits and Eurobonds) is generated to cover the management expenses, then the procedure is straightforward. However, the fund may not generate sufficient gross income. Suppose, in

Table 16.6 *Sample tax liability calculation*

Source of income	Income received	Tax deducted at source	Grossed up income	Tax payable
Domestic shares	8000	2000	10000	
Domestic bonds	10000	Nil	10000	
Foreign shares	7500	2500	10000	
Eurobonds	10000	Nil	10000	
Bank interest	10000	Nil	10000	
Total			50000	
Less management expenses			14000	
Taxable income				36000
Tax due @20%				7200
Less tax deducted				4500
Less tax reclaimable[1]				500
Tax payable				2200
Net income				33800

[1]Under an appropriate double taxation treaty, the fund may reclaim the difference between its own tax rate and any higher rate deducted at source – in this case, between 20% and the 25% withheld on foreign shares.

the example given in Table 16.6, the management expenses were 30000 instead of 14000. In this case the tax deducted at source would amount to more than the fund's actual tax liability. Then the question is whether the fund is entitled to reclaim the tax deducted at source from dividends on domestic shares and from interest on domestic bonds. In some regimes such reclaims are permitted while in others they are not. If such reclaims are difficult and protracted, then fund management companies will tend to generate sufficient gross income to cover management expenses in order to avoid making such reclaims.

A fund's income tax liability calculation might look something like Table 16.6, assuming that the rates of tax were as shown in the Table 16.5.

Differential income tax rates may be problematic
If the tax regime sets the tax rate for fund income at a lower level than would apply to direct purchases of securities, then it creates an incentive for investors to channel all securities purchases through funds. This may be desirable in the initial stages of development of a fund industry where a government is keen to develop a culture of savings. However, in the long run it is also likely to have undesirable side effects. One is that affluent investors will almost certainly try to establish funds under their own control and run them as private portfolios in order to benefit from the lower tax rate.

If tax is payable on income paid through funds, but not on bank deposits or government bonds, for instance, funds are unlikely be able to compete effectively with these lower risk investments since diversification and professional management are unlikely to be strong selling points for funds which invest in relatively risk-free assets.

Policy on taxation of fund capital gains

The main reason developed economies introduce capital gains taxes is to deter investors from evading tax by converting income into capital gains; even in these countries, however, capital gains are often permitted to be tax-free provided they do not exceed a specific annual figure. Conversions of income into capital will only start to occur in conditions where a considerable degree of financial sophistication has developed and where a significant number of people would benefit from them.

Complexities of capital gains tax

Taxes on capital gains can cause even more complexities for funds and their investors than taxes on income. The main reason is that in many jurisdictions, capital gains in the hands of individuals are taxed at a lower rate than income, or not taxed at all, or exemptions are given for small gains in any given year. This creates an incentive for individuals (and funds) to convert income into capital gains, and anti-avoidance provisions may become necessary to counteract this. The fact that under most regimes funds could not pay these gains out to investors as income would not matter, since investors who wished to convert the gains locked into the fund into cash could simply sell sufficient shares to obtain the cash equivalent of the gain. In today's capital markets such income-to-capital conversion strategies are relatively easy to devise.

Starting from the principle of fiscal transparency, this suggests that the fund itself should pay no capital gains tax on its realised profits but that individual investors should be liable to capital gains tax when they sell their fund holdings. But if the situation of the direct investor is considered, who owns a portfolio of securities and manages them actively, he will realise gains and incur capital gains tax on his profits from time to time. If the investor is permitted to hold fund shares or units indefinitely without incurring any capital gains tax, while the fund itself incurs no tax on its internal realised gains, and the individual only becomes liable to gains tax when he sells his fund shares, this does in fact represent a concession for the fund investor as compared with the direct investor in securities. The extent of the concession is unquantifiable because it depends on the behaviour of the individual investor in securities. For example, if he trades actively he will incur tax sooner than if he adopts a 'buy and hold' strategy, particularly if long-term gains are subject to lower or to tapering rates.

The US approach is to require funds to distribute all realised gains in the year in which they arise, and tax the investor on these at the appropriate rate, which may vary with the amount of the gain, whether the gain is short or long and the investor's income. This is a complex way of handling the problem in countries whose tax collection system and investors' sophistication are not of the highest order, and in which tax compliance may be low. Even in the USA the system is believed to cause some distortions and potentially inequitable treatment of certain shareholders in mutual funds, and there have been some attempts to change the system so that any distributed gains that are immediately reinvested would benefit from a deferral of tax until the gain from shares of the mutual fund itself is realised. The famous founder of the Vanguard Group of the USA, Jack Bogle, once said:

> 'The tax issue is the black sheep of the mutual fund industry – like the cousin who can't get her life together or the uncle who drinks too much – best kept out of sight and out of mind'[6]

However, considering the alternative regime, which is that the fund is subject to tax on its realised capital gains, while the investor is also subject to gains tax when he sells, and the investor receives no relief or credit for capital gains tax already paid, then this does represent a form of double taxation which penalises the fund investor as compared with the direct investor.

The different approaches to the taxation of gains

To date, no country has found an entirely equitable, simple and cost-effective approach to capital gains tax, primarily due to the 'conversion' problem. There are three main approaches to the issue and one hybrid solution.

The European approach

Many – but not all – European jurisdictions grant funds exemption from capital gains tax on their realised investment gains. Usually this exemption is subject to the restriction that the gains are not paid out to investors but are retained within the fund and reinvested. The individual investor may or may not be subject to capital gains tax on the profit when he sells his fund shares. Basically this taxation policy represents taxation revenue deferred rather than foregone.

The US approach

The USA – under the 'pass-through' system – makes both short-term (under 12 months) and long-term capital gains (over 12 months) subject to tax in the hands of the fund investor and not the fund. In order to deal with the 'conversion' problem, short-term gains are taxed at the investor's income tax rates, which are higher than long-term capital gains rates. All gains, therefore, are distributed gross of tax, as are dividends and interest.

Complete exemption approach

In less developed economies, governments may prefer simply to exempt individuals' capital gains from taxation altogether. This is unlikely to result in any substantial loss of tax revenue: even in developed economies, capital gains taxes on individuals raise insignificant amounts of revenue as compared with income taxes.

Use of a tax credit: the hybrid solution

A compromise solution is possible, whereby the fund bears capital gains tax at a lower rate than individual investors (say half the normal rate) and passes on a credit of this amount to an investor when he sells. But perhaps the individual investor is for some reason not personally liable to the tax (which will depend of course on the specific gains tax regime). Then he will have to make a tax reclaim. Moreover, suppose that the regime taxes capital gains as additional income, and that there are several progressive income tax rates. Then there are issues about how the tax credit given by the fund will be applied against the individual's tax liability. And there are also difficulties regarding losses carried forward from previous years (if the regime permits this) and their offset against fund gains. So such a compromise solution certainly adds to the complexity of the tax system.

Some countries whose taxation authorities levy taxes on capital gains permit individuals to make a capital gain of up to a certain limit in any one tax year without having to pay tax on this gain. This has the effect of exempting many people from the need to pay capital gains tax to which they would otherwise have been liable.

Effect of the chosen taxation base of funds' capital gains

Where funds are subject to capital gains tax, the variations in the taxation of capital gains may be rather wider than those in the taxation of income.

Deemed cost of acquisition

In general, a gains liability occurs when an asset is sold for a price higher than was originally paid for it. Whatever the rate of tax, there is the complex issue of what the fund's original cost of acquisition of the asset is taken to be, bearing in mind that several purchases of the same security may have been made over several days or indeed several years. It is also likely that, in the case of a security held for many years, there may have been sales as well as purchases and other events which may have affected 'cost' – such as rights and scrip issues, mergers and reconstructions. There are three options for the basis for capital gains taxation: last in first out ('LIFO'), first in first out ('FIFO') and average cost ('AC').

Under international accounting conventions, all three methods are equally valid. Legislation may not lay down which basis funds must use but leave it to fund management companies to decide. In general the average cost method is the simplest and least prone to distortions in use by funds.

The FIFO method, which assumes that the price of the first securities bought is the taxable base for gains or losses on the first sale of the same securities, will obviously result in large tax liabilities in conditions of high inflation unless some form of indexation of costs is permitted. If so, the government will publish an index which may be used to uplift the nominal cost of assets to a higher cost which is used as the basis for computing liability to capital gains tax. Even when such indexation is permitted, the rules for its application may still result in some taxation of 'paper' or nominal gains. This can result in erosion of a fund's assets, and even where the effect is small, it represents an arbitrary imposition. Depending on how taxation is accounted for, it may also disadvantage ongoing investors in a fund at the expense of outgoing investors.

The LIFO method, which assumes that the price of the last securities bought is the taxable base for the first securities sold, is less vulnerable to inflation within a normal range but as a system is better suited to single infrequent asset transactions. Where a fund buys shares at differing prices over a period of time and sells the shares in equal tranches over an extended period, the application of LIFO will produce arbitrarily variable tax liabilities on each sale.

Where capital gains tax is to be paid either by a fund, or by the investor as a result of the requirement to distribute all gains annually, there may be an element of inequity, in that knowledgeable investors may be able to avoid large unrealised gains locked up in the fund by selling their fund shares or units before those gains are realised.

In contrast, the average cost method effectively averages the tax rate across all purchases and sales. As a system it is therefore least likely to produce relative disadvantage for incoming, outgoing or ongoing investors in a fund.

Ability to offset gains and losses

Another issue in relation to funds' capital gains tax liabilities (and indeed those of fund investors) is the ability to 'net out' losses against gains. This means that, where assets have been sold at a loss during the current tax year (or sometimes aggregated over previous tax years), these losses can be deducted from gains realised in the same year, thus reducing the capital gains tax liability. The ability to offset losses against gains, within specific parameters, is given in most developed market fund taxation regimes but sometimes is not applied in emerging economies, where it is probably most needed.

Indexation for inflation
It is common to permit indexation of capital gains against inflation in both developed and developing markets, either within the fund (if capital gains tax applies) or in the hands of the investor. This will, clearly, reduce the liability to capital gains tax.

'OFFSHORE' DOMICILES AND TAXATION

As mentioned in other chapters, traditionally it was popular to create funds in offshore domiciles (many, but by no means all of these are islands) that only levied very low, or no, taxes. Where onshore tax rates were high, the relative risk of tax evasion through use of offshore domiciles was outweighed by the relative advantages of paying low or no tax.

However, these offshore centres were often popular for other reasons also: for instance, they often permitted funds to invest in asset classes that were not open to onshore funds. So if management company Y due to local regulation could not form a money market fund in country X, it could create a sister firm in Luxembourg, which would launch a money market fund whose shares or units would then be sold to investors in country X by management company Y. These funds gave rise to the term 'round-trip' funds – which is still true of many of the offshore funds based in Luxemburg and Dublin.

In recent years tax rates have tended to move down and greater focus on money laundering and other initiatives has made use of onshore, rather than offshore, domiciles more attractive than they used to be. However, these centres are still commonly used, particularly for vehicles for institutional investors or for investment in assets not permitted to onshore funds.

It is conceivable that the tax treatment of funds could be very attractive – they might not be subject to any tax at all (true in Egypt, for instance) – but still not attract a large number of investors. Reasons for this are explored in the next chapter, which looks at how funds are governed and how the conflicts of interest that can arise are controlled.

Those who would like to test their grasp of the contents of this chapter should turn to the self-test questions at the back of the book.

NOTES

1. For instance: PricewaterhouseCoopers and FEFSI (2003) *Discriminatory Tax Barriers Facing the EU Funds Industry – A Progress Report* and KMPG Ireland's *Funds and Fund Management, Regulation and Taxation* reports covering 70 countries.

2. *Country Report for Australia*, IIFC Conference, October 2002, Investment and Financial Services Association, Sydney.
3. *Fundamentals*, 11(2), Investment Company Institute, Washington June 2002.
4. *Economic and Statistical Overview 2001*, Association Française de la Gestion Financière (AFG-ASSFI), Paris.
5. 'According to value' or value based.
6. Internationally issued bonds sold to investors outside the country in whose currency the bonds are denominated.
7. The Vanguard Group® shareholder letter, September 1997.

17

Fund Governance

This chapter looks at a current hot topic: the issue of how investment funds are governed (basically, how decisions are made) and the conflicts of interest that can arise between fund investors and those who operate funds, and their affiliates.

INTRODUCTION

Governance refers to the range of institutions or practices by which authority is exercised: in the funds sector, these need to be designed to ensure that those who operate funds serve the interests of those who own them, rather than putting their own interests, or those of their affiliates, first.

A wide variety of conflicts of interest can arise in relation to collective investment funds, as encapsulated by the following comment, made by John K. Thompson and Sang-Mok Choi, in their paper on fund governance:[1]

'The collective investment sector is characterised by complex agency relationships as well as asymmetry in market power and information. The risk is present that some participants in the collective investment process will abuse agency relationships.'

These conflicts arise due to three key factors:

- Profitability: management companies will wish to make as much profit as possible from their activities in managing funds although this can reduce returns to fund investors: for example, in general, the management company's commercial interest dictates that charges made to funds and the fees earned from them are as high as competitively possible. The investors clearly would prefer that these charges should be as low as possible, since the charges made to funds will reduce the returns that investors receive from them.
- Need for new business: the desire of a management company to enlarge the funds under its management not only by an increase in value resulting from investment returns, but also by selling more units or shares may tempt the management company to misrepresent past or future returns, to mislead people

as to levels of risk or to manipulate fund valuations or to indulge in high-pressure sales methods.
- Misuse of investors' money: worst of all, because it is potentially the most damaging, is the temptation for management companies to use the substantial funds under their management, information about whose investments is asymmetrically in their favour, to benefit themselves or their affiliates at the expense of the investors.

Some more specific examples of these conflicts are illustrated later in this chapter.

COMPONENTS OF FUND GOVERNANCE

The key components of fund governance are:

- Law and regulation.
- Codes of conduct.
- Reputational risk and competitive pressures.

Each of these is explored in more detail below.

Legal and regulatory requirements

The first component of fund governance results from governing law and regulation, which:

- Establishes the legal forms that funds may take and the resulting responsibilities and duties of the various parties.
- Mandates certain forms of disclosure.
- Establishes rules governing the conduct of the business of funds, their management companies and service providers. These rules will include provisions that either prevent management companies entering into activities where conflicts of interest arise, or will specify how they should behave in such circumstances.
- Requires 'third-party supervision' by the depositary or trustee; supervision by the regulator and often internal supervision of regulated firms by compliance departments.

Commonly law and regulation also will define penalties to be applied in cases of failure to comply, which may vary from warnings through fines to withdrawal of authorisation.

No one fund governance structure protects investors better than other structures[2]

It is worth noting that, measured by incidence of fund scandals reported to and reviewed by IOSCO,[3] occurrence of conflicts and breaches identified by regulators are fairly evenly distributed among all types of legal and operational structures throughout the world, with no major concentration of breaches within any one structure or in any one country (refer to Chapter 3 for more information on fund governance structures). Thompson and Choi's exhaustive examination of fund governance structures[4] concludes:

> 'The OECD countries have used a variety of governance structures in the CIS[5] sector. The fact that very few countries have had any crises in the CIS sector and that CIS have become major repositories of wealth would suggest that existing governance mechanisms are adequate and that public confidence is high. At the same time the fact that fraud and misallocation of funds occurred in several European countries before the introduction of adequate legal frameworks and that a serious systemic crisis arose in Korea, where adequate standards were not effectively enforced, provides evidence that such safeguards are needed. At the same time, once a body of acceptable standards has developed and governance structures matured to the point where those assigned an oversight role can compel participants to apply those standards, it becomes very difficult to demonstrate that any particular system provides better investor protection than others.'

In developed markets, the net governance outcome of most permitted fund structures is broadly the same. The directors, trustee, or depositary of the fund essentially supervise the day-to-day conduct of the fund management firm or investment adviser, while the regulator sets entry requirements and standards of conduct for all these entities. The regulator, in effect, delegates much of the day-to-day responsibility for ensuring compliance to these 'third-party supervisors'; this is realistic and practical since they see more of the day-to-day activity of a fund management company than a regulator possibly can. In many ways, a trustee or a depositary may be more effective than fund directors because they see each and every securities transaction carried out by a management company on behalf of the fund at the time or very shortly after it occurs, whereas directors meeting perhaps every other month or even less frequently, may receive only summaries of activity and those a fairly long time after the event.

Power to dismiss the management company

It might be argued that pressure for a fund management company to perform is perhaps stronger where the directors of a corporate fund or trustee of a trust type fund have the power, in the final analysis, to dismiss and replace the fund management company. The exercise of the power of directors, however, is problematic both because even independent directors could be subject to capture by the management company and because in some cases directors are not independent anyway. In the unusual structure of an open-ended investment company permitted in the UK, for example, the management company is permitted to be the single 'authorised corporate director' ('ACD') of a fund, without the inclusion of any independent directors, so is unlikely to sack itself. Many observers regard this provision as a weakening of investor protection and a setback to good governance. However, its proponents point out, rightly, that fund management companies have little room for exploitation because the rules of operation of the fund are set out in advance, with any major changes requiring a vote of investors, and that fund management companies will suffer loss of business if they fail to achieve fund objectives.

The capacity of a board of directors or a trustee of a fund to dismiss or replace a management company does not really exist in the case of the contractual form of fund (although the regulator can and may assume powers to replace management firms in this case). However, no more and no fewer scandals have been associated with this form of fund than with corporate or trust funds that arguably have a stronger governance structure in terms of powers of the directors or trustees of corporate or trust funds and stronger voting rights for fund investors.

Moreover it has to be said that while there are examples of fund directors or trustees changing management companies, it is not a common occurrence, as noted in characteristic style by the famous 'Sage of Omaha', Warren Buffett:[6]

'[Investment company independent] directors and the entire board have many perfunctory duties, but in actuality have only two important responsibilities: obtaining the best possible investment manager and negotiating with that manager for the lowest possible fee. When you are seeking investment help yourself, these two goals are the only ones that count, and directors acting for other investors should have exactly the same priorities. Yet when it comes to independent directors pursuing either goal, their record has been absolutely pathetic.

Many thousands of investment-company boards meet annually to carry out the vital job of selecting who will manage the savings of the millions of owners they represent. Year after year the directors of Fund A select manager A, Fund B directors select manager B, etc.... in a zombie-like process that makes a mockery of stewardship. Very occasionally, a board will revolt. But for the most part, a monkey will type out a Shakespeare play before an 'independent' mutual-fund director will suggest that his fund look at other managers, even if the incumbent manager has persistently delivered substandard performance. When they are handling their own money, of course, directors will look to alternative advisers – but it never enters their minds to do so when they are acting as fiduciaries for others.

The hypocrisy permeating the system is vividly exposed when a fund management company – call it 'A' – is sold for a huge sum to manager 'B'. Now the 'independent' directors experience a 'counter-revelation' and decide that manager B is the best that can be found – even though B was available (and ignored) in previous years. Not so incidentally, B could also formerly have been hired at a far lower rate than is possible now that it has bought manager A. That's because B laid out a fortune to acquire A, and B must now recoup that through fees paid by the A shareholders who were 'delivered' as part of the deal'.

Codes of conduct

The second component of fund governance is the development and adoption of codes of conduct by funds or their management companies or service providers: these are usually voluntary though they may come into existence as a preferable alternative to threatened statutory regulation. Codes are often developed and applied by fund-related trade associations and are common in the areas of:

- Fund advertising and promotions.
- Categorisation of funds.
- Calculation and portrayal of fund performance and performance standards.
- The role of investment funds as shareholders or bondholders in the governance of the issuers in which they invest.

Such codes often have the disadvantage that compliance with them is voluntary and that the penalties for failing to comply with them may not be great. For instance, expulsion from a trade association for failure to comply with its code may have little impact if the organisation's regulatory authorisation would continue. Such expulsions will also have an impact on the financing of the trade association, since it will be dependent upon its members' subscriptions. However, publicising such expulsions could lead to loss of reputation (see below), which may be a stronger incentive to comply.

Before discussing this third – reputational – component, it is worth highlighting the fact that the role of funds as shareholders or bondholders in other companies has been the focus of increasing attention in recent years, as the whole area of corporate governance[7] has become a hot topic. Funds are, of course, unusual in that governance applies at two levels – the level of the fund itself and the level of the companies in which the fund invests.

Codes of conduct governing funds' role as investors are increasingly common, often covering:

- Ensuring the compliance of companies in which funds invest with relevant codes relating to corporate governance.

- The responsible exercising of funds' voting rights.
- Ensuring that mechanisms are in place to ensure that funds' votes are exercised.
- Tracking funds' voting records.
- Maintaining effective communications with investee companies.
- Disclosure of fund policy towards investee company governance and of voting policy in fund prospectuses and annual reports.
- Disclosure of other relevant fund policies, e.g. on environmental or social issues (SRI) in prospectuses and reports.
- Training staff in corporate governance matters.

It is worth noting that classical investment funds have, traditionally, sold a company's shares when they disagreed with its decisions, rather than taking issue with such decisions. In recent years, however, a more pro-active approach to investee company governance has been pioneered, by organisations such as the California Public Employees Retirement Scheme (better known as 'CalPERS'), which has a systematic approach to getting involved in the governance of those companies in its investment portfolios which are performing badly: apparently with positive results. It is worth noting, however, that CalPERS is a huge defined benefit pension scheme (covering around 1.3 million people, with around 1600 employees and administrative expenditures of around US$245 million[8]) with an investment portfolio valued at US$132.6 billion[9] that is well able to support the cost of such involvement, which can involve taking legal action, which is rarely cheap. The same may not be true of smaller funds. In addition, the benefit of such action cannot be guaranteed.

Reputational risk and commercial pressures

A third component of fund governance is reputational risk: that is, the fact that fund firms cannot afford to be seen to fail to operate properly and compliantly – if they are, investors will become disaffected and leave and the fund management company will lose its business. This produces a purely commercial pressure on errant fund management firms either to improve; or to exit the business by sale to another firm or by closing down the business.

The existence of such pressure, however, is critically dependent upon:

- First, people understanding what a fund (and its management company and service providers) should do and becoming aware that failure is occurring – therefore clarity, quality and timeliness of disclosure, and quick, easy and cheap access to information are key.
- Second, people being able to act upon such knowledge – that is, being able to exit from the fund (if they cannot exit, then they cannot bring this commercial pressure to bear). Open-ended funds are therefore much more subject

to this discipline than closed-ended funds, though closed-ended funds can be liquidated upon a vote; or converted into open-ended funds (if their assets are liquid enough) from which investors are able to exit if they so wish.

- Third, that access to markets is open and fair and so is competition within them: so investors can have confidence that if they are unhappy with their current management firm, they can move to others that have met fully disclosed and consistently applied criteria for authorisation.

While these three factors are present in most developed markets, in general they are likely to be partially or wholly absent from emerging markets, which is partly why, the authors believe, investment funds do not develop successfully in some of these countries. However, it is worth noting that the absence of these factors results from failures in public, not just private, sector governance.[10]

To summarise, quoting Thompson and Choi's examination of fund governance:

'Adequate disclosure enhances the capability of investors to undertake independent scrutiny. In cases where inadequate governance procedures are in place or where standards are not observed investors can take legal action or lodge complaints with regulators. Perhaps most importantly, any practice that leads to diminished returns to investors will lead to a decline in funds under management. Particularly in advanced competitive markets, this is the sanction most feared by CIS operators.... [11] The two basic factors that enhance the capability of the market to monitor operators are the degree of competition among suppliers and the access of investors to information. In most markets competition is growing markedly – a powerful factor in aligning the interests of investment managers and CIS promoters with those of investors.'

SOME SPECIFIC FUND GOVERNANCE PROBLEMS

The last section of this chapter covers a highly sensitive area, since there is ample scope for abuse both in the process of investment management and in the process of advertising, marketing, sales and distribution of funds. Much of legislation and regulation aims to curb such abuses, in order to create and maintain market confidence.

Investment management

Many conflicts of interest can arise in the area of investment management, in relation to individual employees of fund management companies and in relation to fund management companies or their affiliates, either of whom may benefit themselves at the potential cost of fund investors. In order to deal with the first eventuality some fund management companies bar employees from undertaking any personal transactions in securities, requiring them to commit their own money either to investment funds managed by their employer or to a discretionary account under someone else's management. This is unpopular but can be justified in two ways:

- It keeps them from the temptation of profiting personally at the expense of the fund.
- It keeps their attention fixed on their work and prevents them wasting time worrying about their personal dealing positions.

Alternatively, employees may be permitted to undertake transactions in securities but only through a designated dealer, whose records can then be used to identify if abuses may have taken place.

Despite the attention given to the type of abuse that can damage shareholder and unitholder value by legislators, regulators and management companies, there are still regular cases of malpractice. This is because such abuses are hard to detect and there is an almost infinite variety of ways that knowledgeable professionals can use their position and skill to abuse the rights of holders of the funds, which they manage. Some examples of these are outlined below.

- 'Front running': one of the simplest ways for an investment manager to profit personally from his position is 'front running', where the manager purchases a security for himself immediately before the fund makes a purchase of the same security. The fund's large purchase is likely to push up the market price of the security, enabling the manager to sell his holding at an immediate profit. Or the manager may simply pass on the information about an impending deal to a trusted associate and share the profits. Where house rules bar the practice of front running, managers may resort to the use of associates or offshore accounts to escape the rules. A comprehensive telephone recording and monitoring system can act as a deterrent, but mobile phones may be used to circumvent these.
- 'Insider dealing': as substantial investors in securities, funds will be treated as institutional investors and their management companies may possess price-sensitive information before it is publicly disclosed. This too provides managers with the opportunity to trade personally on advantageous terms. Such 'insider dealing' is a criminal offence in many developed markets, but is hard to detect and hard to prove in court. Requirements for personnel of management companies to deal only through the companies' dealing desks are designed to help to identify occurrence of such dealing.
- 'Warehousing': there are also situations in which fund managers can have financial incentives to exploit the investors in their funds. These are more likely

to arise when the fund management firm is a part of a financial conglomerate which has subsidiaries engaged in corporate activity in the stock market. For example, the conglomerate may be engaged in seeking to mount a take-over for a particular company. Rather than use its own cash to purchase shares, it may instruct the fund managers to purchase shares in the target company for all its funds. In this way a substantial stake, committed to the potential bidder, can be accumulated at no cost or risk to the conglomerate. Even where market and take-over rules require the disclosure of share stakes by associates or people acting in concert, each fund's stake may be held below the threshold above which disclosure is required. This practice, known as 'warehousing', may be beneficial for investors if the bid occurs, but if it does not, the shares may have to be sold at a loss or held as a poorly performing investment.

- 'Rat trading': unless rules specifically forbid this, or market practice prevents it, it is possible for a fund manager to purchase a large block of shares on behalf of both himself and a number of funds under its management, and to allocate the shares to the respective parties only some time after the deal. This enables the manager to allocate the shares showing profits to its own account and the shares showing a loss to a fund's account: a practice known as 'rat trading'. Where rules bar the undertaking of trades on behalf of the fund manager (or its parent or associates) for its own account together with transactions for one or more funds, the ability to 'late-book' or allocate shares to funds some time after the transaction still gives the fund manager the opportunity to 'massage' the performance of funds it wishes to appear successful by allocating to them the larger proportion of shares showing immediate gains.

- 'The dustbin': in some markets issues of new securities are underwritten: a bank or broker-dealer takes an underwriting fee and in return guarantees that all the securities will be taken up at an agreed price. It will then seek buyers for those securities. If it fails to find sufficient buyers, and it looks as if the shares will trade at below the issue price, the bank or broker-dealer may instruct its affiliated fund manager to subscribe for the shares on behalf of its funds, transferring any loss from its own books at the expense of the investors. This practice is known as 'tail-end underwriting'. Similarly, if a bank or broker-dealer buys an issue of securities (a 'bought deal') and then attempts to place them, it may seek to use any funds under its control to take up any that are unwanted and avoid incurring a loss on its own account. Clearly here the management company or its affiliates is avoiding failure at the cost of its funds' investors rather than itself.

- New issues: its position as a large institutional investor will lead to the fund management company being offered attractive investment opportunities. In rising markets, new share issues can often be predicted to produce quick and sometimes substantial profits. The fund management company will be offered participation in such issues and will have the right to allocate them among its funds. It is therefore relatively easy for it to give an upward boost to the performance of any one fund, especially a relatively small one, by allocating all attractive new issues to it at the cost of other eligible funds.

All the above actions, designed in one way or another to enable the fund management company or individuals within it to profit at the expense of the investors whose money they manage, are illegal in most countries. But they all happen: in several cases within highly respected asset management businesses and all within the last decade.

Advertising, sales and distribution

'Commission-driven selling of these products remains the norm, leading to persistent concerns about consumer detriment and to consequent regulatory intervention. Recent research by the FSA[12] found statistically significant evidence of advisers recommending one provider's offering over another because it paid a higher commission.'[13]

This pithy comment by the author of a UK government-commissioned report illustrates well the concerns of regulators about methods of marketing and selling by fund management companies (and others) to retail investors, who are relatively unsophisticated in financial matters.

These regulatory concerns fall into several categories:

- Misrepresentation or manipulation of past performance (refer to Chapter six), whereby a management company may lead a potential investor to believe that future returns will be in line with past returns, or whereby the returns may be made to look better than they actually were.
- Failure to point out the risks of certain types of products, which may appear to offer attractive yields or guaranteed returns.
- Persuasion of distributors to sell particular products using high commissions or other inducements.

All these may have the result that investors only realise too late that they have invested in a product they did not understand and that may have been inappropriate for their needs.

There are numerous cases of major mis-selling as a result of misrepresentation of return or risk in countries as diffuse as the UK, the USA, Japan, Korea and India, most of which eventually caused some form of financial crisis and cost someone, often the taxpayer, money as compensation was paid out as a result of regulatory action or government embarrassment.

The examples of conflicts of interest reviewed in this chapter – and others quoted elsewhere in this book – illustrate how easy it is for abuses to occur, even in markets where regulators are both competent and have sufficient resources and powers to be effective. Where regulators are weak and fund management companies are well connected, there is little risk of perpetrators of such abuses being called to account; as a consequence funds will have a poor reputation and will be attractive only to those with an 'inside track'.

The next chapter of the book brings all the previous chapters together, looking at how fund management businesses are managed and at the importance of connectivity between the three key parts of the business – administration, investment management and marketing.

NOTES

1. *Governance Systems for Collective Investment Schemes in OECD Countries*, Financial Affairs Division Occasional Paper No1, OECD, Paris, April 2001.
2. For further elaboration, see: Chapter 9, Governance of Investment Funds, *Financial Sector Governance*, Mark St Giles and Sally Buxton, The Brookings Institution, Washington DC, 2002.
3. *Conflicts of Interest of CIS Operators*, IOSCO, Madrid, May 2000.
4. *Governance Systems for Collective Investment Schemes in OECD Countries*, Financial Affairs Division Occasional Paper No1, OECD, Paris, April 2001.
5. Collective investment scheme (in the context of this quote, open-ended funds).
6. 2002 letter to Berkshire Hathaway shareholders.
7. Defined by OECD as 'the system by which business corporations are directed and controlled', *OECD Principles of Corporate Governance*, OECD, Paris, 1999.
8. Facts at a Glance – General Facts, CalPERS website, January 2003.
9. As at the end of October 2002: Facts at a Glance – Investments, CalPERS website, January 2003.
10. For further elaboration, see: Chapter 5, Public Sector Governance and the Private Sector, *Financial Sector Governance*, Jeffrey Carmichael, The Brookings Institution, Washington DC, 2002.
11. Fund management companies, in this context.
12. Financial Services Authority, London.
13. *Sandler Review of Medium and Long Term Retail Savings in the UK*, HM Treasury, London, June 2002.

18

Managing the Business

INTRODUCTION

This chapter looks at the business aspects of managing funds: that is, operating the business that is responsible for the investment management, administration and marketing of funds. This may be done through a business which is set up to manage either investment funds alone (a 'fund management company') or investment funds in conjunction with other types of portfolio managed on behalf of institutional and retail clients if that is permitted by legislation (often referred to as an 'asset management company'). For the purposes of this chapter, the terms 'fund management company' and 'asset management company' will both be used more or less interchangeably, since both can usually manage investment funds.

Law and regulation usually establishes specific requirements for eligibility of such entities for authorisation as fund or asset management companies: these may concern their precise legal nature (corporate, partnership), permitted range of activities, eligibility of shareholders, minimum capital and required resources and personnel amongst other factors (refer to Chapter 4).

BUSINESS CONCEPTS

Those who own and manage investment fund management businesses have three main concerns:

- Their ability to create and manage a sufficient range of products to satisfy the needs of the market and to ensure that the returns to investors are at least competitive with other products on the market.
- Their ability to distribute the products to the market in sufficient volume in a way that is cost-effective.
- Their ability to keep costs down and to enable the benefits of economies of scale to flow through to the bottom line.

The profit and loss account for such a business is very simple in theory. Income is broadly derived from initial sales charges, annual management fees, performance fees and redemption fees. Costs are largely those relating to salaries, systems, office expenses and marketing. The difference between the two is profit. In practice though, however simple the profit and loss account statement appears to be, asset management businesses are not easy to manage, and it is as easy to make losses in some market conditions as it is to make profits. This is because, while almost all the costs, with the exception of marketing and advertising, are fixed, the income is both variable and hard to predict. This gives ample scope for management to be too optimistic about future business prospects in bull markets and increase fixed costs which are not, in the event, covered by increased income; or to spend large sums on marketing a new fund or service, sales of which do not live up to expectations.

Another aspect of any asset management business is that there are very significant economies of scale, particularly at the investment fund end of the business. Massive investment in the technology of processing large numbers of small transactions can pay off handsomely if volumes increase, but can prove to have been an expensive mistake if the systems fail to perform adequately or volumes do not materialise. It is thought that in the last few years several asset management companies in Europe have invested tens of millions in developing on-line dealing in funds based on their own websites: however, evidence indicates that increasingly such dealing is largely done through centralised fund supermarkets or consolidators (for which asset management companies also have to develop or buy systems interfaces) so this investment may have been wasted.

Asset management is a highly valued business at certain times

The management of investment funds (and other types of institutional and private portfolios) is a business, which, if it is well managed, can be a highly profitable one for its owners, not only in terms of current profitability and dividends, but also in terms of the future capital value of the business. This arises from the attribution of a capital value to the future streams of revenue derived from the contracts to manage funds, which in turn gives a fund management company a measurable market value. In recent times, the rule of thumb for this valuation in developed markets has tended to be between 2% and 4% of the value of funds under management, although the market conditions prevailing since 1999 will have affected this valuation adversely, and a number of asset management companies offered for sale have failed to find a buyer. Thus, a fund management company with funds under management of 1000 million would theoretically be valued at between 20 and 40 million.

The actual figures paid to acquire asset management businesses will depend on overall market conditions, the structure of the business, the type of funds managed and the client base, as well as current or likely future profitability. Clearly an asset

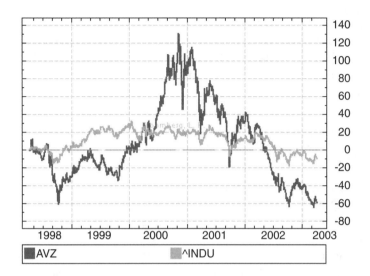

Figure 18.1 *Share price of a leading listed investment management company (AMVESCAP) in good times and bad*
© 2003 Bloomberg L.P. All rights reserved. Reprinted with permission. Visit www. Bloomberg.com

management business, which only manages funds for its parent shareholder(s) and their affiliates and is therefore dependent on them, would be worth less than one that has a broadly diversified client base. There has also been a tendency to value retail businesses more highly than ones that are predominantly institutional, since institutions can become nervous at ownership changes and start quickly to look around for a new manager, whereas retail fund investors are more inert. A number of fund and other asset management companies are listed on exchanges and their prices can be used as a point of reference.

However, given their dependence on economic and financial factors outside their control, and in particular the health of securities markets, the profits from and the value ascribed to asset management businesses can be volatile. So there are some points in the economic cycle at which the value the market ascribes to asset management businesses will be high and others at which it will be low. Figure 18.1 charts the price of a well-known listed asset management company during the bull market of the late 1990s and the bear market of 1999 onwards.

Managing a fund or asset management business is not as easy as it might seem

In some respects, a fund management company appears a simple kind of company to manage. Conceptually it is. Revenues are derived from initial charges on new

sales of products or redemption fees and from annual management and performance fees, while fixed costs are composed mostly of wages and premises, and
variable costs (confined mainly to marketing and sales) are completely within the
control of the management company. The difference between revenues and costs
is profit, which should continue to grow provided that funds under management
continue to increase as a result of new sales and/or a rise in market values, and
provided that costs are kept under control.

However, there are several reasons why the management task is not quite as
simple as described in the last paragraph.

- The processes involved in fund management all have to be integrated in terms
  of functions and systems, and all are time-critical with severe business and
  regulatory penalties for breakdowns and delays; heavy investment in systems
  is needed.
- Competition is very fierce, since the 'retail' market is now regarded as the
  most interesting and consistently profitable area for investment management
  companies.
- In the 'institutional' market, those responsible for advising trustees and directors with whom to place their funds keep a sharp eye on asset management
  companies and are quick to advise their clients to make a change if performance or service deteriorates.
- Compliance with increasingly tough regulations in the many different countries
  in which the company may operate is expensive and complex.

Forecasting is difficult

The main complication is that while it is relatively easy to predict and control
costs, forecasting and controlling the level of revenues is notoriously difficult.
Revenues may depend on several relatively unpredictable factors:

- The level of securities markets will determine the amount of revenue from
  annual management charges – assuming that these are charged as a percentage
  of net asset value, the normal way of charging. Successful forecasting therefore
  will depend on being able to predict the level of different securities markets for
  as long ahead as the period for which budgetary forecasts are being made.
- Successful or unsuccessful investment performance will not only partially determine the level of funds under management but will also influence the ability
  of the manager to attract new clients or subscriptions; by contrast, a consistently poor set of investment results over a long period or a market downturn
  will cause clients to withdraw their funds and look elsewhere for better opportunities.
- Unpredictable political and economic events and changes in taxation will shape
  the perceptions of investors and encourage or discourage clients from investing
  or cause them to disinvest.

It is also difficult for those responsible for managing the management company to determine what products and services should most appropriately be offered. Given the increasingly international nature not only of investing, but also of the investment management and investment fund business, it is very tempting for larger management companies to try to offer every type of product and service everywhere; but just as is the case in any commercial company an excessively large range of products will almost certainly result in the efforts of the firm being spread too thinly with the result that none of the activities is as profitable as it should be. As classical management theory has it, the most consistently profitable companies are those that concentrate on a core business and try to offer the same basic range of products in every market, perhaps with different names. The pan-European ice-cream market, dominated by one company, is a good example.

A business most of whose costs are mainly fixed, which tend to drift upwards in good times, and all of whose revenues are variable has a highly leveraged stream of profits. A fall in revenues can quickly obliterate profits unless costs are adjusted downwards too; this is not an easy or quick process, since a very high percentage of fixed costs are people.

Companies are unwilling to shed good people so long as they maintain the hope that things will get better, since they will have invested a lot in training them and may be afraid that they will not get them back when times improve.

There are a number of ways that management companies attempt to deal with high fixed costs. One is to 'lose' fixed expenses by charging all costs that can be charged to a fund directly to a fund, ensuring that they are not borne out of the management company's revenues. This may, of course, have the effect of raising the total expense ratio of the fund, which has implications for the firm's competitive position. The other is to turn fixed costs into variable costs which is explored further later in this chapter.

Asset management businesses can easily find themselves wrongly positioned

Financial markets and fashions change quickly. It is easy for today's highly successful business segment to be tomorrow's problem child. Some real examples of how wrong decisions might have been in hindsight are as follows:

- Who would have thought that the prominence and success of Japan's financial markets in the mid- to late 1980s could have turned into a decade-long bear market? Excessive commitment to either Japanese investments or Japanese clients would have turned out to have been a poor business decision in retrospect; many asset managers are now pulling out of Japan altogether.
- The failure by many leading European asset managers to have an adequate presence in the USA in the late 1990s during what has been called the 'bull

market of the century' was another example of bad strategic decision making, although they were eventually, after 10 years, proved right.

- In the second half of the 1990s telecommunications, media and technology firms were regarded as sure fire winners; by late 2002 the NASDAQ index of telecoms had fallen by more than 90% from its early 2000 peak and the German Neuer Markt, a predominantly technology focused market, had closed; a heavy commitment to the technology sector would have caused terrible damage to a firm's reputation and profits.
- It is also possible to waste large amounts of money in the expectation of developments that are much slower to come to fruition than anticipated; the integration of European markets for investment funds was in sight in 1985, at the time of the passage of the first EU Directive on collective investment funds, and was still expected at the turn of the millennium. Management companies that had committed themselves to a major expansion in expectation of the development of a pan-European market would have suffered additional costs without attendant revenues.
- Emerging markets often appear to have a bright future, but that can be a trap. In 1996–97 many regarded Russia as an exceptional investment and business opportunity. Then in 1998 the equity market fell by 90% and the government repudiated its domestic debt. At least one heavily committed manager had virtually to close its almost valueless funds. But later, when least expected, Russia turned out to be a star market when other markets were falling.
- It would, at the time of writing, be easy to be mesmerised by the prospects for the investment fund business in China, with its 1.17 billion[1] people, all of whom are high savers holding collectively the equivalent of US$1.17 trillion[2] in low-interest bank deposit accounts waiting to be converted to investment funds. Whether this market turns out to be the gold mine expected remains to be seen.

While the difficulty of making predictions is a constant feature of the lives of managers of asset management businesses, not only in the management of portfolios but in the management of the business too, at the same time they must face strong competition. In the retail markets of developed countries in recent years competitive pressures have meant:

- Competition for distribution has driven commission payments to advisers and salespeople up, reducing retention of initial and annual management fees by management companies.
- Thinner margins have required larger and larger funds under management for break-even to be achieved; in the UK between 1980 and 2000 the average size of a fund increased from around $15 million to $200 million;[3] in the USA in the same period the average size increased from $238 million to $852 million.[4]

- The generation of sufficient sales to meet revenue targets has required a large commitment to advertising, marketing, customer service and distribution.

The risk of failure is high.

Maximising the likelihood of success and minimising the risk of failure

As in any other business it is important for senior management to be clear about what it is trying to achieve. Its objective may depend on the objectives set by the owners of the management company. Examples of these objectives are:

- Building up the value of funds under management as rapidly as possible by focusing on particularly fashionable sectors, with an eye to the profitable sale of the business in the relatively near term.
- Building a sound, diversified business in the long term without immediate concern about creating short-term value.
- Providing services to customers of the parent company or group, without too much regard for where the profit falls, since there will often be cross-subsidies from using existing group facilities at low or no charge (this would typically be the aim of a bank or other financial institution with a wide range of products which it offers to its customers).

Whichever of these objectives (or others) is chosen, the mission statement will shape the plan and the budget. Failure to have a clear objective, as in any other business, will result in diffusion of effort. The definition of an objective and a route form the basis for the assessment of the company's ability to meet the targets and the steps necessary to do so.

The ability to achieve the objective and fulfil the mission statement will be subject to obvious constraints, such as:

- The availability of resources or the ability to tolerate lower profits or losses to finance expansion – which in the case of management companies of investment funds will mean incurring losses which represent the initial costs of developing new products, of entering new markets or of investment in systems to support those strategies.
- The availability of sufficient numbers of competent trained staff, notably those who have met regulatory requirements, if the regulatory regime requires particular qualifications.
- The need to achieve profitability at some stage in the near future or at a later date.
- The external environment – the level and direction of markets, investor confidence, the availability of savings and competition.

Above all success will depend on the ability of senior management to have a clear vision and to implement realistic plans to achieve it, while remaining able to adapt to a rapidly changing environment.

ORGANISATION AND KEY MANAGEMENT ISSUES

The way in which a business is organised, with clear responsibilities and reporting lines, is the basis for effective implementation and management. Figure 18.2 shows a typical organisational structure for an asset management business; naturally each company will organise itself slightly differently, but the main elements will always be present, whatever they are called and however they fit into the organisational structure (though some activities may be outsourced, see later).

It should be remembered that it is not merely the formal organisational and control structure which is important, it is rather the way in which successful integration and management of the range of relationships is achieved, which is the key to effective delivery to the client and to cost control.

Within the internal organisation chart there are an important series of interdepartmental relationships that need to operate harmoniously. Among these are many which can give rise to tensions and problems. It is the duty of senior management to manage the organisation in such a way that tensions are minimised and the whole works harmoniously towards an agreed set of objectives, which are established in the planning and budgeting process.

There may also be a varying number of external relationships with service suppliers, distributors and the financial markets themselves. These often important

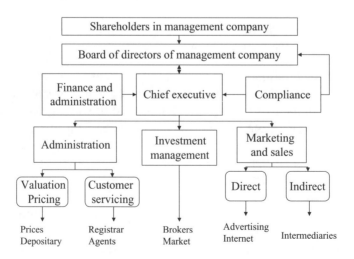

Figure 18.2 *A typical organisational structure*

delegated or contractual relationships need to be managed in a way that avoids conflicts and misunderstandings, the resolution of which may prove costly.

Management of the business: connectivity is important

All three parts of the business – investment management, administration and marketing (whose activities are covered in detail in other chapters) – must work effectively together. If they fail to do so, mistakes will be made which will cost money and possibly give rise to regulatory penalties. Some examples of these are set out below.

Investment management relationships
There is inevitably an important set of relationships between investment management, the portfolio accounting department, and the depositary or trustee, since the last have to complete the transactions which have been initiated by the investment managers and then to ensure that the portfolio is kept up to date for transactions, capital actions and the receipt of income, is valued at the appropriate times and that dealing prices for sales and redemptions are calculated correctly.

This set of relationships is one of the most important within management companies and has sensitive regulatory implications if incorrectly carried out. There are a number of things which can go wrong, each of which may result in an incorrect price for issue or redemption being calculated and used. These are covered in more detail in Chapters 7, 9 and 10, but a brief example of this is:

- The investment manager fails to notify investment accounting of a transaction.
- The depositary refuses to settle transaction since it has not been notified.
- The next valuation will be incorrect.
- The dealing price will be wrong.

This is a serious administrative problem, which arose from the failure to pass accurate and timely information along the chain of internal departments and external organisations. The introduction of the most modern systems, using straight-through processing will ensure the timely passage of data along the information chain but cannot completely eliminate human error.

Marketing relationships
Clearly it is important for marketing to communicate effectively with investment management and administration: particularly in relation to the development of ideas and plans for new funds or services where the development of the idea, the assessment of asset availability to deliver the idea, the systems and administrative support needed to make it happen and the development of a marketing plan and

budget will require input from all three areas. An example of the sort of glitches that can arise is:

- Marketing fails to notify administration of a new launch, so they are unprepared for the onslaught of applications.
- They also fail to advise investment management of the new fund launch, so they are unprepared to manage the money as it arrives.

The desirable build up in customer support for the products of a particular management company is not achieved simply by a series of smart advertisements and the expenditure of large budgets. Success takes time, patience and organisation. Good co-ordination between departments has been stressed, but also good co-ordination between the different parts of a marketing and distribution strategy will also make most effective use of the budgets that have been agreed.

The aim of senior management in managing the marketing department is to ensure that sales are maximised for the minimum expenditure and that money is not wasted on harebrained marketing schemes.

One of the hardest decisions for senior management to take is when to increase the spend on marketing and when to reduce it. In periods when financial and securities markets are in decline and sales are hard to make, an obvious reaction is to cut the spend on marketing and advertising, the one major variable cost in a fund management company's profit and loss account. This is relatively painless in that it does not usually involve many unpleasant redundancies, which are an inevitable consequence of deeper cost-cutting exercises.

But experience has shown that to disappear from the marketplace, however beneficial that may be for short-term profits, may not be the best long-term strategy for a number of reasons:

- The market forgets quickly.
- Customers become concerned that their fund management companies are going out of business.
- Sales agents or financial advisers recognise that the company has ceased to support their efforts and will turn elsewhere.
- It is expensive to re-enter a market once abandoned.

The most successful asset management businesses are always visible through good times and bad, although in bad times they will be spending significantly less than when they can achieve an immediately profitable return on their marketing expenditure. Effective senior management will have the vision to resist the inevitable attempts by their finance director to kill marketing expenditure at the first sign of a downturn.

Shareholder and unitholder dealing, administration and servicing relationships
This department is at the front line between the company and its customers. As such its standards and services will be those by which the whole firm is judged. In common with any organisation which is processing and recording large amounts of data there is considerable scope for error, given that a major fund management company may have millions of share or unitholders carrying out thousands of transactions a day.

The sort of glitches than can arise here include:

- Administration fails to tell marketing that take up of a new fund is poor, so marketing fails to review its current strategy and spend (the opposite of course can also arise – marketing are not told that take up is very high, so continue advertising despite the fact that administration can barely cope).
- Administration fails to tell investment management that there have been major redemptions from a fund, so there is a lack of cash available to meet said redemptions.

Given that this part of the business is dependent on IT and systems and requires an increasingly large investment into those, particularly if the firm is international in its scope, it has become increasingly attractive for all but the very large fund management companies to outsource part or all of this function to specialist firms which are able to achieve economies of scale and continue to invest in the very latest equipment and systems. Their operations do not need to be located in expensive city centre locations and therefore most such companies are based in cheaper out-of-town locations, where not only rents, but also salaries, are lower. The largest suppliers of administrative services will offer a complete package that will include:

- share and unit dealing
- issue and redemption
- registration
- portfolio accounting
- preparation and dispatch of reports to share and unitholders
- pricing
- compliance reporting
- interfaces to fund supermarkets
- operation of 'wrappers'.

Increasingly, in developed markets, depositary clearing companies or fund supermarkets and consolidators will stand between a fund management company and its distribution networks. While these may be able to reduce transaction costs significantly, they also break any direct link between the fund management company and its ultimate customers.

As will be seen later, use of an outsourced service and of centralised clearing and settlement mechanisms will permit, to some extent, fixed costs to be turned into variable ones and thus a reduction in the critical break-even point of the management company.

Finance

In addition to all the other accounting and bookkeeping functions which are present in a fund management company, which relate to portfolio accounting and share or unitholder administration, the firm will need to have its own books of accounts kept. Accounting for a fund management company and planning and budgeting are vital management control functions, which not only record the progress of the company in financial terms but also provide the tools for responding to the budgetary requests from different departments and for allocating the available resources between them.

It has already been pointed out that budgeting and forecasting the likely revenues of a fund management company is difficult. This is true in the context of an established business in a known market but doubly true when a decision is taken to enter a new market (in the business not in the investment sense), in which there will be a number of variables and uncertainties that are outside the experience of the senior management.

To some extent, entering a new market, while it can be analysed logically using the same tools as those applied to forecasting in a more familiar market, is an act of faith. It will involve losses until new customers and sales justify that faith; or may end up having been a completely wrong decision. Strong nerves, deep pockets and a committed board and major shareholder are needed for this kind of expansion, which is why merger or acquisition may be the preferred option.

Each business area will report its results against budgets and targets to the finance division, which will monitor progress. A strong finance department is an asset to any business, particularly to a business as international and complex as fund management.

Management company administration

In addition, as with any other company, a fund management company will have its own administrative needs, covering human resources, IT and systems, etc. These may fall within a single division of finance and administration or may be a separate division.

Compliance

In the increasingly international context in which fund management companies operate, compliance with laws and regulations is no longer simply a matter of knowing and obeying the law of one country, but of many – bearing in mind also that the regimes of some countries can also impinge on how fund management companies and service providers such as custodians conduct themselves in others. It is one of the major concerns of senior management to ensure that the fund management firm remains in compliance, since the consequences of failure to do so – fines or public censure – can not only be expensive, but extremely damaging to the reputation and hence the future profitability of the company.

There is always a conflict between the compliance department and all other parts of the business; compliance is perceived as usually coming up with the answer 'no' to the question 'can we do X?' and is thus regarded by operational departments as an unreasonable drag on their pursuit of legitimate business and profit.

In Figure 18.2, the compliance department is shown as reporting directly to the chief executive, which is a measure of its importance and its need to be seen as independent from other line operating departments. Its function is twofold:

- To ensure that the company remains in compliance with all relevant legislation and files reports regularly with the proper authorities.
- To ensure that the internal organisation and operation of the management company is such as to ensure that it can consistently demonstrate that it does comply with the relevant regulations and that staff are fully aware of their regulatory responsibilities.

Among the tools it will use to fulfil its functions are:

- Monitoring of all new legislation and regulation as it is issued (no mean task in itself).
- Development of internal procedural manuals for all relevant departments, which set out in detail the functions that need to be performed and the correct and compliant way of performing them.
- Requirements for written undertakings by staff that they have read and understood the company's internal rules of conduct as applied to their particular jobs.
- Regular staff training to keep personnel up to date with changes in legislation and regulation or with the regulatory requirements of new markets which the fund management firm proposes to enter.
- Internal compliance inspections designed to ensure that procedures laid down in internal manuals are being followed.
- Maintenance of a register of complaints from customers and regular analysis of this to ensure that complaints are dealt with and that there is not a regularity in the pattern of complaints which points to some systematic weakness.
- Regular review of the fund management company's published and broadcast materials including advertisements, prospectuses and reports to ensure that they have all the required contents and do not make statements which are misleading or incorrect or omit required contents.
- Regular meetings with a compliance committee of senior managers from different parts of the firm to report problems and agree solutions.

The director of compliance and his department are the first point of contact for the regulator, and one of their duties will be to maintain a good and open relationship with the relevant people there. This department will also be in the front line if the regulator decides to conduct an inspection or an investigation.

An increasingly onerous area within compliance is dealing with money laundering regulations, which are developing internationally as a result of efforts to reduce tax avoidance or evasion and impede movement of funds by criminals and terrorists.

PLANNING AND BUDGETING

The decision to start up an investment fund management business in an emerging market or a decision by an existing fund management business to enter a new market will be determined by an overview of the potential within that market to run a profitable business and of any significant drawbacks or constraints. The following skeleton for such a strategic analysis may be useful.

- *Demand* – what is the amount of household savings and their current deployment; what are the competitive products?
- *Supply* – are there suitable assets in which to invest?
- *Appropriateness of legal and regulatory framework* – do laws and regulations adequate for the creation and operation of investment funds exist?
- *Competence, powers and capacity of the regulatory body* – are these sufficient to ensure a fair and open market and that funds can enjoy the confidence of investors?
- *Law enforcement capacity* – are governing laws competently and fairly enforced by courts of law?
- *Availability of distribution channels* – are there distribution channels through which investors can receive information and subscribe for funds?
- *Existence of competent and experienced staff* – are there people of suitable calibre and quality to operate the business?
- *Financial market infrastructure* – does the necessary market infrastructure exist and is it reliable and cost efficient?
- *Money transfer and payment services* – what is the quality, cost and reliability of these?
- *Accounting standards* – do appropriate accounting standards for funds exist?
- *Taxation matters* – is there an appropriate taxation regime for funds?
- *Media* – what is the quality and impartiality of local or national media in relation to advertising and information dissemination?

Having made a broad strategic decision, then a detailed plan will be needed.

Analysis

External
External factors will have a major influence on the company's ability to meet its goals. Factors that should be considered, together with any dangers and opportunities they present to the company, include the following.

Prospects
- How much do people save? Is the ratio rising or falling?
- Does the public have confidence in funds? What could happen to improve or reduce confidence?
- What products does the public prefer? What might make them change their preferences?
- Do taxes currently give individuals incentives to use or avoid funds and is this likely to change?

The economic and legal background
- Is the legal regime for joint stock companies and funds firmly established? Are major changes likely? If so what would be the effects?
- What is the nature of existing markets for securities? Are there likely to be improvements in security, clearing systems, listing procedures, stock exchange membership, or corporate governance that would increase public confidence in markets?
- How stable is economic policy? Are stop-go policies or a high rate of inflation possible? Are short-term interest rates likely to be raised in defence of the currency exchange rate?
- What scenarios appear most likely for the performance of the relevant markets?
- What are the implications of very poor and very good performance?

Competition
- Which competitors appear likely winners over the next few years? Why? What elements of their strategies could be worth imitating?
- What other firms are likely to enter the market in the foreseeable future? Will they have large capital resources or captive distribution? Could they cut existing management companies off from a significant number of potential customers?
- What gaps are there in the market for products or methods of reaching prospects?

Internal
This analysis of the external environment then leads on to a similar internal analysis applied to the company itself. Here the answers should be more precise and specific, especially in terms of any perceived threats or opportunities.

Customers
- Who are the existing or potential customers?
- What are their characteristics in terms of gender, family, age, income, location, wealth, affiliations, employment, etc?
- What are customers' views of the company or its parent company? Its image? Its products? Its performance? Its service?
- Is the situation of the customers, in terms of income, employment and wealth, improving or deteriorating? Will this change?

Ownership
- Does the company have stable ownership for the foreseeable future?
- Does the company have sufficient capital for its current needs? Is more capital available if needed?
- What return on capital is required and how soon? What proportion of profits do the owners wish to withdraw?

Brand
- Does the company have a brand image?
- Is it well known for any particular characteristic or policy? Can this be exploited more or better?

Distribution
- Does the company have partners to assist in distribution?
- Are these arrangements stable?
- Is there potential for new partnerships or channels?

Skills
- How does the company rate its skills in marketing, investment, administration and customer care?
- How does it compare with its nearest rivals?
- What strengths can it exploit better?

Products
- How do the company's products compare with those of competitors in terms of design, performance and charges? How does the average performance of its products compare with its rivals'?
- How quickly is the company capable of launching a new product?
- Is the existing range of products adequate in terms of the needs of existing customers? In terms of the needs of prospects?

This part of the analysis should involve as many people as possible and can be undertaken on a departmental basis and down to the smallest functional unit within a department. If employees are involved in this analysis, it will be much easier to persuade them to 'own' the budget that emerges from the planning process and this in turn will make the budget far more accurate.

Creating the budget

The planning process is intended to produce a budget that shows in money terms the effect of the company's moves to meet its objectives. The senior management of a fund management company will have a number of specific concerns in creating the budget.

Stability of earnings

The greatest potential weakness of a fund management company is the fluctuation of revenues and profits as a result of market movements. In particular, fund management companies with a large volume of open-ended funds are exposed to a market fall in two ways: the decline in the value of the assets reduces management fees and revenues; and the fall may encourage more investors to redeem their holdings, thus further reducing funds under management and hence revenues.

For many fund management companies, building a portfolio that includes closed-ended as well as open-ended funds is therefore a desirable strategic objective. Even though the value of closed-ended funds also falls in falling markets, investors cannot exit the funds, so revenues are more stable.

Opportunities to launch closed-ended funds will depend on the supply/demand situation, since it is virtually impossible to launch new closed-ended funds at times when similar existing closed-ended funds are trading at wide discounts to their net asset values.

Fund management companies therefore need to have an overall objective in terms of the balance of open- and closed-ended funds and to take advantage of market conditions to achieve this.

The need to grow funds under management

Economies of scale have a profound influence on the investment fund business. They give fund management companies strong incentives to expand funds under management, since costs should rise by a relatively much lesser amount; and a very high proportion of the extra revenues therefore represents profit. This results in two principal trends: the launch of many new funds and a steady move to larger business units.

In some markets it sometimes seems that there are more funds being offered than there are investors to make them profitable. The trend is for an increasing number of funds to be launched during bull markets or in response to demands from the marketing department or from intermediaries for something new. But often their total size may remain small, unless they are particularly distinctive either in their objective or their performance, since they are duplicating many other funds already available in the market.

Sometimes mergers between fund management companies will result in consolidation as the merging companies eliminate duplication in their ranges. Bear markets also give rise to consolidation because managers will try to reduce costs by merging uneconomic funds. Nonetheless, there are arguably too many funds on the market (at the end of 2002 results were reported for just over 53 000 open-ended funds worldwide[5]), many of which are not generating good profits for their management companies and are potentially confusing investors. It is noticeable that in most developed markets the sales of mainstream funds, domestic equity growth or income, international growth, quality bond or money market account for a fairly high proportion of funds under management and sales. Such funds can be sold in most weathers and therefore have the potential to grow to substantial sizes.

Factors that will affect revenues and costs

Fund management company profits are highly leveraged as the theoretical example in Figure 18.3 shows.

The main factors affecting profits are revenues and costs.

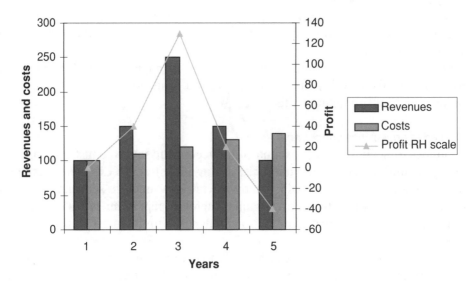

Figure 18.3 *Management company leverage*

Revenue

The revenue of the fund management company is principally dependent on the amount of funds managed on which annual fees are earned, expressed as a percentage of the total value of funds managed, and on the amount of new sales which will either themselves bring an immediate contribution to profits through the retention of part of the initial sales charge or which will add to the total of funds managed. Performance fees, if permitted, and redemption fees may also be a factor but are usually less significant.

The construction of a budget and the accuracy of the prediction of the outcome will therefore depend crucially on two factors:

- The predicted level of and the returns produced by the various markets in which the funds under management invest – bond, money markets and equity markets at home and abroad.
- The amount of new sales (less redemptions) that are expected during the budget period.

This is the most difficult part of the budget process. The prediction of the behaviour of financial markets is an inexact science. But in order to produce any kind of budget it is necessary to make an attempt. The alternative, which is less satisfactory, is to assume a scenario in which only sales, less redemptions, are taken into account, and there is an assumption of no market movement.

Costs

While the future revenues of a fund management company are very difficult to predict for the reasons given above, and their variance around any central assumption is likely to become greater the further into the future the prediction is made, the costs are relatively predictable and controllable. In principle, they are also almost all fixed costs. So most management companies make great efforts to turn fixed costs into variable costs and to ensure that any fixed costs that they cannot deal with in this way are kept as low as possible.

Turning fixed costs into variable costs

The key fact about the structure of fund management profitability is that a significant portion of costs are fixed and do not alter quickly in direct proportion to changes in sales volumes or in response to increases or decreases in the market value of funds managed. Thus a management company's profits are subject to considerable 'operational leverage'. If costs remain relatively constant and funds under management grow, profits will rise faster than the increase in funds under management. The opposite is also true. A decline in the value of funds under management will reduce revenues much faster than costs. This is illustrated in Figure 18.3, from which it can be seen that profits are powerfully leveraged by fixed costs. Unfortunately, it is relatively hard to change the fixed costs of the management company quickly.

Methods of converting fixed into variable costs include:

- Outsourcing: the desire for greater adaptability and flexibility has led some fund management companies in developed countries to subcontract (or 'outsource') large parts of their administration to specialists. Specialist administrators (also known as 'third-party administrators' or 'TPAs') are also usually prepared to agree to a mix of fees and charges, which are partially fixed and partially variable. Also centralised clearing and settlement organisations, which act as routers of orders between distributors and managers, may help to reduce transaction costs, since charges are related to the number and volume of transactions rather than absorbing fixed overheads. A management company is thus able to transfer part of the risk resulting from fluctuations in markets or sales to another organisation that is prepared to assume some of that risk. Typically the companies that offer such specialist services have grown out of either shareholder registration operations or from custodians or are developed from broader securities market transaction, clearing and settlement systems. In developed markets, such companies increasingly tend to offer a comprehensive package so that a customer can outsource to one company rather than to a number of outside suppliers.
- Variable pay for senior executives and investment managers: another way to turn fixed costs into variable costs that is common in the investment management business is to remunerate senior staff in ways other than through fixed salaries. This enables fixed salaries to be kept down. Because they require the staff of the company to share the risks and rewards that result from volatile market conditions, such remuneration systems may also help to attract more dynamic and enterprising people into the organisation. Some of these methods are:
  - bonuses related to the overall profits of the management company: these are usually appropriate to the most senior people whose actions can significantly affect profits;
  - bonuses related to the investment results or returns of the funds managed: these are usually appropriate for investment managers;
  - bonuses related to sales targets: these are appropriate for internal sales and marketing staff;
  - share options which grant participants the opportunity to buy shares in the management company at some point in the future at a fixed price.
- Sales and marketing commissions: apart from the bonuses related to sales targets mentioned in the previous paragraph, it is possible to convert sales costs in part to variable costs through the payment of commissions expressed

as a percentage of sales value achieved. Typically those who can be paid in this way will be prepared to work on a 'no sale, no payment' basis and include:

- individual direct salespeople;
- firms of independent financial advisers and brokers;
- branches of the parent company.

Of course the management company cannot rely totally on the efforts of these organisations, but will need to maintain a centrally planned marketing and advertising budget which will be a variable cost. The extent to which this expenditure is pruned in difficult times is the subject of much debate. It is always tempting for senior managers to minimise the effect of a market fall on profits by cutting out all advertising expenditure, using the justification that it is not going to produce immediate sales; but as has already been pointed out, ongoing visibility is important to investor confidence.

- Subcontracting investment management: it is rare but not unknown for fund management companies to subcontract investment management as well as all the other functions described in this section. There are plenty of independent investment managers eager to undertake investment management for a fee related to the value of the funds: they too have fixed costs and the addition of third-party contracts of this kind is very attractive for them. A management company might consider this option in respect of new funds investing in foreign countries or specialist sectors in which it has no expertise of its own. Using such a subcontractor would avoid incurring extra fixed costs in the form of new hirings of its own investment managers.

Clearly, depending on the extent to which subcontractors are used, the management company may be left with a substantially reduced proportion of overhead costs in relation to total costs. Fixed costs can be controlled in the normal ways by efficiency and good information.

If a fund management company took advantage of all these opportunities to outsource specialist functions, it could create a 'virtual' management company, which carried out no day-to-day functions at all, but simply provided the entrepreneurial skill, the capital, the regulatory cover and perhaps the brand name. Such virtual management companies do exist, usually created by an organisation with an existing customer base and a strong brand name – a major retail chain for example.

The budget in practice
Table 18.1 shows a very simplified headline budget for a fund management company. The budget assumes a start up business with no funds under management at the beginning of the period shown.

Table 18.1 *The Growth Fund Management Company budget ($ million)*

Years	1	2
Opening fund	0.00	487.20
Gross sales (1)	620.00	820.00
Net sales (2)	495.00	545.00
Initial charge 5% (3)	31.00	41.00
Cost of sales (4)	25.00	30.00
Net investment (5)	464.00	504.00
Market movement (6)	1.10	1.10
Closing fund (7)	487.20	1065.12
Average funds managed (8)	243.60	776.16
Management charge 2% (9)	4.87	15.52
Revenues (10)	10.87	26.52
Expenses (11)	8.00	12.00
Profit before tax (12)	2.87	14.52

(1) Total sales on which initial charge of 5% is deducted
(2) Sales net of redemptions
(3) Income from initial charge
(4) Marketing and agents' commissions
(5) Net sales less total initial charge
(6) Market movement is assumed to be 10% per annum in a straight line and therefore is shown as 5% on the average funds managed
(7) Amount of funds managed at the end of the year
(8) The average amount of funds managed during the year (opening fund + closing fund)/2
(9) Management charge on average funds under management
(10) Revenues are the total of the annual management charge + retained initial charge (initial charge less cost of sales)
(11) Operating expenses
(12) Profit before tax = revenues less expenses

The budget format used here is an accounting and not a cash flow format. For example, the payments of the annual charges by the funds may be spread unevenly through the year; payments for the office leases may be quarterly in advance, etc. These cash flow factors will need separate consideration, especially in relation to their impact on capital adequacy.

Of course the budget is a somewhat idealised version of reality in which sales increase steadily and the market rises by 10% per annum. The truth is likely to be substantially different, so this budget represents a methodology not a likely outcome.

Budget methodology

This is a 'macro' budget; each functional unit within the company should also have its own 'micro' budget. The creation of the company's budget is through a combination of 'top-down' strategic direction from the directors and 'bottom-up' planning for implementation by managers of the business units.

In practice each of the business unit's budgets have to be co-ordinated since none can be set independently. The common starting point is sales/income. Any given increase (or decrease) from previous levels should have similar effects throughout the organisation. The managers of business units then need to work through the implications in terms of personnel, premises, systems, etc.

Through effective use of technology, draft budgets can be widely distributed and co-ordinated. Senior managers should have access to the detailed budgets of the smallest business units so that they have a firm grasp of costs and the changes (or lack of changes) in costs resulting from any increase (or decrease) in sales.

Table 18.2 shows one example of a budget from a functional unit, probably the most significant for budgetary purposes, the sales department.

Of course it is likely that each of the funds, the growth fund, the income fund and the bond fund will have different charging and sales commission structures, so the predicted sales patterns and volumes will have implications for the budgetary lines which deal with income from initial and annual charges and sales commissions. The bond fund is likely to have lower charges so the high sales predicted will have less effect on the bottom line than if the high sales had been of the growth fund which is likely to have higher charges.

Budget control

Conventional budget control is through feedback. Performance is recorded and measured against budget. Variances from the budget lead to action. Constant monitoring of performance against budget is used to keep senior managers informed of the state of the company.

The problem with this is that in the fund management business, change can be very rapid. By the time the data has been analysed and presented to managers, opportunities may have been missed. So ideally feedback should be supplemented by 'feed forward', whose objective is to react to change as it happens, to anticipate events and to adapt plans continuously.

In a sense this merely recognises that there is a continuum of possible outcomes for the sales/revenue line in the budget, and that the likelihood of a figure set at the start of the year being achieved is quite low. One answer adopted by many fund management companies is to produce a set of budgets based on different sales/revenue lines and carry out a sensitivity analysis, showing the effect on profit of different scenarios. For example, if the projection was for sales of 800000, budgets would also be produced for sales of 600000 and 1000000. Producing these would give senior managers clear ideas about what the sensitivity of the profit and loss account to varying sales might be, so that appropriate action could be taken quickly if the decision was made to switch the budget basis at any point during the year.

Table 18.2 *Budgeted sales and redemptions for the next financial year*

	Sales forecast									
	Opening year					Next year				
	Q1	Q2	Q3	Q4	Total year	Q1	Q2	Q3	Q4	Total year
Growth Fund										
Sales	20	30	20	20	90	30	40	40	50	160
Redemptions	0	10	5	10	25	10	15	20	10	55
Net	20	20	15	10	65	20	25	20	40	105
Income fund										
Sales	30	30	20	30	110	30	40	40	30	140
Redemptions	0	0	10	10	20	30	10	10	20	70
Net	30	30	10	20	90	0	30	30	10	70
Bond fund										
Sales	100	100	150	70	420	70	100	200	150	520
Redemptions	0	0	50	30	80	40	20	40	50	150
Net	100	100	100	40	340	30	80	160	100	370
Total sales all funds					620					820
Total net sales					495					545

While budgets are necessary, they must not be too rigid, and must be capable of being reviewed, revised and over-ridden during the course of a year.

Using the budget as a management tool

The usefulness of the budget as a management tool depends on the extent to which people throughout the organisation are committed to the budgeting process. Managers can, as in any other organisation, to a large extent sabotage the process by playing budgetary games, for example by building slack into their budgets. They may, for example, exaggerate costs in order to be able to accommodate pressure for cuts, or set easily achievable sales targets. This will actually be a rational solution for individual managers to adopt if the following circumstances prevail:

- There is great pressure not to overspend budgets, and sanctions are applied to those who do so.
- There is no system for reviewing or adapting budgets during the year.
- Senior managers are excessively concerned with meeting the budget rather than dealing with the problems faced by the cost centres.
- Budget holders are dealt with in isolation, individually, so that the budget process is seen as a game between the individual and the company.

It is therefore the responsibility of senior managers to convince managers throughout the organisation that it is worthwhile co-operating and producing realistic figures. Careful thought should be given to incentives to encourage managers to adopt the right attitudes, in particular bonuses based partly on departmental targets and partly on the success of the company as a whole.

TRENDS IN FUND MANAGEMENT

Although this chapter endeavours to give an insight into the way profitability can be achieved by fund management companies, and the way in which the managers think about their business, there are some other bigger trends that need to be understood.

The search for size: mergers and multinationals

Management of investment funds has tended, as a result of regulation, custom and practice, to be trapped within domestic boundaries. This is changing.

There is a belief that size is a benefit in management of funds, and as a result there has been a trend for fund management companies to grow by acquisition.

This trend is particularly accentuated at the point at which fund management companies have reached a limit to their growth in one market and this in turn has led them to seek to become multinational.

Multinational operation requires the possession of investment management capability spanning all world markets, and in many cases this means offices in several countries at least. There is an incentive to spread these costs over the largest possible volume of assets. The attractions are:

- The costs of enhancements in systems can be spread over a larger volume of funds, which generate greater revenues (see below).
- The management company can resell products developed for a domestic market internationally in much larger volumes.
- Similar funds can be merged to form larger ones.
- Economies in staffing, offices, advertising and marketing and administration can produce cost savings.
- The diversification of distribution and a customer base across several countries or even continents may produce greater stability in revenues.

All of these factors provide a powerful incentive to amalgamate and to sell products to a multiplicity of markets. Those who have been successful, however, have found ways to achieve this end without the need to proliferate products designed for different countries' regulatory systems. There are signs that success is being achieved within the EU, the only grouping of large markets with common standards, by management companies which offer a single range of products, domiciled in one jurisdiction – typically Luxemburg, Dublin or even the UK – across all markets. There are also a number of technical systems designed to permit many funds with different structures to share common portfolios or administrative systems.

There is, however, still a place for small specialist management firms, and the case for massive size is yet to be proven. In particular, the risk of contamination needs consideration. A problem with operations in one part of the world may lead to loss of confidence in other countries. Regulators now co-operate far more actively internationally. If they become concerned about one aspect of a company's international operations, this may lead to pressure from regulators in other countries as well.

Financial conglomerates aim to provide a range of services

The largest fund management firms are now part of integrated investment management groups which also manage pension and other institutional funds, and which in turn are often (but not always) owned by multinational and multifaceted financial groups within which there are banks, insurance companies and other financial service providers. This conglomerate approach stresses the need to provide a whole package of financial services, which can meet all the needs of a particular customer in a 'one-stop shop'.

Fund management companies have been seen as desirable components of financial conglomerates because their earnings have been judged as relatively stable, compared with revenues from investment banking and corporate finance, which ride the roller coaster of securities markets. As compared with pension funds, which require regular briefings and presentations from investment managers, investment funds and their individual investors are undemanding clients in respect of investment managers. So the retail sector has become increasingly fashionable.

For this reason, stock market-listed fund management companies can receive high share ratings compared with banks, though their shares also show more volatile movements reflecting the fact that their earnings are directly affected by movements in share prices generally. Given the operational gearing inherent in the investment funds business, commentators have sometimes pointed out that investors might be better off if they bought shares in fund management companies rather than in the funds they manage.

Those who would like to test their grasp of the contents of this chapter should turn to the self-test questions at the back of the book.

NOTES

1. *The Little Data Book*, World Bank, 2002.
2. People's Bank of China, February, 2003.
3. Author's calculation based on Investment Management Association data.
4. Author's calculation based on Investment Company Institute data.
5. *Worldwide Mutual Fund Assets and Flows* Q4, Investment Company Institute, Washington DC, 2002.

Concluding Note

This book cannot hope to be a complete guide to every aspect of investment funds in every country. Each fund industry is a result of different legal and fiscal environments and, increasingly, of regional trading blocs like the EU, MERCOSUR and NAFTA.

For those who want to find out more about funds, see the references given at the end of this book. In addition, there are a large number of websites of regulators, trade associations and information providers, including academic institutions, where further detailed information can be found (start from the authors' website: www.cadoganeducation.co.uk where many of these sites are identified).

The authors hope that this generic review of how the investment funds business works worldwide contributes towards the understanding and the development of this rapidly growing and changing sector.

It is likely that the bear market, which started in 1999, and the economic conditions which have accompanied it, will have a profound impact on the fund management business. Not only have equity prices fallen more steeply than at any time for 30 years but this fall has been accompanied by conditions of near deflation which have driven interest rates to their lowest in living memory.

Fund managers mostly failed to anticipate the scale of the falls in the market and those pension funds and insurance companies that remained strongly committed to equities are experiencing problems of solvency.

Savers and investors have been shaken by this adverse combination of circumstances and have shown signs of losing faith in institutional investors.

It is not easy to predict the outcome of the substantial rethinking and re-engineering that is undoubtedly occurring within the fund management business, but some early signs of potentially significant trends can be identified.

MAKING PROFITS IS NOT AS EASY AS THEY THOUGHT

Conglomerates, including financial holding companies, banks and life assurance companies which enthusiastically embraced the investment fund management business as a natural adjunct to their existing business, and as a profit cash cow, have become disillusioned and as a result have tried to sell off their fund management businesses; it is therefore a buyers' market, and sale prices for investment fund management businesses have fallen sharply. This is partly a result of their realisation that distribution may be more profitable than continuing to operate in an overpopulated manufacturing sector.

DISTRIBUTION IS KING

Those financial institutions with substantial retail distribution capability, typically banks and insurance companies, are beginning to understand that their customers may want a wider range of choice than a single line of own-branded products. They are also realising that their large customer base and distribution capability is a saleable commodity. So they are beginning to offer a selected range of products from a wide range of management companies in addition to their own. Similarly insurance companies, which offer links to investment funds through pension or life assurance products, are increasingly offering a choice of links to other funds than their own through multi-manager funds, or by enabling policy-holders to choose from a range of different funds.

The effect of this, and the increasing dominance of independent financial advisers as distributors in some markets, have resulted in many fund management companies becoming more like product wholesalers with little or no contact with the ultimate customer, who is 'owned' by the distributor. This shift in market power resembles the development of the relationship of supermarkets to consumer goods manufacturers, which has been a feature of the last 20–30 years in most advanced countries.

ECONOMIES OF SCALE AND COST REDUCTION ARE MORE IMPORTANT THAN EVER

Not only is reduction and containment of cost necessary for management companies at a time of falling profits, but lower total expense ratios (TERs) will be essential in order to provide acceptable returns to investors in the future. Whereas a TER of 2.5% could be ignored in an era when annual compound returns were 12% to 15%, such a high TER would bite deeply into the 5% to 7% returns that are widely predicted for the immediate future. Size and economies of scale accompanied by a massive investment in systems is believed to be the key to success. However, the risk associated with major IT projects has been well illustrated in all fields of state and private sector activities; not all projects will succeed.

A reduction in the internal costs of management companies, however, has been paralleled by the increasing demands of the distribution networks and the clearing and settlement organisations, as they realise the full extent of their market power, not only for up-front commissions but also for 'trail' fees which are payable to them by the management company so long as their clients remain loyal.

BOUTIQUES AND HEDGE FUNDS

At the other end of the scale, there is a proliferation of investment boutiques and hedge funds. Started by people who have fallen out of large fund management companies, either by accident or by design, the boutiques' investment management strategies seem to offer some salvation to investors disillusioned with the losses they have suffered elsewhere. The concept of absolute return achieved by the application of a variety of very active management styles, which aim to offer protection against market gyrations and a real return in all conditions, is attractive to those investors for whom more conventional actively managed long-only or index funds have turned out to have had feet of clay. Even some of the largest management companies have jumped on this bandwagon with specialist 'hedge fund' or 'absolute return' offerings. While 'hedge funds' are estimated to account for less than 5% of the total value of investment funds worldwide, moves by some regulators to allow them to be sold more openly to a wider selection of investors may accelerate the trend.

The outcome of these trends cannot accurately be predicted. It is certain, however, that big changes are afoot, which will alter the landscape of the investment management industry in the coming years. Despite this, the basic principles for the technical operation of collective investment funds are unlikely to change as dramatically. So it is the authors' belief that, whatever changes there may be in the business model, the technical aspects of the operation of investment funds that have been covered in this book will remain substantially unaltered.

Self-test Questions

CHAPTER 1

1.1. Who do collective investment funds intermediate between?
1.2. Does an investor in a collective investment fund accept full market risk?
1.3. Between 1990 and 1999, which group of institutional investors had the strongest annual average growth rate of financial assets: investment companies, pension funds or insurance companies?
1.4. Which is the largest collective investment funds market in the world?
1.5. Name five key factors in collective investment funds' popularity.

CHAPTER 2

2.1. Name three key functions required by regulation for the operation of a fund.
2.2. Who is usually responsible to fund investors for the conduct of the business of a corporate fund?
2.3. What are the three key activities of a fund management company?
2.4. What is the main role of a custodian?
2.5. What is the key difference between a custodian and a depositary or a trustee?

CHAPTER 3

3.1. What are the four different legal structures used for funds? Which one of these is not used for publicly offered funds?
3.2. Does a closed-ended fund have an obligation to redeem?
3.3. Does an open-ended fund have fixed capital?
3.4. Give the three commercial reasons why most funds are externally managed.

CHAPTER 4

4.1. What are the four key components of a regulatory system?
4.2. What is self-regulation?

4.3. Name five of the 10 key fund regulatory principles identified by IOSCO.

4.4. What are the four key areas of regulatory activity?

CHAPTER 5

5.1. What are the three main asset classes available for securities investment funds?

5.2. Which organisation normally carries out investment management of an investment fund?

5.3. Is an index tracker fund an actively managed or a passively managed fund?

5.4. Is deciding what exposure to have to money market instruments, bonds or equities an asset allocation decision or a stock selection decision?

5.5. What is a typical figure for the maximum value of any one open-ended fund that can be invested in the equities of a single issuer?

CHAPTER 6

6.1. What is 'total return'?

6.2. Is it more appropriate to compare offer to bid price based or offer to offer price based fund performance against an index?

6.3. Where short-term fund performance is shown, why do regulators often require fund performance also to be shown over five years or since inception?

6.4. What is the median performing fund?

CHAPTER 7

7.1. What is net asset value per share or unit?

7.2. Why is liquidity of fund assets important to valuation?

7.3. How often are open-ended funds valued?

7.4. Name four reasons why errors arise in valuations.

CHAPTER 8

8.1. Is an initial charge a recurring charge on a fund?

8.2. What is the normal basis on which an annual management fee of a fund is levied?

8.3. What is the difference between 'shareholder (or unitholder) fees' and the 'total expense ratio'?

8.4. Why do no-load funds often levy tapering back-end loads?

CHAPTER 9

9.1. If a new investor pays too much to buy units in a fund, will this 'concentrate' or 'dilute' ongoing fund investors?

9.2. Is an open-ended fund which quotes an offer and a bid price for its units or shares a 'dual-priced' fund or a 'single-priced' fund?

9.3. Is a dilution levy included within a single price for a fund share or unit?

9.4. Is a person buying shares or units in a fund at an unknown price buying on a historic or a forward priced basis?

CHAPTER 10

10.1. In what instance is creation and cancellation of fund shares or units different from issue and redemption?

10.2. What are the three main ways of recording ownership of fund shares or units?

10.3. What is 'in specie' redemption?

10.4. What is the difference between an accumulation share or unit and an income share or unit?

CHAPTER 11

11.1. What are the three main reasons for selecting funds to be marketed?

11.2. Name the seven main activities undertaken by the marketing division.

11.3. What is the key difference between retail and institutional business?

11.4. What fund management group has a distinctive brand in your domestic marketplace?

CHAPTER 12

12.1. Name three direct distribution channels.

12.2. Name three indirect distribution channels.

12.3. Which category of distribution channel (i.e. direct or indirect) is more under the control of the management company?

12.4. Costwise what is the main merit of an indirect distribution channel?

CHAPTER 13

13.1. What are the four key communications to investors that regulators require should be made?

13.2. Why do reports and accounts for closed-ended funds exclude a statement of movement of shareholders' or unitholders' funds?

13.3. Why are fund net asset values and prices required by regulation to be disclosed?

13.4. Why is tracking complaints important?

CHAPTER 14

14.1. What terms are used to describe the two different approaches to fund product development?

14.2. Name three factors causing constant change to the product development environment.

14.3. Name the three basic investment objectives of funds.

14.4. Name four factors in fund product profitability.

CHAPTER 15

15.1. Why are fund accounts different from ordinary company accounts?

15.2. Why are income and capital required to be separately accounted for?

15.3. What does the statement of total return tell a holder of fund shares or units?

15.4. What does a statement of movement of shareholders' or unitholders' funds show?

CHAPTER 16

16.1. Name the two main taxes affecting funds.

16.2. What is the principle of 'tax neutrality' or 'transparency'?

16.3. What is the difference between the US 'pass-through' approach and the European 'imputation' approach?

16.4. Characterise your local forms of fund in EEE/TTT terms.

CHAPTER 17

17.1. Identify the three areas in which conflicts of interest between investors and fund management companies arise.

17.2. Name three components of fund governance.

17.3. Name two common subjects for codes of conduct in the funds sector.

17.4. Why is there a temptation to manipulate fund performance or its representation?

CHAPTER 18

18.1. Are most management company costs fixed or variable?
18.2. Are most management company revenues fixed or variable?
18.3. What does management company revenue mainly derive from?
18.4. Name three methods of turning fixed costs into variable costs.

Answers

CHAPTER 1

1.1. Savers and borrowers.
1.2. Yes (except in the case of a guaranteed fund).
1.3. Investment companies.
1.4. USA.
1.5. Reduction of risk through diversification; reduction of cost through economies of scale; professional management; investor protection; flexibility.

CHAPTER 2

2.1. Custody, audit, compliance.
2.2. Board of directors of the fund.
2.3. Administration, investment management and marketing.
2.4. Safekeeping of fund assets.
2.5. A custodian has no supervisory role; both depositary and trustee have a supervisory role.

CHAPTER 3

3.1. Corporate, trust, contractual and partnership. Partnership structure is not used for publicly offered funds.
3.2. No.
3.3. No.
3.4. Future value; economies of scale; diversification of revenue flows.

CHAPTER 4

4.1. Primary legislation; regulator; regulations issued by the regulator under the primary legislation; the Courts or Ombudsmen.

4.2. System of regulation and supervision undertaken by an organisation whose members are the practitioners of the business being regulated and who finance that organisation.

4.3. Fund structures; custodian, depositary or trustee; eligibility of management companies; delegation; supervision; conflicts of interest; asset valuation and pricing; limits on investment and borrowing; investor rights; marketing and disclosure.

4.4. Establishing rules and regulations; licensing and authorisation; supervision and monitoring; investigation and enforcement.

CHAPTER 5

5.1. Money market instruments; bonds; equities.

5.2. Fund management company (or investment adviser).

5.3. Passively managed fund.

5.4. Asset allocation decision.

5.5. 5%.

CHAPTER 6

6.1. Total distributions paid and increase/decrease in net assest value per unit or share in a specified period.

6.2. Offer to offer.

6.3. To prevent a misleading impression of performance being given.

6.4. The middle performing fund (e.g. 50 of 100).

CHAPTER 7

7.1. The net asset value of the fund (assets less liabilities) divided by the number of shares or units in issue.

7.2. The more liquid a security the more likely it is that reliable market prices will be available for valuation purposes.

7.3. Usually daily but at a minimum once every other week.

7.4. Using the wrong price for assets; mathematical errors; incorrect input of a price; failing to include or exclude a security that has been bought or sold; incorrect cash balance; incorrect accruals; dividing by the wrong number of shares or units in issue.

CHAPTER 8

8.1. No, it is a one-off charge upon purchase of shares or units.

8.2. A percentage of annual average net asset value.

8.3. Shareholder or unitholder fees represent the initial or entry or exit charges for a fund; the total expense ratio is the annual operating cost of a fund ('total shareholder cost' or 'effect of expenses' calculations include both of these sets of costs).

8.4. In order to deter redemption and ensure recovery of the cost of acquisition of the investor.

CHAPTER 9

9.1. Concentrate.

9.2. Dual priced.

9.3. No (but a dilution adjustment – not levy – is included in a swinging single price).

9.4. Forward-priced basis.

CHAPTER 10

10.1. When a management company (or other entity) acts as a principal in the sale and redemption of shares or units.

10.2. Bearer; materialised (certificated); dematerialised (electronic).

10.3. When redemption is made through transfer of ownership of a proportion of the fund's portfolio rather than by cash payment of the equivalent value.

10.4. An accumulation share or unit retains the value of distributions paid within its price whereas an income share or unit pays out such distributions (though these may be reinvested in new shares or units).

CHAPTER 11

11.1. Competitive edge; tax advantage; 'hot' or fashionable investment sector.

11.2. Management; researching markets; developing the brand; developing products; advertising; promotions; creating and maintaining databases.

11.3. Retail – large numbers of small amounts; institutional – small numbers of large amounts.

11.4. Your call (usually there aren't many).

CHAPTER 12

12.1. Company's own or affiliated sales forces; branch networks; direct advertising/marketing.

12.2. Financial advisers; sales networks; fund supermarkets; discount brokers; introducers.

12.3. Direct.

12.4. Commissions are only payable upon a sale.

CHAPTER 13

13.1. Prospectus; annual report and accounts; semi-annual report and accounts; NAV and/or price.

13.2. Because they have a fixed not variable capital so there is no ongoing movement of shareholders' or unitholders' funds.

13.3. So potential investors can establish the prices they are likely to have to pay to buy and existing investors can establish the current value of their investment or the price they could get if they wished to sell.

13.4. Indicates if systems, procedures or information given are inadequate and could be improved or if a specific problem has arisen.

CHAPTER 14

14.1. Investment led and marketing led.

14.2. Consumer preference changes; legal changes; fiscal changes; competitive pressures.

14.3. Income, growth and balanced (both income and growth).

14.4. Chargeability of launch and operating costs to the fund and retention of initial and annual charges by management companies; volatility of fees; life of fund; ability to charge performance fees; ability to levy redemption fees; risk of conversion; loss of contract; ability to take (higher) 'wrapper' fees; duration of holding; size of holding; ability to charge costs to funds not management company.

CHAPTER 15

15.1. Because a fund does not have employees, offices, equipment, work in progress, etc.

15.2. Because tax law often requires one to be distributed (income) but the other to be retained (capital gains) and/or because they are often taxed at different rates.

15.3. The results of the investment performance of the fund in terms of income and of capital and costs of operation.

15.4. The impact on the size of the fund of sales and redemption of shares or units.

CHAPTER 16

16.1. Income tax; capital gains tax.

16.2. An investor investing in assets indirectly through a fund should be no worse off taxwise than an investor investing directly in the same assets.

16.3. In the USA income is taxed only in the hands of the investor; in Europe income taxes withheld at source are issued with a credit which is used to offset fund and investor tax liabilities.

16.4. Your call.

CHAPTER 17

17.1. Profitability; need for new business; misuse of investors' money.

17.2. Laws and regulations; codes of conduct; reputational risk, competitive pressures.

17.3. Fund advertising; fund categorisation; fund performance; corporate governance.

17.4. In order to sell more units or shares and obtain more fees.

CHAPTER 18

18.1. Fixed.

18.2. Variable.

18.3. Initial charges and annual charges (sometimes also performance and redemption fees).

18.4. Outsourcing; variable pay; paying commissions on sales; contracting out investment management.

References

Association Française de la Gestion Financière (AFG-ASSFI) *Economic and Statistical Overview 2001*, Paris.

Association of Investment Trust Companies (January 2003) *Statement of Recommended Practice for Financial Statements of Investment Trust Companies*, London.

Buffett, Warren (2002) Letter to Berkshire Hathaway shareholders, Omaha.

Buxton, Sally and St Giles, Mark (2002) Governance of investment funds, Chapter 9, *Financial Sector Governance*, The Brookings Institution, Washington DC.

CalPERS (January 2003) *Facts at a Glance – General Facts*, www.calpers.ca.gov, Sacramento.

CalPERS (January 2003) *Facts at a Glance – Investments*, www.calpers.ca.gov, Sacramento.

Carmichael, Jeffrey (2002) Public sector governance and the private sector, Chapter 5, *Financial Sector Governance*, The Brookings Institution, Washington DC.

Carmichael, Jeffrey and Pomerleano, Michael (2002) *The Development and Regulation of Non Bank Financial Institutions*, World Bank, Washington DC.

Cornick, Tim (2001) *The International Guide to Marketing Investment Funds*, Editor, Finance and Investment Research Ltd, London.

Davis, E. Philip (1995) *Pension Funds*, Clarendon Press, Oxford.

European Union Council Directive of 20 December 1985 (85/611/EEC), on the co-ordination of laws, regulations and administrative provisions relating to undertakings for collective investment in transferable securities (UCITS) as amended, Brussels.

FEFSI (European Federation of Investment Funds and Companies) *The State of the European Investment Funds Industry*, Brussels.

FEFSI (European Federation of Investment Funds and Companies) Worldwide Mutual Funds Assets and Flows, Fourth Quarter, 2002, Brussels.

Feri Fund Market Information Ltd (2002) *European Fund Market Yearbook*, London.

Financial Services Authority (January 1997) *Statement of Recommended Practice for Financial Statements of Unit Trusts*.

Financial Services Authority (November 2000) *Statement of Recommended Practice for Financial Statements of Authorised Open Ended Investment Companies*.

Financial Services Authority (January 2002) *Polarisation: Consumer Research*.

Halzman, Robert and Stiglitz, Joseph E. (2001) *New Ideas about Old Age Security*, World Bank, Washington DC.

HMSO *Financial Services Act 1986*, London.

HMSO *Financial Services and Markets Act 2000*, London.

IOSCO (1994) *Principles for the Regulation of Collective Investment Schemes*, Madrid.

IOSCO (1997) *Principles for the Supervision of Operators of Collective Investment Schemes*, Madrid.

IOSCO (2000) *Conflicts of Interest of CIS Operators*, Madrid.

IOSCO (2003) *Performance Presentation Standards for Collective Investment Schemes*, Madrid.

IOSCO (2003) *Regulatory and Investor Protection Issues Arising from the Participation by Retail Investors in (Funds of) Hedge Funds*, Madrid.

Investment Company Institute *A Guide to Understanding Mutual Funds*, Washington DC.

Investment Company Institute (2002) *Fundamentals*, 11 (2), Washington DC.

Investment Company Institute (2002) *Fundamentals*, 11 (4), Washington DC.

References

Investment Company Institute (2002) *Fundamentals*, 11 (5), Washington DC.

Investment Company Institute (2002) *Mutual Fund Fact Book 2002*, Washington DC.

Investment Company Institute (2000) *Perspective*, 61 (3), Washington DC.

Investment Company Institute (2002) *Worldwide Mutual Fund Assets and Flows Fourth Quarter 2002*, Washington DC.

International Accounting Standards Board (March 1985, as amended) *IAS 32: Financial Instruments: Disclosure and Presentation*, London.

International Accounting Standards Board (December 1998) *IAS 39: Financial Instruments: Recognition and Measurement*, London.

KMPG Ireland (2002) *Funds and Fund Management*. Regulation and taxation reports covering 70 countries.

Markowitz, Harry M. (1952) Portfolio Selection, *Journal of Finance*, March.

Moore, Philip (1997) *Islamic Finance*, Euromoney Books, London.

Newlands John (1997) *Put Not Your Trust in Money*, Chappin Kavanagh, London.

OECD (1999) *Principles of Corporate Governance*, OECD, Paris.

OECD (2001) *Institutional Investors Yearbook 2001*, OECD, Paris.

PricewaterhouseCoopers and FEFSI (2003) *Discriminatory Tax Barriers Facing the EU Funds Industry — A Progress Report, Brussels*.

Sandler, Ron (June 2002) *Sandler Review of Medium and Long Term Retail Savings in the UK*, HM Treasury, London.

Sharpe, William F. (January 1963) A simplified model for portfolio analysis *Management Science*.

Sharpe, William F. (September 1964) Capital asset prices, *Journal of Finance*.

Wagner, Wayne H. and Lau, Sheila (November/December 1981) The effect of diversification of risk, *Financial Analysts Journal*.

Stutchbury, Oliver Piers (1964) *The Management of Unit Trusts*, Thomas Skinner & Co.

Thompson, John K. and Choi, Sang-Mok (2001) *Governance Systems for Collective Investment Schemes in OECD Countries*, Financial Affairs Division Occasional Paper No 1, OECD, Paris.

Ward, Sue (1995) *Managing the Pensions Revolution*, Nicholas Brealey Publishing, London.

Index

Index compiled by Terry Halliday